a movie a day

a movie a day

A Year's Worth of Fascinating Films and Fun Facts

STEVE UHLER

BERKLEY BOULEVARD BOOKS, NEW YORK

A Berkley Boulevard Book
Published by The Berkley Publishing Group
A division of Penguin Putnam Inc.
375 Hudson Street
New York, New York 10014

Book design by Tiffany Kukec
Cover design by Pamela Jaber
Cover photograph by Marc Tauss

PRINTING HISTORY
Berkley Boulevard trade paperback edition / November 2001

Visit our website at
www.penguinputnam.com

Library of Congress Cataloging-in-Publication Data
Uhler, Steve.
A movie a day : a year's worth of fascinating films and fun facts / Steve Uhler.—Berkley Boulevard trade paperback ed.
p. cm.
ISBN 0-425-18175-8
1. Motion pictures—Miscellanea. 2. Motion picture actors and actresses—Anniversaries, etc. I. Title.
PN1998.U38 2001
791.43—dc21
2001035476

PRINTED IN THE UNITED STATES OF AMERICA

10 9 8 7 6 5 4 3 2 1

Thanks to the following people, for their inspiration, faith, assistance, patience, and support:

Michael Bowen, Felicia and Mitou Brings, Sheree Bykofsky, Judy Creasman, Lanie and Marly Frasier, Chris Garcia, Cristina Herrera, Betty Ann Hillman, Doug Joachim, Tara Lewis, Holly Morgan, John Morgan, Glen Moorman, Richard Roeper, Jody Seaborn, Cindy Synodinos, Jean Synodinos, Joyce Uhler, and, last but not least, my favorite son, Jeremy Zamecnik.

This one's for Dad.

introduction

1. Pick a date. Any date.

2. Now, turn to that date in this book. (It's easy—everything's chronologically listed.)

There. You've just been introduced to my book.

Just what kind of book is this, exactly? Is it a movie guide? A trivia book? An almanac?

Well, kind of, sort of, and that, too.

As a film critic and video columnist for a metropolitan newspaper, it can be a daunting challenge to come up with fresh material as an alternative to the standard-issue movie reviews.

One week in the middle of April, I was browsing through a video store and noticed James Cameron's *Titanic* available on DVD. Normally it wouldn't have appealed to me—in fact, the movie will never appeal to me, but that's another subject altogether. What was strange was that I noted that the date was April 14—the very same day the real *Titanic* had actually gone down in the Atlantic on that cold night in 1912. On a whim, I decided to rent the movie and drink a toast to those long departed at the same time. I invited a few friends over; we had a little seafood, a couple of drinks (with plenty of ice, in honor of the occasion), and settled in to go down with the ship.

The next day, it occurred to me that I might find, for any given day of that month, some piece of obscure history or trivia or anniversary or birthday—and at least one movie to go with it. So I wrote a movie column, "April Anniversaries"—and the response was overwhelming.

Readers from as far away as Australia and India responded. I received more mail than for any previous column.

One thing led, as they say, to another—and soon I had embarked on a quest to find a historic anniversary and thematic movie for every day of the year. As you'll see, my criteria for inclusion were highly subjective and, it's been alleged, somewhat biased.

The one passion that ties it all together is movies. And this is a book for movie-lovers of all kinds—all of those "lovely people out there in the dark," as Norma Desmond phrased it in *Sunset Boulevard.*

Maybe it's best not to think of this as a book at all; think of it more like a collection of small treasure maps, strewn with jewels (both real and costume), and scattered where you may least expect to find them. Treasure maps may not always lead to treasure—but they do lead to adventure.

I hope you have even half as much fun reading and using *A Movie a Day* as I did researching and writing it. And who knows? You may indeed find a true treasure or two. I know I did.

january

january 1

Eggs-actly What the Doctor Ordered

Welcome to the first day of the rest of your life.

Not to put too fine a point on it, but the start of a new year can be a little overwhelming. It's a clean slate—a blank, white canvas filled with nothing but open space and infinite possibilities. So you need something that lets you feel good about yourself and the world you live in—to inspire you while it entertains you. What you need is a feel-good movie that reminds you that all things are possible for you: love, freedom, joy, success in the face of adversity . . . a movie that uplifts your spirit as it puts a smile on your face; a film that will make you feel like all things are possible without hitting you over the head with a lot of existential juju. What you need is . . . **Chicken Run** (1999).

For the chickens who live at grim and joyless Mrs. Tweedy's Chicken Farm, there's little time to question life or pursue happiness amidst the never-ending pressure to lay eggs. But Ginger, a resourceful, independent-thinking hen, dreams of somehow escaping to a better life. All of her schemes and plans to escape under the dreaded fence fail, until one day she glimpses a flying rooster—and decides the best way to escape is *over* the fence. She recruits Rocky, the rooster (voiced by Mel Gibson in his best performance in years), to help them concoct an escape plan that will succeed where others have failed before.

Cowriters and codirectors Peter Lord and Nick Park have fashioned a magical film for all ages, literally built out of clay. There is enough warmth and wit in Karey Kirkpatrick's enchanting, hilarious story for at least three movies—packed with smart, savvy jokes that both kids and adults will appreciate.

The bottom line is this is a great feel-good movie—a wonderful, no-pressure way to start the new year. If chickens can dream, chickens can fly. And so can you.

And just to cover a few more bases, here are some additional possibilities to help get you over some potential New Year's Day humps, with suggested movies:

If you're feeling hung over and want to keep this morning's resolution to stop drinking, watch **The Lost Weekend** (1945) . . . followed by **Clean and Sober** (1958) as a chaser.

If you're beginning to wonder whether you made the right choice by marrying your high school sweetheart: **Peggy Sue Got Married** (1986).

If you think you'll never find that ideal life companion to share the rest of your days with: **Marty** (1955); **Sleepless in Seattle** (1993); or **Hannah and Her Sisters** (1986).

If you're resolved to create a new you through vigorous resolve and discipline: **Pumping Iron** (1976) or **Rocky** (1976).

If you're resolved to create a new you through plastic surgery: **Death Becomes Her** (1992).

If you've made a resolution to lose weight: **Thinner** (1999).

If you're thinking, "Good God. Another year working at . . .": **Bagdad Café** (1987).

If you're thinking, "Screw it. I just wanna watch a football movie!": **Any Given Sunday** (1998).

If you find yourself thinking, "Chuck it all, I'm going to live on a tropical island.": **Cast Away** (2000), followed by **Swiss Family Robinson** (1960).

If you find yourself wanting to erase your entire existence and start from scratch: **Heaven Can Wait** (1978).

If you find yourself merely wanting to forget last night . . . : **About Last Night . . .** (1986).

If you find yourself deeply wanting to believe that somehow we can all get along: **Beautiful People** (1999).

If you want to believe that one person can make a difference: **Erin Brockovich** (2000).

If you think there's no way to start over: **Starting Over** (1979).

Lastly, if you find yourself wistfully recalling a particular year from your youth, rent your favorite movie from that year and revel in the memories one last time before facing the new day.

Have a great year. I'll be here for you each day.

january 2

Life in the Slow Lane

America slowed down—for a while, anyway—on this day in 1974, when an overly prudent President Richard Nixon imposed a mandatory nationwide speed limit of 55 mph. Overnight, those who had been freely speeding along the San Diego Freeway or zipping over what was left of Route 66 at 75 mph found themselves puttering along next to Ramblers and VW microbuses. The law was more or less adhered to for a few years, until disgruntled states and citizens began to put their foot on the gas.

Commemorate the anniversary of the 55-mile-an-hour speed limit, and take a ride with **Speed**, the runaway (pardon the pun) box office hit of 1994. Dennis Hopper plays an embittered ex-cop and demolitions expert who rigs a city bus with explosives that will detonate and kill all the passengers aboard if the bus ever slows down to below 50 mph (he must not have been a Nixon man). Keanu Reeves had his best screen role yet as an L.A. SWAT cop who climbs aboard for the ride, along with last-minute-recruit bus driver Sandra Bullock, in her breakthrough role.

You'd think an action movie set aboard a lugubrious bus in congested L.A. traffic would be a bit cumbersome, but the movie is as light on its feet as its star. First-time director Jan De Bont never lets the pace flag, topping the action bits one on top of the other. Suspenseful, action-packed, inventive, and funny, *Speed* is that rare, guilty pleasure, an intelligently constructed, dumb action thriller. Go ahead . . . hit that accelerator and hang on tight. It's going to be a bumpy ride.

january 3

Keep This Movie Under Wraps

Famed Egyptologist Howard Carter spent most of his professional life in search of a pharaoh's tomb—and on November 4, 1922, he discovered more than he ever dreamed of: the long-lost tomb of Pharoah Tutankhamen—located, suitably enough, in Luxor's Valley of the Kings. King Tut, who was only a teenager when he died, ruled Egypt from 1333–1323 B.C. In the years following Carter's discovery, his team unearthed a cornucopia of priceless treasures, statues, and jewelry.

But on this date in 1924, after excavating for two years, he uncovered the pièce de résistance: the solid gold sarcophagus of the king himself, with the mummified remains within. It was the archeological find of the century.

The obvious choice to commemorate this occasion? **The Mummy**—no, not the creaky 1931 original Universal picture with Boris Karloff (who only appears as the title character for a scant few seconds!). Instead, gorge on the sumptuous big screen junk-food version of *The Mummy* (1997). Most audiences were expecting an updated remake of the original horror flick, but what they got was a rousing comedy-adventure-romance along the lines of *Indiana Jones* meets *Gunga Din.* Brendan Fraser continues to prove his movie mettle with his winning portrayal of a refreshingly naïve and nonchalant soldier of fortune, deftly juggling the clichés of both hero and comic relief. The deep-orange cinematography is gorgeous, particularly in letterbox. Like the title character, the plot begins to unravel toward the end—but it's a diverting, fun ride getting there.

january 4

Deviate from the Usual

As one of Rome's last and most deviant emperors, Caligula was nothing if not a colorful character. He killed his own father, admitted a horse to the Senate, married and impregnated his sister, and then killed both mother and her unborn child. He was notorious for his fearsome rages, aberrant hobbies, and inventively gruesome tortures. His constituency was understandably apprehensive about his mood swings, and on this day in A.D. 41, Caligula was stabbed to death. By just about everyone in Rome.

But his well-deserved reputation for perversity and depravity outlived him. In 1979, *Penthouse* publisher Bob Guccione, a man who knew a thing or two about perversity and depravity himself, decided to branch out from publishing trash into filming it, and decided the debauched tale of Caligula would make for some steamy adult entertainment. **Caligula** (1979) became billed as the first A-budget, major star porn film. Determined to make the first big-budget porn film, Guccione hired Gore Vidal to script it (Vidal later insisted his name be removed), lined up an impressive A-list of actors, including Peter O'Toole, John Gielgud, and Malcolm McDowell (in the title role) and spiced it up with some genuine X-rated orgies and over-the-top gore sequences. The result is one of the most controversial, inept, and vile movies ever, and one of the most eye-opening historical films you'll ever see. There are two versions on DVD: the 122-minute R-rated cut and a two-and-a-half-hour X-rated "director's cut." Ah, the glory that was Rome. Prepare to shower after watching.

For a more enlightened, restrained, and considered look at Caligula, seek out the excellent BBC *Masterpiece Theater* miniseries from 1976, **I, Claudius**. Derek Jacobi became a star with his sympathetic portrayal of the stuttering hero, who is smarter than he lets on and rises through the ranks of Roman society to become emperor. Along the way he must contend with the often lethal whims of his unpredictable nephew, Caligula, memorably played by John Hurt. One of the greatest—and certainly most literate—miniseries of all time, *I, Claudius* raised the bar for years to come.

january 5

Ride Lonesome Tonight

His first role on film was an instant classic. As Boo Radley, the feeble-minded, misunderstood boogey man who becomes an unlikely hero in 1962's *To Kill a Mockingbird,* he was onscreen for less than three minutes, but he left an indelible impression. From there, he took on an endless string of supporting character roles—as a catatonic soldier in 1963's *Captain Newman, M.D.*, as a repressed Southern bank teller carrying on an affair in *The Chase* (1966), as icy but loyal lawyer Tom Hagen in *The Godfather* (1972). He seldom took lead roles, but when he did, he was brilliant. Many actors consider him the single greatest movie actor of the last fifty years bar none, the heir to Spencer Tracy.

Robert Duvall was born this day in San Diego, California, in 1931. Celebrate by watching any of his layered, masterful performances: his taciturn, down-on-his-luck country singer who finds redemption and love in Bruce Bereford's elegiac *Tender Mercies* (1983; for which he won an Oscar for Best Actor), his gung-ho, surf-happy Col. Kilgore in 1979's *Apocalypse Now* ("I love the smell of napalm in the morning!"); his blustering, bullying warrior-in-peacetime Bull Beecham in *The Great Santini* (1980).

But if you'd really like to savor Duvall at the top of his form, and want to get totally lost in one of the greatest Western epics ever made, watch him as the love-struck, life-embracing, over-the-hill Texas Ranger Gus McCrae in the epic miniseries, **Lonesome Dove** (1986). Yup, it's six hours long—but it's about the most engrossing and rewarding six hours you'll spend in front of your TV. Tommy Lee Jones costars as Gus's obstinate old saddle pal, Woodrow Call, who joins with Gus, their old buddies Deets and Jake Spoon (Danny Glover and Robert Ulrich), and young Newt (Rick Schroeder) on an epic cattle drive from Texas to Montana. Along the way they encounter a psychotic half-breed Indian named Blue Duck (Frederick Forrest), Gus's old love Clara (Anjelica Huston), water moccasin nests, outlaws, buffalo herds, and apocalyptic storms. It's a stunning achievement for a made-for-TV movie, easily outclassing most cinematic Westerns—a rousing adventure, a bittersweet romance, a comic fable, a saddle soap opera. But what is remembered after the closing credits is the twinkle in Duvall's eye as he grins and says, "It's not death I'm talkin' about, Woodrow—*it's life!*"

january 6

Stay Holmes This Evening

"Come Watson, come! The game is afoot."

—Sherlock Holmes

According to his creator, Sir Arthur Conan Doyle (who should know), the world's greatest detective, Sherlock Holmes, was born on this day in 1854. Early biographical details are sketchy (and far-fetched; see Chris Columbus's *Young Sherlock Holmes* (1985) for details on the detective's first case). Holmes has become as much a movie icon as a literary one. The most ubiquitous Holmes was Basil Rathbone who, along with Nigel Bruce as his blustering companion, Dr. Watson, starred in a series of potboilers for Universal Studios in the '30s and '40s—the best of which is the first, *The Hound of the Baskervilles* (1939). After *Hound,* the series rapidly went downhill, eventually putting the sleuth in modern dress and outwitting the Axis powers with plots that had nothing to do with Conan Doyle's masterful short stories.

With a little Holmesian deduction, though, you can track down some intriguing cinematic variations on the great detective. George C. Scott gave one of his finest and most touching portrayals as a deluded modern-day judge who believes he *is* Sherlock Holmes in the delightful and wistfully romantic *They Might Be Giants* (1971). Joanne Woodward is Dr. Mildred Watson, who is assigned to help cure him but ends up teaming up with him in this inventive spin on Sherlockian lore. In Nicholas Meyer's ingenious, revisionist *The Seven-Per-Cent Solution* (1976), Dr. Watson (Robert Duvall) takes his good friend Holmes (Nicol Williamson) to Vienna to kick his cocaine addiction with the help of a radical and controversial doctor named Dr. Sigmund Freud (Alan Arkin), and the three team up to solve a kidnapping. Comic actor Gene Wilder put his own singular spin on the mythos with the fitfully amusing *The Adventure of Sherlock Holmes' Smarter Brother* (1975).

But the most original Holmesian movie is Billy Wilder's **The Private Life of Sherlock Holmes** (1970). At once a spoof and a respectful, loving, informed homage, *Private Life* is vintage Wilder and vintage Holmes. Robert Stephens makes a splendid Holmes, and the plot—which involves the Loch Ness monster, dwarves, and dead canaries—puts a terrific spin on the Holmes myth while honoring it at the same time. A far cry from Wilder's typical cynicism, this is a lush, almost romantic movie that delves into how Holmes became so distanced from his human emotions. A forgotten masterpiece—or, rather, a lost masterpiece; apparently, approximately a quarter of the movie was removed by studio editors before it was released, and Wilder was incensed. The missing reels have never been recovered. Somebody call in Sherlock Holmes.

january 7

Peek into This Cage

As a struggling young actor, his career didn't start out promisingly. His slightly goofy, hangdog looks didn't help, but he did have some great connections. Having Francis Ford Coppola as an uncle couldn't have hurt.

Happy birthday today to Nicholas Coppola, born this day in 1964 in Long Beach, California. After dropping out of high school, he landed his first acting job on TV in 1981. He got a bit part in 1982's *Fast Times at Ridgemont High.* The next year he changed his name to Nicolas Cage, and things began picking up. He began making big impressions in small movies like *Rumble Fish* (1983) and *Birdy* (1984). His unique mix of mopey vulnerability and surliness earned him a cult following, and he developed a reputation as an artist who would go to bizarre extremes for his craft—getting two teeth pulled for *Birdy,* slashing his arms for *Racing with the Moon* (1984), and eating a live cockroach (his own suggestion) in *Vampire's Kiss* (1989). He really broke through to mainstream Hollywood with three consecutive hits: directed by his uncle Francis in *Peggy Sue Got Married* (1986), playing an inept but well-intentioned kidnapper in *Raising Arizona* (1987), and as Cher's pizza-tossing paramour in *Moonstruck* (1987).

Celebrate his birthday with any of those three great performances—or catch his Oscar-winning performance in **Leaving Las Vegas** (1995). As a washed-up alcoholic screenwriter bent on drinking himself to death in Las Vegas, Cage delivers an edgy, literally suicidal performance that is simultaneously sympathetic, funny, and raw. Elizabeth Shue costars as the hooker who tries to save him from himself. An extraordinary, no-holds-barred performance from one of the most unpredictable actors of our generation.

january 8

Good Rockin' Tonight

Could Elvis act?

That's kind of like asking whether or not Einstein could play basketball. It's kind of a moot question. Elvis was . . . well, *Elvis!* And Elvis Aron Presley was born on this day in 1935 in Tupelo, Mississippi; his twin brother, Jesse Garon, died in childbirth.

If he'd never made a single Hollywood movie his reputation would still be undiminished. But, for better or for worse (and mostly worse), Elvis did make movies. As an actor, he lacked nuance, depth, shading, decent roles, diction, and timing; on the plus side, he had a face like a trailer park Adonis (helped along with a streamlined nose job and jet-black dyed hair) and undeniable charisma. And in Hollywood, those two out of eight ain't bad.

For a while, Elvis strove to be taken seriously as an actor. At his audition for producer Hal Wallis, it's been said that he reenacted James Dean's entire part from *Rebel Without a Cause,* mumbling in his Mississippi drawl. He looks adrift in his first film role, as Richard Egan's kid brother in *Love Me Tender* (1956). He even got a death scene at the end. But Hollywood never quite knew how to handle Elvis, and Col. Tom Parker didn't want to tinker with a successful franchise. And so began the homogenization and neutering of Elvis, as he appeared in a series of films that became more formulaic and limp as he grew increasingly indifferent, finally walking through the interchangeable parts in a detached, dismissive haze.

But when he was young, lean, and hungry, the charisma carried him. And he occasionally tapped into his own primal appeal in such stretches as *King Creole* (1958) and *Wild in the Country* (1961). But his best film, both musically and dramatically, is **Jailhouse Rock** (1957), made when he still gave a damn and had something to prove. Elvis plays Vince Everett, a nice enough kid who lands in prison after he accidentally kills a man in a barfight. Elvis was still young and beautiful, and got to do all the by-now-patented Elvis-isms. He rocked, he crooned; he was shy and awkward; he was tough and tender; he was a hillbilly juvenile delinquent with a sneer that was as endearing to young girls as it was threatening to their parents. His rocking version of "You're So Square" in trunks by the swimming pool is a highlight, as is the iconic title number. (Contrary to popular myth, Elvis did not choreograph the other dancers in the famous "Jailhouse Rock" dance sequence, but the set piece was structured around his moves.)

january 9

A Rocky Beginning

"Yo, Adrienne!"

On this day in 1976, after years of trying to get his screenplay off the ground, Sylvester Stallone finally began shooting the movie that would become his ticket to stardom and his one inarguable masterpiece—a simple tale of a "ham and eggs" boxer who gets a shot at the heavyweight championship and finds love. Stallone had shopped his story around Hollywood with the proviso that he be the star. His perseverance paid off in a big way; the low-budget movie went on to become a box-office smash, surprising industry wags by winning an Oscar for Best Picture, and spawning four sequels. The parallel between Stallone's own good fortune and cinematic alter ego did not go unnoticed.

Stallone never really topped **Rocky** (1976), one of the great "underdog" movies of all time. He wrote himself the best role of his career with the character of a simple-minded boxer with a heart of gold, Rocky Balboa. The story is implausible, but it succeeded because of its tremendous heart and emotion—even if it does pile the sentimentality on a bit thick. Burgess Meredith got the best part of his late career as Rocky's curmudgeony trainer, and Talia Shire embarked upon her second "gravy train career" role (the other being Connie Corleone in the *Godfather* trilogy) as Rocky's mousey wife, Adrian. The *Rocky* sequels got worse and worse, but the original is a genuine '70s cultural touchstone and still packs an uplifting emotional punch.

january 10

Did His Friends Call Him "Buff"?

Buffalo Bill wasn't much of an Indian fighter, buffalo hunter, or scout, but he was a hell of an entrepreneur and showman. For over twenty years he starred in and produced Buffalo Bill's Wild West Show, traveling the U.S. and Europe long after the real West had been tamed. But audiences still went in droves to see the unique six-gun circus, featuring such real-life over-the-hill gang members as Annie Oakley and Sitting Bull. With his flowing wavy white locks of hair, finely cultivated mustache, and immaculate buckskin jacket, Buffalo Bill looked like a cowboy as imagined by Busby Berkley.

But on this day in 1914, the old cowboy finally went to that great "home on the range" and joined the Ghost Riders in the Sky. When informed by his doctor that he had only thirty-six hours at most to live, he took out a deck of cards and played till the end. Observe the passing of a part of the American West with **Buffalo Bill and the Indians** (1976), director Robert Altman's unceremonious salute to the fraudulence and hucksterism of good ol' American celebritydom. Paul Newman gives a winking performance as William F. Cody—entrepreneur, con man, and yarn spinner par excellence, who pretty much invents the character Buffalo Bill. Altman delights in exposing showbiz pretensions, and he finds the original ripe subject here— delightfully exposing the seedy reality that lurks behind America's popular well-polished myths. Eccentric supporting performances from Burt Lancaster, Will Sampson (as Sitting Bull), Geraldine Chaplin (as Annie Oakley), and Harvey Keitel add to the fun.

january 11

Hail, Albania

On this date in 1946, the People's Republic of Albania was officially established. Happy birthday, Albania.

Commemorate the momentous anniversary with Barry Levinson's biting political comedy **Wag the Dog** (1997). Robert DeNiro stars as Capitol Hill spin doctor Conrad Brean, who gets called in to the White House to manage a PR crisis: The president has been caught having a sexual liaison, and the country needs to be distracted from the issue. (Right. As if that could ever happen!) Conrad decides what the country needs is a huge distraction—like, say, maybe going to war. Not a real war, but a staged smoke-and-mirrors campaign to deflect public attention, complete with rumors, denials, video footage, and patriotic anthems written by Willie Nelson. So Brean concocts a diversionary, phony war with Albania to distract the country's attention from the emerging scandal.

"Why Albania?" asks an aide (Anne Heche).

"Why not? What do you know about 'em?"

"Nothing."

"Precisely. They seem shifty. They seem standoffish. I mean, who knows from Albania? Who trusts Albanians?"

Brean recruits the services of one Stanley Motss (Dustin Hoffman, doing a dead-on impression of homage to producer Robert Evans) to "produce" the "pageant." Motss delivers the goods, and more. A little too much more for his own good.

Wag the Dog left a bitter taste in the public's mouth when it was initially released; it hit just a little too close to the truth, and the public was both weary and wary of the then-ongoing Monica Lewinsky/Bill Clinton scandal. But seen on the small screen, with Hilary Henkin and David Mamet's screenplay properly distanced from history, *Wag the Dog* emerges as a delightfully subversive little comedy.

But rest easy, it's a fable. It could never really happen. Really. No. *Really*.

january 12

Holy Hollywood, Batman, We're on the Big Screen!

ABC Television Network was in dire straits in 1966, running a distant third place in the ratings war behind rival networks NBC and CBS. The underdog network was willing to try anything to win over young viewers and ratings—including making the first TV series about a comic book hero since *Superman* was hoisted on invisible wires in the 1950s. The network recruited producer William Dozier, who had previously adapted *Dennis the Menace* for TV, to oversee production.

On this date in 1966, *Batman* debuted on ABC—a tongue-in-cheek, anything-goes series showcasing the adventures of Gotham City's Caped Crusader. Gone was any semblance of dark, noirish elements of the original Bob Kane comic strip—replaced by bright candy-colors, outrageous puns, wildly tilted camera angles, cheesy sets, "special guest villains," and over-the-top emoting by series stars Adam West (as millionaire Bruce Wayne, a.k.a. Batman) and Burt Ward (as Bruce's youthful ward, Dick Grayson, a.k.a. Robin the Boy Wonder). The camp show became a mainstream hit, appealing to both youngsters and savvy adults.

It was almost inevitable that a quickie feature-length film would be made to cash in on the phenomenon before it died. **Batman: The Movie** premiered at the Paramount Theater in Austin, Texas, on July 30, 1966. In addition to West and Ward, it featured many of the top villains from the series: the Joker (Caesar Romero), the Riddler (Frank Gorshin), the Penguin (Burgess Meredith), and Catwoman (Lee Merriwether). The movie has its admirers; there is a small but vocal cult who consider it superior to Tim Burton's dark 1989 version. Be your own judge. But it's a refreshing and evocative journey back to the candy-colored pop sensibilities of the '60s. *Boff! Thwack! Socko! Crunch!*

january 13

Pass the Buck

Today is National Blame Someone Else Day. Observe the occasion by passing gas in a crowded elevator and scowling at the person standing next to you. Then watch Alfred Hitchcock's film **The Wrong Man** (1956). In a noirish change of pace for the Master, Hitchcock decided to film a story that actually happened, about a young jazz musician and family man who is falsely accused of a crime. Shot in a calculated, cool, somber style, with none of Hitch's usual passages of brevity, it's one of the Master's lesser-seen works. Henry Fonda stars as the hapless victim of mistaken identity. Hitchcock films the nightmarish scenario in an almost documentary-like manner, at a brisk clip. A chilling and still all-too-relevant indictment of a "justice" system gone awry.

january 14

Slam Punk

On this night in 1978, controversial rock group the Sex Pistols kissed it all good-bye with their last concert ever, at Winterland in San Francisco. During the final show, Johnny Rotten provoked and taunted the crowd, "Ever get the feeling you've been cheated?" Punk rock had suffered its first implosion.

By the time the Sex Pistols had burst onto the music scene in 1976, rock 'n' roll had become corporate-sponsored pablum and insipid disco music. It was no longer the rebellion against the machine; it *was* the machine. But with their epochal album *Never Mind the Bollocks: Here's the Sex Pistols*, lead singer/instigator Johnny Rotten and the Sex Pistols single-handedly revolutionized rock and gave it a second infusion of life with such anthems of anarchy as "Pretty Vacant" and "Anarchy in the U.K." The Sex Pistols were together less than two years and made only one album. Musically, they were unbearably inept—but music wasn't the point. It was attitude. The Sex Pistols pioneered the genre that would be labeled "punk rock," influencing such later disciples as the Ramones, the Clash, Patti Smith, and Devo.

Of course, such a volatile, combustible concoction couldn't last. At least in the eyes of the media, the group couldn't help but become a parody of themselves. After the defection of bass player and head psycho Sid Vicious, there was little to do but mop up the blood.

Their final concert of this night was recorded for posterity, and it is one of the highlights in **The Filth and the Fury** (2000), the often entertaining, sometimes annoying documentary that chronicles the formation and dissolution of the Sex Pistols. Packed with vintage performance, interview, and newsreel clips, *The Filth and the Fury* is fascinating, funny, disturbing, enlightening. Director Julien Temple also directed the Sex Pistols' earlier cinematic opus, *The Great Rock 'n' Roll Swindle* (1980).

january 15

If She's a Virgin, How Can She Be a Queen Mum?

It was the stuff of royal British soap operas: illegitimate child of royal lineage ascends to throne. On this day in 1558, two months after the death of her half-sister Queen Mary I of England, twenty-five-year-old Elizabeth Tudor was crowned queen of England at Westminster Abbey in London. The daughter of Henry VIII and Anne Boleyn, Elizabeth was declared illegitimate after the execution of her mother, but was pressed into royal service upon the death of her half-sister. Under her reign, England prospered like never before (and seldom since)—establishing a permanent Protestant church, destroying the formidable Spanish Armada, sponsoring Sir Francis Drake's circumnavigation of the world and expeditions to the North Coast. A writer named William Shakespeare found the atmosphere particularly inspiring, and the English Renaissance flowered. Whether or not the queen herself was ever deflowered is a questionable point; she never married, earning the sobriquet "the Virgin Queen."

Commemorate the coronation with **Elizabeth** (1998), featuring an appropriately regal and independent Cate Blanchett in the title role. The emphasis is on how this smart, savvy woman managed not only to survive many attempts on her life, but to thrive as one of the most headstrong, dynamic, and effective world leaders ever. With Geoffrey Rush as the nefarious spy Walsingham and Joseph Fiennes as Elizabeth's vexing temptation. Talk about Girl Power.

january 16

I'll Drink to That

By and large, a dark day in American history. On this date in 1920, Prohibition was officially declared and became the law of the land. Overnight, alcohol became an illegal substance, the nation went dry, and otherwise law-abiding citizens became felons, choosing to risk jail by frequenting speakeasies. It was the age of bootleggers and gangsters, and no studio reflected that element of the times with more panache and energy than newly formed Warner Brothers.

No gangster flick of the '30s Prohibition era shot up the house like **The Roaring Twenties** (1939). James Cagney, then at the height of his career as screen tough guy, stars as one of three World War I soldiers returning home to New York, only to find rampant poverty and unemployment. Cagney finds himself reluctantly drawn into bootlegging by his ruthless friend, played by Humphrey Bogart. Cagney becomes a kingpin, and Bogie his back-stabbing nemesis. One of the greatest gangster flicks of all time, magnificently directed by the undisputed master, Raoul Walsh. Almost makes you nostalgic for Prohibition. Almost.

january 17

He Was What He Was

Popeye the Sailor made his official bow this day in 1929 in hundreds of newspapers in the comic strip *Thimble Theater,* a modestly successful daily strip written and drawn by iconoclastic cartoonist E. C. Segar. Popeye's appearance was brief and dramatic—he showed up only in the final panel—but he became a huge hit with readers across the U.S.A. He became so popular that Segar reformatted the strip to star him.

Thus began Popeye's long and memorable career in the collective consciousness of Americans and spinach lovers everywhere, supported by a cast of characters who went on to become icons themselves, including girlfriend Olive Oyl, adopted toddler Swee' Pea, nemesis and romantic rival Bluto, mooching hamburger addict Wimpy, the crony Sea Hag, and the lovable Jeep. Popeye went on to appear in a classic series of cartoons for the Fleischer brothers, where generations of fans were first introduced to Popeye's guttural, mumbling voice and Olive Oyl's high-pitched whine.

Years after Segar's death, another artistic iconoclast, Robert Altman, had the crazy notion of doing a live-action movie based on the character and was savvy enough to cast Robin Williams in the title role. Altman's **Popeye** (1980) was very much based on Segar's original conception. Williams makes a wonderfully convincing Popeye, and Shelley Duvall is Olive Oyl personified—it is quite simply the role she was born to play. The town of Sweethaven is lovingly, whimsically, surreally rendered. *Popeye* is one of the strangest musical comedies ever made, with an appropriately quirky score by Harry Nilsson, featuring such oddities as Olive's ode to Bluto, "He's Large." A strange little movie that is a wacky universe unto itself, a homage from one artistic iconoclast to another.

january 18

Cary On

"To succeed with the opposite sex, tell her you're impotent. She can't wait to disprove it."

—Cary Grant

Archie Leach was hardly an ideal name for the screen's most suave and sophisticated leading man. So Archie, born this day in Bristol, England, in 1904, eventually changed his name to Cary Grant.

When he was twelve, his mother suffered a nervous breakdown, and he found a new home in a troupe of traveling acrobats. He moved to America in 1920 as a tumbler, and began his rise to stardom literally doing back flips.

It seemed Cary Grant could do anything well and effortlessly—in both public and private life. For a couple of years in the '30s he shared a Beverly Hills mansion with fellow actor Randolph Scott, and nobody thought it strange. Late in his career, in 1967 he waxed rhapsodic about the spiritual and medicinal benefits of LSD, and nobody really raised much of a stink, not even Art Linkletter. No one in movies had Grant's charm, class, and savoir faire. He was underappreciated as a comic actor, making it look so effortlessly easy. But marvel at his perfect comedic timing, particularly in his films with Katharine Hepburn, *Bringing Up Baby* (1938), *Holiday* (1938), and *The Philadelphia Story* (1940). Next to Spencer Tracy, Grant was Hepburn's best screen partner.

But his best performance may be his most atypical—as a ne'er-do-well small-time Cockney crook in **None but the Lonely Heart** (1944). After his seemingly effortless comedy successes, Grant desperately wanted to show the dark side beneath his light and breezy demeanor. When con man Grant finds out his mother (Ethel Barrymore) is dying, he attempts to mend his ways. A brave performance, Grant shows the humanity and vulnerability beneath his trademark bravado and charm. The film failed abysmally at the box office, though, and Grant went back to the formula with which his audience was most comfortable. Written and directed by Clifford Odets.

january 19

Take Another Little Piece of Her Art

She had a voice that sounded like the bottom of a bottle of Southern Comfort, and she had the credentials to back it up.

Janis Joplin was born this day in Port Arthur, Texas, in 1943. The quintessential "ugly duckling" and outsider, she started building a modest reputation as a folk singer around Austin, Texas. She moved to San Francisco during the Summer of Love and found herself singing rock and blues with several bands—eventually hooking up with Big Brother and the Holding Company, where she became lead singer. After her incendiary performance at the 1967 Monterey Pop Festival, the world of rock had seldom been so smitten so soon as it was with the ballsy, boozing blues singer who could work your mojo and break your heart in the same moment. Within five years she had burned herself out, dying alone in a hotel room, her trusty bottle of Southern Comfort at her bedside. She left $2,500 in her will for her friends to throw a party in her memory.

Her life story served as the template for Bette Midler's film debut in *The Rose* (1979). But celebrate the birthday of the Queen of Dem Kosmic Blues by watching the real thing at her finest in **Janis** (1974). Director Howard Alk's documentary on the legendary singer is a cornucopia of riches. All her watermark performances are here, including her career-defining moment at the Monterey Pop Festival, along with her appearance at Woodstock, plus revealing interviews, newsreel footage, and unexpectedly affecting moments such as her appearance on *The Dick Cavett Show,* when she announced her intention to attend her high school reunion. She went, too—and was still the odd girl out.

january 20

A Friendship Remembered

On this day in 1980, the *New York Times Magazine* published Sydney Schanberg's memoir, *The Death and Life of Dith Pran,* which recounted the author's friendship with his Cambodian interpreter Dith Pran during his coverage of the war in Cambodia. They were separated during the fall of Saigon, when Western journalists fled and were forced to leave behind their native assistants—often to face death by the Khmer Rouge. Schanberg spent years searching for his friend—not knowing that Pran had, in fact, finally managed to escape to freedom.

The inspiring story is recounted in **The Killing Fields** (1984). Sam Waterston does a solid, sober, restrained job as Schanberg. S. Ngor, who plays Dith Pran, is immensely effective; it's worth noting that his own life closely mirrored that of the real-life character he was portraying. This film also marked the debut of an intense newcomer named John Malkovich, in his first major movie role as a suicidal photojournalist.

january 21

Why You Never Heard of Louis XVII

Louis the XVI wasn't the most popular king in the history of France—which is why, on this day in 1793, he was executed by guillotine in the Place de la Revolution in Paris. By most accounts, he was ill suited for his job; a pleasant enough aristocrat, he was simply in over his head and the victim of bad timing, a weak economy, unfortunate circumstance, geneology, and numerology. His wife, the cake-loving Marie Antoinette, suffered the same fate as her husband nine months later.

Commemorate the end of the French aristocracy with **Start the Revolution Without Me** (1970), an underappreciated spoof that revolves around

Louis's court and the intrigues of the French Revolution. Gene Wilder and Donald Sutherland are genuinely funny together as two sets of twins separated at birth who find themselves on opposing ends of the revolution—one pair on the side of the aristocracy, the other pair members of the peasantry. It's the kind of silly comedy that brings to mind what is best about Mel Brooks. A breezy farce, with Wilder and Sutherland making two splendid pairs, written and directed by Bud Yorkin, who would go on to cocreate *All in the Family* with Norman Lear. Orson Welles appears as the narrator—for the first five minutes. That was all the filmmakers could afford him for.

january 22

Thank the Man Who Invented Movies

If any man can be said to have invented the visual language of modern movies, it is David Wark Griffith, born this day in 1875 in La Grange, Kentucky.

He began as a barnstorming actor using the stage name Lawrence Griffith, playing supporting roles in various slap-dash traveling theatrical troupes throughout the South. His courtly manner and distinguished voice did not overcome his somewhat unattractive physical appearance, and he tried playwriting. He failed at that, too—until he decided to try his luck peddling his stories around New York in hopes of selling a story idea suitable for the newfangled fad called moving pictures. At the newly launched Biograph Studios, he found work as both actor and writer, soaking up everything he could about the exciting new medium. He was a quick study, developing a phenomenal, instinctive understanding of motion pictures. Soon he was directing one- and two-reelers for the company, literally inventing the language of film as he went along.

At Biograph, he stopped actors from giving the over-the-top "stage" performances that were prominent at the time, recognizing that the camera exaggerated expression. He developed inherently cinematic techniques—moving the camera, changing angles, cross-cutting, and incorporating parallel action, close-ups, and rhythmic editing. He almost single-handedly liberated movies from the stage, from whence they had come, and opened a world of possibilities. In *The Birth of a Nation* (1915), his epic saga of the American Civil War and its effects on a Southern family, he created what many historians regard as the single most important film in the development of cinema. But it was—and remains—controversial for its depiction of the KKK, portrayed as heroic vigilantes.

Griffith's next project was to be his ultimate masterpiece—and grandest failure. Celebrate the birth of the man who invented modern movies with the grandiose **Intolerance** (1915)—an astonishingly ambitious work of art, huge in scale, and still breathtakingly impressive. Griffith audaciously tells four separate stories simultaneously—a retelling of the Passion Play, the storming of Babylon, the Huguenots, and a "modern-day" tale—gradually blending them together like a fabric in a majestic four-part climax. Griffith used film as a multinarrative form that was astonishing in its reach and scale.

Inevitably, the monumentally ambitious film bombed at the box office, and it ruined Griffith financially. He went on to make several more masterpieces—most notably the poetic *Broken Blossoms* (1919) and the historical epic *Orphans of the Storm* (1921); both starring the luminous Lillian Gish—but found himself left behind when talkies arrived, an anachronistic symbol of the old days. He died penniless, proud, and soused, in the Knickerbocker Hotel in 1948, forgotten by all but a few old-timers.

january 23

Here's Lookin' at You, Bogie

During his service with the navy during World War I on board the *Leviathan*, the sailor's lower lip was injured during a shelling, and he talked with a noticeable lisp for the rest of his days. But if anybody ever made a lisp sound manly, it was Humphrey Bogart, born this day in 1899 in New York City.

If any actor comes close to the illusory, iconoclastic heart of the American cinema, it's Bogie. The AFI voted him #1 in their list of the 100 top movie stars. But his lineage was misleading. He was born the son of a successful Manhattan physician, and sent to Phillips Academy in preparation for medical studies at Yale, but was expelled due to disciplinary problems. He joined the navy during World War I, and after his discharge found himself drawn to the theater, working his way up from office boy to stage manager and eventually to actor. When he started acting in off-Broadway plays, he was invariably cast as a second juvenile lead.

The struggling actor got his big break when he was cast as gangster-on-the-run Duke Mantee (at the insistence of influential star Leslie Howard) in *The Petrified Forest* (1936). Thereafter, he took a series of secondary roles to Jimmy Cagney—who invariably killed him off before the last reel. But in 1941, director Raoul Walsh saw something special and noble in Bogart, and cast him as veteran criminal Roy "Mad Dog" Earle in **High Sierra** (1941). It was Bogie's first starring role. Suddenly, the Bogart persona was there, intact: tough but sympathetic, distant but romantic, even tender. It remains one of his most impressive performances.

Bogart went on to other memorable, immortal performances—*The Maltese Falcon* (1941), *Casablanca* (1943), *The African Queen* (1951), masterful turns all—but his insightful, sorrowful performance as the noble outlaw in *High Sierra* was never surpassed. He created a bad guy who was cool, heroic, sympathetic, and loyal. Taut direction and great location photography make this one of the greatest heist films ever—and something more. *High Sierra* also provided a breakthrough part for Ida Lupino, touching and tough as the tagalong girl who loves him.

january 24

A Golden Opportunity

Carpenter James Marshall had just been hired by landowner John Sutter to build a waterwheel-powered sawmill on Sutter's parcel of land near what is now appropriately named Eureka, California. On this day in 1848, Marshall was walking beside the river bank when he noticed something. "My eye was caught with a glimpse of something shining at the bottom of the ditch," he later recalled. "It made my heart thump, for I was certain it was gold. Then I saw another. After taking it out I sat down and began to think right hard."

If he'd really thought it through, he may have decided to keep his mouth shut. But he didn't—and within six months over four thousand miners had arrived, and the Gold Rush was officially on. Marshall didn't profit from it; he died penniless.

Commemorate his discovery and the '49ers Gold Rush with the last full-blown Hollywood musical, **Paint Your Wagon** (1969). On the surface, it's easy to see why it was Hollywood's last big musical; any movie that casts Lee Marvin, Clint Eastwood, and Jean Seberg in the main singing roles has a self-destructive perversity you've got to admire. *Paint Your Wagon* is a big, clumsy, lumbering drunken bear of a movie musical. Lee Marvin stars as craggy Ben Rumson, a cantankerous gold prospector who teams up with a naïve young Easterner simply named "Pardner" (a kinder, gentler Eastwood) panning for gold. Their mining camp sprouts up into a veritable boomtown, No Name City. When lovely Jean Seberg comes to town, Marvin marries her, but soon she finds herself attracted to his young partner. So everyone embarks on a happy three-way marriage. (Hey, it was 1969, folks!)

Paint Your Wagon is more a boisterous, blustering comedy than a musical—and most of its music is classifiable as comedy, especially when Lee Marvin is singing (his croaking version of "Wanderin' Star" is simultaneously ludicrous and affecting). But damn if it isn't fun. Harve Presnell's rendition of "They Call the Wind Maria" is one of the film's few true musical highlights.

january 25

All Opposed?

Today is Opposite Day. Celebrate the occasion by bringing out your opposite nature—the yang to your yin—with **Dr. Jekyll and Mr. Hyde,** the quintessential parable of the repressed opposite within all of us.

Ah, but which Jekyll and Hyde to watch? Silent film buffs can enjoy John Barrymore's critically acclaimed performance in *Dr. Jekyll and Mr. Hyde* (1920)—especially for his now-hilarious transformation scenes, which were accomplished without the aid of special effects or makeup—just Barrymore contorting his face and body. There have been countless film versions before and since, but most agree the best screen version is **Dr. Jekyll and Mr. Hyde** (1932) with Fredric March in the starring role(s). Director Rouben Mamoulian brings a hallucinatory intensity to the story, and March delivers what is arguably his finest screen performance as the humanitarian doctor who delves into mysteries best left unexplored. Later, Spencer Tracy did a skillful job in yet another *Dr. Jekyll and Mr. Hyde* (1941), with Ingrid Bergman looking particularly fetching as his mistress. The whole Jekyll and Hyde theme got inverted when Jerry Lewis made his one undisputed masterpiece, *The Nutty Professor* (1963), which in turn spawned the Eddie Murphy remake over thirty years later. The tale also got skewered with Steve Martin, who manages to "absorb" Lily Tomlin's spirit in *All of Me* (1984), with Martin doing some of his most amusing physical schtick ever as his male self tries to subdue his female half.

january 26

Aussie What You Mean

Today is Australia Day. Watch *Crocodile Dundee* (1986) if you like—that's perfectly OK, mate. But I'd suggest a radically different view of Australia:

Nicolas Roeg's visually mesmerizing and haunting **Walkabout** (1979). An in-depth look at the harsh glories of the Australian outback, *Walkabout* is a film unlike any other, visually seductive and dreamlike in its approach. Director Roeg has an uncanny ability to readjust the viewer's internal clock and cultural compass. This story of two English schoolchildren (Luc Roeg and Jenny Agutter) lost in the outback after their father abandons them and kills himself plays like a languorous dream. When the two wanderers come across an Aborigine boy on his "walkabout"—a rite of passage into manhood involving months of solo survival—they become dependent on the seemingly primitive being to get them back to civilization. With no common language, the trio embark on a journey back to "civilization," which has irrevocable changes for all. *Walkabout* casts a spell—sometimes unspeakably beautiful, sometimes chilling—packed with unforgettable images and with an ending that is at once ironic and heart-wrenching. *Walkabout* is a journey you'll long remember.

january 27

A Little Night Movie

He was the ultimate child prodigy, the son of a stern taskmaster father who played the violin and a doting mother. The toddler mastered the piano at two and composed his first minuet at four; by 1780, he had been decorated by the Pope, played for England's King George III, had proposed to Marie Antoinette (she turned him down because she was only eight at the time), and eventually became the court composer for Emperor Joseph II. He was born this day in 1756 in Salzburg, Austria, and was christened Johannes Chrysostomus Wolfgangus Theophilus. But we know him better as Wolfgang Amadeus Mozart, arguably the greatest and most prodigious composer who ever lived.

Mozart was popular in his life, but he had his detractors—most significantly the envious Antonio Salieri, his rival composer at court. Salieri had talent, discipline, and devotion; Mozart had genius and the ability to toss off masterpieces seemingly without effort. Salieri envied Mozart, perhaps even loathed him. But did he hate him enough to commit murder?

That's the premise for director Milos Forman's excellent movie based on Peter Shaffer's successful play, **Amadeus** (1984), which swept the Oscars that year, winning Best Picture, Best Director, and Best Actor. *Amadeus* celebrates Mozart's life, music, and times—bringing it all to vivid life in a film that is alternately funny, speculative, and magnificently musical. Tom Hulce is a totally unexpected Mozart—called "Wolfy" by his wife—giddy, fun-loving, bawdy, and with a laugh like a hyena on helium. His rival Salieri is played with petulant indignation and envy by F. Murray Abraham, who won a Best Actor Oscar for his tortured portrait of a man who devotes his life and art to God and can't understand why his Master bestows His gifts on a hedonistic oaf like Mozart. The film does take liberties; the whole Salieri murder conspiracy, while a very effective hook, is fiction. In all probability, Mozart died of typhoid fever, not poison, at thirty-five. Still, *Amadeus* is an enthralling rumination on genius—both on those to whom it is seemingly randomly bestowed and on those who suffer and sacrifice and never attain it. And whoever wrote that music score should've gotten an Oscar. A vibrant, invigorating, lushly imagined modern masterpiece.

january 28

The Promised Land of Milk 'n' Money

The city of Beverly Hills became formally recognized by the Golden State of California on this day in 1914, and property values were never the same again.

In 1844 a Spanish woman named Maria Rita Valdez managed to score one of the great deals of the century when she acquired controlling interest of 4,500 acres of tumbleweeds, sagebrush, sheep meadows, and lizards for a grand total of $17.50. In 1912, a group of German investors decided to build a hotel—dubbed the Hotel Beverly Hills—on the property to attract visitors. By sheer luck and fortuitous timing, the fledgling film industry arrived months later, and business at the hotel was booming. When movie royalty Mary Pickford and Douglas Fairbanks decided to build their legendary home, Pickfair, on a hill overlooking the hotel, the town's reputation was made. Within a few years, John Barrymore, Charlie Chaplin, Greta Garbo, and the rest of Hollywood royalty had nestled into cozy coexistence in paradise. As the film industry ensconced itself in Hollywood, Beverly Hills became, in essence, the suburbs for the industry's well-to-do.

Commemorate the illustrious real estate transaction with **Down and Out in Beverly Hills** (1986), Paul Mazursky's potent and funny satire of southern California customs and values. Based on the French film *Boudou Saved from Drowning, Down and Out* follows the tale of a homeless, eccentric, but charismatic bum (Nick Nolte) who manages to get adopted by a typically atypical Beverly Hills family, headed by wire hanger manufacturing mogul Richard Dreyfuss and his spoiled wife, played with great gusto by Bette Midler. Mazursky skewers the Southern California lifestyle with both wit and compassion, and Nolte reveals previously unknown comedic talents in his role as the manipulative but amiable bum.

january 29

What Do Ya Wanna Do Tonight, Marty?

"Dogs like us, we ain't such dogs as we think we are."

—Marty

Paddy Chayefsky, one of the great screenwriters of the twentieth century, was born on this day in 1923, appropriately enough in the Bronx. As a young man after World War II, he wrote his first play, a musical, while recuperating from injuries incurred by a German land mine while in the service. After the war, he began writing radio and TV dramas, specializing in stories that dealt sympathetically with the lives of ordinary people, portrayed in a realistic way. After moving to the big screen, he went on to write the acerbic film *The Hospital* (1971), with George C. Scott as the literally impotent head of a beleaguered hospital; the epochal and Oscar-winning *Network* (1976); and his last film as (uncredited) screenwriter, *Altered States* (1980), starring William Hurt and directed by Ken Russell.

Honor Chayefsky's celebration of the common man with his most famous work, **Marty** (1955), the tale of a lonely New York butcher who finds love with a plain-looking girl, but who is afraid to tell his friends and mother. It was originally produced as a television play starring Rod Steiger and later as a full-fledged Hollywood movie with Ernest Borgnine (who won an Oscar for Best Actor). The Hollywood version is great, but the original teleplay is even better. Steiger delivers one of his greatest performances ever—and that's saying plenty—all on live TV. But no matter which version of *Marty* you watch, it'll be an evening well spent.

january 30

Gandhi but Not Forgotten

For an icon recognized around the world as a nonviolent visionary of peace and compassion, Mohandas Gandhi was kind of a killjoy. Birth control advocate Margaret Sanger commented on his "ruthless determination to destroy pleasure wherever he saw it." (He even wanted to outlaw sex between a husband and wife!) His record as a husband and father was abysmal. He steadfastly refused to educate his wife and children, even though he had financed his own education by selling off his wife's jewelry. When she contracted pneumonia in 1944, he refused medical treatment, insisting her fate was in God's hands. She died three days later. This didn't stop him, however, from taking medication when he himself contracted malaria months later.

But he went from fallible human being to fallen martyr on this day in

1948, when he was assassinated in Delhi by a Hindu extremist who opposed Gandhi's benevolent attitude toward his country's Muslim population.

As a symbol, Gandhi is potent; as a man, he was decidedly flawed. In **Gandhi** (1982), director Sir Richard Attenborough (trying hard to be David Lean) jettisoned Gandhi's more objectionable traits for a more audience-friendly icon. Still, it makes for fine entertainment, and Ben Kingsley is suitably beguiling in the title role. *Gandhi* is magnificently filmed with awe-inspiring cinematography and lavish attention to period detail. But as far as the true man, the film certainly chooses to turn the other cheek.

january 31

My Boats Is U-boats

On this date in 1915, Germany announced its policy of unlimited submarine warfare in the Atlantic, and declared that it was prepared to attack any and all ships in "disputed" waters—including commercial passenger ships. Three days later, the U.S. broke off diplomatic relations, and hours after that, an American liner was sunk by a German U-boat. Then Germany delivered the coup de grace by sinking the *Lusitania,* on May 7, 1915, thus ushering in America's involvement in World War I.

The German U-boat (from the German *Unterseeboot*) figured prominently in both world wars. But life aboard them was nearly unimaginable. The average boat was 150 feet long, carrying three officers and a crew of thirty, with bunks for only half. There were no refrigerators; it was brutally hot on the surface and freezing cold on the bottom. The entire crew would go weeks without bathing, scrunched together in extremely tight quarters like sardines, and the odor—a foul stench of oil, body odor, and feces—was horrendous.

Das Boot (1984) is a movie that will literally have you gasping for breath and clutching your own arms. A harrowing depiction of life aboard a German U-boat during the last days of World War II while it patrols the Atlantic,

Das Boot puts you uncomfortably close to the action. Wolfgang Petersen's epic originated as a television drama and was expanded for theatrical release. His direction is extraordinary—although most of the action takes place in the cramped environment of the fragile U-boat, Petersen's fluid Steadicam creates a visceral sense of tension that pulls you into the picture. An almost unbearably suspenseful film.

february

february 1

Rent a Ford

On this day in 1895, Sean Aloysius O'Feeney was born in Cape Elizabeth, Maine. He often introduced himself by saying, "My name is John Ford. I make Westerns."

Well, yeah . . . and a guy named Stradivarius made fiddles.

When Orson Welles was asked who his favorite film directors were, he replied, "The modern masters. By that, I mean John Ford, John Ford, and John Ford."

In his long and distinguished career, John Ford directed films that have become the American gold standard—and not just Westerns. With 1939's *Stagecoach,* he pretty much invented, defined, and refined the modern Western in one fell swoop, as well as making a young USC football player named Marion Morrison into John Wayne. His movies are filled with characters who evolved into American archetypes (*Young Mr. Lincoln; The Man Who Shot Liberty Valance*), a stunning yet subtle flair for visuals (it sometimes seems as if God created Monument Valley just for him), and a sense of morality which could at times be problematic (see how his treatment of Native

Americans evolves from *The Searchers* to his late-career apology, *Cheyenne Autumn*).

Choose from several of his many masterpieces: the precedent-setting and still exciting *Stagecoach* (you'll get so caught up in the Indian attack sequence you may not notice that they're going the wrong way on the screen); the refined and shaded *My Darling Clementine;* his beautiful blarney valentine to his Irish homeland, *The Quiet Man* (1952); or, my personal favorite, **The Grapes of Wrath** (1940), Ford's magnificent adaptation of John Steinbeck's classic story of the Oklahoma farmers migration from the dustbowl to the promised land in California during the Depression. The lyrical cinematography (by Greg Toland, who would shoot *Citizen Kane* two years later) perfectly captures the stark plainness of the migrants, and Ford's direction is elegiac while staying, for the most part, remarkably free of sentimentality. Henry Fonda delivered one of his greatest performances as Tom Joad, the conscience for a whole country. His final farewell speech to Ma Joad (Jane Darwell) was done in one take.

february 2

Groundhog Day

Ever wondered where such a goofy holiday as Groundhog Day came from? It stems from an old German legend that says that if the sun shines on this day, also known as Candlemass Day, six more weeks of winter will follow. Don't ask me how the groundhog got involved.

Whether or not you see your shadow today, celebrate the occasion with—what else?—**Groundhog Day** (1993). Bill Murray stars in his best screen role yet as arrogant, misanthropic TV weatherman Phil Connors, who is assigned to cover the annual Groundhog Day festivities in Punxatawney, Pennsylvania—"the weather capital of the world"—only to find himself lost in some sort of time warp, having to relive the same twenty-four hours over and over . . . and over. Murray is endearingly smarmy in one of his best roles, and Andie McDowell is good as the coworker he's trying to seduce. A consistently witty, inventive, delightful comedy from writer/director Harold Ramis *(Ghostbusters)*.

february 3

The Day the Music Died

Twenty-two-year-old rock pioneer Buddy Holly's plane went down in a snowy cornfield in Mason City, Iowa, this night in 1959. Also on board were rising teen rock star Ritchie Valens and DJ-turned-novelty performer J. P. Richardson, better known as the Big Bopper. A young Waylon Jennings, touring with the group at the time, lost a bet—and his seat—on the plane that night. Before his death, Holly wrote some of the greatest pop songs of the golden era, including "That'll Be the Day," "True Love Ways," and "Rave On."

Commemorate the occasion by watching **The Buddy Holly Story**, the immensely enjoyable if slightly sanitized 1978 screen bio. A lot of its infectious energy and drive come from the uncanny, evocative performance of Gary Busey in the title role. Although taller than the real Holly by a good twelve inches, Busey somehow *becomes* the young, politely rebellious rocker from Lubbock, Texas. The story may not be historically accurate (there were actually three other Crickets, not two), but the mythology is right. As Holly, Busey sang and performed the musical numbers live on camera (along with fellow Cricket costars Charles Martin Smith and Don Stroud), contributing a real sense of electricity that other rock musicals sorely lack.

Make it a double bill with **La Bamba** (1987), starring Lou Diamond Phillips as Ritchie Valens, the young Mexican American who had two Top 10 hits ("La Bamba" and "Donna") before dying at seventeen in the same plane crash that claimed Holly. Phillips is good, but the movie is really carried by the performances of Esai Morales as his rebellious and envious older brother and, in a layered and captivating performance, Elizabeth Peña as his mother. Directed by Luis Valdez, who occasionally escapes the confines of the genre with some striking sequences—particularly the opening sequence, a black-and-white flashback of a basketball game interrupted by a plane crash.

february 4

It Hearst to Be in Love

Steven Weed and his fiancée were spending a quiet evening watching TV in their Berkeley apartment on this night in 1974 when the doorbell rang. Weed got up to answer and found himself confronted by three strangers—two men and a woman—who assaulted him and elbowed their way inside, making off with his girlfriend in a hail of bullets. They shoved her into a car and disappeared into the night. The girl happened to be nineteen-year-old newspaper heiress Patricia Hearst, granddaughter of the famous millionaire William Randolph Hearst and daughter of Randolph Hearst, prestigious publisher of the *San Francisco Examiner.*

In a tape recording sent to a local radio station, the captors identified themselves as members of the Symbionese Liberation Army and said they had captured Patty as a "prisoner of war" in order to protest "the crimes her mother and father have committed against the people of America and the world." They demanded that Randolph Hearst, among other things, give away two million dollars' worth of food to be distributed to the poor. When he did, they demanded an additional four million.

Things got even stranger when Patty Hearst emerged to take part in a bank robbery near Sacramento in April with the radical group. She was caught on videotape brandishing an automatic weapon and sporting a radically chic black beret. She issued a taped message in which she claimed she had changed her name to Tania (after a Bolivian woman who had died with Che Guevara) and joined in the fight against capitalist oppression of the poor and disenfranchised.

And that was just the beginning to one of the strangest criminal stories in the annals of American crime. Commemorate the anniversary of Patty's abduction by watching writer-director Paul Schrader's **Patty Hearst** (1988). Natasha Richardson gives a cool, convincing performance as Hearst in this gritty account of her kidnapping, torture, brainwashing, and eventual capture. A fascinating, at times unbelievable story; the kind of tale that, if it had been fiction, would have prompted incredulousness in audiences.

Today Patricia Hearst is Mrs. Patricia Hearst Shaw, a married mother living in Connecticut who finds herself most often recognized as an author and actress (she has appeared in several John Waters movies). She never discusses her time with the SLA.

february 5

Enjoy a General Disaster

On this day in 1927, silent screen clown and genius Buster Keaton released his masterpiece, **The General,** possibly the greatest silent comedy of all time—and it promptly bombed at the box office.

During the Civil War, young Southerner Johnny Gray (Keaton) risks his life as he pursues his beloved railway engine, stolen by Northern spies. The ensuing chase makes for what is arguably the greatest silent screen comedy ever made. It has it all—brilliant comedy, suspense, action, unbelievably enveloping period detail, a love story, and the single longest sustained chase ever put on film. It also has the single most expensive visual joke in the history of movies—a locomotive crossing a wooden bridge and collapsing into the river below.

Seen today, *The General* is still brilliantly, breathlessly creative and fresh. The period detail is faithfully re-created—Keaton's sense of time and place were never better; the images often look like Mathew Brady daguerreotypes come to life.

Sadly, after the failure of this movie, Keaton's career began its long decline; by the 1930s he was an alcoholic, had lost creative control of his movies, and was reduced to playing second banana to Jimmy Durante. He did live long enough to see a revival of interest and appreciation throughout the '60s up until his death in 1966.

Unfortunately, this masterpiece fell into the public domain back in the '60s and has been dubbed many times. Catch the digitally remastered Kino Video version if you possibly can—the images are jaw-droppingly vivid and alive.

february 6

A Birthday Babe

Happy birthday to the "Sultan of Swat," George Herman "Babe" Ruth, born in Baltimore, Maryland, this day in 1895. He endured a troubled childhood (he was abandoned as an incorrigible child and left to be raised by priests) and became one of the ultimate sports icons of all time. In his twenty-two major league seasons he hit 714 home runs and played in ten World Series. And, by all accounts, he was one of the most colorful sports heroes ever, with a hearty, gluttonous appetite for life.

He's been the subject of two very different screen bios—the highly fictionalized whitewash, *The Babe Ruth Story* (1948), starring William "Life of Riley" Bendix, and the more realistic, warts 'n' all portrait in **The Babe** (1991). Bendix played the Babe as a simpleton—a gifted, good-hearted oaf. John Goodman delivers a splendid, big-barreled performance as the life-grabbing, hard-hitting (in more ways than one) Ruth, while still maintaining the geniality that the Babe projected. Here he emerges as a glutton for life who abuses alcohol, has outbursts of violence, and cheats on his wife. In short, the prototype of a modern American sports hero. A surprisingly effective movie, even if you don't know a ball from a strike and couldn't care less. (If you'd like to see how the real Babe fared in front of a movie camera, catch 1942's *Pride of the Yankees,* with Gary Cooper as Lou Gehrig and Ruth appearing in a cameo as himself.)

february 7

Beatles Invade America

On this day on a cold winter morning in 1964, the Beatles arrived at JFK Airport for the first of three scheduled appearances on *The Ed Sullivan Show,* and Beatlemania arrived in the U.S.A. A crowd of over three thousand—mostly teenage girls—was on hand to welcome them. Before they sang a note, the group charmed jaded Big Apple reporters at the airport with their repartee and witty, off-the-cuff answers to demeaning questions.

"Will you sing for us?"

John: "No, we need money first."

"We hear that Detroit is organizing a 'Stamp Out the Beatles' campaign. What are you going to do?"

Paul: "We're putting together a 'Stamp Out Detroit' campaign. . . ."

"Do you ever get haircuts?"

George: "I had one yesterday."

"What do you think of Beethoven?"

Ringo: "He's great. 'Specially his poems."

"How do you find America?"

John: "Turn left at Greenland."

And from then on, for anyone who was there, the British Invasion had begun, in both earnest and in jest.

Celebrate the beguiling phenomenon that was Beatlemania—magically captured in **A Hard Day's Night** (1964), the group's unexpectedly inventive and funny film debut. Andrew Sarris called the film "the *Citizen Kane* of jukebox musicals," but it is a lot more enjoyable than that lofty description would imply. Initially planned as a black-and-white quickie exploitation flick to cash in on the group's popularity, *A Hard Day's Night* transcended its purpose and its genre to become an enjoyable and buoyant masterpiece. Filmed as a *faux-verité* "day in the life" of the group (written by fellow Liverpudlian Alan Owen), *A Hard Day's Night* managed to capture pop culture lightning in a bottle, portraying the Beatles as a kind of mod, musical version of the

Marx Brothers. Director Richard Lester made the most of his limited resources; the film is brimming with energy and inventive sight gags. His use of hand-held cameras and framing of musical sequences served as a veritable Bible for future music videos. Packed with memorable bits: the still-exhilarating "Can't Buy Me Love" montage with the group cavorting on an open field ("Sorry we hurt your field, mister"); George's confrontation with a stiff-shirted marketing guru; and, best of all, Ringo's wistful solo sojourn beside the River Thames. (He later confessed to being hung over during the shooting of that sequence.) At once a vivid snapshot of a long-ago era and a still-fresh musical comedy, *A Hard Day's Night* remains the Beatles' most enchanting cinematic legacy.

Top off the night with a remarkable find. If you'd like to vicariously experience their actual arrival in the U.S.A. on this date, it is memorably brought to life in a true cinema verité video, **The Beatles: The First U.S. Visit** (1994). Filmmakers David and Albert Maysles followed the Beatles during their four-day trip to América. What results is a fascinating documentary, revealing how insulated and surrealistically isolated the boys were from the real world—which was going mad just outside their doors. As George later ruefully remarked, "Everybody got to see the Beatles but us." Here's his chance. *The First U.S. Visit* features all of the *Ed Sullivan* performances in pristine condition. Fab.

february 8

Get Ahead, Lose a Head

Imagine a melodramatic Hollywood costume drama all about a beautiful young woman who becomes queen of Scotland when she's only six days old, and then queen of France, too, by virtue of blood ties, by the time she's seventeen. She gets overly ambitious and begins to covet the English throne when she's only eighteen. The plot thickens when her husband dies and she is convicted of his murder. She's put into prison, but escapes with the help of her confederates and loyal subjects. . . .

It happened to Mary Stuart, who ruled as Queen of Scots from 1542 to 1567 and as queen of France from 1559 to 1560. By all accounts, Mary, Queen of Scots, was a headstrong woman—but on this day in 1587 she became a headless one.

Observe the occasion with **Mary, Queen of Scots** (1971), an austere production featuring a luminous performance from Vanessa Redgrave in the title role. Raised in France by her mother's Catholic family, Mary inherits the Scottish crown after her mother's death. This doesn't sit well with her Protestant half-brother Stuart (Patrick McGoohan, suitably nefarious) or England's equally Protestant Queen Elizabeth (Glenda Jackson). The sort of vedy prestigious British costume drama that they just can't afford to make anymore. Predictably, both Redgrave and Jackson are superb.

february 9

Look! Up in the Sky! It's a Bird! It's a Plane! It's . . .

The Adventures of Superman debuts on TV this day in 1953, and tens of thousands of impressionable young baby boomers start jumping off their mattresses with arms outstretched and bath-towel capes trailing behind. One of the first TV series created for syndication, it was also one of the first to be filmed in color (after its first season). Baby boomers memorized the opening credits, which became a cultural mantra: "Look! Up in the sky! It's a bird! It's a plane! It's . . . *Superman!*" Stalwart B-movie actor George Reeves starred as the Man of Steel, a.k.a. mild-mannered reporter Clark Kent. The stories and special effects were cheesy even for their time—but the series went on to become a touchstone for a generation.

The series actually had a "dry run" as a movie—a very modest movie—called *Superman and the Mole Men* (1952), which featured the leotarded Reeves being a Good Samaritan to underground alien midgets who carried around futuristic vacuum cleaners. Reeves actually won the part because of his chin, which resembled the way Superman was drawn in the comics.

Superman: The Movie eventually made it to the big screen in 1978, launching the career of Christopher Reeve as the Man of Steel. The first installment, helped along by a two-million-dollar cameo by Marlon Brando as Superman's Kryptonian father, Jor-El, was a huge hit and spawned three sequels, each worse than its predecessor. Seen today, *Superman: The Movie* seems very much a product of its time. The special effects, impressive at the time, now seem sluggish and dated, and the film is almost halfway over before Superman ever makes it to Metropolis (although Gene Hackman makes a marvelously malevolent Lex Luthor).

The best version of Superman on the screen didn't feature an actor at all—it was a series of seventeen dazzling animated cartoons produced by the Fleischer studios between 1941 and 1943. The Fleischer's animated Superman performed all the dazzling feats he could do in the comics but not in the movies—like lift an ocean liner or divert a shower of meteors—and he did it with style. The breathless adventures were shown as short subjects before the main feature film in theaters across the country. Max and Dave Fleischer were the anti-Disneys—producing high-quality, innovative Art Deco–drenched animation that absolutely burst off the screen in an explosion of color. The entire series is available for home viewing as **The Complete Superman Collection** (Bosko Video).

february 10

Have a Fields Day

"It was a woman drove me to drink.
And I never had the courtesy to write and thank her."

—W. C. Fields

William Claude Dunkenfield—better known as W. C. Fields—was born on this day in 1879, and dogs and children suffered his wrath for decades after.

His eccentricities, foibles, and pet hatreds are well documented. A world-class misanthrope, he trusted no one and had more phobias than a textbook on psychology. But he took his eccentricities, prejudices, and fears and turned them into some of the funniest film footage ever run through a projector.

Commemorate the birth of the great man with **It's a Gift** (1934), where Fields, as much-put-upon, small-town-grocer Harold Bissenette ("pronounced Bis-o-*nay!*"), dreams of moving to the sun-drenched orange groves of California. But he gets no support from his henpecking wife, self-absorbed teenage daughter, and bratty ten-year-old son. The extended sequence where he tries to get a good night's sleep on the front porch after being evicted by his wife is classic; only Chaplin could have squeezed so many laughs from such a simple premise. *It's a Gift* is one of Fields's funniest films—if not *the* funniest. Which makes it easily one of the greatest comedies ever made, and one of the most insightful satires of the American Dream ever committed to film.

february 11

A Vision for the Faithful

On this day in 1858, Bernadette Soubirous, a fourteen-year-old French peasant girl who could neither read or write, was out gathering firewood with her two sisters near Lourdes. As her sisters crossed a small stream, Bernadette was left behind for a moment—and heard a sound which she later described as being "like a storm." She looked up to see an apparition of a lady dressed in white with a blue sash, and with a yellow rose on each foot, standing before her. The apparition did not speak, but made the sign of the cross and disappeared.

The next time the vision appeared to Bernadette, she spoke, telling the girl to urge the local priests to build a chapel there. She then told the girl to drink from the spring and pointed to a pool of muddy water. Bernadette dug into the ground, and fresh water appeared.

Bernadette returned every day and on each occasion but two, the vision appeared. Whenever Bernadette asked who the lady was, the apparition would only smile in response. One day the woman answered, *"Que soy era Immaculada Conceptiou"* ("I am the Immaculate Conception").

Bernadette reported her vision to a local priest, who asked the peasant girl if she knew what the words meant. She did not. The phrase had only been applied to the Virgin Mary four years before and was only known within the circles of the clergy. The priest was convinced of Bernadette's vision, and soon the faithful were flocking to the grotto in Lourdes. The Church later confirmed the apparitions as genuine, and to this day the shrine and spring waters have been said to cause miraculous healings.

The Song of Bernadette (1943) is a sensitive and moving re-creation of the story which almost plays like a religious fairy tale. Sensitively directed by Henry King, and with a near-ethereal performance by Jennifer Jones as the girl who sees the Virgin Mary. Jones won an Oscar for Best Actress that year for her role as Bernadette. A timeless and moving tale of the power of faith. Vincent Price is good in a change-of-pace role as a priest. (That's Linda Darnell as the apparition.)

february 12

Young and Abe-le

"A man of steel and velvet,
who is as hard as a rock and soft as a drifting fog,
who holds in his heart and mind the drifting paradox of terrible storm and peace unspeakable."

—Carl Sandburg, describing Abraham Lincoln

Abraham Lincoln was born this day in 1809 near Hodgenville, Kentucky—and, yes, he really was born in a log cabin.

He has been portrayed on screen more often than any other U.S. president. D. W. Griffith filmed the first talkie bio, *Abraham Lincoln* in 1930, and Lincoln also figured prominently in his previous *Birth of a Nation.* In 1939's *Abe Lincoln in Illinois,* Raymond Massey looked like Lincoln but acted like Mt. Rushmore. Much more entertaining and elegiac is 1939's **Young Mr. Lincoln**, directed by John Ford. When John Ford approached Henry Fonda to portray the lanky prairie lawyer in a film biography of Lincoln's early years, the intimidated actor declined, until Ford convinced him he wouldn't be playing a saint—he'd be playing an uneducated backwoods storekeeper who rode on a jackass.

His protestations aside, Ford was obviously in awe of the sixteenth president. Lincoln is presented as a saintly everyman with an endearing, self-deprecating sense of humor, a sharp wit, and a wily, aw-shucks approach to justice. The film follows Lincoln from log splitter to storekeeper to country lawyer to politician. The highlight is Lincoln's defense of an accused murderer, based on a real-life incident where a witness testified she had seen Lincoln's client commit a murder under the light of the moon. The canny lawyer produced an almanac proving there was no moon on the night of the crime, and the accused was acquitted. Although Ford's direction and tone borders on fawning, it is Henry Fonda's humanistic, humorous, and humble portrayal of Lincoln which lingers and makes this motion picture so memorable. Fonda gave us the Lincoln of our collective aspirations, dreams, and imaginations. Honest, Abe.

february 13

Been to Confession Lately?

Today is National Confession Day. I confess I have no idea where it came from, nor do I care.

Observe the occasion with—what else?—Alfred Hitchcock's **I Confess**

(1953). Montgomery Clift stars as a Catholic priest who faces the death penalty because he refuses to divulge incriminating information he heard in the confessional, and the circumstances point to him as the prime suspect. Not one of Hitch's typical roller coaster rides, *I Confess* is one of his more serious artistic endeavors, more of a character study than a thriller or mystery. Still, the Hitchcock style is much in evidence, and the black and white, holy noir atmosphere is evocative and steeped in symbolism. Clift is great—there is still the ghost of his youthful beauty in evidence—and Karl Malden began a long career playing cops in this movie.

february 14

Follow Your Heart

Valentine's Day. Here's hoping you're all lucky enough to have someone to spend it with.

Aside from politics and sushi, no subject is more subjective than romance. One man's meat might be another man's poison, and one woman's poetry may be another's pornography. Hey, there's no accounting for taste or for love.

Romantic hint: If you want to score some romantic points with your paramour, rent the very first movie you ever saw together, and give him/her a foot rub while he/she is watching. At $3.50 or so, a very affordable evening—and he/she will thank you/me for it in ways that you/he/she/me can all appreciate.

Can't remember that first movie?—or would rather *forget* that first movie? With that in mind—and also the fact that love at twenty is different from love at forty (at least, the way I remember it . . .)—here are a few random suggestions.

AGES 10 TO 13:

A Little Romance (1979), an absolutely enchanting French pastry of a movie about two young runaways in Paris who find companionship and guidance in the person of an old con artist, endearingly played by Laurence Olivier. **The Little Mermaid** (1989), the charming story of Ariel, a headstrong mermaid who is curious about life above the water, and who falls in love with a seafarer. **Beauty and the Beast** and **Cinderella.** Yes, I know there may be some post-feminist recriminations over these two animated Disney classics, but they are lush and lovely to behold.

AGES 13 TO 18:

William Shakespeare's Romeo + Juliet (1996), Baz Luhrmann's MTV-style update of the classic romance, transferred to modern-day gang warfare in "Verona Beach" and starring Leonardo DiCaprio and Claire Danes as the star-crossed lovers; **The Princess Bride** (1987), the enchanting comic fable based on William Goldman's cult classic novel, with Cary Elwes and Robin Wright heading an eclectic and hugely enjoyable cast; **Titanic** (1997), James Cameron's box-office blockbuster romance set aboard the ill-fated ocean liner. With Leonardo DiCaprio, Kate Winslet, a hokey script, and great effects.

AGES 18 TO 30:

Shakespeare in Love (1997), its inventive "what if?" plot centering around Shakespeare's early love life and how *Romeo and Juliet* came to be written, showcasing Gwynyth Paltrow in a wonderful performance and Joseph Fiennes as young Will, and filled with lush scenery and repressed Elizabethan hormones; **There's Something About Mary** (1997), the Farrelly Brothers' smash hit comedy with a sweet, romantic heart at the core of its anything-goes comedy; Steve Martin's romantic comic update of *Cyrano de Bergerac,* **Roxanne** (1987), or his equally amusing and laugh-packed **L.A. Story** (1991).

AGES 30 TO 40:

When Harry Met Sally (1989), Rob Reiner's amiable romantic comedy charting ten years between Billy Crystal and Meg Ryan, is like a less-filling

Woody Allen movie—lots of laughs, sharp observations about the differences between men and women, and plenty of beautifully composed shots of Manhattan; **Moonstruck** (1987), Cher's Academy Award–winning performance as a thirty-something woman who finds love with pizza tosser Nicolas Cage ("Get over it!"), is a romance for borderline cynics and burnt-out dreamers; **Sleepless in Seattle** (1997), with Tom Hanks and Meg Ryan as two lonely people on opposite coasts brought together by Hanks's son; **Casablanca** (1943), the definitive movie romance starring Humphrey Bogart and Ingrid Bergman as two ex-lovers reunited in war-torn Casablanca, has more heart and great lines than any other movie ever made; **The Taming of the Shrew** (1967), an energetic rendering of Shakespeare's comedy of romance starring Richard Burton and Elizabeth Taylor; **Modern Romance** (1980), comedian Albert Brooks's hilariously neurotic but therapeutic take on relationships; and just about any Woody Allen movie—**Annie Hall; Play It Again, Sam; Hannah and Her Sisters; Manhattan; Everyone Says I Love You.**

AGES 40 TO 50:

Robin and Marion (1976) is a funny, inventive, and ultimately affecting film about Robin Hood returning to Sherwood Forest and his beloved Maid Marion twenty years after going to war for King Richard. Sean Connery makes a wonderful middle-aged Robin and the luminous Audrey Hepburn is Maid Marion ("You didn't write!" scolds an angry Marion, to which Robin replies truthfully, "I don't know how."). A magical rumination on what happens after "happily ever after," which is both uproariously funny and heartbreakingly romantic, *Robin and Marion* has it all—romance, comedy, action, and an ending that will pierce your heart; **The Way We Were** (1973), charts the years-long stormy relationship between ill-suited lovers Barbra Streisand and Robert Redford in this classy depiction of a volatile romance; **An Affair to Remember** (1957), the tear-jerker that inspired all those Nora Ephron movies.

AGES 50-PLUS:

The African Queen (1951) costars Humphrey Bogart, in an Oscar-winning performance as a hard-drinking steamboat skipper and Katharine Hepburn, the prudish but stalwart traveling companion he gradually falls in love with; **The Bridges of Madison County** (1997), wherein sensitive but taciturn photographer Clint Eastwood falls for neglected housewife Meryl Streep, and both the rewards and terrible burden of adultery are artfully balanced; **On Golden Pond** (1981) stars Henry Fonda and Katharine Hepburn as a long-time couple knowing that their autumns together are growing fewer and shorter. When their daughter (played by Jane Fonda, in her only performance ever with her dad) and grandson arrive for a visit, the two discover the courage to face what lies ahead. **Guess Who's Coming to Dinner** (1967) is largely recalled today for its "social theme"—the complications of a mixed marriage. But what comes through today is the tremendous love between Tracy and Hepburn as the parents of a daughter who's going to marry a young African-American med student (Sidney Poitier). When Tracy looks at Hepburn and toasts their years together at the end, those tears are for real.

No matter what you watch tonight, viva l'amour.

february 15

Legend of a Profile

John Barrymore—"the Great Profile"—was born this day in 1882—too early for what could have been a phenomenal career in motion pictures. As it was, he was still plenty successful.

The youngest son of stage matinee idol Maurice Barrymore and American actress Georgia Drew, and youngest brother of fellow thespians Ethel and Lionel, John was one of the handsomest young men ever to grace the theater footlights. His Hamlet and Richard III are the stuff of theater legend—as is his tempestuous, anecdote-laden private life. He walked through most of his film roles as the character of "John Barrymore," a concocted persona of flamboyance, impeccable diction, and a profile that the camera adored—at least in his early years. His silent film roles—like in *Don Juan* (1926) and *Dr. Jekyll and Mr. Hyde* (1920)—capture his astonishing beauty. But by the time talkies arrived, Barrymore was already over fifty, and his once-magnificent physique and memory were beginning to show the ravages of a self-indulgent lifestyle of women, parties, and booze. Lots and lots of booze.

Still, he managed to create a few brilliant performances on film before he literally drank himself to death in 1942. His Mercutio in *Romeo and Juliet* (1936) may be overage but is still robust and full of life, and his doomed jewel thief who falls in love with Greta Garbo in the all-star *Grand Hotel* (1932) is gallant and touching. But the film that best captures Barrymore's hammy brilliance—and ingratiating gift of self-parody—is the screwball comedy, **Twentieth Century** (1934). Barrymore plays Oscar Jaffe, a pretentious and egomaniacal theater director extraordinaire who discovers and mentors unknown actress Mildred Plotnik (Carole Lombard), and changes her name to Lily Garland. She becomes a huge star and leaves the egomaniacal Oscar to go to Hollywood; his career tanks. When they meet again on a cross-country train, Oscar maneuvers to get her name on a contract. Barrymore simultaneously makes fun of the acting profession (playing a character who has been acting for so long he's no longer capable of distinguishing acting from reality) while honoring it. Director Howard Hawks, who insisted on Barrymore for the role over the protestations of studio brass, keeps the madcap action going full throttle. And the dialogue by Ben Hecht and Charles MacArthur snaps, crackles, and pops with wit. Barrymore is nearly matched by the delightful Carole Lombard as the fiesty diva.

february 16

Have a Sonny Day

Let us now pause to praise those born with negligible talent and no particular genius, but blessed with a surplus supply of tenacity, ambition, luck, good timing, and drive, striving and working their way to greatness.

Salvatore Bono—called Sonny by his loving mum—was born this day in Detroit, Michigan, in 1935. While working as a delivery boy in Los Angeles, one of the stops on his route was Phil Spector's recording studio. The ambitious twenty-something ingratiated himself to the brilliant but eccentric record producer and talked his way into an assistant engineering job. A quick study with a good ear but a nasal, whiney voice, Sonny absorbed the nuts and bolts of Spector's methods, managing to help work out arrangements and actually even writing a hit Spector-ish song, "Needles and Pins." He met and fell in love with a fifteen-year-old backup singer named Cherilyn LaPiere. They formed a duo called Caesar and Cleo, got married, changed the act's name to Sonny and Cher, and took off for the top of the charts with Sonny's catchy 1965 ditty, "I Got You, Babe." In the early '70s, they became stars of a hit TV variety series, which lasted until their divorce in 1974.

You know the rest of the story. After Sonny and Cher fizzled, Sonny opened a restaurant in Beverly Hills. When that eventually failed, he ran for mayor of Palm Springs—and won. Then he went on to become a U.S. congressman. In America, a little talent and a lot of tenacity can take you a long, long way.

Commemorate the birth of one of the patron saints of enterprise and perseverance with a double bill of Bono: In **Good Times** (1966), the duo's sole excursion into the movies as a team, Sony and Cher play themselves, with George Sanders as a Hollywood tycoon who keeps dreaming up different parts they could play. Tracy and Hepburn they weren't—they weren't even George and Gracie—but here they still display the goofy charm that would take them to the top of the Neilsons with their later TV series. *Good Times* also has the distinction of being the first movie ever directed by

William Freidkin, who would later go on to direct such seminal movies as *The Exorcist* (1973) and *The French Connection* (1971). Then, if you can stand the homage, ponder **Chastity** (1969), Sonny Bono's sole effort as screenwriter and Cher's first starring role. She plays—surprise!—a free-spirited young girl named Chastity. That's about all you need to know, except that here's your opportunity to see Cher with her original nose.

february 17

A Warrior at Peace

"I cannot think that we are useless or God would not have created us. We are all the children of one God. The sun, the darkness, the winds are all listening to what we have to say."

—Geronimo

He became famous and feared as an Apache warrior and leader, and to this day his name evokes passion, strength, and respect. Born in what is now western New Mexico in 1829, he acquired a reputation as a fearless warrior after he returned home from a trading excursion into Mexico in 1858 and found his wife and three children murdered by white soldiers. He vowed to kill as many white men as he could, and from that day he was driven by a series of visions. He believed he was impervious to bullets. For fifty years he fought brilliantly against the white man; at one point over one-quarter of the entire U.S. Army was assigned to track him and his small band of twenty-eight, and he avoided capture for years. He was the last Native American leader to effectively defy the government's attempts to take the Indians from their rightful land.

He spent his final days, an old fighter tamed and subjugated by the U.S. government that he had so effectively battled years before, charging a dollar to pose for pictures with visitors, tourists, and dignitaries, until he died on this day in 1909 at the ripe old age of eighty. He was right all along. He had indeed been immune to bullets.

Relive his glory days as the most revered and feared Apache warrior of all time in **Geronimo: An American Legend** (1993). In one of his most restrained and cohesive films, director Walter Hill paints a vivid and haunting portrait of the warrior and his tempestuous times. Wes Studi, as Geronimo, delivers a solid, layered performance, but the real star of the film is Jason Patric as the cavalryman who is used as a liaison between Geronimo and the whites. Far from your typical cavalry vs. Indians shoot-'em-up, Walter Hill's memorable movie is a sad and instructive history lesson. Gene Hackman and Robert Duvall deliver great supporting turns.

february 18

Rollin' Down the River

Generally acknowledged to be the quintessential Great American Novel, Mark Twain's *Adventures of Huckleberry Finn* first rolled off the printer's press on this day in 1885.

The free-wheeling satirical story of a young orphan on the run from the law on the Mississippi has been filmed countless times, but the best version may well be MGM's **The Adventures of Huckleberry Finn** (1939), starring Mickey Rooney as the precocious runaway who takes off on a raft down the Mississippi River, accompanied by his best friend and protector, the runaway slave Jim (Walter Connelly). Rooney was at the peak of his popularity—in fact, he was the most popular star in America—and MGM spared no expense in the prestigious adaptation. Great family entertainment. Feel free to smoke a corncob pipe while you're watching.

february 19

Rally 'Round the Flag

On this day in 1945, on a small island 650 miles from Tokyo, thirty-thousand Marines landed on the Japanese-occupied island of Iwo Jima in the Pacific. In the battle that followed, the Japanese were nearly decimated and Americans lost over two-thirds of their troops. After weeks of bloody fighting and terrible losses, the Marines finally took control of Mt. Suribachi. Four Marines raised the American flag, and AP photographer Joe Rosenthal snapped a photo that would become nearly mythic. He later admitted that the photo was staged.

The same might be said of John Wayne's career as the quintessential tough all-American soldier—it was pretty much staged. Contrary to popular opinion, John Wayne did not personally win World War II. He didn't even fight in it. Unlike fellow Hollywood stars Jimmy Stewart, Glenn Ford, and Clark Gable, the Duke managed to avoid serving in the armed services, preferring to do his patriotic duty on the comfortable sound stages of Hollywood. Some say he did more for American morale by staying home; that's one backhanded compliment to his abilities as an actor.

Sands of Iwo Jima (1949) is vintage Wayne (the role earned him his first Oscar nomination) and vintage World War II propaganda. As tough U.S. Marine Sgt. Stryker, Wayne is not one of the soldiers who raises the flag—he gets killed by a sniper's bullet before it goes up, just as he's lighting up a victory cigarette (and they said smoking those things wouldn't kill you). One of those quintessential American propaganda movies where all the "Japs" are cartoon characters and all the American soldiers are straight and upright, *Sands of Iwo Jima* is still undeniably entertaining in a manipulative way—and a lesson in negative Hollywood typecasting that should not be forgotten. Directed by silent film veteran Alan Dwan.

february 20

Shoot a Little Pool with the Greatest

No less an authority than Orson Welles dubbed Jackie Gleason "The Greatest." Whether he was talking about his appetite or his talent is anybody's guess.

Jackie Gleason was born this day in 1916 in Brooklyn, in a tough neighborhood. His father abandoned the family when he was eight, and his mother died when he was sixteen. Hanging out in pool halls and bars, Gleason understood well the lives of poor working stiffs who talked big and dreamed big but would never break out of their humdrum jobs. He drew on these memories when he created one of the most endearing and enduring comedic characters in television history: blustery bus driver Ralph Kramden of *The Honeymooners.*

Gleason made his biggest mark in television, but he had a long history with the movies. He was a contract player for Warner Brothers in the 1940s, playing supporting roles in several movies, including a small part with Humphrey Bogart in *All Through the Night* (1942). But Hollywood didn't really know what to do with his oversize, boisterous talents. After he had established himself as a huge TV star in the '50s, he took Hollywood on his own terms and delivered several fine performances in films like *Requiem for a Heavyweight* (1962), *Papa's Delicate Condition* (1963), and *Gigot* (1962), which he also wrote. But Gleason was never better than in **The Hustler** (1961). Paul Newman stars as "Fast" Eddie Felson, a hotshot pool hustler who is hungry to beat the best—and the best is Gleason as Minnesota Fats. Their marathon showdown midway through the film is so drenched in atmosphere you can almost smell the sweat and old coffee. Newman overacts (a rare occurrence for him), but Gleason is magnificent and understated—elegant, confident, and every inch the poolroom champion. Gleason obviously drew from his youth in this mesmerizing portrait of a king who rules a shadowed and seedy kingdom. A masterful character study, moody, dark, and on the money. Six ball, corner pocket.

february 21

A Voice Silenced

"Power never takes a back step—only in the face of more power."

—Malcolm X

While standing to deliver a speech at the Audubon Ballroom in Harlem this day in 1965, African-American activist and leader Malcolm X was assassinated by several Black Muslim extremists who were angered over Malcolm's recent defection from the Nation of Islam. Or so the official story goes; to this day, many unanswered questions surround the murder.

As both a man and an icon, Malcolm X remains a cultural lightning rod and an enigma of seeming contradictions—angry militant, enlightened prophet, Harlem pimp, religious radical, galvanizing orator, dedicated family man. Spike Lee was the ideal director to tell his story in the impressive bio-pic **Malcolm X** (1992). Denzel Washington delivers an astonishing, incendiary performance as the charismatic Malcolm—ever-evolving, compassionate, angry, militant, enlightened. From his zoot-suited pimping days in Harlem in the 1940s to his imprisonment, where he first became converted to the Islamic faith, to his rise as a disciple of Elijah Muhammad, the Supreme Leader of the Nation of Islam, to his life-changing pilgrimage to Mecca, Lee's film intelligently examines the life of one of the twentieth century's most charismatic and incendiary leaders. Lee admirably restrains himself from his typically showy style, flawlessly integrating the various phases of Malcolm's often contradictory life into a cohesive whole. A magnificent accomplishment all around.

february 22

Buy George

The father of our country, George Washington, was born this day in 1732 in Virginia.

I cannot tell a lie: For someone with such a noble title as "father of our country" and the distinction of being the first president of the United States, old George wasn't the hottest of film properties. Lincoln gets the John Ford treatment, Jefferson gets the juicy sex scandals, but Washington . . . well, aside from a fairly wooden-toothed TV miniseries starring Barry Bostwick and a token appearance in the musical *1776,* Washington's film legacy is negligible.

But don't be dissuaded; celebrate his birthday with the delightful comedy **George Washington Slept Here** (1942). Jack Benny stars in one of his best film roles as a city-loving husband whose antique-loving wife (Anne Sheridan) buys a colonial home in the country. The selling point: George Washington once slept there. The bad news: Nobody's been there since, and the place is falling apart. Benny delivers one-liners with his typically great timing, and his interplay with the locals is priceless. The movie served as the template for such future rural comedies as *Mr. Blandings Builds His Dream House* and the TV series *Green Acres.*

february 23

Take That, Yankee Dog!

On this date in 1942, soon after the U.S. had entered World War II, the coastal hamlet of Santa Barbara, California, was invaded by the Japanese navy. And all because of a cactus.

Well, not exactly. A Richfield Oil Company refinery was shelled by one lone Japanese submarine just offshore this night in 1942. Very little damage was done and no one injured. It turned out that the commander of the submarine, Kizo Nishino, had worked at that very refinery years earlier as a tanker captain, and had fallen on a cactus plant, much to the amusement and teasing of his coworkers. Seems Captain Nishino had a short sense of humor and a long memory. He vowed revenge one day. And on this day, he got it. . . .

But the incident, amusing as it was, understandably scared nearby residents and the rest of California. Steven Spielberg ran with the incident in his box office bomb, **1941** (1979). Spielberg took the event, tweaked it with an anything-goes script by Robert Zemeckis, moved the locale down the coast about fifty miles to Los Angeles, and hired on a massive cast including Dan Ackroyd, John Belushi, Warren Oates, Toshiro Mifune, Christopher Lee, and Treat Williams. The result was Spielberg's biggest bomb ever, so critically lambasted that few people bothered to see it. Seen today, it's still far from Spielberg's finest hour, but it has its clunky charms, not the least of which is Belushi's samurai pilot.

february 24

A Champion of Clay

In those days, his name was Cassius Clay, and on this day in 1964 he captured the Heavyweight Championship of the World from Sonny Liston, and the world of boxing was changed forever. A scrappy, cocky, and impossibly handsome young man, Clay was nothing if not self-assured. He went on to be ordained a Black Muslim minister, change his name to Muhammad Ali, and become arguably the greatest sports icon of all time.

The ever-humble Ali starred in a movie of his own life story, *The Greatest* (1977), a film that, despite his charismatic presence, floats like a lead balloon and stings like a moth. Robert Duvall and Ernest Borgnine are wasted in supporting turns, and Ali himself had the sense to retire from acting—his one defeat—after this well-basted turkey.

Instead, celebrate the first victory of the man many call "The Greatest" by watching **When We Were Kings** (1996), Leon Cast's fascinating documentary of what many consider Ali's finest hour—the "Rumble in the Jungle" with George Foreman in Zaire in October 1974. With commentary by Spike Lee (who wasn't there) and Norman Mailer and George Plimpton (who were). A fascinating time capsule that captures Ali at his peak.

february 25

A Real Lady-killer

His real name was Henri Landru, but the public knew him as Bluebeard. He made his living in France by placing ads in the paper saying, "Widower with comfortable income desires to meet widow with a view to matrimony." Over three hundred well-to-do spinsters replied, and between 1915 and 1919 he murdered ten of his newly acquired wives and burned their bodies in his stove. Today is the anniversary of his execution by guillotine in 1922.

There have been many films inspired by his nasty deeds, including Edgar G. Ulmer's low-budget, B-movie masterpiece *Bluebeard* (1944), with an unusually subdued and effective John Carradine as the lady-killer, but the best homage came from Charles Chaplin, of all people, in **Monsieur Verdoux** (1947). This decidedly black comedy pretty much helped destroy Chaplin's career in America. In *Verdoux,* fans of the Little Tramp were shocked to see Chaplin as a suave villain who kills women for money. It didn't help that at the time the film was released Chaplin was in the middle of a scandalous paternity suit brought by actress Joan Barry and under attack for his leftist political views.

Monsieur Verdoux was originally proposed to Chaplin by Orson Welles, who was slated to direct until the always autocratic Chaplin decided to handle it himself. Although the direction is stagey and static, and the script windier than Chicago in April, *Monsieur Verdoux* is a revolutionary, almost subversive movie, daring and often brilliantly, bleakly funny. Martha Raye steals the film whenever she's on-screen as the clutzy and brassy Annabella, a potential victim who simply refuses to die. She's actually funnier than Chaplin, and that's saying a lot.

february 26

The Bug That Conquered America

On this day in 1936, automotive history took a giant leap forward with a very small car: the Volkswagon debuted. It soon became a staple mode of transportation in Europe, and when it was imported to the U.S., the ubiquitous "Bug" soon became a beloved icon and an affordable means of transportation, particularly among younger people who enjoyed an "alternative" lifestyle. In the early '60s, a series of brilliant TV commercials spotlighted its unique properties; one classic spot shows a very young and perplexed Dustin Hoffman searching in vain for the missing engine.

Celebrate the unveiling of a cultural icon with Woody Allen's futuristic comedy **Sleeper** (1973). Allen plays a musician who is cryogenically frozen and awakes two hundred years later. *Sleeper* may be Allen's out-and-out funniest film. He joins with underground rebel Diane Keaton to overthrow the futuristic government, discovering the joys of the "orgasmatron" along the way. What has all this got to do with Volkswagons? Not much, really—but there is one gag that is probably the best endorsement the VW Beetle ever had. I won't spoil it; just enjoy. And if you still can't get enough, watch Walt Disney's family-friendly pic **The Love Bug** (1964), about a talking VW named Herbie. It was so successful it actually spawned a series of sequels. They can drive you buggy.

february 27

The Best-Laid Plans . . .

Author John Steinbeck was born this day in Salinas, California, in 1902. He would always return to the Salinas Valley—in his life and in his novels *Tortilla Flat, East of Eden, The Grapes of Wrath,* and in his underrated and heartbreaking *Of Mice and Men.*

All of them have been made into movies—and many of them are great. *Tortilla Flat* (1942) stars Spencer Tracy in a delightful comedic performance as a lazy ne'er-do-well companion to love-struck John Garfield in Monterey; *East of Eden* (1955) is really only the second half of Steinbeck's epic tale about how a patriarch's sins destroy his sons Cal and Aaron (read Cain and Abel), but it was the first starring role for James Dean (as young Cal); and *The Grapes of Wrath* (1939) is possibly John Ford's greatest movie, featuring a triumphant performance by Henry Fonda as Tom Joad.

But **Of Mice and Men** (1939) is a beautiful tone poem of a film—honest, filled with the simple dreams of the common man, and heartbreaking. Burgess Meredith gives the performance of his career as George, the wandering and philosophical migrant worker who is caretaker to his companion Lenny (Lon Chaney, Jr.)—a giant bear of a man who has the mental capacity of a child, loves to caress soft things, and, tragically, does not know his own strength. Together, they get jobs as workers on a farm in the Salinas Valley, and George goes in with some other farmhands in a scheme to buy a piece of land for themselves. But the fates conspire against the two. A heart-wrenching film of simple dreams, and of both the strength and the fragility of the human spirit; have your tissues handy. Lovingly directed by Lewis Milestone, and produced by Hal Roach, of all people, who was best known for his Laurel and Hardy comedies.

february 28

Oui, Three Kings

The Persian Gulf War was one of the shortest American wars on record, and one of the most controversial. On this day in 1991, Operation Desert Storm officially ended with the "liberation" of Kuwait. The ground war had lasted one hundred hours, with 148 American soldiers killed and 458 wounded in combat. On paper, it was one of the most successful deployments of military might ever.

David O. Russell's **Three Kings** (1999) is set during the closing days of the conflict, as the Gulf War is winding down and soldiers are celebrating their dubious victory and preparing to return home. Four American soldiers (leader George Clooney, Mark Wahlberg, Ice Cube, and live-wire redneck Spike Jonze) decide to go home with more than just sand in their shorts, and journey into the Iraqi desert to retrieve millions in stolen Kuwaiti bullion. What begins as a typical macho heist flick à la *Kelly's Heroes* evolves into one of the most layered films of the decade, mixing humor, action, and history in a lively cross-genre-ational adventure/comedy. A startlingly original movie.

march

march 1

Volunteer for Some Laughs

On this day in 1961 President John F. Kennedy created the Peace Corps by executive order. Within months, thousands of volunteers had signed up to go away to far-off "Third World" countries to help with housing, medical, and farming projects. The pay was minimal, but it was, and remains, one of JFK's greatest contributions.

Celebrate the anniversary of the Peace Corps with **Volunteers** (1985)—one of Tom Hanks's lesser-known early comedies, but still a fun diversion. Hanks plays ne'er-do-well Ivy League playboy and compulsive gambler Laurence Bourne III (his Boston accent is a bit dodgy), who tries to escape his bookie by boarding a plane full of Peace Corps volunteers heading for Thailand. Once there, he spends more time teaching the locals how to cheat at cards than how to plant crops. Hanks's scenes with costar John Candy (as Tom Tuttle of Tacoma) are the best in the film; this was the second time they worked together (the first time being in 1984's *Splash*). It was on the set of this movie that Hanks began his romance with leading lady Rita Wilson; they married the following year. Like the Peace Corps itself, *Volunteers* is uneven, but worthwhile.

march 2

Seuss Who?

Where would the English-speaking world be without Dr. Seuss? His real name was Ted Geisel—and he was born this day in 1904 in Springfield, Massachusetts. The gentle but eccentric writer had an enormous and delightful influence on baby boomers and readers everywhere with his classic tales *Green Eggs and Ham* (the result of a $50 bet with publisher Bennett Cerf over whether or not Seuss, could write a story using just fifty words), *The Cat in the Hat, Horton Hears a Who,* and countless others—including his modern-day Christmas classic, *How the Grinch Stole Christmas.*

As a big-budget movie, *Dr. Seuss' How the Grinch Stole Christmas* (2000) is an admirable effort to combine Hollywood star power with the unique and singular spirit that was Dr. Seuss. Jim Carrey is virtually unrecognizable under layers of latex as the misanthropic title character, and director Ron Howard has come up with an eye-popping Whoville. But try as it may—and it tries mighty hard—the film pales in comparison to Chuck Jones's classic animated TV version, *How the Grinch Stole Christmas* (1966), with Boris Karloff narrating and supplying the voice for the Grinch. Jones and Seuss collaborated closely to combine the best of both worlds—Seuss's patented rhyming whimsy and designs and Jones's celebrated Warner Brothers cartoon style.

Celebrate Seuss with a real one-of-a-kind film oddity—**The Five Thousand Fingers of Dr. T** (1953), a delightful and inventive fantasy. Dr. Seuss cowrote it with screenwriter Allan Scott, but the overall feel is definitely Seuss. Nine-year-old Bart (Tommy Rettig) resents his piano lessons, imagining his stern teacher, Professor Terwilliker (Hans Conreid), as a madman bent on enslaving five hundred little boys at a giant keyboard to endlessly practice Terwilliker's own masterpiece for eternity. Bizarre, surreal, and absorbing for both kids and savvy adults, this is a rare cinematic treat from the imagination of one of the greatest writers for the child in all of us.

march 3

Escape from It All

One of the great escapes in the annals of American crime took place on this date.

In February 1934, the law had caught up with flamboyant outlaw John Dillinger—for a while, anyway. Charged with the murder of Chicago policeman William O'Malley (Dillinger's only kill), the charismatic Dillinger was extradited to Crown Point Jail in Crown Point, Indiana—where he congenially posed for waiting newspaper photographers upon his arrival, jovially draping his arm around the hapless sheriff's shoulder. When reporters asked the criminal why he looked so unconcerned, he replied that he would be out from behind bars soon enough.

On March 3, 1934, he made good on his word. Somehow, Dillinger managed to procure a piece of wood carved to resemble a pistol and painted with black shoe polish. It was realistic enough to allow the brazen criminal to bluff his way through several guards and past six jailhouse doors. He then incarcerated every policeman in the building and, to add insult to injury, drove away in a police car past more than one hundred guards who ringed the facilities. The man had unquestionable style.

Overnight, Crown Point Jail became known as "Clown Point Jail." Understandably, the escape only added to the luster that was Dillinger's in his own brief lifetime.

Relive the daring escape by watching **Dillinger** (1973), an underrated B picture written and directed by John Milius and starring the late, great Warren Oates as Dillinger. Milius does an even better job of bringing the '30s to life than Arthur Penn (*Bonnie and Clyde*) did—the souped-up getaway cars are a kick, and the legendary escape from Little Bohemia is vividly recreated. Add to that a hyper performance by a very young Richard Dreyfuss as the whiny, murderous "Baby Face" Nelson, Cloris Leachman as "the Lady in Red" who betrays the outlaw, and Ben Johnson as wily and determined G-man Melvin Purvis, and you have a cinematic stew that's a B-movie buff's feast.

march 4

Send in the Clones

It all came to a head with a sheep named Dolly, who became the first animal to be successfully cloned. Soon, speculation was rampant on when—not if—the first human would be cloned. The medical, ethical, and moral issues often overlapped and conflicted, and the topic is still volatile and highly controversial. On this day in 1997, President Bill Clinton signed legislation banning federally-funded human cloning research.

The key words here are *federally funded.* Hmmmm . . . ever wonder what's going on behind closed doors at *private* companies?

Early on in **The 6th Day** (2000), Arnold Schwarzenegger is primping in front of his mirror on his birthday. Flexing his biceps and scrutinizing his wrinkles, he sighs, announcing, "I'm getting too old for this." It's a knowing wink to his audience, a self-effacing joke in homage to his longevity as an action film hero.

The year is 2024. Adam Gibson (Arnold) is a helicopter pilot who snags a lucrative contract with Replacement Technologies, a biotech company specializing in nonhuman cloning—but which is (surprise!) secretly producing illegal human clones. During a supposedly routine eye exam, Arnold's brain is scanned for every piece of information and a sample of his DNA is extracted. Through plot machinations that are about as murky as the issue of how clones can be harvested in water, they make a duplicate Arnold. *The 6th Day* tosses equal parts of *The Matrix, Blade Runner,* and *Invasion of the Body Snatchers* into a blender and presses the "edit" button. The embryo for a thought-provoking premise exists, but the movie ultimately purees the moral and ethical issues of cloning in favor of typical Arnold shoot-'em-ups, car chases, and killing. Lots of killing. But whenever a bad guy's number is up, he gets another one, thanks to the magic of cloning. It's Hollywood's duplicitous way of trying to placate its critics, saying, "Look, this isn't really violence. It's just *clone* violence—they're not *really* human, see? They get to come back." We should all be so lucky.

But *The 6th Day* is not without humor. Rodney Rowland is amusing as a punk henchman with the appropriate name of Wile E. Coyote, who keeps getting knocked off in a variety of messy ways, only to be repeatedly revived as a clone of himself who suffers recurring psychosomatic pains from his old injuries. *The 6th Day* is part mindless escapism, part clever sci-fi—and Schwarzenegger delivers one of his most relaxed performances. At least, I *think* that's Arnold Schwarzenegger. . . .

march 5

Feel In-Clined?

Country music—and American popular music—lost one of its most distinctive voices too soon when singer Patsy Cline died in a plane crash on this day in 1963, near Camden, Tennessee. She was thirty years old, but had already created a legacy worthy of a lifetime.

Cline had one of the most arresting, plaintive voices in music—at once passionately strong and achingly vulnerable. She was the first country music artist to cross over successfully—almost inadvertently—into pop. Listen to her legendary renditions of "Walkin' After Midnight," "I Fall to Pieces," and "Crazy," and you know you're in the presence of greatness.

Her story is recounted in the bittersweet film bio **Sweet Dreams** (1985), which stars Jessica Lange in an Oscar-nominated performance. The narrative focuses mostly on her troubled marriage (Ed Harris is excellent as her husband) and rise to the top of the charts before her premature death. A Hollywood version of a country-western soap opera, redeemed by the authenticity and sincerity behind the performances. Patsy Cline's original performances are used throughout.

march 6

Texas Alamo'd

In the predawn hours of this day in 1836 in San Antonio, Texas, a veritable swarm of Mexican troops launched a massive attack on a dilapidated adobe mission occupied by a small, ragtag band of resistance fighters for the Republic of Texas. Every schoolboy knows the story of the battle of the Alamo—how 180 brave men fended off 5,000 of Gen. Santa Anna's troops, with the holy trinity of Col. William Travis, Jim Bowie, and Davy Crockett at the forefront of the battle.

But, as is always the case with history, the real story was more complicated. The Mexican government, which legally owned the area of Texas, had graciously allowed the so-called Texicans squatters' rights, allowing them to live on their land—but after a while the colonists banded together against their hosts. Many of the defenders of the Alamo weren't patriots in the usual sense of the word; they were mercenaries, land speculators, and, most surprising of all, slave owners—a dubious business for so-called freedom fighters. The Mexican soldiers—usually portrayed as fresh-uniformed, disciplined, and formation-perfect—had just traveled hundreds of miles on foot from Mexico over torturous terrain, were poorly armed, had no food, and were exhausted. And to really put a hole in the legend, there's controversial evidence that Davy Crockett surrendered during the final conflagration, only to be run through with a bayonet at Santa Anna's orders.

Wherever the truth lies, the battle for the Alamo conjures vivid images of patriotism, sacrifice, and bravery on both sides—and makes for ideal movie material. Movies like *The Last Command* (1956) and *The Alamo: Thirteen Days to Glory* (1977) are intelligent and reasonably factual recountings, but for sheer big-budget blockbuster entertainment you can't top John Wayne's propaganda-fueled testosterone fest, **The Alamo** (1959).

It had long been a dream of the Duke's to film the saga and direct it himself, and he literally spent years in preparation, putting his entire personal fortune on the line. He constructed an identical full-scale version of the

Alamo just outside of Bracketville, Texas (which is still standing as of this writing; it's also been used in *Lonesome Dove* [1989] and *Barbarosa* [1982]). The entire set covered four hundred acres, utilized over 1 million adobe bricks, and had over 200,000 square feet of structures. Wayne cast himself as Davy Crockett (a much older Crockett; Wayne was in his fifties at the time, the real Crockett in his thirties), Richard Widmark as Jim Bowie, and odd-man-out British actor Laurence Harvey as Col. William Barrett Travis.

Although the script occasionally lapses into flowery Hollywoodisms (particularly Wayne's patriotic speech, "Republic. I like the sound of the word.") and out-of-place macho "humor," Wayne did a yeomanlike job in the director's chair (rumored to have been assisted and advised by mentor John Ford). The final battle is vividly staged, and Harvey makes for an appropriately vain and arrogant Travis. It's simple-minded and overlong, but Wayne's attention to detail is admirable. (Well, there are a *few* lapses; keep a sharp eye out for the mobile trailers in the background—and the soldier falling onto the mattress!)

march 7

A Divine Exit

Three-hundred-pound, forty-two-year-old actor Harris Glenn Milstead—better known as the transvestite performer Divine—died this day in 1988 of natural causes due to an enlarged heart. His timing was unfortunate: He was about to become the mainstream star he'd always dreamed of and strove to be. His last movie, *Hairspray,* had just opened to surprising success and rave reviews. He was just beginning to enjoy the fruits of his years of labor.

Years earlier, Divine and old Baltimore high school chum John Waters decided to make a movie, and the two hit it off immediately. With Waters writing and directing and Divine starring, they produced a series of cult classics, each one striving to be more tasteless than the last: *Mondo Trasho* (1970), *Multiple Maniacs* (1970), *Lust in the Dust* (1985), and, notoriously, *Pink Flamingos* (1972), where Divine actually ate—well, if you don't already know, you may want to watch the movie. Or maybe not. Divine played virtually every role in drag—with the sole exception of his performance as the villain in Alan Rudolph's *Trouble in Mind* (1986).

Commemorate the passing of a true American original with the movie that made him a mainstream star—albeit posthumously: **Hairspray** (1988). Ricki Lake (in her film debut) plays Tracy Turnblad, a "typical" teenager in 1962 Baltimore. Divine plays her supportive mother, Edna. When Tracy becomes a hit on the local TV dance series, *The Corny Collins Show,* she earns the wrath of bitchy queen-of-the-hop Amber Van Tassle. Although fairly mild stuff by John Waters standards, *Hairspray* is a delightfully candy-colored nostalgia-fest tinted in deep kitsch.

Divine is, if not divine, endearingly amusing, and the eccentric supporting cast includes Sonny Bono, Deborah Harry, Jerry Stiller, Mink Stole, Rick Ocasek, Pia Zadora, and the great Ruth Brown as Motormouth Maybelle.

march 8

A Marriage Made in Hollywood (I Do, Take Two)

It was a marriage made in Tinseltown heaven: Nice, bland, unassuming guy marries wholesome, ambitious all-American gal and goes all the way to the White House. They live happily ever after. Long slow fade to black.

On this day in 1952, B-movie actor Ronald Reagan (then newly divorced from Jane Wyman) married B-movie actress Nancy Davis—and went on to prove that there *are* second acts in American lives.

Commemorate the romantic anniversary with the only film they ever made together (discounting their epic eight-year-long miniseries in the White House), **Hellcats of the Navy** (1957). Reagan plays a rugged U.S. submarine commander assigned to destroy Japanese merchant ships. He gets into conflicts with his first officer (Arthur Franz) and falls for Nancy. Together, Reagan and Davis didn't exactly ignite the screen with passionate sparks of sexual chemistry. They were no Tracy and Hepburn; they were Ron and Nancy. And the best was yet to come.

march 9

Slip Yourself a Mickey

OK—so he wasn't the classiest or most sophisticated literary exponent of the decade, but the 1950s belonged to Mickey Spillane, the pugnacious tough-guy pulp writer who created Mike Hammer, the quintessential pugnacious tough-guy detective. Spillane was born this day in 1918 in Brooklyn, New York. He probably came out swingin'.

Drink a birthday toast (bourbon, and the cheaper the better, doll) to the Mick and watch the best cinematic adaptation of one of his books, Robert Aldrich's fever dream–induced, over-the-top noir cult classic, **Kiss Me Deadly** (1955). Detective Mike Hammer (Ralph Meeker) picks up a hitchhiking damsel-in-distress (a young Cloris Leachman) clothed in nothing but an overcoat, who implores the detective to "remember me." Next thing you know, she's murdered, and Hammer is sucked into a predicament where he spends more time getting the crap beat out of him than solving the case. Plenty of baroque action, drenched in an outrageous, schizoid blend of film noir and cold war '50s paranoia. A mesmerizing supporting performance by the aptly named Gaby Rodgers, who never made another film again, but leaves an indelible impression here. A noir film like noir other.

march 10

Bells Are Ringing

On this day, in his Boston lab in 1876, distracted research scientist and compulsive tinkerer Alexander Graham Bell spilled acid on his worktable. When a few drops ran off into his lap, he painfully spoke into a contraption he'd been fiddling with lately, saying, "Mr. Watson, come here, I want you," through clenched teeth. It was the first time a human voice was carried over wire, and the telephone was born. At least, that's the well-known story.

Contrary to the stale old 1930s joke, Don Ameche did not invent the telephone. But Ameche did play his most famous role in **The Story of Alexander Graham Bell** (1939), Hollywood's entertaining screen bio of the inventor, all wrapped up in nice production values and a nice supporting cast. A young and very likeable up-and-coming player named Henry Fonda plays Bell's young assistant, Mr. Watson. Not exactly historically accurate but, gosh, could you imagine a two-hour movie about a guy just sitting around waiting for the phone to ring?

march 11

A Love Eternal

According to William Shakespeare (who should know), Romeo Montague and Juliet Capulet were wed on this day in 1302 in fair Verona. The marriage itself didn't last long, what with both parties committing suicide and all, but it definitely took the #1 spot in the annals of the Hit Parade of Great Romances.

The timeless, tragic tale has been filmed countless times. A lavish, big-budget 1936 version from MGM was hampered by an overage Leslie Howard and Norma Shearer in the leads, but John Barrymore made a wonderfully mischievous if slightly over-the-hill Mercutio (Barrymore was over fifty years old, and Howard and Shearer in their midthirties!). The teen tragedy was also reconfigured into the popular 1960 musical, *West Side Story*—the tale told this time with a jazz score and choreographed by dancing teenage New York inner-city gangs. In the midst of the swinging '60s, Italian director Franco Zefferelli made a fine, energetic mod version, *Romeo and Juliet* (1968), having the savvy stroke of genius to use actors who were actually the same age as the characters, and the film was an unexpected box office hit with teens. Its theme song even became a Top 40 hit.

But the romantic old chestnut was given a revolutionary, radical chic makeover in Baz Luhrmann's extravagantly over-the-top music video–cum–gangsta romance, **William Shakespeare's Romeo + Juliet** (1996). Set in our day, Luhrmann did a majestic job injecting cinematic life into the hoary hormonal romance, pumping up the volume, adrenaline, and intensity; the entire film plays like an extended MTV video—but with a damn good screenwriter who wasn't around to collect the royalties. Teen gang warfare is rampant in "Verona Beach" as young Romeo (Leonardo DiCaprio) and Juliet (Claire Danes) play out the tragedy—all in Shakespeare's unadulterated text. Dazzling visuals, sumptuous sets and colors, kinetic energy, and a hip-hop score all combine to make this an exciting, experimental, and enormously successful attempt to bring Shakespeare to a new audience—even, arguably, a new medium. Too bad those two nice Italian kids couldn't work it out.

march 12

Hit the Road, Jack

"A true writer should be an observer and not go around being observed. Observing—that's the duty and oath of a writer."

—Jack Kerouac

Happy birthday today to the heppest of the hep, Jack Kerouac, born this day in Lowell, Massachusetts, in 1922. He more or less invented the Beat movement of the late '40s and '50s, and became (whether he liked it or not, and he didn't) its patron saint. He wrote what is arguably the single most influential modern American novel, *On the Road*—the closest thing to a Bible for an American iconoclast. It is said that he wrote the entire book in three weeks' time—using a single long strip of paper, endlessly rolling out of his well-beaten Underwood typewriter—fueled by amphetamines, booze, and coffee. The truth is that he worked for years on it.

His playful, alliterative command of the English language was astonishing—all the more so when you consider that English was a second language to him; his parents were French-Canadian. As a young man he spent some time in the navy but was discharged due to his schizoid personality. He became a merchant seaman, and then a vagabond, from which he began to gather the experiences that he brought to such stunning effect in his novels.

He was rugged, handsome, and the quintessence of cool. But after his literary success, he became increasingly reclusive, spending his last years living with his mother and drinking himself to death, distrustful and wary of the generation of Beatniks he had spawned.

On the Road, like all of his other works, is virtually unfilmable. But Kerouac has inspired countless filmmakers, drawn to his restless gypsy spirit, to create works from *Easy Rider* (1969) to *Lost in America* (1985) to *Road Trip* (2000). The closest Hollywood ever came to filming a Kerouac book was *The Subterraneans* (1960), starring a bland George Peppard as Kerouac's proxy and Roddy McDowall as a Beat poet who sleeps standing up and comes up with such bons mots as "Life's a party an' everyone else is a party crasher!" Predictably, Hollywood watered down everything even remotely risqué about Kerouac's story (the black girl with whom the book's protagonist falls in love is transformed into white French waif Leslie Caron), and its author rightfully and indignantly disavowed it. On the plus side, it does boast brief appearances by Art Pepper and Art Farmer—the only "Art" apparent in this fiasco.

Heart Beat (1979) is a small, forgotten gem starring John Heard as young Kerouac and big, ambling Nick Nolte perfectly cast as Jack's partner in beatitude, Neal Cassidy (who served as the template for the character of

Dean Moriarty in *On the Road*). Anyone expecting an evocation of the Beat Movement will be disappointed; the focus of the film is on the threesome of Jack, Neal, and Neal's wife (and Jack's occasional lover), Carolyn Cassady, played by Sissy Spacek. Most of the story takes place in post-war American suburbia, not "on the road." Still, Nolte is fabulous, and the always-riveting Ray Sharkey costars. Much harder to find—but worth seeking out as a beatific curiosity—is Jack himself doing the off-camera narration that drives *Pull My Daisy,* a sort of twenty-minute existentialist Beat short with pals Allen Ginsberg and Gregory Corso.

For a glimpse of the real article, check out **Kerouac** (1984), director John Antonelli's documentary-cum-reconstruction of the author's life. Mixing dramatizations of events from Kerouac's life with fascinating interviews and archival clips, *Kerouac* is a shorthand but fascinating insight into the contrarian author. The interviews with Kerouac's friends and contemporaries (Lawrence Ferlinghetti, Allen Ginsberg, William Burroughs, Gregory Corso) are illuminating, and the brief clips of Kerouac (reading excerpts from his works on *The Steve Allen Show,* grumbling his way uncomfortably through TV chat sessions) are tantalizing, revealing—and ultimately sorrowful.

march 13

Where the Road Began

On this day in 1940, the very first Bing Crosby–Bob Hope *Road* picture, *The Road to Singapore,* premiered at the Paramount Theater in New York. The film was not originally conceived for the two stars; the script was actually created for George Burns and Gracie Allen, who passed, then it went to Fred MacMurray and Jack Oakie, who also passed. Finally, it was offered to Hope and Crosby, who had not worked together before but had each generated success separately. Once on the set, they discovered a wonderful chemistry and rapport together that proved more than the sum of its parts. Hope's rapid-fire delivery balanced perfectly with Bing's laid-back repartee and casual crooning, and their mutual ability to ad-lib—usually in an attempt to top the other—was endearing. The film was a huge hit and spawned six follow-ups.

Revel in the fun of the very first *Road* picture with **The Road to Singapore** (1940). Bing and Bob play two Americans who decide to swear off women and live the good life in the South Sea Islands. They didn't figure on Dorothy Lamour, a showgirl who's being abused by bad guy Anthony Quinn. Naturally, both Bing and Bob fall for the same girl. So begins one of the longest three-way romantic tug-of-wars in film comedy history, which would last for nearly twenty years and several sequels. *Singapore* may not be as funny as subsequent entries in the series (*Road to Morocco* and *Road to Utopia* are the best of the series), but it's still a breezy escape from reality with two of the most pleasant companions imaginable. See where the Road began, and then enjoy the rest of the trip.

march 14

The Greatest Opening Shot Ever

> *"I don't think it's a masterpiece. I think it's the greatest B movie ever made."*
>
> *—Charlton Heston*

What is generally acknowledged to be the most famous and influential opening shot in movie history—Orson Welles's stunning three-minute opening sequence for *Touch of Evil*—was shot on this day in 1957. It has since become the textbook example of a continuous tracking shot: It begins with a close-up of someone's hands placing a ticking bomb into a car, then pulls back to follow the car through the streets of a backwater Mexican border town, while simultaneously tracking two newlyweds (Charlton Heston and Janet Leigh) as they walk a parallel course. The shot glides effortlessly through streets, up over ramshackle buildings, and finally rests on a border guard as the young couple literally cross over into another world. As they lock lips, the car explodes. Whew! The shot has been copied many times, by everyone from Martin Scorsese (in *Goodfellas*) to Robert Altman (in *The Player*).

It was the very first day of filming, and studio execs were hovering around the set, monitoring Welles. It was the director's first Hollywood directing assignment in years, and his profligate reputation preceded him. As the hours passed and Welles coordinated the logistics of the shot, the watch-checking bean counters became increasingly nervous; Welles had yet to shoot a single frame. Then, just as the sun was strategically setting and the sky was perfect, Welles commanded, "Action!" The crane swept and danced, following the complex, choreographed action flawlessly, and the three-and-a-half-minute continuous shot went off without a hitch. "Cut! Print!" Welles boomed after the shot was completed. He then turned to the impressed studio execs. "We're three days ahead of schedule."

The irony is that upon release of the film, Universal Studios plastered the opening credits over the entire sequence, thus distracting the viewer's attention from the intricate work. Thankfully, the restored version is now available.

Revel in Welles's audacious filmmaking talents by watching **Touch of Evil** (1957). Originally, Welles was only set to act, until Charlton Heston suggested he direct. Welles had become persona non grata as a director, but at Heston's insistence, Universal took a chance, and Welles delivered the goods with one of the most distinctive, dizzyingly inventive movies ever, the last word in film noir.

In one of his best screen performances, Welles plays corpulent, corrupt cop Hank Quinlan, who has a nasty habit of framing suspects for crimes. Trouble is, he's usually right about their guilt. Janet Leigh's ordeal in a dilapidated hotel (run by loony Dennis Weaver) anticipates her stay at the Bates Motel two years later. A great supporting cast, including Marlene Dietrich as a fortune-telling madam who takes one look at the bloated Welles and intones, "You're a mess, honey. You should lay off those candy bars."

march 15

The Ides of March

"Beware the Ides of March."

—*William Shakespeare,* Julius Caesar

If Julius Caesar had heeded those words of advice we might all be wearing togas today.

On this infamous and unlucky day, the emperor Julius Caesar was stabbed to death by a group of conspirators, among them his good friend and advisor, Brutus. Mark the occasion with a Caesar salad and by watching Joseph Mankiewicz's film adaptation of Shakespeare's **Julius Caesar** (1960). Mankiewicz did an admirable job of paring down the play to its essence and making it filmable. He was helped by a stellar cast. Marlon Brando actually articulates his lines as Marc Antony, and he looks every bit the noble Roman. James Mason is an impressively torn and conflicted Brutus, and John Gielgud gives what is arguably his finest screen performance as the manipulative Cassius. Enjoy the movie. Just don't invite a lot of friends over to watch it with you, and keep the knives in the drawer.

march 16

Hey, Laaaddyyyy!

"I'm an American icon."

—*Jerry Lewis*

With an ear-piercing shriek that would only improve with age, Jerry Lewis entered the world this day in 1925 as Joey Levitch.

His mother and father were vaudeville performers, and he pretty much had show biz in his blood. He started his career lip-synching to records onstage—not the most auspicious of show biz beginnings. But his career took off when he met up with a struggling Italian crooner named Dean Martin, fresh from a nose job in Toledo. The two teamed up onstage, Martin trying to sing and the monkeylike Lewis causing endless mayhem, and the chemistry was immediate and highly combustible. Martin and Lewis became the biggest sensation of the '50s . . . bigger than Ike, bigger than Sputnik, bigger even than Elvis among the young.

The team went on to make a series of successful films for producer Hal Wallis at Paramount Studios—some of them actually entertaining: *Hollywood or Bust* (1956), *The Stooge* (1953), and *Artists and Models* (1955). But even the best Martin and Lewis films never captured their manic, anything-goes onstage energy. (To see them in their full anarchic, antic glory, seek out the old *Colgate Comedy Hour* TV shows, which they hosted in the mid '50s.)

When the team broke up acrimoniously in 1957, Jerry went it alone, taking his "idiot" character into increasingly surreal surroundings. He began to direct himself, impressively so, in *The Bellboy* (1960) and *The Errand Boy* (1961). But his most perfectly realized role, and his greatest achievement as a comedic actor and director, is the brilliantly Freudian **The Nutty Professor** (1963). Jerry plays Dr. Julius Kelp, a nerdy, bespectacled, buck-toothed college science teacher, who secretly longs to be a swinging he-man. In a witty takeoff on *Dr. Jekyll and Mr. Hyde,* Kelp concocts a potion that transforms him into obnoxious, suave lounge lizard Buddy Love. Critics at the time thought the character of Buddy Love was a poison-pen valentine to ex-partner Dean; in retrospect, the character proves a frighteningly accurate harbinger of the real-life Jerry to come.

Lewis gives a terrific dual performance and fills the screen with some hilariously surreal sight gags. He never made a better movie. Even viewers who don't enjoy Jerry will be impressed.

march 17

Feeling a Little Green Today?

Today is St. Patrick's Day, named after the patron saint who, according to legend, drove the snakes from Ireland.

Ironically, St. Patrick wasn't really Irish—he was born in Wales and kidnapped and sold in Ireland as a slave. After learning the language, he escaped and sought refuge in the church. He was eventually ordained as a deacon, then a priest, and finally a bishop. Pope Celestine sent him back to Ireland to preach the gospel, where evidently he did much traveling—as places bearing his name all across Brittany, Cornwall, Scotland, Wales, and Ireland attest to.

You don't have to be Irish to be enchanted by the blarney-bedecked film **The Quiet Man** (1952)—but it helps. No other movie so lyrically captures the breathtaking beauty of the Irish landscape—and no other movie is stuffed with a more stereotypical Irish stew of characters. John Wayne gives one of his best performances as Sean Thornton, an American boxer who comes back home to his birthplace in Ireland after accidentally killing a man in the boxing ring and vowing never to fight again. Once in the picture-perfect hamlet of Innisfree, he meets the lovely and fiery Mary Kate (Maureen O'Hara). It's love at first sight for both, but things get complicated when Kate's brawling bear of a brother (Victor McClaglen) refuses to hand over her dowry. Sean must either give up the woman he loves or fight for her honor. Every shot is like a postcard from the Irish Tourism Board; the Irish countryside never looked so lush and beautiful. The sexual chemistry between Wayne and O'Hara is so palpable it jumps off the screen. Have a pint and sit back, sing one more round of "I'll Take You Home Again, Kathleen," and enjoy one of the most picturesque romances ever filmed. Directed by Sean O'Feeney, better known by his Americanized alias, John Ford (who won the Oscar for Best Director that year).

march 18

Come One, Come All!

Before movies, before TV, before radio, there was the circus. And the greatest of them all was Barnum and Bailey—"the Greatest Show on Earth." And the Greatest Show on Earth opened this day at New York's Madison Square Garden in 1881.

Showman and con artist extraordinaire P. T. Barnum had the reputation, the marketing savvy, and the chutzpah. He knew how to package an act, even when the act wasn't so package-able. (He once paired two average-height men and charged people to see them as "the world's smallest giant and the world's tallest midget, together on one stage.") While Barnum had the showmanship, James Bailey had the money and the acts. When they decided to pool their resources, they created the world's most successful traveling circus.

Celebrate the bygone magic of the circus with Cecil B. DeMille's over-the-Big-Top salute to circus life, **The Greatest Show on Earth** (1952). *SEE*—stalwart hunk Charlton Heston as the rough-and-tumble circus owner who will do anything to make sure the show goes on. *SEE*—Cornel Wilde's buff six-pack abs as he plays a high-wire artist defying gravity, death, and Gloria Grahame. *SEE*—Jimmy Stewart as Buttons the Clown, who never once removes his makeup during the entire picture because he's actually a doctor wanted for murder. *SEE*—cameos from Bob Hope, Bing Crosby, and more. Colorful, brassy, and packed with real-life circus entertainers (including clown immortal Emmett Kelly), *The Greatest Show on Earth* is the next best thing to being there. It's a *movie*—not a *film*—so don't forget the popcorn and peanuts.

march 19

Viva Las Vegas

You have to wonder what Nevada's prime industry would be if it wasn't gambling. Nuclear waste storage? On this day in 1931, the state of Nevada passed legalized gambling, and an American dream was launched in all its sequined, sun-soaked splendor.

Of course, Nevada begat Las Vegas, and Las Vegas—as both a dream and a backdrop—begat countless movies. The list is endless; some of the more memorable include *Honeymoon in Vegas, The Godfather, Bugsy, Indecent Proposal, Showgirls, Fear and Loathing in Las Vegas, Sister Act, Rain Man, The Rat Pack, Very Bad Things, Ocean's Eleven,* and *Leaving Las Vegas.* The Flintstones even got into the act in the atrocious *Flintstones in Viva Rock Vegas* (2000).

But one of the best Vegas movies ever is Martin Scorsese's **Casino** (1995). Scorsese delivers a fictional account of the mid '70s fall of the mob in Vegas as seen through the eyes of Sam "Ace" Rothstein, played by a steely-eyed Robert DeNiro. Sharon Stone delivers a searing performance as DeNiro's ex-hustler, drug-addled wife, Ginger. And what an eclectic supporting cast: In addition to another great turn by Joe Pesci as Roth's loose-cannon enforcer Nicky, look for Steve Allen, Dick Smothers, Don Rickles, Frankie Avalon, and Joe Bob Biggs in cameos. And just for the hell of it, why not rent **Viva Las Vegas!** (1964) just to see Elvis do the title song, one of the great movie themes ever—if not one of the greatest movies ever.

march 20

This Is One Addictive Movie, Released in the Nick-o-Tine

It was a stunning turnaround for the tobacco and cigarette industry. On this day in 1997, after decades of denials, the Liggett Group, manufacturer of L&Ms, Larks, and Chesterfields, finally 'fessed up and admitted that cigarettes were addictive. What's more, they acknowledged that they—and their much larger brethren in the cigarette conspiracy—had consciously marketed their product to children. The Liggett Group was far from the world's largest manufacturer of cancer sticks—Phillip Morris had the biggest market share—but they were the first to finally admit to a decades-long conspiracy.

Commemorate the occasion by snuffing out that cigarette and watching **The Insider** (1999), a movie that's a fascinating exposé of both the cigarette industry and the broadcast media. Al Pacino gives an atypically restrained performance as veteran *60 Minutes* producer Lowell Bergman, who is out to expose the tobacco industry, even if it costs him his career. He forms an uneasy alliance with Dr. Jeffrey Wigand (Russell Crowe, in a revelatory turn), a former tobacco executive recently fired by his employer, one of the largest tobacco companies in America. Desperate for money to cover the medical insurance for his asthmatic daughter, Wigand accepts a job as a paid consultant for a story Bergman is working on about unethical practices within the tobacco industry. What begins as a temporary alliance turns into much more; the two men find out that the powerful cigarette lobby will stop at nothing to save their billion-dollar-a-year industry, and the media will stop at nothing to protect itself. Terrific performances (including a scene-stealing Christopher Plummer as *60 Minutes* correspondent Mike Wallace), and a scathing script by Eric Roth and Michael Mann make *The Insider* a provocative, suspenseful, sobering, and often shocking experience.

march 21

A Movie That Led to Freedom, Not Escapism

On this day in 1989, an extraordinary event in the annals of justice occured—all thanks to a single motion picture. Randall Dale Adams was released from prison after serving eleven years for the 1976 murder of a Dallas police officer—and he owed his freedom to a movie.

Adams specifically owed his freedom to filmmaker Errol Morris. Morris, a documentary filmmaker, heard about Adams's unjust incarceration and began doing his own investigating—on film. The resulting documentary, **The Thin Blue Line** (1988), not only garnered several awards from impressed critics (the New York Film Critics and the National Board of Review both pronounced it "Best Documentary")—it was so convincing that Adams's conviction was overturned, and he was freed.

The Thin Blue Line is far from your standard dry documentary fare; director Morris creates a delightfully bizarre piece of investigative filmmaking, as well as a slightly wacky thesis on the nature of truth. His highly stylized reconstruction of the crime, interrogations of legal experts, and interviews with shifty and unreliable witnesses are at once funny and disturbing, fascinating and repulsive. If David Lynch ever made a documentary, it might look something like this. An intelligent, original film investigation like no other, it will leave you moved, relieved, upset, angered, amused . . . and entertained.

march 22

Birth of a Ham

William Shatner is the patron saint of ham actors. To some, he is a parody of the profession, with his signature pregnant . . . pauses, inflections on the unexpected syllable, and overwrought, hand-wringing delivery. To some (particularly his costars) he is reportedly a bullying, egotistical prima donna; but to most of us he is and always will be Captain James T. Kirk of the starship *Enterprise* in *Star Trek.*

He was born this day in 1931 in Montreal, Quebec. He appeared in numerous movies of the '50s in supporting roles and second leads, including *The Brothers Karamozov* (1958) and *Judgment at Nuremberg* (1961). He starred in *The Intruder,* a startling 1961 Roger Corman quickie about small-town prejudice and hatred, as a hate-fanning stranger in town. In TV, he memorably portrayed an airline passenger who sees a gremlin crawling on the wing of the airplane in an episode of *The Twilight Zone.*

But he finally hit pay dirt in 1966 when he was cast as the captain of a starship in the TV series *Star Trek* by series creator and producer Gene Roddenberry, after original star Jeffrey Hunter bowed out. The show achieved only modest ratings and was canceled in its third season. Shatner went on to star in a series of B-budget movies and TV movies like *Kingdom of the Spiders* and *Crazy Mama* (where he appears in a nude scene with costar Angie Dickinson). But in reruns *Star Trek* became a huge hit—enough to convince Paramount Studios to invest in a big-screen version in 1979, ten years after the original series was canceled. *Star Trek: The Motion Picture* (1979), directed by Robert Wise, was a big, overblown bore that somehow managed to become enough of a hit to justify a sequel.

The sequel became the best of the series (the aging crew went on to film five more installments), deftly mixing action, adventure, comedy, drama, and state-of-the-art FX. **Star Trek: The Wrath of Khan** (1982) was cleverly written and directed by Nicholas Meyer. You don't have to be a fan of the TV series to enjoy the exciting story, great special effects, and effective turns from the familiar supporting cast, including DeForrest Kelly as Dr. "Bones" McCoy and Leonard Nimoy as that personification of pure Vulcan logic, Mr. Spock. It's also Shatner's finest performance. For once, he underplays, and is all the more believable because of it. Almost as importantly, his toupee fits. And Ricardo Montalban, as the justifiably pissed-off Khan, goes *mano a mano* with Kirk in one of the screen's great all-time ham-offs.

march 23

No Wire Hangers!

Ever since the day she was born (on this date in 1904), Lucille LeSueur was determined to succeed—and in a big way. She was not conventionally beautiful, but she was a tigress in more ways than one, clawing her way to the top. Beginning as a waitress and shop girl, she won a Charleston contest in the '20s and began a dancing career. She changed her name to Billie Cassin, after her stepfather. (At around this time, she also appeared in a few porn films, which she later tried desperately to suppress.) She was dancing in a Broadway chorus line when she caught the attention of an executive from MGM who saw potential.

She was awarded a contract with MGM, the most prestigious studio in the industry. But her name still wasn't right. In a brilliantly tawdry display of marketing savvy, the studio launched a national publicity contest to find her a name. The winning entry: Joan Crawford. The public had created and named its monster.

The struggling would-be actress managed to get herself bit parts in legitimate theater and films. And she managed to be pretty damn good in them. She delivered a light and lively performance in Harry Langdon's silent comedy classic *Tramp, Tramp, Tramp* (1925) and became a national sensation—and scandal—as the freewheeling flapper in *Our Dancing Daughters* (1928).

With the advent of talkies, the upwardly mobile actress gave a vulnerable performance in MGM's epic *Grand Hotel* as Wallace Beery's put-upon secretary (1932). As the years went by, she morphed into an icon. Like a canny alien, she kept mutating and evolving into a new image, a next phase, a different skin, that thrived for nearly a half century. She was underrated as an actress; witness her compelling turns in *Rain* (1932), *The Women* (1939), *Mildred Pierce* (for which she won an Oscar), and *Johnny Guitar* (1954), which was nearly her last good performance in a good picture.

They're all great performances—but save them for another day. Instead, savor one of the all-time worst hit movies ever, **Mommie Dearest** (1981) featuring Faye Dunaway as Crawford, under tons of makeup that makes her look like Charles Pierce. Based on the memoirs of Crawford's adopted daughter, Christina, *Mommie Dearest* is a high camp, way-over-the-top exposé of the actress as melodramatic stage villain, and Dunaway chews the scenery like a raptor in heat. Highlights include the fiftyish Crawford substituting for her own daughter on a popular daytime soap opera late in her career and a hilarious sequence when she tells it like it is to the Pepsi-Cola board of directors ("Don't fuck with me, fellas!"). This is one terrible movie—so god-awful it transcends its own trashiness to become something bordering on the sublime. A clean-sweep winner of the Golden Raspberry Awards for 1981, including Worst Picture, Worst Actress, Worst Supporting Actress (Diana Scarwid as Christina), and Worst Screenplay. Enjoy. And scrub yourself up afterward.

march 24

Escape from It All

Stalag Luft III in Sagan, Poland, was proud of the fact that it was escape-proof. It had been built in 1942 to be the last word in German ingenuity. Surrounded by two ten-foot barbed-wire fences, and literally built on sand—impossible, the Germans believed, to tunnel through. On top of that, they had planted listening devices fifteen feet beneath the ground that could detect any disturbance. But the Germans had underestimated the Allies' ingenuity. Under the leadership of British officer Harry Day and Spitfire pilot Roger Bushell, six hundred prisoners dug three separate tunnels—code-named "Tom," "Dick," and "Harry"—all an incredible thirty feet below the surface.

On this date in 1944, two hundred men, equipped with compasses, maps, and impressively forged papers, began crawling toward freedom. But the would-be escapees had miscalculated the length of the tunnel; it came up one hundred yards short of the forest, in plain view of the Germans. Still, seventy-six prisoners managed to escape before a sentry discovered the hole and stopped the escape. Three actually made it back to England; the rest (including Bushell) were captured and executed.

The Great Escape (1962), director John Sturges's macho movie salute to the efforts of Allied prisoners to escape Stalag Luft III, is one of the major all-star action flicks of the '60s. The testosterone-swelled cast is headed by Steve McQueen as Capt. Hilts, "the Cooler King," a taciturn loner who is determined to bust out to freedom at any cost. Also starring Charles Bronson (convincing as a claustrophobic tunnel digger), Donald Pleasence as a nearsighted forgery expert, James Garner, Richard Attenborough, David McCallum, and a woefully miscast but still amusing James Coburn (whose Australian accent has to be heard to be disbelieved). The last hour is a nail-biter, and features one of the great action sequences of the '60s—McQueen's bid for freedom aboard a motorcycle in the German countryside. McQueen did his own stunt-driving, much to the horror of the producers. The film lifted him to superstar status. (Coincidentally, today is also McQueen's birthday.)

march 25

The Force Was Running a Little Low That Day

On this date, not so long ago (1976, to be precise) on a film set far, far away (Tunisia), George Lucas began filming a project that would come to be titled *Star Wars.*

The first day of production was not an easy day. His two lead actors, a couple of androids dubbed R2-D2 and C3PO, refused to cooperate (actually, it was Tunisian radio signals jamming their electronic devices). And the young hero's name wasn't quite right, either: Luke Starkiller. But Lucas persevered—and changed the lead character's name to the more benign and mythic-sounding Luke Skywalker—and one of the most phenomenal pop culture success stories of the century was off to a slow but eventful start.

Star Wars took everyone by surprise and set the tone for an entire generation of films to follow, including two sequels (*The Empire Strikes Back* [1980] and *Return of the Jedi* [1983]) a woefully misguided prequel (1999's *Star Wars Episode One: The Phantom Menace*), and countless imitators. The entire franchise morphed into more of a cultural merchandising phenomenon than a movie.

But go back and savor where it all began, with **Star Wars** (1977), and delight in the original story of naïve but honorable young Luke Skywalker, Princess Leia, and devil-may-care renegade pilot Han Solo. Lucas managed to squeeze enough great effects, thrills, laughs, romance, and derring-do for three films into one movie. (His colleague Steven Spielberg took extensive notes, then made *Raiders of the Lost Ark,* taking Harrison Ford along with him.) Alec Guinness keeps things anchored yet mystical as Luke's wise old mentor, Obi-Wan Kenobi—a part that the actor himself was, quite vocally, ashamed of. And Harrison Ford broke through to superstar status with his ingratiating portrayal of the cocky mercenary pilot with a sentimental streak, Han Solo. Bring out the snacks—this is a popcorn movie if ever there was one. This is why they call 'em "movies."

march 26

Who Done It

If anybody could have filmed Pete Townshend's lugubrious rock opera, *Tommy,* it was '60s cinema's enfant terrible, Ken Russell. And, for better or worse, he did.

The movie version of **Tommy** (1975) premiered on this day in London in 1975—to very mixed reviews. The loose (very loose) story of a deaf, dumb, and blind boy who becomes a pinball wizard was composed by Townshend and performed by the Who in the original two-LP set recorded in 1969. Along with *Jesus Christ Superstar* it launched the thankfully short-lived fad of composing rock operas—which generally were neither rock nor operas. *Tommy* had the benefit of at least having solid bollocks, thanks to the Who's reputation.

Does the movie version succeed? Depends on how you feel about the material and Ken Russell's everything-but-the-kitchen-sink directorial gifts. (I defy anyone not to be moved one way or the other by Ann-Margret's bean-bathing scene!) The Who's lead singer, Roger Daltrey, starred in the all-singing title role—and an eclectic supporting cast alone makes the movie worth seeing: Tina Turner, Ann-Margret, Jack Nicholson, Eric Clapton, Elton John (on stilts, no less), Oliver Reed, and, as the sleazy Uncle Ernie, the Who's manic drummer, Keith Moon, better known as "Moon the Loon." Musical highlights include "See Me, Feel Me, Touch Me," and "Pinball Wizard."

march 27

Shaked Alaska

It was the single most violent earthquake in U.S. history. On this day in 1964, an earthquake measuring a hefty 9.2 on the Richter scale hit Anchorage, Alaska, literally splitting the city in half. Fissures twelve feet wide ran through the streets. And what followed was even more frightening: A tsunami caused by the quake descended on the city like a hammer of water. In all, 131 people died that day.

Tremble at the power of Mother Nature—and the gimmick called Sensurround—with the so-hokey-it's-fun '70s cheese-fest **Earthquake** (1974). When it was originally released to theaters, it was marketed as the first (and, so far, last) film in Sensurround, a complex multichannel sound system that actually caused the entire theater to rumble. Unless your TV is equipped with Sensurround, you'll have to settle for watching an earthquake pretty much level Los Angeles, along with the reputations of its cast members, Charlton Heston, George Kennedy, and, in her last screen role, Ava Gardner. Cowritten, believe it or not, by Mario Puzo.

march 28

A Movie That Radiates Suspense

Call it good timing or call it bad timing. Call it a fluke or call it a warning. Call it art imitating life.

Any way you call it, on this day in 1979, in the town of Middletown near Three Mile Island, Pennsylvania, there was what is euphemistically called "an incident." A valve in a nuclear power plant got stuck in the open position, letting water evaporate from the cooling system of the plant's #2 reactor. Misunderstanding what was happening, workers stopped the flow of water to the core, and the temperature skyrocketed. When they reversed the procedure, the fresh water shattered the now white-hot uranium fuel rods, allowing radiation to escape.

Scarcely two weeks later, **The China Syndrome** (1979) was released to theaters all across America—a movie about an "incident" at a seemingly fail-safe nuclear energy plant in California. The parallel was almost too close for comfort.

It was certainly too close for comfort for the Nuclear Regulatory Commission. It may not be provable in a court of law, but there's a good chance that the one-two punch of Three Mile Island and *The China Syndrome* spelled the end of nuclear power's image as a viable, safe power source for the American public.

The China Syndrome is more than a historic curiosity. It's a taut, suspenseful, all-too-believable thriller told with a literate, believable script, tight direction by James Bridges, and stellar performances. Jane Fonda has one of her best roles as a frustrated TV journalist who is tired of the puff pieces she has been assigned and is eager to break a real story. She gets her wish when a standard PR assignment at a nearby nuclear power plant turns into a near-meltdown. Convinced there's a cover-up (and with good reason), she interviews long-time company man Jack Lemmon, who finds himself torn between his nagging conscience and his loyalty to the company. It all builds to a suitably nail-biting conclusion.

Reminds me of an old saying that adorned countless bumper stickers back in the '70s: "Nuclear thinking and unclear thinking are the same thing. Depends on how you use the UN."

march 29

The War Nobody Won

A double anniversary for the U.S. in Vietnam: On this day in 1971, 1st Lt. William L. Calley was found guilty of the murder of twenty-two Vietnamese civilians in what became known as the My Lai Massacre, one of the most infamous atrocities of an atrocity-filled war—and exactly two years later, on this same date, the last U.S. troops left Vietnam. During the decade of American military involvement there, the U.S. spent over 110 billion dollars, and over fifty-seven thousand soldiers lost their lives.

The Vietnam War was the most divisive war in U.S. history. It has been the subject of numerous films, too many to list here. The first movie about the Vietnam War made for American audiences—and the only movie made about the war while it was going on—was John Wayne's horribly misguided *The Green Berets* (1966), a blatant right-wing propaganda piece. Postwar films of note include Michael Cimino's *The Deer Hunter* (1978) and Stanley Kubrick's *Full Metal Jacket* (1987). But the most prolific and significant moviemaker on the Vietnam War has been Oliver Stone. A veteran of the conflict, he has written and directed *Born on the Fourth of July* (1989), *Heaven and Earth* (1983), and, most notably, **Platoon** (1986). Charlie Sheen plays a naïve grunt plunged into the insanity of the ground war in Vietnam. The ideological division back home in the U.S. is evident in the makeup of his platoon; it's split into two warring factions, embodied by Staff Sgt. Bob Barnes (Tom Berenger), a gung-ho killing machine, and Sgt. Elias (Willem Dafoe), the pacifistic spiritual center of the movie. Sheen is torn between the two. At once awesomely brutal and poetic, *Platoon* is a blistering experience.

march 30

Birth of a Ladies' Man

Arguably the silver screen's most prodigious lothario, Warren Beatty had, by all accounts, an enviable love life before settling down into domestic bliss and family with wife Annette Bening. It would be easier to compile a list of women he *didn't* court (let's see . . . there's Marjorie Main and, um . . . Margaret Hamilton and, um . . .) than those that he did (Julie Christie, Joan Crawford, Goldie Hawn, Natalie Wood, Diane Keaton . . .). Somehow, in between his libido-fueled liaisons he managed to make some movies, many of them pretty damn good. He became a star with *Bonnie and Clyde* (1967), and even his failures—like *Ishtar* (1987), *Mickey One* (1965), and *Love Affair* (1994)—have been fascinating. He has branched out into an impressive and successful career as auteur, writing, directing, and starring in *Reds* (1981), *Heaven Can Wait* (1978), and *Bullworth* (1998).

He was born this date in 1937. It's only fitting to celebrate his birthday today by watching **Shampoo** (1975), in which he plays a compulsively womanizing hairdresser in Nixon-era Beverly Hills. It's a role that comes dangerously close to self-parody, but Beatty pulls it off with naïve charm and a tussled sense of duty that is endearing and ultimately affecting. A landmark film, and a unique time capsule of Hollywood and America in the late '60s.

march 31

Requiem for the Queen of Tejano

She was "the Queen of Tejano Music," a fabulously talented Mexican American girl who rose to the top of the music charts. Her 1993 LP, *Selena Live* won the Grammy for Best Mexican American Album—and she was beginning to break into the big time. Her music was getting mainstream airplay, and she was becoming not just a successful Hispanic pop artist, but a pioneer crossover artist, as well.

Selena was only beginning her mercurial rise when, on this day in 1995, she was fatally shot by her employee and business partner, Yolanda Saldivar, at the Days Inn Hotel in Corpus Christi, Texas. Saldivar had first seen the young singer at a concert in San Antonio and became a fan. She organized the official Selena Fan Club, became Selena's friend and confidant, and eventually head of Selena, Etc. Boutiques. Yolanda had a past record of having stolen nearly $10,000 from Dr. Faustino Gomez, who had employed her in the 1980s. Selena's father became suspicious that Yolanda was embezzling thousands of dollars from Selena, and, allegedly, Selena confronted Saldivar on this fatal morning in 1995.

Jennifer Lopez delivered a career-igniting performance in the title role of **Selena** (1997). Admittedly and shamelessly a biased and adoring account of her life (Selena's father, Abraham Quintanilla, produced the film), *Selena* does a commendable if predictable job of celebrating the singer and what she gave to her musical culture and heritage. Edward James Olmos delivers a charismatic performance as her stern but supportive father and manager (and, again, let's bear in mind who produced this film). Lopez, playing a virtual idol, was straight-jacketed here—but succeeds admirably in balancing her own characteristics with those of the already-iconic character whom she is portraying. She went on to prove herself capable of far more in later roles.

april

april 1

Make a Fool of Yourself

"The first of April, some do say
Is set apart for All Fools' Day
But why the people call it so
Not I nor they themselves do know."

—Poor Robin's Almanac, *1760*

April Fools' Day, for those of you with a penchant for pursuing meaning behind meaningless things, probably derives from a change in the calendar year about five hundred years ago. Before 1564 it was traditional to honor the new year with a solid week of partying, but the calendar was different then—the new year began on March 25, and the biggest celebration fell on April 1. Fifteen sixty-four marked the first year in which the first day of the new year was January 1. People who forgot the new day for celebrating were called "April fools." Over the years, the date has become the traditional day of playing practical jokes on unsuspecting victims.

Celebrate April Fools' Day with a film oddity that is right in the spirit of the occasion—Orson Welles's last completed film, the witty, mischievous, and little-seen **F for Fake** (1975). In 1977, author Clifford Irving managed to publish *The Autobiography of Howard Hughes,* a splendid hoax that he perpetrated on the entire world. He may have gotten the idea from his next-door neighbor, a masterful art forger named Elmyr de Hory—a man who could fake a Picasso so accurately that it fooled the artist himself. Welles, no stranger to trickery (he began as a magician, and his infamous "War of the Worlds" radio broadcast was one of the great pranks of all time) pieced together this fascinating rumination on trickery using existing footage of both Irving and de Hory, as well as shooting new footage himself. The result is one of the most entertaining of his films—a wonderful sense of mischief pervades the whole beguiling movie. And, yes, there's an April Fools' joke—but I'm not giving it away. Discover it for yourself.

Can't find *F for Fake*? As a standby, consider **The Game** (1997), director David Fincher's original and stylish Rubik's Cube of a movie starring Michael Douglas as Nicholas Van Orton, a millionaire investment banker whose estranged brother (Sean Penn) gives him a birthday present that is more than meets the eye. Soon Van Orton's world is turned upside down as he tries to figure out what the game really is, if he lives long enough. Clever screenplay by John Brancato and Michael Ferris.

april 2

Take a Detour into Crime

It was a day like any other day in Los Angeles in 1965 . . . spring was in the air but who could see it through the smog and what difference would it have made anyway? Washed-up Hollywood B-movie actor and never-quite-star Tom Neal had fallen on hard times, was living in a cheap dilapidated apartment, and all the days looked the same. His reputation for hard living and hard drinking had made him virtually unemployable in the industry. On top of all that, he was paranoid and suspicious that his wife, Gail, was having an affair.

The story he told the police was that she tried to kill him and the gun went off accidentally; the prosecution's version of that same story was that he had shot her in the head while she slept on the couch. Strangely, the gun itself vanished. Either way, accidentally or on purpose, on this day in 1965, Tom Neal killed his wife, along with whatever chance he had for a better future.

The irony was thick. Years before, he gave one of the all-time great noir performances as a down-on-his-luck drifter who meets one bad dame too many, who gets a bad hand dealt him, and who accidentally kills his lover in the movie many consider the greatest film noir ever, the classic **Detour** (1946). B-movie director Edgar G. Ulmer, working on a poverty-row budget, created a bitter, dark, compelling masterpiece on the vagaries of fate. Neal is appropriately dim as the luckless hero, but it's Ann Savage (an appropriate name if there ever was one) who steals the show as the brassy bitch Neal picks up hitchhiking in California. All in all, it's an amazing movie, drenched in the darker hues of human nature; like watching a bad traffic accident, you're compelled to look.

Neal, sentenced to one to fifteen years for manslaughter, was paroled in 1971, but died August 7, 1972. In a typical piece of Hollywood stunt-casting, his son, Tom Neal, Jr., played his old part in a 1992 remake of *Detour.* He hasn't been heard from since. Like father, like son.

april 3

"Mommy" Wasn't the Last Word He Mumbled

Marlon Brando was born this day in Omaha, Nebraska, in 1924, the son of a father who was a traveling salesman and a mother who acted in community theater. There was a method to his mumbling, and he went on to become the single most influential film actor of his age.

After being expelled from military academy in Minnesota, he attended the Dramatic Workshop in New York, gradually getting supporting parts in Broadway shows. In 1947, he exploded into stardom on Broadway with his incendiary performance as brutish but vulnerable Stanley Kowalski in Tennessee Williams's *A Streetcar Named Desire.* Hollywood beckoned, and his first role was as an embittered paraplegic in *The Men* (1950), followed by a brilliantly realized reprise of his role in *A Streetcar Named Desire* (1951), directed by Elia Kazan.

Audiences had never seen anything quite like him. Positively primal, grunting, scratching himself whenever and wherever he happened to itch, Brando was compulsively watchable, projecting a raw sexuality that leaped off the screen. Throughout the '50s he exerted enormous artistic force, with varied showcase roles in such films as *The Wild One* (1954), *On the Waterfront* (1954), and *Viva Zapata!* (1952) and impressively enunciating every Shakespearean syllable as Marc Antony in *Julius Caesar* (1953). He fell into slack performances throughout the '60s, then had one of the great comebacks in film history as Don Vito Corleone in *The Godfather* (1972) and the grieving middle-aged American in Bertolucci's *Last Tango in Paris* (1972). They're all monumental performances. You've likely seen most of them.

Every film buff has been exposed to Brando's much-touted acting acumen, but have you ever seen Brando's sole effort as director? For a special change of pace, celebrate Brando's birthday with the only film he ever directed and starred in, **One Eyed Jacks** (1961). A fictionalized take on both Billy the Kid and the theme of betrayal, set in the Old West, it was originally going to be directed by Stanley Kubrick, but Brando took over the reins at the last minute; apparently some of Kubrick's footage still survives in the final cut. Brando plays bank robber Rio, who is betrayed by his partner and surrogate father, Dad Longstreet (Karl Malden in one of his most nuanced performances). Released from a Mexican prison after five years, Rio tracks down his old partner, now the sheriff of a small coastal town in California. Rio plots revenge and begins an affair with Longstreet's daughter (Pina Pillicer).

One Eyed Jacks is a muddled psychological study but a fascinating cinematic Rorschach test into Brando's bizarre psyche. (Naturally, he includes a mandatory whipping scene; Brando often took a beating at the box office.) He had the inspiration to film his movie on the beautiful Monterey Peninsula on the California coast, giving the picture a sand-swept, bleached-out oceanspray ambience that is unusual in a Western. Gorgeously shot, uniformly fine acting (except for the miscast Pillicer), and far from your average shoot-'em-up. A great supporting cast includes Tim Carey, Ben Johnson, Slim Pickens, and Elisha Cook, Jr.

april 4

Gloria's Swan Song

"We didn't need dialogue. We had faces then."

—Gloria Swanson, as faded film star Norma Desmond

Her public thought she'd live forever. Even *she* thought she'd live forever, appearing on countless talk shows in her doddering old age, imperiously pontificating on the benefits of enemas and health foods. But on this day in 1983, Gloria Swanson, one of the last of the great silent-screen divas, shuffled off her mortal coil.

She had seen it all, though, by the time she left us. She started out as one of Mack Sennett's Bathing Beauties in the early 1920s. With her short stature and perky energy, she soon got noticed and became a star—one with a finely tuned gift for both comedy and drama. In the halcyon days of silent film, she was rivaled only by Mary Pickford and Lillian Gish. She became, in fact, the most successful and highest paid actress of the silent screen. C. B. DeMille had made her a star, inevitably casting her as a newlywed wife whose attention wanders. She quickly grew to exert more and more control over her own films (surreptitiously assisted by her clandestine lover, Joseph P. Kennedy)—most notably when she hired notorious but brilliant film director Erich von Stroheim to direct her in *Queen Kelly* (1928), and then walked off the picture before it was completed, firing von Stroheim and seizing possession of the film reels.

After the arrival of talkies, she pretty much retired from the screen—until, of course, her career-defining performance as aging silent film star Norma

Desmond in Billy Wilder's **Sunset Boulevard** (1950). William Holden costars as a down-on-his-luck Hollywood screenwriter who ends up hiding from creditors in Norma Desmond's eerie and magnificently decrepit Hollywood mansion. "I know you," he says, recognizing the film star. "You're Norma Desmond. You used to be big." "I am big," she replies grandly. "It's the pictures that got small."

Soon Holden finds himself a kept man, writing a "comeback" script for Norma under the thumb of the overbearing star. Wilder's dark, gothic movie is both a bleak comedy and a noirish tragedy, and Swanson's performance proved to be the most memorable of her career, earning her an Oscar for Best Actress. (*Sunset Boulevard* also garnered Best Picture, Best Actor [Holden], and Best Director.)

By the way, von Stroheim, the director Swanson had fired twenty-five years earlier, plays her butler and ex-husband, Max. A brief piece of silent film footage starring Swanson is projected during a sequence in the mansion. It's an excerpt from *Queen Kelly,* the very film that von Stroheim had directed and Swanson had taken away from him.

april 5

The Greatest Film Actor Ever?

The story goes that when the tall and lanky Katharine Hepburn was first introduced to the short and stocky Spencer Tracy on the set of their first picture together, she imperiously looked down her aristocratic nose and observed, "You're rather short, aren't you?" To which he responded, smiling confidently, "Don't worry. I'll cut you down to size."

As an actor, Spencer Tracy cut everyone down to size. Frequently cited as the screen's all-around greatest actor (Laurence Olivier thought Tracy the best), he projected a seemingly effortless, masculine naturalism, rock solid. Though not conventionally handsome, and never a heartthrob (he had a face for Mt. Rushmore), Tracy conveyed more strength and conviction than a dozen Erroll Flynns. You never see Spencer Tracy acting; roles bent to the force of his willful personality like mountains came to Muhammad.

He was born on this day in 1899. His early films were spent playing cocky tough guys (*20,000 Years in Sing Sing,* 1932) or second banana to top-billed Clark Gable (*San Francisco,* 1936). He won the Academy Award as Best Actor for his performance as the life-embracing Portuguese fisherman Emanuel in *Captains Courageous* (1937) and again the following year for his performance as Father Flanagan in *Boys Town* (1938). He could handle tough, physical roles, as is evidenced by his great showing in the lush, testosterone-fueled *Northwest Passage* (1940). His comedic timing and naturalism were unparalleled in such comedy classics as *Adam's Rib* (1948; his best film with Hepburn) and the charming *Father of the Bride* (1950). In his later years he rounded out his remarkable career with typically great performances in *Bad Day at Black Rock* (1954), *Inherit the Wind* (1961), and *Guess Who's Coming to Dinner* (1967).

You really can't go wrong with Tracy; the number of astonishingly good performances in great movies is staggering. For an interesting Tracy double feature, catch him at two points along the long arc of his career: in his early masterpiece, **Captains Courageous** (1937), followed by his magnificent solo portrayal in **The Old Man and the Sea** (1958).

april 6

The War That Was Supposed to End All Wars: Take One

On this date in 1917, the U.S. formally declared war on Germany and entered into World War I. Triggered by Germany's sinking of the Cunard ship *Lusitania* off the coast of Ireland, killing 1,198 people on May 7, 1915, the U.S. Senate voted 82 to 6 and the House of Representatives endorsed the declaration by a vote of 373 to 50.

Observe the sober anniversary with one of the greatest antiwar films ever made, Lewis Milestone's unforgettable **All Quiet on the Western Front** (1930), based on the classic novel by Erich Maria Remarque. At the instigation of their gung-ho schoolteacher, seven German youths enlist in the army and go to the battlefields in World War I, their imaginations filled with visions of patriotism and glory. Stuck in the trenches and experiencing the horrors of war firsthand, they quickly see there's no glory in it. An emotionally wrenching antiwar film that has lost none of its power in the ensuing decades, *All Quiet on the Western Front* is at once poetic and gritty, graphic and shocking. Lew Ayres excelled with the performance of his lifetime as the naïve enlistee through whose eyes we, the audience, come to see the horrors of war. A masterpiece of film as not only an art form, but as a potent weapon—the kind of weapon that can give the word *propaganda* a good name. (The film was withdrawn during World War II to discourage pacifism.)

april 7

A Birthday You Can't Refuse

Happy birthday today to one of the great mavericks of cinema, Francis Ford Coppola, born this date in 1937 in Detroit, Michigan. He filmed his first movie on an 8mm camera at the age of ten after recuperating from a year-long bout with polio. In 1962 he finagled a job as assistant director and all-around errand boy for the patron saint of struggling young filmmakers, Roger Corman. After directing a low-budget horror flick in Ireland, he directed his own lighthearted coming-of-age comedy, *You're a Big Boy Now* (1967). Hollywood noticed and entrusted him to direct two films, *Finian's Rainbow* (1968) and *The Rain People* (1969). Both flopped, and Copolla was on the verge of bankruptcy when he signed on to direct *The Godfather* (1972), one of the biggest moneymakers ever. And one of the great roller-coaster directorial careers in Hollywood was off to an auspicious start.

Over the years, Coppola has directed some of the most audacious, daring, and occasionally successful movies in the American oeuvre (*The Godfather,*

Part II [1974]; *Apocalypse Now* [1979]), and quite a few that paled, flailed, and failed with audiences (*One from the Heart* [1982]; *The Cotton Club* [1984], *Gardens of Stone* [1987]). But one of his greatest achivements is one of his most rarely seen experiments, a brilliant, taut, and unsettling piece called **The Conversation** (1974). In one of his most complex performances, Gene Hackman plays Harry Caul, one of the top surveillance experts in the country, a deeply moral man in a deeply sleazy business who feels guilty about what he does for a living: invading people's privacy. When wealthy businessman Robert Duvall hires him to trail his wife (Cindy Williams), whom he rightfully suspects of having an affair, Caul stumbles across a murder plot. All is not what it seems in this labyrinthine puzzle of a movie, which is not so much a thriller as a fascinating character study of a man who has misplaced his moral compass. Featuring Harrison Ford in a rare role as a heavy and the late John Cazale as Harry's worshipful assistant. *The Conversation* was one of the first—and still the best—of the paranoiac thrillers. The DVD release carries a fascinating feature-length commentary by Coppola.

april 8

Can Love Kill?

As lead singer and writer for Nirvana, Kurt Cobain spoke for a lot of the disenfranchised youth of the early '90s. Sensitive, gifted, indulged, troubled, and drug-addled, he had trouble adjusting to the pressures of celebrity. According to some, he also had troubles adapting to his mercurial and codependent wife, Courtney Love, lead singer for Hole. On this day in 1994, Cobain's body was found in an upstairs room over the garage of his home near Seattle, Washington. Dead by a single shotgun blast to the head, the official verdict was suicide.

Or was it?

Maverick director Nick Broomfield set out to investigate the life of the troubled rock star, and emerged with **Kurt and Courtney** (1997), a film so controversial it was withdrawn from exhibition at the Sundance Film Festival at the insistence of Courtney Love's lawyers. Small wonder: Broomfield disputes the theory that Cobain committed suicide, and he tracks down just about everyone who agrees with him—and the evidence keeps coming around to Courtney Love. *Kurt and Courtney* is packed with a cast of seedy characters that would do David Lynch proud: "El Duce," who claims Love offered him $50,000 to off her husband; Tom Harrison, a private detective who claims to have worked for Love; and, most startling of all, Love's own father, Hank Harrison—an articulate man who has no trouble accepting the theory that his daughter killed Cobain.

Like the couple it documents, *Kurt and Courtney* is a fascinating mess of a film. Broomfield—who bears an unsettling similarity to the sleazy reporter played by Robert Downey, Jr., in *Natural Born Killers*—doggedly pursues his increasingly wacky theories by interviewing the most unreliable, drug-frazzled group of incoherent conspiracy nuts ever. Sometimes his efforts become side-splittingly funny: After trying for months to track down Courtney Love and grill her on camera, he morphs into a fawning fan in her presence and loses his opportunity. He's continuously making false claims that he's "with the BBC," and more often than not he has to keep prodding his interview subjects into coherence, as several of them appear to be nodding out on the verge of narcolepsy.

But beneath the ineptitude and far-fetched theories, there emerge glimpses of a troubled marriage, in a troubled society, inhabited by desperate people. Judge it for yourself. And pray that Nick Broomfield never decides to interview you.

april 9

And They Say Cheetahs Never Prosper. . .

Happy birthday today to Jiggs the Chimpanzee—one of four original chimps employed to play Tarzan's best pal, Cheetah, in the series of classic

Tarzan movies starring Johnny Weissmuller. As of this writing, Jiggs is still alive, if not exactly still swinging, at sixty-eight years old—one of the longest surviving chimps on record—and residing comfortably in (where else?) Palm Springs, California. Unfortunately, he is not granting interviews.

Celebrate his birthday by watching one of his finest performances, in **Tarzan's New York Adventure** (1942). Tarzan, Jane, and Cheetah visit the Big Apple in search of Boy, who has been kidnapped by an evil circus owner. Naturally, Manhattan is no match for the King of the Jungle when he's PO'd. Though it's not one of the best-remembered Tarzan pictures, it is one of the most enjoyable of the series. It's still amusing to see the Ape Man's reaction to being stuffed into a wool suit. Best of all, *Tarzan's New York Adventure* boasts one of Cheetah's finest performances; he outacts Johnny Weissmuller by a mile. And, like the late Keith Moon, he had a real flair for trashing posh hotel rooms.

april 10

A Revolutionary Film Bio

Emiliano Zapata was one of the great revolutionaries of the twentieth century. A poor, illiterate, but charismatic Mexican farmer, he raised an army of indigenous people in southern Mexico under the slogan "Land and Liberty." A tireless worker for the return of land to the Mexican people, Zapata was a reformer who became an idol to the poor, resisting no less than three Mexican presidents. On this day in 1919, he was assassinated by a government envoy who had come under the ruse of peace negotiations. Like Eva Peron, in death he became an icon to his people.

Marlon Brando gave one of his best performances in **Viva Zapata!** (1952), the life story of the Mexican revolutionary who led a peasant revolt only to be corrupted himself by power. Anthony Quinn nearly outshines Brando in his fiery performance as Zapata's brother (he won a well-deserved Oscar that year for Best Supporting Actor); he certainly outshouts him.

Excellent direction by Elia Kazan, and a sympathetic screenplay by John Steinbeck.

april 11

Take It Easy—Doolittle Tonight

George Bernard Shaw's celebrated play *Pygmalion* premiered this night in London in 1914. The story of erudite Professor Henry Higgins's bet with a colleague that he can make a lady out of a guttersnipe, and fool society, was an immediate hit with audiences, who fell in love with the character of Eliza Doolittle, the Cockney flower seller whom he tutors and transforms—and who changes her mentor along the way.

The popular play was made into a successful and faithful movie in 1938, *Pygmalion,* starring Leslie Howard and Wendy Hiller, with Shaw contributing to the screenplay. But the play's popularity really exploded when composers Lerner and Lowe transformed it into one of the most popular Broadway musicals ever written, *My Fair Lady.*

Spectacular sets, beautiful costumes, enchanting musical numbers, buoyant direction from George Cukor, and stellar performances all add up to make **My Fair Lady** (1964) one of the last great Hollywood musicals and winner of an impressive eight Academy Awards, including Best Picture, Best Director, and Best Actor. Rex Harrison is to the manor born as stuffy Professor Henry Higgins, and Audrey Hepburn is predictably luminous as Eliza, who rises from guttersnipe to socialite under his tutelage (her voice was dubbed for the musical numbers by Marni Nixon). Stanley Holloway is jovial as Eliza's Falstaffian father, and Wilfrid Hyde-White is a perfect foil as Harrison's colleague. Eliza's would-be suitor who sings "On the Street Where You Live" is none other than a very young Jeremy Brett, who would later receive acclaim for his performances as Sherlock Holmes in the BBC TV series. And if you can't get "Wouldn't It Be Loverly" out of your head for the next few days after watching, well . . . there are worse things to have floating around between your ears.

april 12

The Shot That Divided a Country

The bloodiest war in our history, the American Civil War was triggered by an event that happened on this day in 1861. Fort Sumter, a government stronghold in South Carolina's Charleston Bay, was attacked by Confederate forces under the command of General Pierre G. T. Beauregard. Three days later, President Abraham Lincoln issued a proclamation for 75,000 volunteer soldiers to help quell the Southern "insurrection." By the time the war ended four years later, over 620,000 Union and Southern soldiers had given their lives.

Observe the occasion by watching one of the most compelling and gloriously executed documentaries ever done: Ken Burns's great epic, **The Civil War.** Originally broadcast on PBS in 1990, *The Civil War* is an exhaustive, miraculously detailed insight into the conflict. Thousands of rare photographs provide memorable images, and the voice-over narratives of various participants of the events—reading excerpts from letters or documents—are profoundly affecting. A monumental achievement, well worth spreading out over two evenings.

If you're not quite up for eleven and a half hours (conveniently divided into nine separate episodes) of riveting but arduous entertainment, seek out John Huston's seldom-seen **Red Badge of Courage** (1951), based on the novella by Stephen Crane. Audie Murphy (the most decorated soldier of World War II) gives a fine performance as the nameless young soldier who finds himself in a literal trial by fire at the battle of Chancellorsville. Huston evokes the dreadful confusion of battle superbly—the ragged infantries, the dust and noise, the marches, the enemy emerging from clouds of smoke like figures in a nightmare. A visceral, bare-bones film directed by a gifted craftsman at his peak.

april 13

"Houston, We Have a Problem"

Up until this day in 1970, everything had gone swimmingly for the U.S. space program. Alan Shepard had made the first successful space flight by an American, John Glenn had orbited the earth in Friendship 7, and Neil Armstrong had walked on the moon.

Today was to be Apollo 13's day.

And it was. But not in the way anybody had planned it. Five hours after liftoff, astronauts Jim Lovell, Jack Swigert, and Fred Haise had just signed off from a ship-to-earth interview when an oxygen tank onboard the spacecraft exploded. Suddenly, there was a very real possibility that Apollo 13 may not make it home safely, if at all.

Ron Howard's **Apollo 13** (1995) manages to overcome a seemingly insurmountable problem: How to generate an entertaining, suspenseful, and emotionally satisfying movie out of a story most people know the ending to? But it does. Scenes alternate between the three crew members in space limbo, their resourceful backup teammates at Cape Kennedy who scramble to do the impossible, plus a few satirical swipes at the media—all juggled expertly. Tom Hanks gives his usual excellent performance as Lovell. An inspiring movie that evokes a genuine patriotism other movies only aspire to. Look for the real-life Lovell in a cameo as the navy captain welcoming the astronauts aboard the recovery ship.

april 14

Witness a Titanic Disaster

In the minutes just before midnight on this night in 1912, the world's largest luxury cruise ship, the *Titanic,* struck an iceberg off the coast of Newfoundland while on her maiden voyage from England to New York. Within the next few hours, the *Titanic* sank to the bottom of the sea, taking with it over fifteen hundred lives. Of the 2,340 passengers aboard, only 745 were saved. There were only enough lifeboats for half of the passengers and crew, and many of those left the decks of the *Titanic* only half full.

Everyone's seen James Cameron's soggy, waterlogged epic *Titanic* (1998)—and I won't try to dissuade you from seeing it again if that's your choice. Just try not to notice what a horribly written script it has. Ignore such plot holes as the fact that the famous paintings shown as sinking on the *Titanic* can't be in two places at once (the bottom of the ocean and hanging in a museum today). Overlook the nonexistent chemistry between the two young stars, who together generate about as much heat as the iceberg that does the ship in. Wave aside the fact that if Cameron had jettisoned the hokey love story and concentrated on virtually any one or more of the real-life participants, he might have had something glorious. Well, I suppose he did have something glorious: *Titantic* was the biggest hit of the year. But as a movie, *Titanic* lives up to its name: It's huge, full of bilge water, and takes about three hours to sink.

But for a far more emotionally satisfying experience, try watching the gripping British film, **A Night to Remember** (1958), instead. Clocking in at just over two hours, it's significantly shorter than Cameron's elephantine epic, but infinitely richer in content. What it lacks in majesty and special effects, *A Night to Remember* more than makes up for in a literate, compelling, compassionate, and (mostly) historically accurate story line—focusing on the courage, humanity, and despair of an ensemble of voyagers—most of whom will never return. Screenwriter Eric Ambler did a magnificent job in adapting Walter Lord's book of the same title. Featuring a young David McCallum (later Illya Kuryakin on TV's *Man from U.N.C.L.E.*) as a crew member.

april 15

Tax Day

Observe the event by renting **How to Steal a Million** (1966) and submit it as a tax deduction. The luminous Audrey Hepburn plays an art forger's daughter who teams with a debonair thief (Peter O'Toole) for a museum heist to restore her father's reputation and honor. Sparkling dialogue, dazzling sets, a frothy script, and fabulous costumes (Hepburn could wear a Hefty Trash Bag and make it look fetching). One sophisticated comic caper that will steal your heart.

april 16

A Trampy Film That's Pure Gold

He was the most influential comic artist the movies ever produced, and arguably the most important cinema artist, period. He rose from an impoverished, abused childhood that could have come right out of a Dickens novel to being the single most recognized film figure in the world.

Charles Spencer Chaplin was born this day in the tenements of London in 1889. His rise from a miserable childhood (his father abandoned the family, his mother went insane and was confined to an asylum, and he and his half-brother, Sidney, were separated and sent away to horrific workhouses) to world-renowned icon is a story that can't begin to be told in a movie—though Richard Attenborough tried in *Chaplin* (1992), an all-star film bio helped in no small measure by the impressively beguiling performance of Robert Downey, Jr., as Chaplin.

If you've never seen a Chaplin film, you're missing one of the great joys of filmdom. His early two-reelers for Mack Sennett allowed him the space, spontaneity, and freedom to grow as an artist in an incredibly short time. By the time he had signed with Mutual in 1916 he was the single most popular movie star in the world and was producing works of greatness: *The Vagabond, Easy Street,* and *The Emigrant* are masterful short comedies—deftly mingling brilliantly inventive slapstick, pointed social commentary, and pathos. He expanded into feature films: the seriocomic pic *The Kid* (1921), the bittersweet film *The Circus* (1928), the exquisitely romantic *City Lights* (1931), and the borderline social statement that is *Modern Times* (1936). But the film he most wanted to be remembered by, and his overall masterpiece, is **The Gold Rush** (1925). Chaplin's iconic Tramp is "the Lone Prospector" in the frozen north during the Klondike Gold Rush. Packed with priceless bits (Chaplin's celebrated "Oceana Roll" dance using two biscuits; being caught in a cabin teetering on the precipice of a cliff; sharing a meal of a boiled shoe) and pathos (Chaplin filmed from the back as he enters a boisterous, crowded saloon, an outsider wanting to belong; his New Year's Eve dinner which nobody attends), *The Gold Rush* is Chaplin's most sustained work.

Chaplin never again had such a command of the camera and such an expansive, naturalistic canvas to work on. *The Gold Rush* is that rare thing—a truly epic comedy.

april 17

All's Farrow Love and War

On this date in 1980, Woody Allen had an eventful lunch with actress Mia Farrow at Lutece restaurant in New York to discuss a possible part in a movie, and it became the start of a twelve-year union both onscreen and off. Farrow even went so far as to needlepoint this date on a sampler rug that adorned Woody's bedroom wall for years—at least until 1992, when the two estranged partners engaged in one of the most acrimonious and public breakups in history

But it was a productive partnership while it lasted; they collaborated on eleven films, including some of Allen's best work: *The Purple Rose of Cairo, Zelig, Crimes and Misdemeanors, Radio Days,* and *Broadway Danny Rose* (in which Farrow delivers her most atypical performance as a whiny, spoiled gangster's moll). Commemorate their first date with one of their finest film collaborations—**Hannah and Her Sisters** (1986). Farrow gives one of her best screen performances as Hannah, the eldest and most steadfast and stable of three sisters in Manhattan (where else?). Hannah is married to Elliot (Michael Caine), who develops a major crush on Hannah's younger sister Lee (Barbara Hershey). The crush leads to an affair, which threatens everyone's happiness. One of Allen's finest films, if not his best; his unparalleled ability to distill comedy, drama, and insight out of the peccadillos of the human condition is uncanny. Packed with great one-liners. (When asked how, in a world with a benevolent God, there could be Nazis, Allen's father replies, "How the hell do I know why there were Nazis? I don't even know how the can opener works!") The exceptional cast includes Dianne Wiest in a flat-out movie-stealing role as odd-sister-out Holly, a struggling actress who can land neither a role nor a man; Max Von Sydow as Lee's dour mentor and lover; and Allen himself as Hannah's ex-husband Mickey, a hypochondriac who finally has a real brush with his mortality. Allen's hilarious search for spiritual fulfillment in Catholicism, complete with Wonder Bread and mayonnaise, is hilarious. An astonishingly rich, funny, insightful work—and with the most optimistic denouement of any film in the Allen canon.

april 18

Shake 'n' Bake Tonight

San Francisco has always had a reputation as a promiscuous town—and on this day in 1906 the earth moved for everybody. The San Francisco earthquake and the disastrous fire that followed left 503 dead. But, as it always does, the City by the Bay rose from the ashes like a phoenix, rebuilding and reinventing itself all over again.

Remember the earth-shaking event by watching **San Francisco** (1936), one of those classic, impressively budgeted MGM spectacles—this one starring Clark Gable as a cynical saloon owner in love with Jeanette MacDonald, and Spencer Tracy as—surprise!—an Irish priest and Gable's best buddy. The Barbary Coast melodrama is thick as the San Francisco Bay fog, and the earthquake sequence packs a wallop, utilizing still-impressive editing and special effects. They don't make 'em like this anymore; you too will feel the earth move.

april 19

Heart Attack of Darkness

The year was 1977, and the previous few months had been a disastrous experience for actor Martin Sheen. He had signed on to star as Captain Willard in *Apocalypse Now,* Francis Ford Coppola's epic adaptation of Joseph Conrad's classic adventure story, *Heart of Darkness.* Coppola had taken the original novel, which takes place in Africa, and envisioned placing it in the context of the Vietnam War. That was about the last coherent idea he had.

No sooner had Coppola moved his entire production unit to the Philippines (as a stand-in for Vietnam), then things began to fall apart. The weather was horrifically uncooperative, disease and jungle sickness were rampant, pretty much the entire company was ingesting mammoth proportions of drugs, stimulants, and alcohol (all recorded on film in wife Eleanor's documentary, *A Filmmaker's Apocalypse*)—and Coppola kept revising the script until the film pretty much became an epic improvisation in the jungle. For one scene where Willard is supposed to be going stir-crazy, Coppola got the teetotaler Sheen drunk. In a stupor, Sheen crashed his fist through a mirror, cutting an artery and severing a tendon. Things went downhill from there, with dysentery, mosquitoes, snakes, bad water, and a crazy, megamaniacal director. Sheen suffered a massive coronary and was administered the last rites.

It was on this day, after weeks of recuperation, that a shaky Sheen returned to the set to continue shooting. He wished he'd dropped out. The first scene to be shot was Willard's arrival at the compound of Col. Kurtz, the renegade officer whom he has been assigned to eliminate. Kurtz was to be played by Marlon Brando, who also showed up this day for his first day of work. Coppola was aghast to find the actor grossly overweight and clueless as to what the story was about, holding up filming for days with endless discussions on motivation with the drug-addled director. And to top it all off, Dennis Hopper, then the self-proclaimed king of substance abuse, arrived to add his own loony style to the movie as a gonzo photojournalist. Sheen looked around and prayed he'd escape the movie alive.

He did. And, amazingly, **Apocalypse Now** (1979) emerged as one of the watermark movies of the decade—a fascinating, dreamlike, impressionistic forty-million-dollar masterpiece. Somehow, Coppola had pulled it all together and created a magnum opus, a behemoth of a movie that was at once hallucinogenic, violent, and excessively, wildly out of control. One of the few visionary works of the '70s, and a still-astonishing testament to the powers of ego and talent.

april 20

Rue the Day?

The first modern-day "detective story"—wherein the protagonist utilizes deduction and logic to solve a perplexing puzzle—was published on this day in 1841. In Edgar Allan Poe's "Murders in the Rue Morgue," the detective, a gentleman named C. Auguste Dupin, is left to figure out a perplexing crime: How did a murderer get in and out of a room without disturbing either the doors or the windows? Poe's culprit may have been a little farfetched (an orangutan!), but his methodology wasn't. His almost illogical logic was embraced by Sir Arthur Conan Doyle, who went on to give the world the greatest detective ever, Sherlock Holmes. But it was Poe, usually thought of as a writer of morbid gothic short stories or alliterative poetry, who deserves the credit for starting an entire genre.

Celebrate the birth of the detective story with **Murders in the Rue Morgue** (1932). Originally, director Robert Florey and star Bela Lugosi were to have collaborated on *Frankenstein*—but when Lugosi (then at the height of his popularity due to his performance in the previous year's *Dracula*) balked at the makeup and lack of dialogue, director James Whale got the project and cast unknown Boris Karloff as the monster. *Murders in the Rue Morgue* was given to Florey and Lugosi as an alternate project, and in the process, the "mystery" element was supplanted by a more prominent "horror" ratio, more in keeping with Lugosi's screen image.

Lugosi is effective as Dr. Mirakle, the madman who conducts evolutionary experiments by draining the blood of young women. One scene, which features a prostitute (Arlene Dahl) being crucified as her blood is being drained, still has the power to raise eyebrows; it's amazing that it got past the censors in 1932. The movie, photographed by Karl Freund, is visually in debt to *The Cabinet of Dr. Caligari,* more than the story is indebted to Poe. Still, a nice Grand Guignol spirit of malevolence hangs over this seldom-seen gem.

There's a later version—*Murders in the Rue Morgue* (1971)—that's much more inventive and in keeping with the "spirit" of Poe, although it, too, is far removed from its source material.

april 21

When in Rome . . .

According to legend, Romulus and his twin brother, Remus, founded Rome on this day in 753 B.C. During the next thousand years, the city grew to become the heart of the great Roman Empire, dominating the entire classical world, until Emperor Constantine transferred the empire's capital to Constantinople early in the fourth century.

Celebrate the glory that was Rome with **The Fall of the Roman Empire** (1964), a big-budget, all-star extravaganza packed with great action sequences. The power-hungry son of Marcus Aurelius orchestrates his father's murder, and the Barbarians begin gathering at the gates. A superb cast includes Sophia Loren, Alec Guinness, Omar Sharif, James Mason, and Christopher Plummer.

The same period is re-created—this time with a CGI-generated Colosseum—in Ridley Scott's impressively epic **Gladiator** (2000). Russell Crowe delivers a galvanizing performance as Maximus, the Roman general who becomes a slave and then a gladiator. Breathless battle sequences (the opening one is extraordinary) and an excellent cast (including Richard Harris as the old Marcus Aurelius, and, in his last performance, Oliver Reed as Proximo, the P. T. Barnum of gladiatordom) help make *Gladiator* one of the most literate and epic re-creations of the Roman Empire ever put on film, far above your typical sword-'n'-sandals genre movie fare.

april 22

As the World Turns . . .

The first Earth Day was officially celebrated on this date in 1970. Devoted to spreading awareness of ecological responsibility, the day has since become an annual holiday of sorts. Observe the occasion with **Silent Running** (1971), a truly underrated sleeper, part effects-laden sci-fi movie and part passionate ecology lesson. Bruce Dern stars as an ecologist aboard a spaceship that is carrying the last living remnants of Earth's plant and animal life, contained in three gigantic domes powered by artificial sunlight. When the crew is ordered to destroy the cargo, Dern goes bonkers, killing off his fellow crew members. With the aid of a trio of drones—whom he names Huey, Dewey, and Louie—he sets about rescuing and nursing his precious cargo. Directed by Douglas Trumbull, who supervised the special effects for Stanley Kubrick's *2001*. A truly original, thought-provoking film on the sanctity and fragility of our existence.

april 23

Happy Birthday to the World's Most Successful Screenwriter . . . If Only He'd Lived to Collect the Royalties

William Shakespeare, the most quoted playwright in history and most prolific screenplay writer ever, was born this day in 1564 at Stratford-on-Avon. At least, this is the accepted, traditional date; the earliest documented evidence we have on Shakespeare is his baptism three days later on April 26.

Scores of his works have been adapted to the movies with varying degrees of success. He's probably the most-filmed author of all time; there were even silent film versions of his works—which is kind of like hiring Luciano Pavarotti to do pantomime.

The list of great Shakespearean movies is too long to get into here but these are some highlights: *Henry V* (both Olivier's 1944 version and Kenneth Branagh's 1989 version); *Romeo and Juliet* (the 1936 MGM version with fifty-five-year-old John Barrymore as Mercutio; the lovely, mod 1967 version directed by Franco Zefferelli; and Baz Luhrman's stylishly kinetic *William Shakespeare's Romeo + Juliet* [1996] with Leonardo DiCaprio and Clare Danes); *Othello* (Orson Welles's inventive, austere yet lopsided 1952 version; Olivier's stage-bound 1965 effort; and the 1995 version starring Laurence Fishburne); *Hamlet* (take your pick from over a dozen versions—but see Kenneth Branagh's complete four-hour interpretation and the much shorter, stylish 2000 version with Ethan Hawke as a modern-day Dane in New York City); *A Midsummer Night's Dream* (both the visually stunning 1935 rendering directed by Max Reinhardt and starring Mickey Rooney as Puck and James Cagney as Bottom and the 1999 version with a beguiling Michelle Pfeiffer and an amusing Kevin Kline as Bottom) . . . and that's only the tip of the quill.

How did one man create so much work of such depth, insight, and impenetrable genius? No one will ever know the answer (in fact, there's considerable speculation among literary detectives that he didn't), but **Shakespeare in Love** (1998) is a buoyant, inventive, and winking speculation on the young playwright's early life. *Shakespeare in Love* is an enchantingly whimsical romance, and an absolute feast for anyone who loves the Bard. Joseph Fiennes plays the struggling young writer, who has a bad case of writer's block, and, in Freudian terms, a limp quill. The year is 1593, and Will is struggling with his latest opus, tentatively titled *Romeo and Ethel, the Pirate's Daughter*. His path and destiny cross with Viola Lesseps, a young actress who disguises herself as a boy to get a part in his latest play (Gwyneth Paltrow in her Oscar-winning role). Great support from Geoffrey Rush, Ben Affleck, and Judi Dench (Best Supporting Actress winner) and a dazzlingly inventive script cowritten by Tom Stoppard (who also wrote the Shakespeare-inspired *Rosencrantz and Guildenstern Are Dead*) make *Shakespeare in Love* enchanting entertainment. It also won an Academy Award for Best Picture. Maybe that Shakespeare guy had something going on after all.

april 24

It Must've Been Painful Giving Birth to an Ego That Big . . .

Hello, gorgeous! Barbra Streisand was born Barbara Joan Streisand on this day in 1942 in Brooklyn, New York.

No matter what your feelings are for Ms. Streisand, she cannot be ignored. She is the reigning female superstar of the last fifty years, a diva from Brooklyn who took America by sheer talent and force of will. She is the closest thing we have to American royalty, having inherited the highly combustible torch left by Judy Garland. Unlike Judy, though, Streisand knows how to get just what she wants.

In addition to her stunning musical achievements, Streisand has made—and increasingly controlled—numerous movies of merit, including *The Way We Were* (with Robert Redford; 1973), *Yentl* (1983; she also directed, produced, and cowrote), and *The Prince of Tides* (1991; she also produced and directed).

Her big break came on the night of March 20, 1964, in New York—and nobody was going to rain on Barbra Streisand's parade. It was the opening night on Broadway for a new musical based on the life of popular 1940s comedienne and singer Fanny Brice, *Funny Girl*—and, in the title role, the young and fiercely talented Streisand seized destiny by the throat. Overnight, she became the toast of the Broadway stage—and started on her way to becoming the most celebrated diva of our time.

Celebrate Streisand with the film **Funny Girl** (1968), shot four years later, with Barbra reprising her starring role for the big screen in her most buoyant and entertaining movie. Directed by William Wyler (his only musical), the film was a huge box office success, earning Streisand an Academy Award for Best Actress (sharing the award that year, in the only Oscar tie in history, with Katharine Hepburn). More than any of her other movies, *Funny Girl* captures the beguiling combination of talent and charisma Streisand can put across—sass, humor, a breathtaking voice that's a force of nature, vulnerability, and her unique look. As Brice, Streisand is funny, energetic, open, vulnerable, and endearing—and she sings her ass off. Omar Sharif is both greasy and smooth as her amore, Nicky Arnstein, compulsive gambler and inevitable heartbreaker. Streisand's songs are masterful set pieces: "My Man" and "People" are transcendent moments, and was there ever a more stirring moment in her whole canon than when she sings the last verse of "Nobody's Gonna Rain on My Parade" from a boat in Manhattan? A fabulous reminder of why she deserves her diva status. Enjoy La Streisand in the glorious culmination of everything she did best. Funny girl, indeed.

april 25

"From a Place You've Never Heard of . . . Comes a Story You'll Never Forget"

On this day in 1915, one of World War I's most famous—and tragic—battles took place. Under the orders of Winston Churchill (who was then first lord of the Admiralty), Australian and New Zealand forces (ANZAC) landed at the small Gallipoli peninsula on the coast of Turkey and launched a disastrous, misguided attack on the Turkish stronghold. Churchill had woefully miscalculated and underestimated the tenacious Turks (their leader, Mustafa Kemal, went on record as saying to his troops, "I don't order you to attack; I order you to die"). Due to a combination of bad timing and inept planning, the ANZAC troops suffered an overwhelming 90 percent casualty rate. To this day, April 25 is the most important holiday in Australia.

Peter Weir's **Gallipoli** (1981) is a wrenching re-creation of the battle and an enormously moving rumination on war—but it is not a war film, per se. It's an absorbing story of friendship. Two competitive young Australian friends, Archie (Mark Lee) and Frank Dunne (Mel Gibson, in the role that brought him to international attention), decide to enlist in the Tenth Light Horse Regiment, though the war is far away in Europe. As they're walking to a recruiting station in the flat, featurless Australian outback, they come across a prospector. When they tell him they're going to enlist, the grizzled man wonders what the war in Europe has to do with Australia. "Because if we don't stop the Germans there," Archie insists, "they'll come over here." The prospector looks around at the vast emptiness of the Australian desert and declares, "They're bloody welcome to it."

Gallipoli is ravishingly shot—particularly the early training sequences in Egypt—and emerges as one of the most passionate antiwar films ever made. Gibson's final footrace to deliver an urgent message that could save his best friend's life will have your heart pounding like a hammer.

april 26

Funny, He Doesn't Look Like He's from Japan

He was supposed to be a combination of a gorilla and a whale, but he looked an awful lot like a man in a rubber suit. On this day in 1956, **Godzilla, King of Monsters** (1955) opened in the U.S. The cheesy production from Japan was laughably inept; TV star Raymond Burr was recruited to shoot separate footage (as a hospitalized reporter recounting the story in flashback) so there would be an Anglo face in the film for its American release.

But filmgoers all over the world somehow related to the tale of a monster awakened from a million-year nap by an atom bomb, destroying Tokyo with his radioactive breath. Surprisingly, the film grossed over two million dollars in the U.S.A.—a substantial hit in those days. Thus began the most popular series of "Atom Age" monster movies, spawning countless sequels. In 1998, Hollywood made a big-budget version that had all the charm of a six-hundred-ton kidney stone. Celebrate Godzilla's birthday with his first film—and try not to get stepped on.

april 27

Woody Does It Again with *The Thin Man*

Director W. S. "Woody" Van Dyke was legendary around Hollywood for his speed and economy; he was known as "One-Take Woody." On this day in 1934 he broke his own speed record, finishing up his latest movie in an incredible sixteen days.

No one had any idea that it would be one of the most successful hits of the 1930s, spawning five sequels and bringing a breath of fresh air to a tired genre, the detective film. **The Thin Man** (1934) was a detective film like none before it. Instead of the world-weary lone gumshoe pounding the rain-drenched streets and back alleys, *The Thin Man* features William Powell and Myrna Loy as married sleuths Nick and Nora Charles, two sophisticated and perpetually inebriated lovebirds who live in quiet affluence in their spacious Manhattan apartment with their dog, Asta. The chemistry between the two costars is nothing sort of magic. Their witty banter and affectionate repartee—largely fueled by a never-ending series of drinks and a script packed with great one-liners—enhanted audiences.

The Thin Man is more of a delightfully droll screwball comedy than a thriller. In fact, solving the case is almost an afterthought; the film is actually a free-wheeling ninety minutes of amiable banter, endless martinis, and the nonpareil charm of urbane William Powell in what would become his best-known role. Many fans mistakenly believed Powell played the title character, but "the Thin Man," an inventor, was actually played by Edward Ellis. Although the Thin Man gets killed in the first movie; the producers kept references to him in the titles so audiences would recognize each sequel as a Nick and Nora Charles caper.

april 28

This Crew Is Revolting

They were mad as hell and they weren't going to take it anymore. And on this day in 1789, there was a mutiny on the *Bounty*.

On December 23, 1787, the British ship HMS *Bounty*, under the command of Captain William Bligh, had set sail for the West Indies, under orders to bring back a huge cargo of one thousand breadfruit trees. To make room for the returning shipment, the ship's crew had been drastically reduced to a skeletal forty-seven. This meant double-duty rotations, and the voyage was exhausting. When they finally reached the island of Tahiti, the crew enjoyed twenty-three days on shore in paradise with accommodating locals. When it came time to leave, they were understandably reluctant to go back to their previous shipboard conditions.

On this date in 1789, a rebel crew led by Fletcher Christian took over the *Bounty*, set their captain adrift in a lifeboat with a handful of loyal sailors, and set course for nearby Pitcairn Island. The crew didn't count on the captain's resilience. In one of the most magnificent nautical feats ever, their tenacious former commander managed to pilot his way across four thousand miles of uncharted ocean to Timor in the small lifeboat. The mutineers were tracked down and brought to justice, and Bligh went on to serve as governor of New South Wales in Australia, retiring a much-decorated rear admiral. Popular history has pegged Captain Bligh as a monster—largely based on Charles Laughton's unforgettable portrayal—but the real-life Bligh was more hero than villain. Fletcher Christian, on the other hand, was no hero. He kidnapped twelve Tahitian women and six men to take with him and his mutineers to Pitcairn; they later retaliated by killing him.

The famous mutiny inspired three movies, each with a different take on history: 1935's original **Mutiny on the Bounty** with Charles Laughton as a sadistic Captain Bligh and Clark Gable as his rebellious first officer, Fletcher Christian; the 1962 remake, filmed on location with Marlon Brando as a decidedly foppish Christian, Trevor Howard as Bligh, and Richard Harris as a rough crew member; and **The Bounty** (1984), with Anthony Hopkins as a considerably more complex Bligh and Mel Gibson as a considerably less complex Christian. Of the three, the original 1939 version is the most entertaining (Laughton's Bligh is one of the screen's classic tyrants, and he relishes every unsavory moment), but *The Bounty* wins for accuracy. Hopkins gives a subdued yet intense performance as the tough-minded, resourceful Bligh, and the period detail and life aboard ship are accurately drawn. The sequence where the *Bounty* attempts to round Cape Horn is a nail-biter.

april 29

Thank You and Good Evening

After a long and productive career as one of the most popular and successful directors in history, Alfred Hitchcock died on this night in 1980 at the age of eighty-one.

In 1904 London, when young Alfred was five years old, his father gave him a letter sealed in an envelope and instructed the lad to deliver it to the local police constabulary. The boy, following instructions, walked to the precinct station and dutifully presented the desk sergeant with the missive. The constable opened it up, read it, and promptly locked the boy in a jail cell. Two hours later he released the frightened child and handed him back the letter, which contained a message for him: "This is what happens to bad little boys."

Some film enthusiasts backhandedly credit Hitchcock as a canny, pandering, clever craftsman who knew what formula the public liked and delivered the goods; others consider him one of the most intuitively brilliant directors of all time. Either way, he was definitely an auteur in a town where such a word was frowned upon. His films skirt the fine line between popular entertainment (*To Catch a Thief, Rear Window,* and *The Trouble with Harry*) and art (*Vertigo, Strangers on a Train,* and the experimental *Rope*).

His masterful manipulations of suspense appear in such films as *Suspicion, Shadow of a Doubt, Psycho,* and *The Birds.*

Hitchcock's darkest, most personal film is undoubtedly **Vertigo** (1958), a film which is the culmination of Hitch's themes of the dark side of obsession, love, and death. James Stewart gives one of his boldest performances as Scottie Ferguson, a San Francisco detective assigned to trail a friend's suicidal wife, Madeleine (Kim Novak). When she commits suicide by jumping from a tower—which Ferguson is powerless to prevent because of his acrophobia (fear of heights)—he becomes wracked with guilt. One day he sees a woman who reminds him of the dead Madeleine, and he becomes obsessed with changing her into Madeleine. *Vertigo* is a fascinating, unsettling labyrinth of a movie, and the most potent examination of obsessive behavior ever filmed. In the gallery of masterpieces by Hitchcock, *Vertigo* stands alone.

april 30

This Spud's for You

On this day in 1952, a fledgling toy company called Hasbro—later to market such immortal toys as Slinky and the ubiquitous Etch-a-Sketch—introduces the very first toy ever advertised on TV: Ladies and Gentlemen, I give you . . . *Mr. Potato Head!*

In those days, they used real potatoes—the glasses, eyes, ears, etc. had sharp plastic spikes, designed to be inserted into the potatoes. But times changed (along with child endangerment laws), and the insertable spikes were replaced by well-rounded safety prongs, along with a plastic potato.

Commemorate the birth of Mr. Potato Head with his first film appearance—in the delightful **Toy Story** (1995), Pixar's computer-generated animation masterpiece. Tom Hanks stars—well, actually Tom Hanks's *voice* stars—as the cowboy toy Woody, his owner Andy's favorite companion. Woody finds himself usurped by the arrival of obnoxious braggart Buzz

Lightyear (Tim Allen's voice), the Toy of Tomorrow—who is totally oblivious to the fact that he's a toy. Woody and his pals—including Mr. Potato Head (Don Rickles)—endeavor to set Buzz straight and reclaim Woody's place in Andy's heart. A wonderfully inventive comedy, filled with in-jokes for knowing adults, *Toy Story* is magical entertainment, and its sequel, *Toy Story 2* (1999), where we get to meet Mrs. Potato Head, is nearly as good.

may

may 1

See the Eighth Wonder of the World

At the time it was the tallest building in the world, a streamlined, towering testament to the American dream, and it instantly became an icon for New York City. On this day in 1931, the Empire State Building opened to the public for the first time. Many called it the Eighth Wonder of the World.

What better way to commemorate the anniversary than by watching the *other* Eighth Wonder of the World, a fifty-foot-tall ape named Kong, ascend the structure, carrying a screaming Fay Wray in one hand and fending off attacking airplanes with the other?

A twist on the classic tale "Beauty and the Beast," **King Kong** (1933) is a timeless fantasy adventure that has still never been topped. A group of filmmakers, including a crusty director (Robert Armstrong), a stalwart hero (Bruce Cabot), and a damsel in distress (Fay Wray) embark on a trip to Skull Island to find the "Eighth Wonder of the World," the mighty Kong. Once there, the group encounters living dinosaurs, a tribe of natives who live in a giant jungle fortress, and, of course, the magnificent Kong himself.

Pay close attention and you'll notice that Kong changes size throughout the film—in one scene he'll be 50 feet tall, in the next 150 feet. Long before the days of CGI, special effects guru Willis O'Brien perfected the art of stop-motion photography, painstakingly shooting the stop-motion sequences frame-by-frame. Kong was actually a sixteen-inch manipulable, fur-covered doll; O'Brien would position the mini Kong, shoot a frame of footage, then carefully reposition the doll for the next shot—a laborious, time-consuming process requiring steady hands and enormous patience. Sharp-eyed viewers will notice that Kong's fur is constantly matted and changing, as if being blown by a breeze—the result of technician's fingerprints on the doll from moving it into position for the next shot.

But all these technicalities disappear while watching the film. To audiences of 1933 and today, King Kong is still the Eighth Wonder of the World. Great score by Max Steiner. (By the way, the two pilots who fire the fatal shots at the end are played by none other than producer Merian C. Cooper and director Ernest Schoedsack. They figured that since they created Kong, they get to destroy him. Little did they know that King Kong would live forever.)

may 2

Choppy Waters

It was the director's first day on the job and nothing was going as planned. The weather wasn't cooperating, the script wasn't ready, and, worse yet, the star wasn't cooperating. And when the star is a twenty-five-foot mechanical great white shark, you've got a big headache on your hands.

On this day in 1974, director Steven Spielberg, still smarting from box office disappointment with *The Sugarland Express,* began production on the summer movie that would change summer movies forever. It was a little horror flick based on a book originally named *Jaws of Death,* but shortened at the last minute by author Peter Benchley to *Jaws.*

Jaws (1974) is generally acknowledged to have launched the modern tradition of the big summer release, and it was the biggest-grossing movie ever up until *E.T.* It's still a fabulous motion picture—exciting, suspenseful, dramatic, and funny. And the trio of leading men—Roy Scheider as Police Chief Brody, Robert Shaw as the salty old seadog Quint, and Richard Dreyfuss as the wiseass rich-kid ichthyologist Matt Hooper—play off each other beautifully. The best scene is perhaps the quietest—the trio's late-night shipboard comparison of scars, followed by Quint's devastating account of his experience on the USS *Indianapolis*—Robert Shaw's finest moment on film. This is truly great acting, understandably obscured by the breathless action sequences that precede and follow it. And Spielberg's taut, teasing direction is nearly flawless. This was filmed back in the days when he wasn't afraid to kill a kid or a dog onscreen. Arguably Spielberg's finest film.

may 3

B-B-Bing Crosby B-B-B-Born

Masterfully casual crooner Bing Crosby would've been remembered as one of the Jazz Age's finest singers even if he'd never made a movie. But his affable demeanor and easygoing charm somehow transcended his rather vanilla looks, and he became one of Hollywood's biggest draws in the 1940s.

He was born Harry Lillis Crosby this day in 1903, in Tacoma, Washington. What is often underappreciated about Crosby is that he evolved into a pretty damn good actor, too. He could handle breezy musicals (*Holiday Inn, High Society, White Christmas*), comedies (*A Connecticut Yankee in King Arthur's Court* and, of course, the *Road* series with Bob Hope), and, most surprising of all, drama. He actually won an Oscar for Best Actor in 1944 for his winning performance as Father O'Malley in *Going My Way,* a pretty drippy picture, but the best showcase for Crosby's unapproachable charm and nonchalance.

But he really deserved it for his brilliant portrayal of a weak, alcoholic actor on the skids in **The Country Girl** (1954). It was a radical departure for him and his image, and perhaps hit a little too close to home. In exposing the fragile and needy ego beneath a performer's easygoing charm and outward self-confidence, Crosby created a devastating portrayal. Grace Kelly gives a revelatory, against-type performance as his long-suffering wife and caretaker, and William Holden is the man who comes between them. Crosby never again took on another challenging role after that, pretty much falling back on the goodwill generated by his buoyant likability.

may 4

Tragedy at Kent State

College campus protests against the Vietnam War were becoming fairly common by 1970. But on this day during a student demonstration rally at Kent State University in Kent, Ohio, everything went tragically wrong. National Guardsmen were called in to "keep the peace," and instead wound up firing live ammo into the crowd, killing four unarmed students. The incident served to further divide the country. **Medium Cool** (1969) captures the turbulence of the times like lightning in a bottle. Robert Forster plays a TV news cameraman, covering the 1968 National Democratic Convention in Chicago, who finds himself drawn into the riots between students and cops. Parts of the film were shot on location at the convention, adding a tangible visceral reality. In fact, director Haskell Wexler was accused of actually starting the riots in order to get some good footage. A fascinating, absorbing political drama, mixing cinema verité with radical politics.

may 5

Bet on the Black

"He has just a long-shot chance," said owner Jack Amiel. He was talking about his horse, Count Turf, who was set to race in the 77th Kentucky

Derby. And the long shot paid off—big time—at 53 to 1 on this day in 1951. The previously unknown, underachieving horse leaped into the lead to win the derby—and with a loose right shoe, to boot.

Celebrate this equestrian long-shot victory with **The Black Stallion** (1979), a so-called children's film that has at least as much magic for adults as for kids. Kelly Reno stars as Alec, a young boy who sees a beautiful black Arabian stallion while on a ship bound for Morocco. When a fire breaks out, the boy and the horse go overboard and wash up on the shores of a deserted island. Over time, they develop a deep friendship. The first half of the film is pure cinema—breathtaking imagery and ravishing cinematography from director Carol Ballard.

Once rescued, they return home, where "the Black," as the boy calls his stallion, shows an unusual talent for speed. Retired jockey and horse trainer Henry Dailey (Mickey Rooney, in a performance that echoes his long-ago turn as a jockey in *National Velvet*) coaches the boy on the finer points of riding, and they decide to enter the stallion in a big race. *The Black Stallion* is a ravishing film—timeless, enchanting, and vastly entertaining.

may 6

I Do, Take One

On this day in 1950, a vivacious, drop-dead gorgeous Elizabeth Taylor, then eighteen years old, married Conrad "Nicky" Hilton, Jr. She promised to love, honor, and obey until death did them part—or until Michael Wilding and Mike Todd and Eddie Fisher and Richard Burton and Larry Fortensky and Senator John Warner and . . .

Celebrate the first of many marriages for Ms. Taylor with the delightful and totally charming comedy, **Father of the Bride** (1950), filmed that very same year—and she never looked more radiant. Liz plays the daughter of proud parents Spencer Tracy and Joan Bennett, and as her wedding day approaches, her proud but flustered pop has to deal with all manner of crises—

from the bridal shower to paying for the wedding—and Tracy is in top comedic form. Still as fresh and funny as the day it was made. Remade forty years later with Steve Martin and Diane Keaton as the harried parents, but without the charm or heart of the original.

may 7

Compose Yourself

On this day in 1840, the greatest of Russian romantic composers, Peter Ilich Tchaikovsky, was born near Votkinsk, Russia. His music is as rich and evocative as his life was tortured. A homosexual in a country where homosexuality was a crime, Tchaikovsky went to extreme lengths to hide his lifestyle, including going so far as marrying a young female fan. The marriage, predictably, was a disaster.

Celebrate the composer's birthday with director Ken Russell's wildly over-the-top screen bio of Tchaikovsky's troubled life, **The Music Lovers** (1970). Russell was already the enfant terrible of British film directors, having successfully directed a series of unorthodox and innovative BBC television films about Debussy, Rousseau, Elgar, Dante, and others. But *The Music Lovers* topped everything with its colorful extravangance. Richard Chamberlain plays the composer, portrayed here as a tortured homosexual who, desperate for peace and domestic bliss, marries a nymphomaniac fan (an incredible, envelope-pushing performance by the great Glenda Jackson). Typical Ken Russell overstatement, packed with extravagent images and fever-pitch intensity bordering on the ludicrous.

There are some truly inventive, stirring musical sequences here—particularly the inventively filmed *Sleeping Beauty* excerpt, where Russell shows how each member of the audience interprets the music as a reflection of his or her personal desires. And the *1812 Overture* dream sequence, complete with heads being blown off by phallic cannons, is undeniably fun. Truth be told, *The Music Lovers* is terrible film making—gauche, over-the-top, and vulgar—but great movie-making. A guilty pleasure; you'll want to bathe in boiling water afterward. Sumptuous cinematography by Douglas Slocombe.

may 8

Make a Devilish Deal

Robert Johnson, King of the Delta Blues, was born on this day in 1911, in Hazlehurst, Mississippi. Considered by many, Eric Clapton among them, to be the greatest blues guitarist who ever lived, his short, mercurial life spawned a legend that has become folklore: the oft-told story of how he gained his musical genius by making a deal with the devil one night at a Mississippi Delta crossroads.

After losing his young wife and son in childbirth, the real-life Johnson was a wanderer and a womanizer, going from juke joint to juke joint throughout the Delta area, before being murdered by a jealous husband on August 16, 1938, at the age of twenty-seven. He recorded only a handful of songs (performed in the only two sessions he ever recorded), now available as the essential "King of the Delta Blues."

The tale of his Faustian bargain served as the inspiration for **Crossroads** (1986) an amiable effort starring teen heartthrob Ralph Macchio as a guitar prodigy who, with the help and advice of a legendary bluesman whom he rescues from a hospital in New York, hits the road for fame and fortune. Joe Seneca gives depth to the old man, and their odyssey together takes on elements of both *Faust* and *Rocky*. Macchio ultimately has to battle the devil in a musical duel for his soul. Music by guitar great Ry Cooder.

Johnson's real life is recounted in **The Search for Robert Johnson** (1992), a TV documentary now available on video and DVD. Blues musician John Hammond travels the Mississipi Delta, talking to those who knew the enigmatic bluesman. Fascinating stuff for devotees (including great renditions of Johnson's classics), but a bit dry for general viewing.

may 9

Irresistible Force, Meet the Immovable Object

"The best time I ever had with Joan Crawford was pushing her down the stairs in Whatever Happened to Baby Jane?*"*

—Bette Davis

Cats and dogs. Palestine and Israel. Ireland and England. Bette Davis and Joan Crawford. What do all of these have in common?

The first shots were fired in the battle of the bitches on this day in 1962 when screen divas Bette Davis and Joan Crawford showed up for publicity photos on the set of their first—and last—film together, *Whatever Happened to Baby Jane?* Contrary to popular rumor, the two women didn't hate each other; they despised, detested, and *loathed* each other. Throughout the filming they alternated between taking verbal potshots at each other and refusing to acknowledge the other's existence. Still, the chemistry was there—the two prima donnas relentlessly scratching and clawing for screen time, better lighting, and top billing—and it came across on the screen. Just their luck that the movie was a smash hit and the studio quickly wanted to reteam them for a sequel, *Hush, Hush, Sweet Charlotte,* but Crawford would have no part of it, and Olivia de Havilland ended up playing the part.

Celebrate the onscreen meeting of the immovable object and the irresistible force with **Whatever Happened to Baby Jane?** (1962). Director Robert Aldrich mixed elements of the Grand Guignol with a scathing if sophomoric satire of Hollywood—sort of a *Sunset Boulevard* on wacky weed. Davis (truly frightening in whiteface) plays former 1920s Hollywood child star Baby Jane, who shares a decrepit old Hollywood mansion with her sister (Crawford), a former movie queen who is now confined to a wheelchair after a mysterious accident. Clips from Crawford's old movies are used to represent her Hollywood past, and both actresses deliver intense performances. Davis, in particular, is a hammy hoot, going joyfully over the top when she serves Crawford her favorite pet as an entree. A masterpiece of kitsch and camp, and the Holy Grail for aspiring cabaret female impersonators.

may 10

Fred Astaire's B'Day

"Can't act. Can't sing. Balding. Can dance a little."

Some nameless movie executive wrote that curt assessment after seeing Fred Astaire's first screen test. The man who wrote it is long forgotten, but everybody remembers Fred Astaire, right?

Right?

Let's face it—there's not much of a market for Fred Astaire these days. And the executive's dismissive critique wasn't totally off the mark. As a screen presence, Astaire simply couldn't compete with Clark Gable or Cary Grant—or even Harpo Marx. The image of Astaire which exists today is an icon evocative of another time and place altogether. And his raison d'être, the movie musical, is as extinct as the dinosaurs.

But the man could dance. And when he did, the real world—and all critical carping—faded into insignificance. Astaire transported Depression-era audiences to an elegant fantasy world of exotic locales, huge art deco sets, impossibly glossy floors, impeccably tailored top hat and tails, lavish gowns, and, above all, passionate, romantic dancing. He looked so natural on his feet that it appeared he could dance before he could think. Astaire in motion was the personification of carefree sophistication, natural grace, and style.

Today marks his birthday. Celebrate it in style with **Top Hat** (1935). It has all the elements that made movie musical magic: a classic score by Irving Berlin ("Isn't It a Lovely Day," "Cheek to Cheek"), superb dance routines (choreographed by Hermes Pan), great comedic support (courtesy of Edward Everett Horton), stunning black and white art deco designs, and, most of all, Ginger Rogers. Astaire and Rogers went together like . . . well, Astaire and Rogers. Katharine Hepburn once said that Astaire gave Rogers class, and she gave him sex. *Top Hat* is the most sexually charged of their films together. Keep an eye out for Lucille Ball in the flower shop scene.

And if you want to slip off your shoes and cut the rug along with Fred . . . who's looking?

may 11

Thai One On

On this day in 1949 the country of Siam ceased to be a monarchy and renamed itself Thailand.

Celebrate the Siam that once was with **The King and I** (1956)—a deliriously romantic musical starring the radiant Deborah Kerr as Anna Leonowens, the real-life English schoolteacher sent abroad to tutor the royal court children of the king of Siam (Yul Brynner in his signature, Academy Award–winning performance) in 1860. Packed with great numbers by Rodgers and Hammerstein, including "Getting to Know You" and the magical "Shall We Dance?" Oh, by the way, see if you can catch one of the great film flubs: an earring keeps jumping from one of Brynner's ears to the other.

And no, that's not really Deborah Kerr's voice doing the singing—it's the ubiquitous Marni Nixon, the world's least-known musical star, who also sang for Audrey Hepburn in *My Fair Lady* and for Natalie Wood in *West Side Story*.

may 12

. . . But What's There Is Cherce

"I don't care what is written about me as long as it isn't true."

—Katharine Hepburn

Theatrical producer Jed Harris called her "inept." Leslie Howard referred to her as "a beanpole," and a writer for *Vanity Fair* called her "the most irritating person I can think of." Algonquin wit Dorothy Parker, after seeing her in a Broadway production, famously remarked, "She runs the gamut of emotions from A to B." As for the lady herself, when asked to describe herself in one word, she considered the question and replied, "Tenacious."

Movies had not seen anything like Katharine Hepburn before—born this day in 1907 in Hartford, Connecticut. She was a thoroughbred, born of noble New England lineage—her father, who committed suicide when she was fourteen, was a renowned surgeon and her mother was a dedicated suffragette and birth control advocate. She was athletic, free-thinking, beautiful, and, as she often said, tenacious. She did college theater at the prestigious Bryn Mawr, and by 1928 had started to appear on Broadway, already gaining a reputation as a difficult actor. RKO offered her a film contract, but she was unimpressed, so she named a ridiculous price. To her astonishment, they agreed. She won her first Academy Award for her third picture. The rest is Hollywood history. When she teamed up with Spencer Tracy for the first of a series of splendid pictures together, Hollywood's most enduring love story began.

Hepburn and Tracy went on to deliver unforgettable performances in numerous films—both together and separately—but the best of their films together is the delightful **Adam's Rib** (1949). As married lawyers on opposite sides of a murder case (he's the prosecutor, she's the defense attorney), their onscreen rapport together is absolutely astonishing. There was never a chemistry so palpable between two actors. Garson Kanin and Ruth Gordon's brilliantly fresh and funny script is a spot-on comment on romantic expectations and the roles men and women are expected to play. Deft direction by the great George Cukor. And for the cherry on top, there's Judy Holliday in her first film performance as the defendant accused of trying to kill her philandering husband. A gold mine of a movie, still fresh, vital, romantic, and mighty funny.

may 13

Get Lost

Chet Baker had it all and blew it. A phenomenally gifted jazz trumpet player of the '50s, he also became a singing sensation with his beguiling voice. Baker's singing was uniquely opaque and blandly romantic—listeners could project onto if whatever interpretations and meaning they liked. In his youth, he was drop-dead gorgeous, a bop James Dean with a hint of Oklahoma drawl. "I was beautiful," he said later. "I should've been a movie star." And he might well have been, except for his self-destructive lifestyle and unrepentant heroin habit. On this day in 1988, in exile from his country and looking more like eighty-five than his actual fifty-eight years, he fell out of a Paris hotel window in a drug-induced stupor.

Just before the end, he starred in a documentary for photographer Bruce Weber, **Let's Get Lost** (1987). It's a fascinating look at a walking contradiction, a man who has been given a gift and, feeling he doesn't deserve it, sets about to destroy both himself and anyone stupid enough to care about him. In some scenes he's brutally candid, in others blatantly lying. A fascinating, gorgeously photographed, but ultimately heartbreaking movie. Those expecting a typically fawning portrait of a jazz legend will be in for a sobering surprise. Chet Baker was a gifted horn player, and he blew it in more ways than one.

may 14

The Force Was with Him

Love him or hate him, no filmmaker has influenced a generation more than George Lucas. Coppola had the aspirations of art, Scorsese the skittish style, Spielberg was the crowd-pleasing Hitchcock of new filmmakers, and DePalma *wanted* to be the Hitchcock of modern filmmakers. But Lucas seemed to loom omnipotently above them all, like a vast, all-powerful puppet master, pulling strings from on high.

He was born this day in Modesto, California—the town that inspired his early hit, *American Graffiti*—in 1944. He forever changed the direction of motion picture-making with the release of *Star Wars* (1977)—a fun film that began as a homage to Saturday morning matinee entertainment, turned into a franchise, and became a cult and then a pop culture milestone. It would be impossible to overstate the importance of *Star Wars*—if only for its influence on countless films to follow.

After *Star Wars,* Lucas became a nearly inaccessible figure. He stopped directing, preferring instead to oversee projects as producer from his kingdom at ILM headquarters in northern California's Marin County. When he finally did emerge to direct a prequel to the series twenty years later in 1998, *Star Wars Episode One: The Phantom Menace,* it wasn't so much directing as conjuring; 90 percent of the film is computer-generated.

For all his commercial success, Lucas is often accused of being technically innovative but lacking substance. He combines the gee-whiz enthusiasm of Spielberg with a boy's love of gadgetry and gimmickry. But early on, he did exhibit heart, depth, and a winning attraction to characters in his early masterpiece—and first box office smash—*American Graffiti.*

American Graffiti (1973) recounts one eventful night in a small California town in the summer of 1962. The focus is on a group of graduating high school students, including nice kid Steve (Ron Howard, in his first post-Opie performance), sensitive cerebral dreamer Curt (Richard Dreyfuss in his most underplayed, nuanced performance), John Milner (Paul LeMat), the overage cool drag runner who will never grow up or leave town, and "Toad" (Charles Martin Smith), the nerdy outcast kid who has the worst—and greatest—night of his young life. Lucas perfectly captures the comedic coming-of-age rituals of those days, along with perfectly re-created period details (the movie inspired the watered-down TV series *Happy Days*). The music score—comprised entirely of rock and pop hits from the era, emanating from the ever-present car radios, commenting on the onscreen action—set a precedent that would forever change motion picture soundtracks, for better or worse. A wonderful supporting cast includes Cindy Williams, Candy Clark, and, as Bob Falfa, the tough new threat in town with a yellow roadster, Harrison Ford. Lucas certainly made more successful movies than *American Graffiti,* but he never made a better one.

may 15

If Ever if Ever a Wiz There Was . . .

If not for an event that occurred this day in 1856, we would never have seen the Yellow Brick Road. L. Frank Baum, born this day near Syracuse, New York, would grow up to write a series of popular children's books, starting with *The Wizard of Oz.* He got the title by glancing at an alphabetical file cabinet, labeled O–Z. It was first published in 1900, and had been filmed at least once before the definitive MGM version of 1939. (One silent version from 1925 featured Oliver Hardy as the Tin Man.)

But let's face it—there really is only one **The Wizard of Oz** (1939). One of my great moviegoing experiences was watching this film at a free public showing on a summer evening at the park behind the public library in the middle of New York City. The whole audience sang along with the movie, collectively "oooohed" when the impressive twister appeared ominously in the background, and hissed when Miss Gulch came to claim Toto.

The Wizard of Oz is, of course, much more than a movie—particularly to baby boomers and their ancestors. You don't need me to give you an excuse to see it again. But here it is anyway.

may 16

And the Oscar Goes To . . .

On this night in 1929, in the Grand Auditorium at the Roosevelt Hotel on Hollywood Boulevard the very first Academy Awards were presented. It was a stellar evening and set the tone for an annual ritual that would become increasingly glitzy—and increasingly long. The first ceremony clocked in at under an hour; recent installments have lasted approximately as long as the Gulf War. Only four awards were handed out that first night—for best picture, director, actor, and actress.

Get hold of the very first movie to win the Academy Award for Best Picture (and the first and last silent film to win)—**Wings** (1928), William Wellman's spectacular tribute to the American flyers of World War I, based on the director's own wartime experiences. Buddy Rogers and Richard Arlen play longtime pals who become pilots and fall for the same woman (ambulance driver Clara Bow). The aerial photography is still breathtaking, and the dogfights exciting and accurate. Anyone who thinks silent films were clunky and static will be converted; Wellman's camera is positively balletic, literally dancing over tables.

may 17

Birth of a Rebel

One of the cinema's true auteur-rebels, Dennis Hopper, was born this day in 1936 in Dodge City, Kansas. An attractive but bland juvenile leading man, he found himself easily cast in early TV dramas of the '50s, usually as a misunderstood teen. In 1955 he was cast in *Rebel Without a Cause,* where he met his muse and mentor, James Dean, and the two became fast friends. After *Rebel,* they were both cast in *Giant,* though they shared no scenes together. Dean's sullen, introspective naturalistic acting style was a profound influence on Hopper. "He said things like, 'If you're smoking a cigarette in a scene, don't act smoking a cigarette. Just smoke a cigarette.'" Dean's death just after completing *Giant* devastated Hopper.

He went on to specialize in spoiled rich kids and psychotic outlaws in Westerns. After he was fired by Howard Hawks (for stubbornly ruining a record fifty-eight takes in front of the frustrated director), his reputation as a difficult actor effectively blacklisted him, and he found himself working for Roger Corman at AIP Studios. While at AIP he met up with Peter Fonda, and the two embarked on a project—"a Western with motorcycles instead of horses"—*Easy Rider* (1968). Hopper cowrote and directed, Fonda produced, and they both costarred along with an up-and-coming actor named Jack Nicholson. *Easy Rider* went on to become a touchstone film of the '60s.

But to see Hopper's ultimate creation, seek out **The Last Movie** (1971). After the unexpected box office success of *Easy Rider,* Hollywood gave Hopper carte blanche on his next project. He promptly gathered together an unbelievable cast (including director Sam Fuller, Peter Fonda, Dean Stockwell, Michelle Phillips, and Henry Fonda—all of them literally hidden in the background of the movie) and crew, flew them all to the Andes in Peru, and started filming. While Hopper ingested a steady diet of hallucinogens, the budget went through the stratosphere and an already complex movie became an incomprehensible mess.

The central idea of the movie was brilliant and intriguing: Hopper plays Kansas, a movie stunt man who is with an American movie crew filming a Western in a remote Peruvian village. The natives become fascinated with the reenactments of murder and violence. After the film company leaves, Kansas stays behind—and the natives begin to emulate what they saw, fashioning "movie cameras" out of bamboo.

Hopper was reportedly whacked out of his proverbial gourd on drugs during filming, and it shows all over the screen. When he returned to the States with his finished film, the execs at Universal scratched their collective heads and buried the movie. For Hopper, it very nearly was the Last Movie. This is one seriously strange piece of cinema, quite impossible to describe. It is at once a masterpiece and a folly, like nothing you've ever seen before (or may want to see ever again). And by all accounts Hopper was certifiably looneytunes. He was very briefly married to Michelle Phillips during this period; she left him after eight days, asking on her way out, "Have you ever considered suicide?"

may 18

You're Gonna Lava This Movie

It had been dormant for hundreds of years, but when it erupted on this day in 1980 in Washington State, Mt. St. Helens sent out a torrent of flaming lava, destroying everything in its path, and sent a black smoke cloud that darkened seven states. Fifty-seven people died. It was a powerful reminder of nature's unsparing, unpredictable majesty.

As geologists and seismologists will attest, there are numerous volcanoes—several in the United States—that have been lying dormant for centuries and will eventually erupt. The effect is fairly convincingly portrayed—in a perfectly hokey Hollywood way—in **Volcano** (1998). A dormant volcano has been bubbling underneath the La Brea Tar Pits in Los Angeles, and before you can say "thar she blows," the city is awash in fiery lava. The tag line for the movie was "the coast is toast." Tommy Lee Jones plays the ultimate fireman, who manages to save part of the city with the help of geologist Anne Heche. And yes, the little girl and the dog live. It's that kind of movie. But the effects are fabulous; who hasn't wanted to see L.A. buried under an ocean of molten lava? Here's your chance.

may 19

Death of an Enigma

While riding through the English countryside on his motorcycle, author and adventurer T. E. Lawrence —better known to the world as Lawrence of Arabia—took a fatal spill while trying to avoid hitting a young boy on a bicycle on May 13, 1935. He was pitched over the handlebars, landing on his head. He lingered for several days before passing away this day in 1935. Though he was only forty-six when he died, he had squeezed several lifetimes into his time on earth.

One of the most heroic, romantic, complex, and enigmatic figures of the twentieth century, Lawrence was a man wholly out of place in his own culture, but who embraced another and changed the world. A brilliant archeologist, mapmaker, writer, soldier, and diplomat, he fought ceaselessly to promote the independence of Arab states. David Lean's magnificent **Lawrence of Arabia** (1962) is a thoughtful, intelligent, epic retelling of his adventures in Arabia—and one of the most gloriously shot epic motion pictures of all time. Peter O'Toole (in what was only his second film appearance) delivered a mesmerizing star-making performance as Lawrence, ably supported by a stellar cast, including a young and handsome Omar Sharif, Anthony Quinn, Claude Rains, and, in a chameleonlike turn as wily Prince Faisel, Alec Guinness. Breathtaking cinematography by Freddie Young and a thoughtful, literate script by Robert Bolt contribute to the film's success. And, of course, there's that expansively evocative theme song.

may 20

It Was a Wonderful Life

Jimmy Stewart was born this day in 1908, in Indiana, Pennsylvania. Surprisingly, he began his film career as a bad guy, playing a murderer in

After the Thin Man, but his aw-shucks disposition sabotaged his efforts. Next, he tried musicals—but his thin, reedy voice and lanky demeanor proved a major handicap. What was a casting director to do with this gawky, gangling young man with the stuttering drawl and shy country-boy demeanor?

But when he finally found his niche—in essence, playing himself—Jimmy Stewart hit paydirt and, ultimately, became more than an actor. He became an icon, America's idealized image of itself. As naïve senator Jefferson Smith in *Mr. Smith Goes to Washington* (1939), as the love-struck store clerk in *The Shop Around the Corner* (1940; later remade as *You've Got Mail*), and as slightly tipsy Elwood P. Dowd in *Harvey* (1950), he personified honor, humility, generosity, and good humor.

But there was more to Jimmy Stewart than the homespun image. After his return from active duty in World War II (where he flew over twenty missions as a bomber pilot over Germany, rising from private to full colonel and, eventually, brigadier general for the U.S. Air Force Reserve), he deliberately broadened his range, downplaying his former sunny image and delving into a secret side that bubbled just underneath. His post–World War II work is often darkly shaded: His vengeance-obsessed cowboy in *Winchester '73,* his iconoclastic loner in *Two Rode Together,* his self-sufficient airplane pilot in *The Flight of the Phoenix,* and, most eye-opening of all, his obsessed detective in Hitchcock's *Vertigo.*

But let's face it—his greatest performance, and his favorite among dozens of great performances, was as small-town savings and loan businessman George Bailey in Frank Capra's **It's a Wonderful Life** (1946). Stewart was still young enough to tap into his old charm, but mature enough to dig deep into the frustration, stifled anger, and pain of a man who considers himself to be a failure. The scene where he begins to abuse his family is heart-wrenching and difficult to watch. Stewart's performance is one of the great performances in cinema—immensely moving, inspiring, sometimes upsetting, but ultimately redeeming and uplifting.

may 21

Watch the Ultimate In-Flight Movie

On this day in 1927, Charles Lindbergh became the first man ever to fly nonstop solo across the Atlantic, from New York to Paris.

When a French-American businessman named Raymond Orteig offered $25,000 for the first nonstop solo flight between New York and Paris, young hotshot pilot Charles Lindbergh volunteered to take him up on his offer. At the time, he was earning his living flying airmail runs between Chicago and St. Louis and had logged hundreds of air miles; before that, he had been a daredevil stunt pilot on barnstorming tours.

His history-making nonstop trans-Atlantic flight began with a muddy takeoff from Long Island's Roosevelt Field on May 20, 1927. The plane, *Spirit of St. Louis,* was a single-engine aircraft with oversized wings and loaded down with all the fuel it could carry. Lindbergh couldn't even see where he was flying; there was no windshield, and he had to lean out of the window to get any view at all. He had nothing to rely on but magnetic compasses and faulty charts. Twenty-eight hours after takeoff, he crossed the English Channel and followed the Seine River to Paris, where he landed at Le Bourget Airport at precisely 10:24 P.M. to the cheers of a crowd of thousands.

The shy Lindbergh instantly became a worldwide celebrity and icon following this record-setting—and daring—feat. Lindbergh's epic flight from New York to Paris is vividly re-created in Billy Wilder's underrated **The Spirit of St. Louis** (1957). In what is pretty much a one-man show, Jimmy Stewart may have been a bit long in the tooth to play the twenty-five-year-old aviator (Stewart was himself nearly fifty at the time of filming), but he still made for an amicably all-American hero. The climactic flight across the Atlantic is suspenseful stuff even though we know he succeeded—no easy accomplishment. But Wilder's unsentimental and economical direction and script (cowritten with longtime partner I.A.L. Diamond) keep things moving. Lindbergh's later controversies and tribulations (his anti-Semitic stance during World War II; the kidnapping and subsequent murder of his infant son in 1932) are ignored altogether. This is strictly a celebration of an American pioneer and icon—and it flies.

may 22

Hello, Larry

Sir Laurence Olivier, considered by many the world's premiere classical actor of his day, bowed into the world on this day in 1907 in Steyning, West Sussex, England. Although critics assert his finest work was on the stage, he left behind a legacy of monumental performances on film, too, before passing into what Shakespeare called "the undiscovered country" on July 11, 1989, at the ripe old age of eighty-two.

His early films—when he set the hearts of young women aflame with his resonant, aristocratic voice and handsome, romantic features—were among his most memorable: his windswept Heathcliff in *Wuthering Heights* (1939), his aristocratic and mysterious Maxim de Winter in Hitchcock's *Rebecca* (1941), and as Lord Nelson in *That Hamilton Woman* (1941; opposite his future wife, Vivien Leigh). When World War II broke out, Olivier volunteered for the Royal Air Force but was turned down. He circumvented the process by joining up with the Fleet Air Arm of the Royal Navy. In 1944 he was discharged from the service and, with codirector Ralph Richardson, supervised the restoration of the Old Vic Theater. It was then he attempted his first film as both director and star, the fabulously successful and stirring *Henry V* (1944; for which he won an unprecedented special Academy Award), which he followed by the equally impressive *Hamlet* (1948; which won him Oscars for Best Actor and Best Picture).

After his final Shakespearean adaptation, *Richard III* (1955), he found himself at a crossroads in his life, but managed to find compelling material. His portrayal of third-rate talent Archie Rice in *The Entertainer* (1960) is brutal and unsentimental; his determined and manipulative Crassus in *Spartacus* (1960) is both showy and understated; and his performances as a mystery writer engaged in a lethal battle of wits with blackmailer Michael Caine in the clever *Sleuth* (1972) and as the former Nazi dentist in New York who drills Dustin Hoffman in *Marathon Man* (1976) make deep impressions. Thereafter, the roles required little but for Sir Larry to show up for one day of filming, then "home for tea." And who could blame him?

Salute Sir Larry with his exceptional **Hamlet** (1948), a labor of love and of craft, and graced with one of the most mellifluous voices in the history of the English language. His is still considered—after several prestigious and honorable attempts since—to be considered the finest film Hamlet. Olivier—as he typically does when directing Shakespeare—keeps the "movie ambience" (i.e., complex sets) to a minimum, and delights in the theatrical, sometimes audacious possibilities inherent in the film medium. A masterful performance by an immortal in his prime.

may 23

A Movie with a Few Holes in It

"Some day they will go down together,
they will bury them side by side.
To a few it means grief, to the law it's relief,
but it's death to Bonnie and Clyde."

—Bonnie Parker, 1933

Bonnie Parker was probably a better bandit than poet, but not by much. She penned the above doggerel and sent it to the newspapers, which naturally printed it in 1933.

Bonnie and Clyde did go down together, on this day in 1934, ambushed in their car by Texas Ranger Frank Hamer and a well-armed posse a few miles outside of Gibland, Louisiana. Authorities removed a total of 187 bullets from their bodies. But, contrary to Bonnie's poetic prophecy, they were not buried side by side; the two outlaws currently occupy plots in separate cemetaries near Dallas.

By the 1960s, Bonnie Parker and Clyde Barrow had been largely forgotten by the public. In their heyday in the '30s, they were second only to John Dillinger in nabbing headlines as they indulged in a savage crime spree across the Southwest. They were not glamorous; Bonnie stood a little over four feet tall, had a hatchet face, and was quick-tempered. Clyde Barrow was a goofball three-time loser with elephant ears and no chin. They were no Robin Hoods, either. By all accounts, they were small-timers, robbing filling stations, cafes, dime stores, and dry cleaners. Clyde once killed a jeweler for ten dollars. Even Dillinger regarded them as idiotic amateurs, going on record as saying, "They give crime a bad name."

But they became immortal when director Arthur Penn filmed the watermark 1967 classic, **Bonnie and Clyde.** Along with Sam Peckinpah's *Wild Bunch, Bonnie and Clyde* opened the floodgates of graphic violence in American cinema. It was widely critized at the time of its release for glorifying sociopaths.

The film's combustible mixture of action, romance, tragedy, and comedy is still startling. Warren Beatty became a bona fide star for his portrayal of the charming but dim Clyde Barrow, and Faye Dunaway made for a far more glamorous Bonnie than the real thing. Gene Hackman was nominated for Best Supporting Actor for his brilliant performance as Clyde's reckless but likable brother, Buck. And keep an eye out for a young Gene Wilder in his first film role, hysterically funny as Eugene, a mortician who is kidnapped by the Barrow gang.

may 24

The Reel Bob Dylan

Robert Zimmerman, a.k.a. Bob Dylan, came into the world this day in 1941. Although a major force in twentieth-century popular music, Bob Dylan's occasional forays into film have proven a mixed bag. His appearance as the enigmatic "Alias" in Sam Peckinpah's *Pat Garrett and Billy the Kid* is a purposefully vague cipher, and his role as the elder statesman of rock in *Hearts of Fire* is a murky, mumbling curiosity at best. His self-written, self-directed magnum opus, *Renaldo and Clara* is a self-indulgent, incomprehensible disaster, either in the uncut four-hour version or the edited two-hour version. He's also put in occasional musical guest shots, most notably in *The Last Waltz* (1976) and *The Concert for Bangladesh* (1972), where he contributed a beautiful performance of "Just Like a Woman."

The best performance by Bob Dylan on film is his performance as Bob Dylan in D. A. Pennebacker's fascinating 1965 documentary, **Don't Look Back,** filmed during Dylan's 1965 United Kingdom tour. Dylan had just released *Bringing It All Back Home,* the album where he first utilized a backup band and offended staid folkies by plugging in an electric guitar. This was his last all-acoustic tour, and he was an artist in transition. Alternately arrogant, childish, biting, clever, and drunk, he's undeniably entertaining. A contemporary critic compared it to "ninety minutes of watching the neighborhood brat blow his nose." Dylan's confrontational interview with a clueless writer from *Time* magazine is classic cinema verité. Also with Joan Baez.

may 25

You Must Remember This . . .

After a troubled preproduction, *Casablanca* begins filming on this day in 1942 on the Warner Brothers lot. At the time, no one associated with it realized that, as time goes by, it is still the most popular romance ever filmed. It was originally titled *Everybody Comes to Rick's* and, as every film buff knows, Ronald Reagan was originally slated to play Rick, the tough proprietor of Rick's Café in war-torn Casablanca. Luckily, he passed, and the part went to Humphrey Bogart—who made the role his own. Bogie's tough, mercenary exterior cannot mask the disillusioned romantic inside when his true love, Ilse, with whom he had an affair years earlier in Paris, walks into his club. "Of all the joints in Casablanca, she walks into mine," he grumbles famously.

Celebrate the anniversary of the first day of filming by watching the final product—one of the greatest Hollywood romances ever filmed. **Casablanca** has more classic lines in it than any other movie—the litany is almost endless. To list them all here would spoil the fun. One line which is *not* in the movie—listen carefully—is the most quoted: "Play it again, Sam." No one actually speaks that famous phrase. (Bergman wistfully asks piano player Sam [Paul Dooley] to, "Play it, Sam. Play 'As Times Goes By'"; later, Bogart, drink in hand, says, "You played it for her, you can play it for me. If she can stand it, I can. Go on, play it.") Ingrid Bergman is positively luminous as Ilse, the wife of Resistance fighter and political activist Victor Laszlo (Paul Henried). Terrific performances (particularly from Claude Rains as Louie, the corrupt chief of police), one of the greatest Hollywood scripts ever (by Howard Koch), a magically evocative setting, and snappy direction from Michael Curtiz all contribute to this film's deservedly legendary status—but it's Bogart and Bergman who lift it into the pantheon of the sublime.

may 26

Duke It Out Tonight

If you're born a beefy boy and your parents name you Marion, you'd better have tough skin. Luckily, Marion Morrison, born this day in 1907, had tough skin. And when he was old enough, he changed his name to the more masculine-sounding John Wayne.

As a football player for USC, he dabbled in the film industry, working as an occasional gaffer and set boy. He began getting small roles in B Westerns on the Republic Studios lot. His acting was stiff, but he made progress from film to film, gradually developing a distinct style of his own. Among the people he met were John Ford, who recognized the young man's potential star power. The director cast Wayne as the Ringo Kid in his Western opus *Stagecoach,* and the rest is history, pilgrim.

Celebrate his birthday with a double feature, the bookends of his film career. Start off with **Stagecoach** (1939), the role that made him a star. John Ford's epic tale of a group of disparate passengers traveling through Monument Valley set the bar for every saddle soap opera to follow. Volumes have been written about its art and its influence; and on top of that, it's a damn entertaining ride. Ford literally made the Western into an art form in this masterpiece, filled with sweeping vistas, innovative camera use, complex character development, and exciting action sequences. Wayne is the Ringo Kid, an outlaw out to avenge the men who killed his brother. Wayne was never more attractive, both sensitive and resolute, and it's no wonder the role made him a star.

Then watch **The Shootist** (1976), filmed almost forty years later and a fitting finale to his career. Wayne plays John Book, a retired gunslinger who finds out he's dying of cancer (he gets the news from James Stewart in a small role as a frontier doctor). Book gets a room at a boardinghouse, run by widow Lauren Bacall, and invites all his enemies to town for a final showdown. Wayne's farewell performance is a fitting valedictory, and a homage to the genre that made him a star.

may 27

Open Your Golden Gates . . .

It may be just a suspension bridge of gaudy orange steel, but to countless Californians it's one of the most beautiful and instantly recognizable landmarks in the world. On this day in 1937, the Golden Gate Bridge was officially dedicated, and the city of San Francisco gained an emblem.

The Golden Gate Bridge has been utilized as an exotic backdrop in several movies—virtually every San Francisco–based movie has at least one shot of it. But it was really exploited nicely in the climax of the James Bond thriller **A View to a Kill** (1985). Christopher Walken made a delightful heavy as Max Zorin, who plots to destroy the Silicon Valley near San Francisco. Zorin kidnaps lovely Stacey Sutton (Tanya Roberts), and is making his getaway in a blimp loaded with explosives: Bond (Roger Moore) grabs the mooring line and hangs on. As the deadly dirigible passes the Golden Gate, Bond wraps the mooring line around one of the uppermost cables of the bridge—leading to a battle for his life atop the bridge in a dazzlingly produced sequence.

may 28

Enjoy a Little Bondage

James Bond's creator was born this day in England, in 1908. The name was Fleming. Ian Fleming. As a young man, he worked for British Intelligence, mostly pushing paper—but he did pick up considerable inside information and lingo. He wrote the children's classic *Chitty, Chitty, Bang, Bang,* but Ian Fleming will be best remembered for creating the preeminent fictitious superspy icon of the cold war, who lasted well beyond the collapse of the Soviet Union: Bond. James Bond. And, like his creation, Fleming preferred his martinis shaken, not stirred.

Fleming lived to see the film version of only one of his Bond stories, **Dr. No** (1963). It became JFK's favorite movie. In Bond films to come, the stories and gadgets and girls got campier. But *Dr. No* is played fairly straight and is all the more effective for it. Other Bond adventures would be bigger and noisier, but this is the closest the series ever came to capturing the essence of Fleming's conception of the suave superspy. Sit back, sip a martini—shaken, not stirred—and enjoy James Bond before he became a camp culture icon.

may 29

Have a Little Hope

He was born Leslie Townes Hope in Eltham, England, this day in 1903. After immigrating to America, he worked as a soda jerk and a newsboy and had a brief career as, of all things, a boxer. He got his start in comedy in vaudeville, then got cast in the Broadway musical *Roberta*. He proved to be a natural for the movies, perfecting a character who was endearingly cowardly yet witty. He was—and remains—Woody Allen's favorite comedian, a fact apparent in Allen's early films.

It's tough to remember now, but there was a time—the late 1940s to be exact—when Bob Hope was fresh, snappy and incredibly funny. He made several near-classics: *My Favorite Brunette* (1947), *The Paleface* (1948), *Monsieur Beaucaire* (1946), and, of course, the popular *Road* series with frequent screen partner Bing Crosby.

But Hope's best film is the hilarious Western parody **Son of Paleface** (1952), a sequel to his hit film of 1948, *The Paleface.* In *Son of Paleface,* Bob is a timid Harvard graduate who goes out West to claim his inheritance, left by his dad, "Painless Potter" the dentist (played by Hope in the original film). He gets tangled up with outlaws, Indians, Roy Rogers, and Jane Russell. Hope has never been better, and snappy direction from the great Frank Tashlin keeps the pace at a gallop.

may 30

You May Be Better Off Taking the Fifth

I have to tell the truth: Today is National Honesty Day. Here's your challenge: Could you get through an entire day without telling one single little white lie?

That's the problem that faces Jim Carrey in the amusing **Liar, Liar**

(1997), and because he's playing a lawyer, he's in double jeopardy. When his neglected son, Max (Justin Cooper), makes a birthday wish that his busy dad would have to stop telling lies for just one day, his wish comes true—much to the embarrassment of his spin-doctoring dad. Carrey deftly mixes his patented physical schtick with a tentative first stab at a more sophisticated script. The results are mixed, but there are still more laughs than in a half dozen Adam Sandler movies. And that's the truth.

may 31

Go Ahead: Make His Day

It took a long time for Clint Eastwood to be taken seriously. He had the curious distinction of becoming an icon before he became an artist. He was born this day in 1930 in San Francisco.

His first movie role was as a lab assistant in the minor sci-fi classic *Tarantula* (1955); he's on-screen for approximately thirty seconds. Back in the days when westerns dominated TV screens, he was cast as amiable cowhand Rowdy Yates in the popular TV series *Rawhide,* where he literally learned the ropes of the genre. After the series was canceled, he accepted an offer to film a trilogy of westerns in Italy for director Sergio Leone. He played a mercenary killer—the "Man with No Name"—in *A Fistful of Dollars* (1964), *For a Few Dollars More* (1966), and *The Good, the Bad and the Ugly* (1967).

The series, which inspired the coining of the term *spaghetti westerns,* became a worldwide hit with mostly male audiences. Not for the last time, Eastwood came under fire for his perceived promotion of violence. But the movies firmly established Eastwood as an unlikely international star.

Back in the U.S., he was cast as San Francisco police detective Harry Callahan in the first of Don Siegal's series, *Dirty Harry* (1971). Again he took a lot of heat for the violence; some called the movie fascist.

He took advantage of his box office clout with his first directorial effort, the tepid Hitchcock homage *Play Misty for Me* (1973). Further directorial efforts followed—and he began refining his talents behind the lens. He began experimenting with new directions and attitudes, directing and starring in such diverse films as *The Outlaw Josey Wales* (1976), the delightfully offbeat and humorous *Bronco Billy* (1980), his ode to a grizzled country music icon, *Honkeytonk Man* (1982), and directing but not appearing in *Bird* (1988), his film homage to jazz pioneer Charlie Parker.

But his best movie is his revisionist Western masterpiece, **Unforgiven** (1992). Eastwood plays William Muny, a former gunslinger, reformed by his loving wife, who dies and leaves him with two children to look after. When a drunken cowhand cuts up a prostitute and has a bounty placed on his head, killer-turned-farmer Muny teams up with his old partner (Morgan Freeman) and an inexperienced young would-be gunslinger called the Scofield Kid (Jaimz Woolvett) to resume his old ways to get money for his children. But in the town of Big Whiskey, they confront sadistic sheriff—and inept carpenter—"Little Bill" Daggett (Gene Hackman in a splendid performance that won him an Oscar). The story is almost an anti-Eastwood movie, graphically depicting how violence begets violence. After the Scofield Kid kills his first man at close range, he's sickened by what he did. "But I guess he had it comin'," he rationalizes. "We've all got it comin', kid," Muny replies. "It's a hell of a thing, killin' a man. You take away everything he's ever had, and everything he's ever gonna have."

Unforgiven is Eastwood's greatest performance—the summing up of everything he's ever done, a coming-to-terms with aging and mortality, a profound and complex rumination on the nature of justice. A masterful script by David Webb Peoples and evocative, elegiac direction from Eastwood make *Unforgiven* one of the great Westerns of all time.

june

june 1

Hello, Norma Jean

Norma Jean Mortenson, born this day in 1926, had, by all accounts, a lousy childhood. Her father, an itinerant baker, committed suicide when she was three, and her mother, a film cutter at RKO Studios, spent most of her time in mental institutions, leaving the young girl to live in a series of foster homes—where she was abused, neglected, and raped. After marrying a twenty-one-year-old aircraft mechanic at sixteen, she attempted to commit suicide.

But her luck changed when she was spotted by an army photographer and asked to pose for a series of pinups. In short order she was introduced to a modeling agency, changed her hair color from brown to blond, and took the name Marilyn Monroe. With her breathy voice, her childish pout, and her indefinable wiggle, she projected a sexuality that was at once wholesome and coquettish, and became the iconic female sex symbol of the century.

The jury may always be out regarding her acting talents, but as an icon, she is unchallenged. And no scene sums her up like the famous shot in *The Seven Year Itch* (1955), where she stands above a New York subway grating to feel the breeze blow up her dress. (By the way, her then-husband, Joe

DiMaggio, was standing on the sidelines during the filming of that sequence, watching and fuming. They divorced not long after.) *The Seven Year Itch* projects the perfect Marilyn—in other words, the perfect fantasy. And therein lies the tragedy of Monroe; she created a mythical persona and lost herself in it.

Perhaps her most endearing performance was as the breathlessly optimistic Sugar Kane in Billy Wilder's legendary comedy **Some Like It Hot** (1959). Marilyn is sexy, endearing, and vulnerable as the cabaret singer who's holding out for the perfect man. It's quintessential Monroe—childlike, winsome, and unbelievably, unattainably sexy. And the dual lead performances by Tony Curtis and Jack Lemmon as two Chicago jazz musicians who inadvertently witness the St. Valentine's Day Massacre and disguise themselves as women to join an all-female orchestra are justifiably legendary. Usually listed as one of the Top 5 greatest comedies of all time, and for good reason. The closing line alone makes it worth watching.

june 2

"Think You Used Enough Dynamite There, Butch?"

According to those who knew him, Butch Cassidy was the most amiable and easy-going of the great Western outlaws—even if he wasn't the brightest. For several years, he and his gang (including Harry Longbaugh, better known as "the Sundance Kid") robbed trains and banks throughout the Mid- and Southwest. Although unquestionably an outlaw, he was an amicable, peaceful one. Butch never killed anyone, had a raucous sense of humor, and enjoyed the high life.

One of his most famous robberies occurred on this day in 1889, when he and his Hole in the Wall Gang robbed the Union Pacific Flyer near Wilcox, Wyoming. The gang flagged down the train and boarded it, quickly making their way to the safe deposit box in the rear car. When the guard refused to open the safe, Butch decided to use dynamite. He blew up the safe . . . and the railroad car . . . and a substantial portion of the $130,000 inside. (Miraculously, the guard escaped unharmed, but understandably shaken.)

The incident is a highlight of one of the most atypical Westerns ever filmed, George Roy Hill's **Butch Cassidy and the Sundance Kid** (1969). It was the first film to team Paul Newman and Robert Redford, and the chemistry was pure magic. As the two likable train robbers they poked fun at the Western genre while putting a fresh spin on it. George Roy Hill's sepia-toned portrait of an idealized, fading time—the sunset of the Wild West—perfectly complements William Goldman's now-textbook screenplay. About the only weak point is Burt Bacharach's treacly score, which is totally at odds with the rest of the movie.

june 3

Now *That's* Extreme Performance Art

Avant-garde artist Andy Warhol was riding the crest of his success as the country's most radical and recognized pop artist when, on this day in 1967, he was shot in the stomach by Valeria Solanis, lesbian head of S.C.U.M. (Society for Cutting Up Men). Warhol had cast the sometimes-actress in his film *I, a Man.* When he refused to film a script she had written, she shot him three times. He lingered on the brink of death for several days before recovering. She got her fifteen minutes.

Commemorate the near-death experience with **I Shot Andy Warhol** (1996), director and cowriter Mary Harron's engrossing account of life at the Factory leading up to the shooting. Lili Taylor is sensational as Solanis, and Jared Harris (son of Richard Harris) is a suitably distant and enigmatic Warhol. And the cast of Warhol's sycophants, hangers-on, and transvestite gofers are all present and accounted for. An evocative reconstruction of a bygone time, and an insightful look at the price—and illusion—of fame.

june 4

Orange You Glad He Came Up with This Scene?

On this day in 1971, Marlon Brando, made up to look like an old man, was attempting to make friends with the three-year-old boy who was playing his grandson in a pivotal scene he was shooting. Brando turned his face away, stuck a couple of orange peels in his mouth, and turned back to the unsuspecting toddler with a huge grin. Instead of the laughter he anticipated, Brando's spontaneous gesture petrified the poor boy. It became one of the watermark scenes in Brando's career—and probably a traumatic event for the young kid which resulted in years of therapy.

It's right there for you to see in **The Godfather** (1971)—as if you'd need another excuse to watch this extraordinary film, one of the finest achievements in American cinema and a true epic crime saga. Mario Puzo's best-selling novel had been the talk of the nation the previous year, when young turk director Francis Ford Coppola was given the assignment to direct it. The producers were reluctant to cast Brando in the role of Don Vito Corleone; the reclusive and eccentric actor was considered troublesome and, worse, washed up. And the producers definitely didn't approve of Coppola's choice of untried young actor Al Pacino to play Don Corleone's youngest son, Michael. But Coppola obstinately persevered, and an American classic was born.

Magnificently shot, written, composed, and acted, *The Godfather* is near-flawless entertainment; it's impossible to walk away from this movie once you start. In addition to star turns from Brando and Pacino, *The Godfather* boasts superlative performances from Robert Duvall as family lawyer Tom Hagen; James Caan as Michael's older brother, the volatile Sonny; and John Cazale as weak link in the genetic chain, brother Fredo. Coppola made two sequels; the second much better than the limp final installment. *The Godfather* has also been reconfigured as part of the all-inclusive *Godfather Saga,* edited together by Coppola from *The Godfather* and *The Godfather,*

Part 2, but the experiment loses something in the reconfiguration. Stick with the original *Godfather*—it's an offer you can't refuse.

june 5

Enjoy a Little Scandal

On this day in 1963, British secretary of war John Profumo resigns his post following allegations that he lied to the House of Commons about his sexual affair with showgirl Christine Keeler, who was also involved with a Soviet naval officer at the same time. The whole sordid affair threatened to topple the entire government of Prime Minister Harold Macmillan, and set the stage for a series of political sex scandals that would become increasingly commonplace in the years to come.

The story serves as the backdrop for the political soap opera–cum–thriller, **Scandal** (1988), the first feature directed by Michael Caton-Jones. Joanne Whalley-Kilmer is riveting as Christine Keeler, the center of the story. Great supporting turns from Ian McKellen as John Profumo and John Hurt, who delivers one of his most impressive performances as Stephen Ward, the socialite who instigated the "Profumo Affair." As Ward, Hurt is alternately sympathetic and vain, manipulative, and kind—it's an unbelievably rounded performance, a textbook examination of human ambition and frailty. Bridget Fonda has her first major supporting role as Mandy Rice-Davies.

june 6

D Day

The Anglo-American invasion of Nazi Europe began in the predawn hours of this day in 1944, as the first assault wave stormed Omaha Beach at

Normandy. Despite careful planning, losses were heavy. After two long hours, the Allies gained the upper hand, and the liberation of Europe was underway.

The watermark event has been re-created and reenacted in several movies, the most expensive and accurate being producer Daryl F. Zanuck's impressive version, *The Longest Day* (1962), which boasted three different directors and an all-star cast including John Wayne, Henry Fonda, Richard Burton, and Robert Mitchum. A monumental technical achievement, Zanuck filmed the movie on the exact locations as the original battles, and it remains the most faithful re-creation of that momentous day.

But the most visceral and realistic depiction of the event goes hands down to the first twenty-five minutes of Steven Spielberg's **Saving Private Ryan** (1998). Spielberg puts you right into the adrenalized thick of the battle—surrounded by exploding mines, whizzing bullets, severed limbs, screaming soldiers. The invasion is the film's set piece, and one of the most intense visual (and aural) experiences ever put on film. After the Normandy beach invasion, the film lapses into the familiar, sentimental, patriotic clichés we've all seen before: Every American soldier is a good, decent G.I. Joe who just wants to go home, and virtually every German soldier is portrayed as either a barbaric, murderous sadist, a sniveling coward, or both. Spielberg makes the mistake of propagandizing an entire ethnic group—as if the German soldiers were really any different from the American soldiers. Still, *Saving Private Ryan* is undeniably powerful, compelling, and well acted. One way or the other, you'll be exhausted by the end.

june 7

The King of Cool

Dean Martin was so cool even Frank Sinatra wanted to be him. Dino made it all look so easy—singing, swinging, acting, seducing, floating through his charmed life with a nonchalance that bordered on narcolepsy. He lived by his own oft-repeated credo: "Fuck everything."

He was born Dino Crocetti this day in Steubenville, Ohio, in 1917. After a brief career as a boxer with the name "Kid Crochet" ("I was paid ten dollars a match," he recalled. "Out of a dozen fights, I won all but eleven"), he fell in with small-time gangsters and got a job dealing cards in local gambling houses. But more than anything else, Dino Crocetti liked to sing—and took off on a series of low-paying gigs in Italian restaurants and dinner clubs. He modeled his style on Bing Crosby's—a smooth, seductive bel-canto baritone that sounded so casual he could've been sleepwalking. After a nose job (paid for by Lou Costello—who, according to legend, never got repaid), he met a young comic named Jerry Lewis. The two teamed up, and Martin and Lewis became the biggest show business sensation of their day. But there was no love lost between the increasingly estranged partners. When the team played their last date together, a misty-eyed Jerry told Dean that he loved him. Dean stared his ex-partner in the eye and said coolly, "You can talk about love all you want, pallie. To me, you're nothing but a fucking dollar sign."

The conventional wisdom of the day was that Jerry would continue on to huge solo success and Dean would fade from view. Dean proved them wrong—delivering a convincingly good dramatic performance alongside the likes of Montgomery Clift and Marlon Brando in *The Young Lions* (1957).

But Dean Martin's golden hour as an actor was in a genre he loved, the western. In **Rio Bravo** (1959), he plays Dude, a washed-up lawman who has fallen into drink and hard times. His old boss, Sheriff John Chance (John Wayne), is in a fix, determined to keep a prisoner in jail despite an impending assault from the man's friends and limited manpower. Dude tries to sober up to lend support, helped along by old Stumpy (Walter Brennan, in full Amos McCoy mode) and young gunslinger Colorado (Ricky Nelson, pretty but vacant). Martin is scruffy and convincing as the recovering alcoholic with the shaky hands, compelling and honest in a monologue about the callow weakness behind the easy-going charm. Eventually, Martin would resort to merely strolling through his roles, but *Rio Bravo* was a revelation, the confirmation of a gifted actor. And he was pretty good with those pistols, too.

june 8

You Can Lead a Horticulture . . .

On this day in 1937, the world's largest flower ever recorded up until that time came into full bloom in the New York Botanical Garden—a breathtaking twelve-foot calla lily. Crowds lined up for hours to see the gargantuan flower, which lasted all of three days.

Audrey is a plant, too—and breathtaking in its own way—in **Little Shop of Horrors** (1960 and 1986). A carnivorous hybrid, Audrey craves human flesh to keep growing—and growing. There are two versions of *Little Shop of Horrors.* Roger Corman's original 1960 version, a spectacularly inventive low-budget masterpiece, was filmed in an astonishing three days, and features a classic cameo by a very young Jack Nicholson as a masochistic dental patient who enjoys the pain. Corman's directorial inventiveness under such tight budgetary constraints rightfully earned him a reputation as the kind of creative filmmaker the industry loves. A marvelously inventive movie, spoofing everything from sci-fi movies to Jerry Lewis to *Dragnet, Little Shop of Horrors* is a textbook example of how to make a hugely enjoyable film on a next-to-nothing budget.

Little Shop of Horrors developed a cult reputation over the years and inspired a Broadway musical in the '70s—which in turn served as the basis for the movie remake. *Little Shop of Horrors* (1986) stars Rick Moranis as shy flower shop assistant Seymour, Ellen Greene (carried over from the original Broadway show) as his girlfriend Audrey, and a scene-stealing supporting bit by Steve Martin as a sadistic dentist. Director Frank Oz keeps the story bizarre but amiable, and Steve Martin's solo number is his finest musical moment yet. Great cameos from John Candy, Christopher Guest, and Bill Murray in the old Nicholson role add to the fun.

june 9

Pryor on Fire

He was hot, but he wasn't supposed to be *that* hot.

Comedian Richard Pryor had been riding the crest of a creative and critical wave of success when, on this day in 1980, he was almost killed in an explosion, catching on fire while free-basing cocaine. The comedian suffered third-degree burns over half of his body and was not expected to live. But after months of tortuously painful treatments, rehabilitation, and skin grafts, he recovered and went on to recount the incident—hilariously—in *Richard Pryor Live on Sunset Strip* (1982).

It wasn't the first time Richard Pryor had played with fire. As a comedian, Pryor walked the razor's edge like no one since Lenny Bruce. Hollywood effectively neutered him, and he found himself a mainstream success. He was highly watchable in several films, most notably *Silver Streak* (1976; his first and best film with screen partner Gene Wilder) and *Blue Collar* (1978).

But Pryor was really in his element onstage in front of a live audience. He transcended the image of stand-up comic by using his amazingly agile body and malleable face to create a virtual gallery of masterful characters, attitudes, and situations. Luckily, his incredible talent is captured in two great films, *Richard Pryor in Concert* (1979) and **Richard Pryor Live on Sunset Strip** (1982), filmed at the Hollywood Paladium two years after his accident.

Concert is brilliant—Pryor's recounting of his heart attack is amazing—but *Live on Sunset Strip* is a revelation—the work of a sober, recovering genius at the peak of his form, facing his demons head-on—honest, brutal, and unrelentingly funny. Pryor knew the pressure was on, facing a live audience for the first time after the accident and arduous recovery in the unblinking lens of a movie camera recording the entire event. As he walks to the stage from the audience at the beginning of the show he looks like a deer caught in the headlights of expectation. But he delivers the goods—whether morphing into a cheetah in Africa or playing his beloved old "Mudbone" character one last time, Pryor's timing and delivery are astonishing. And when he gets to the pièce de résistance—his account of his addiction and the accident —he combines comedy, theater, and therapy to invent an entirely new art. It's the ultimate "performance art," and it's never been more entertaining, brilliant, or laugh-out-loud funny.

june 10

Witch Film to Watch Tonight

On this day in 1692, the first witch execution took place in Salem Village, in the Massachusetts Bay Colony. Bridget Bishop was hanged after being found guilty of witchcraft by a court of law. It all began when two young girls, nine-year-old Elizabeth Parris (the daughter of an influential local reverend) and her friend and cousin, eleven-year-old Abigail Williams, started to experience fits and show signs of hysterical behavior. A doctor was summoned and, based on tales the girls told, determined that they were suffering from the effects of witchcraft. The young girls went along with the diagnosis, and, under pressure from the doctor, named three women whom they claimed were witches. Soon, the girls were joined by other "afflicted" victims, and an ever-widening circle of local residents, mostly middle-aged women, were accused of sorcery and witchcraft. Eventually, nineteen men and women were executed.

Commemorate the mass hysteria that prompted the Salem Witch Trials with **The Crucible** (1996), based on Arthur Miller's successful 1953 play. Although she's a little too old for the part, Wynona Ryder is convincingly wild-eyed as the disturbed Abigail Williams, showing the vulnerability behind her venom. The impressive and versatile Daniel Day-Lewis delivers another solid performance as John Proctor, the object of her hysterical attentions, and Joan Allen is typically brilliant as his victimized wife. The whole cast is perfect, and director Nicholas Hytner's scrupulous attention to period detail pays off in a big way.

june 11

S' Wonderful, S' Marvelous . . . S' Gershwin

George Gershwin was arguably the most influential and brilliant American composer ever—mixing elements of classical music, jazz, and pop into an art form that no one else has matched. His "Rhapsody in Blue" is possibly the single most recognized symphonic piece of the last hundred years. On this night in 1937, he died at the age of thirty-eight of a brain tumor. He was midway through writing the score for *The Goldwyn Follies;* one of his last songs was "Our Love Is Here to Stay."

Celebrate the life of one of America's greatest composers with Gene Kelly's dazzling cinematic interpretation of his work, **An American in Paris** (1951). Kelly plays an ex-G.I. who stays in Paris after the war to study painting. He is supported by rich American Nina Foch, who subsidizes Kelly's efforts in hopes of reciprocated affection, but Kelly falls for petite Leslie Caron, who is engaged to an older man. But the story is inconsequential next to Gershwin's resplendent music and Kelly's spellbinding dancing and choreography. The highlight is the longest single dance sequence ever filmed—the astonishing climactic seventeen-minute ballet to the title song. Other Gershwin classics featured in this great movie include "I Got Rhythm," "Nice Work if You Can Get It," "S' Wonderful," "Our Love Is Here to Stay," and "Embraceable You."

june 12

Justice Delayed

Medgar Evers was one of the most influential and effective Civil Rights leaders in the early '60s. On this night in 1963, while stepping out of his car in front of his Jackson, Mississippi, home, he was shot and killed by an assailant in the darkness. He was thirty-seven years old. The killer, a white supremacist named Byron De La Beckwith, was caught, but released after two hung juries could not reach a verdict. Thirty years later, Evers's widow finally succeeded in getting a new trial, and Beckwith was convicted. He died in January 2001.

Ghosts of Mississippi (1996) reconstructs the fateful day and its long-delayed day in court. Whoopi Goldberg stars as Myrlie Evers, the tenacious widow who unrelentingly seeks justice for her husband's murder, and Alec Baldwin is typically stolid as the assistant D.A. in charge of the case. An intriguing combination of social drama, detective story, and courtroom drama, *Ghosts of Mississippi* does an effective job of squeezing a lot of history into a tight narrative. James Wood delivers a knockout performance as the reprehensible Byron De La Beckwith. Directed by Rob Reiner.

june 13

Trial and Erin

On this day in 1994, Judge LeRoy Simmons of the Superior Court for the County of San Bernardino, California, handed down a decision that would irrevocably affect the outcome of one of the most influential—and inspiring—court cases of our time: the case of the town of Hinkley, California, vs. PG&E. A substantial portion of the population of Hinkley, a small town near Barstow, California, had become sick—the cancer rate was astonishingly high. The charge against PG&E was that it had knowingly misled the citizens about the addition of a cancer-causing chemical, hexavalent chromium (better known as chrome 6), to their water supply. PG&E denied knowledge that it was aware of the dangers of chrome 6 at the time of possible contamination. Judge Simmons's decision effectively laid the ground rules: If it could be proven that PG&E did indeed have foreknowledge that its water supplies in Hinkley were potentially harmful to residents, it could be held liable.

What PG&E didn't count on was the resourcefulness and determination of Erin Brockovich, a local legal secretary who, in the process of doing some basic research on a pro bono case, came across potentially damaging evidence against PG&E. Almost single-handedly, Brockovich unearthed testimonies and evidence against the huge corporation. Largely as a result of her efforts, PG&E ended up settling with the plaintiffs for the astonishing sum of 333 million dollars.

Celebrate the power of one in the inspiring and uplifting **Erin Brockovich** (2000). Julia Roberts delivers a galvanizing performance in the title role, evolving from a desperate unemployed single mom into a one-woman army who doggedly, resolutely fights for justice and brings a major corporation to its knees. Albert Finney costars as her curmudgeonly boss, lawyer Ed Masry, who reluctantly takes on the case and finds himself at the center of the hurricane. Director Steven Soderbergh (*Sex, Lies & Videotape; Traffic*) does a fabulous job in condensing a complex legal story into an entertaining, enlightening, and involving movie experience. Inspiring, uplifting, and surprisingly humorous, *Erin Brockovich* is a testament to the power of a single committed individual. (Keep an eye open for a cameo by the real Erin Brockovich as a waitress.)

june 14

Let Your Attention Flag

Today is Flag Day. Celebrate by watching one of Clint Eastwood's most underrated movies: **Bronco Billy** (1980). In this thoroughly enchanting, comedic film fable, Eastwood plays "Bronco" Billy Anderson, a former shoe salesman who makes a living traveling with a modern-day Wild West show with his ragtag troupe of misfit performers. Billy's great with a lariat and six-shooter, and he always does his best to leave his "li'l pards" with a strong moral lesson. Trouble is, times are tough in a land where the Wild West has been eclipsed by shopping malls and *Star Wars*. Sondra Locke is the spoiled young heiress who takes refuge with the troupe, which gradually softens her up. Eastwood displays a charm and surprising sweet pathos that he never quite equals elsewhere. If Frank Capra had ever filmed a Western, it would've looked a little like this. The sequence where Billy and his gang try to rob a modern-day train on horseback is both funny and whimsical.

You may be wondering what this has to do with flags. Watch the movie and you'll see. Trust me.

june 15

One Good Cop

On this day in 1972, amidst much media hoopla, Detective Frank Serpico of the Eighty-first Precinct in New York City resigned from the police force. He had joined in 1959, proud to be a cop and anxious to do his part. One night while the young rookie and his partner were on patrol, Serpico pulled over a car for running a red light. The suspect apologized and said he was late for work and had failed to see the light. Serpico was about to let him go when the man offered him thirty-five dollars. Serpico returned to his patrol car and informed his partner of the bribery attempt. His partner told him to wait in the car and he'd take care of it. When he returned, he offered Serpico half of the money that he had gladly taken. Serpico refused.

From that point on, Frank Serpico was a thorn of consciousness in the side of crooked cops and became ostracized by pretty much the entire New York City Police Department. It all came to a head on February 3, 1971, during a drug raid in an inner-city apartment house. Serpico was shot point-blank in the face—and his fellow officers did nothing to help him.

His story is vividly brought to life in **Serpico** (1973), starring Al Pacino in a bravura performance as the nonconformist crusader who starts out as an active idealist and ends up weary, worn-out, and deserted. The first of director Sidney Lumet's "corruption" films, followed by *Prince of the City, Q&A,* and *Night Falls on Manhattan.* As he often does, Lumet filmed entirely in New York City, and the story has a kinetic authenticity to it. Pacino gives a heated performance; he's not afraid to show some of the egotistical and alienating behavior of a man who possesses a streak of both self-righteousness and self-destruction.

june 16

Get Down in Monterey

The first—and arguably best—rock festival ever kicked off on this day in 1967. The Monterey Pop Festival was an unprecedented event, bringing together the psychedelic San Francisco scene and the laid-back southern California contingency for three days of "peace, love, and music." It was the music that made history, with a killer lineup of performers, including the Mamas and the Papas, Simon and Garfunkel, Ravi Shankar, Otis Redding, Hugh Masekela and career-making performances from Janis Joplin, Jimi Hendrix, and the Who.

Luckily, director D. A. Pennebaker was there to film the event for ABC Television. The resulting movie, **Monterey Pop** (1969), is more than a time capsule—it's a classic, cathartic snapshot of a music scene that was so diverse and eclectic that it branched out into a thousand genres in the years to come. Joplin's jaw-droppingly passionate rendition of "Ball and Chain" literally made her a star overnight (look for a great shot of Mama Cass Elliott shaking her head in awed disbelief), and Jimi Hendrix's orgasmic sacrificial burning of his guitar scared the bejeezus out of middle-American PTA members. An evocative movie of a cultural and musical event that bordered on a dream. Like the song says, be sure to wear some flowers in your hair.

june 17

A Botched Burglary That Brought Down the President

"Nothing's riding on this except the First Amendment of the Constitution, freedom of the press, and maybe the future of the country."
—Ben Bradlee (Jason Robards, Jr.)

In the early morning hours of this day in 1972, Washington, D.C., police received a call from a security guard at the nearby Watergate hotel and office complex about a burglary in progress. Officers arrived on the sixth floor in time to arrest five men, including James McCord of the Committee to Reelect the President, for burglarizing Democratic Party National Headquarters at the Watergate Hotel: Thus began the domino effect that eventually went all the way to the White House and toppled the presidency of Richard Nixon.

Follow the trail of deceit, corruption, and intrigue in one of the most accurate movies ever made on the fine art of journalistic detective work, **All the President's Men** (1976). Robert Redford and Dustin Hoffman give credible, nonshowy performances as *Washington Post* reporters Bob Woodward and Carl Bernstein, who team up to track down the story of the burglary—and just how deep it goes. Jason Robards, Jr., gives excellent support as crusty editor Ben Bradlee (he received an Oscar for Best Supporting Actor that year). Taut direction by Alan J. Pakula and an intelligent script by William Goldman help make this movie that rarest of genre successes—a suspenseful true-life political thriller.

june 18

Rock 'n' Roll Riot

The first officially recognized rock riot broke out at the National Guard Armory in Washington, D.C., this night in 1956. An audience of nearly five thousand—mostly teens—had gathered to see Bill Haley and the Comets. When Haley took the stage a little after ten P.M., the kids leaped into the aisles to dance, only to be chased by the cops back to their seats. Amidst the dancing, a melee broke out. "It's the jungle strain got 'em all worked up," observed the armory manager. The event made the papers the following morning.

Celebrate that rockin' rebellion with the movie that helped start it all, **The Blackboard Jungle** (1955), the first teen exploitation flick. Bill Haley's "Rock Around the Clock" was its opening theme. In England, the film was outlawed due to "teen riots"; teens literally ripped seats out of the cinema during the opening credits. The movie itself is a fairly compelling drama starring Glenn Ford as a new teacher at a tough inner-city high school. Sidney Poitier is the gifted student with potential who has a chip on his shoulder, but tough guy Vic Morrow steals the picture as the class sociopath. And yes, that is indeed Jamie Farr (*M*A*S*H*'s Corporal Klinger) as a young student.

Make it a rockin' double bill with **Rock, Rock, Rock** (1956), featuring a starring role by legendary DJ Alan Freed, before his tragic fall from grace. A great little quickie exploitation flick, it boasts rare footage and performances of such greats as LaVern Baker, Frankie Lymon and the Teenagers, the Flamingos, and more. Not only that, you get Tuesday Weld, too. Hubba, hubba.

june 19

Get Tuckered Out

It was one of the ballsiest, most radical experiments in automotive history. On this day in 1947, in front of a roomful of photographers, journalists, and curious competitors, auto designer and entrepreneur Preston Tucker unveiled his much-anticipated Tucker Torpedo automobile—a revolutionary car with an engine in the rear and a single revolving headlight. Two days earlier, he had written an open letter to the industry, published in several newspapers, in which he stood his ground against the established giants. Because Detroit choked off Tucker's access to materials, he only managed to produce a few of the unique Tucker Torpedoes before he went bankrupt. The Don Quixote of Capitalism died penniless years later, still trying to launch a follow-up.

Celebrate his vision and tenacity in **Tucker: The Man and His Dream** (1988), a film by another man with vision and tenacity, Francis Ford Coppola. The director, who no doubt identified with his visionary subject, delivers an ingratiating and inspiring story of taking on the suits with stubborn individualism and integrity. Jeff Bridges is dynamic and endearing as the quixotic Tucker, and Martin Landau is affecting as the investor who believes in Tucker but who has an embarrassing and incriminating past behind him. Look for a great cameo by Dean Stockwell as another obstinate American visionary, Howard Hughes.

june 20

Go Bugsy

Benjamin "Bugsy" Siegal was obsessed with class, cash, and success and lived several lifetimes in his short thirty-nine years. He was a savvy and ruthless hit man for Meyer Lansky and the Mob. He once sold a defective explosive compound to Benito Mussolini. He embarked on an expedition to Cocos Island in search of rumored buried treasure, and when he didn't find it, he literally blew up half the island. He hobnobbed with movie stars, hung out with Gable and Grant, and even coached his boyhood pal George Raft on how to play a real gangster. To top it all off, Siegal had movie star good looks himself and probably could have been a star.

In 1945 Bugsy had a vision that everyone else thought was crazy: He wanted to transform a sleepy, barren desert community east of Los Angeles into a glitzy oasis of gambling and show biz. He spent $6 million to build Las

Vegas's first megahotel and casino, the Flamingo, financed in part by his connections with the Mob. But his fatal mistake was skimming a little too much off the top. When developer Del Webb expressed concern over where some of the money was coming from, Bugsy eased his anxieties, responding, "Don't worry. We only kill each other."

And on this day in 1947, while he was sitting in his girlfriend's $500,000 mansion in Beverly Hills, somebody proved him right, blasting a fusillade of bullets into his body through the front window. At the exact moment Bugsy was dying, Meyer Lansky's boys were walking into the Flamingo and taking over.

But it was a sweet life while he lived it. Luckily, Warren Beatty saw the potential for a film about Bugsy Siegal and produced and starred in **Bugsy** (1991). Beatty is both endearing and scary as the mobster, and Annette Bening is sensational as his mistress, actress Virginia Hill. Whether he's trying to better his education through language skills, plotting to kill Mussolini, or juggling a business meeting, a phone call from Virginia, and his daughter's birthday meal, Beatty is unabashedly admiring of the tenacious dreamer. A sparkling script by James Toback and snappy direction by Barry Levinson make *Bugsy* so good it's criminal.

june 21

Working in a Coal Mine

By the 1870s, hundreds of Irish immigrants were toiling away in anthracite mines throughout Pennsylvania. It was a dangerous and poorly paid vocation. Potentially explosive methane gas could be set off by a spark, and in the meantime soot caked on the laborers' lungs in layers. On the average, ten workers died every week.

The Molly Maguires were a "secret society" which became an instrument of vengeance against the oppressive mine owners, the railroad, and company foremen. Legend has it they were named after a tenacious Irish widow who was heartlessly evicted from her land. In their quest for better working conditions, the Molly Maguires sabotaged the mines—destroying equipment, blowing up trestle bridges, and pulling up railroad spikes to derail cars. The company retaliated by hiring the Pinkerton Detective Agency, which in turn recruited an undercover operative, James McParlan, to infiltrate the radical group to obtain evidence against them. For two years McParlan lived with the Mollys, privy to their plans, before testifying. His testimony sent twenty men to the gallows and effectively ended the Molly Maguires. The first eleven were hanged on this day in 1877 in Scranton, Pennsylvania. Was McParlan a hero or a weasel? Were the Molly Maguires heartless terrorists or humanitarian activists?

The Molly Maguires (1969) attempts to answer these questions. And, since it was directed by Martin Ritt (*Norma Rae; The Front*) it does a compelling job of mixing historical fact with Hollywood fiction. The first twelve minutes, a wordless descent into the mines, is a harrowing evocation of the dark, claustrophobic, and dangerous working conditions into which the laborers ventured every day. Sean Connery stars as Jack Kehoe, the charismatic leader of the Molly Maguires, and, in one of his most understated turns, Richard Harris plays McParlan. *The Molly McGuires* shows the fine and ambiguous lines between activism and terrorism, friendship and betrayal.

june 22

End of the Rainbow

Judy Garland died this day in 1969, after stumbling blindly in the bathroom of her London apartment, of an apparent overdose of sedatives. She was forty-six years old, and she lived on the edge through every one of them. In *A Biographical Dictionary of Film,* David Thomson comments astutely that "Garland left deep impressions on many viewers, but ruinous ones on herself."

She was born Frances Gumm on June 10, 1922, in Grand Rapids, Minnesota—a town she tended to romanticize in later life as "a wonderful town." From the age of three, when she began performing professionally with her older sisters as "Baby Gumm," she was destined for a life of performing. Both her parents were frustrated artists, all her siblings were performers, and her mother seemed to live her dreams vicariously through her daughter.

Pushed by her mother, Ethel, Frances and her sisters toured as the Gumm Sisters, although young Frances was always the focus and had the biggest voice. After a 1935 audition, MGM head honcho Louis B. Mayer as much as adopted Frances—and set about the process of reinventing her as Judy Garland.

Once she was under contract to MGM, Mayer wanted to take off some of her baby fat—and promptly forced on her a starvation diet, complete with lackeys whose job was to see to it that she consumed nothing but chicken soup at the studio commissary. Diet pills (supplied by the studio doctor) kept her edgy and awake, so her mother gave her sleeping pills to counteract the diet pills. It's no wonder she was such an emotional mess.

She was a natural-born actress—a truly natural creature of film—who projected such guileless warmth and honesty that she was instantly believable in anything, whether as the young small-town girl in the delightful *Meet Me in St. Louis* (1944) or, nearly twenty years later, as the tortured German hausfrau she played so memorably in *Judgment at Nuremberg.* (1961).

But her greatest performance, the one that utilizes both her acting and her singing talents to their fullest, is in **A Star Is Born**, her 1954 musical remake of the Janet Gaynor/Frederick March drama of 1937, coscripted by Dorothy Parker. Garland should have won Best Actress that year, but didn't. She gives the performance of her life as Vicki Lester, the young singer who skyrockets to stardom thanks to being discovered by rapidly slipping matinee idol Norman Maine (an appropriately charismatic but weak James Mason). She falls in love with the fading star, but her love is not enough to save him from himself. And just to watch Garland perform "The Man That Got Away" alone is worth the price of admission. The film was severely edited before its initial release (the entire twenty-minute-long "Born in a Trunk" musical number was cut); it has since been restored with missing scenes, stills, and audio.

june 23

Think Pink

Today is National Pink Day. The possibilities are as endless as they are potentially headache-inducing. You could watch John Waters's epochal exercise in bad taste, the notorious *Pink Flamingos* (1972), in which Divine and Mink Stole compete for the title of "Filthiest Person Alive," and Divine immortalized himself in the Hall of Gross. There's the *Pink Panther* series with Peter Sellers; all closet Clouseau buffs can hold a marathon. Molly Ringwald fans (Hello, out there?) can savor *Pretty in Pink* (1986), one of John Hughes's best efforts.

But my vote for best way to celebrate National Pink Day is Walt Disney's delightful animated tale of **Dumbo** (1941), featuring the classic "Pink Elephants on Parade" musical number. Filmed after the box office bomb *Fantasia, Dumbo* marked a return to form for Disney—and was a huge popular hit. It lacks any of his cloying aspirations at being artistic and, perversely, thus becomes art. The simple story of an orphaned elephant who can fly because of his giant ears takes to the heights in more ways than one. But the most dazzling sequence is "Pink Elephants on Parade"—a colorful representation of a nasty hangover. Have some bromo handy.

june 24

Starkweather We're Having

Like many teenagers in the late 1950s, Charlie Starkweather was obsessed with James Dean, fast cars, and rock 'n' roll. But Charlie had other, darker obsessions: He was a total psychopath who thought nothing of killing anyone, anytime, anywhere. When he met up with precocious fourteen-year-old Caril Ann Fugate, it was star-crossed young love at first sight, and they roared off into a crime spree that terrified the Plains states area throughout the winter of 1958, robbing and killing at random. The law quickly caught up with Starkweather, and he was executed by electric chair on this day in 1959 at Nebraska State Penitentiary.

The duo's exploits inspired several movies, not the least being Oliver Stone's controversial *Natural Born Killers.* But the best treatment of their sorry tale is Terrence Malick's first feature, **Badlands** (1973). Starring a young Martin Sheen as Charlie (renamed "Kit") and the appropriately-named Sissy Spacek as his acquiesecent girlfriend, "Holly," Malick's camera achieves a kind of elegiac poetry (he would later go on to direct *Days of Heaven* [1977] and *The Thin Red Line* [1998]), and the director's mesmerizing ability makes the mundane seem profound. A disturbing but beautiful film. Featuring the late great Warren Oates as Holly's ill-fated dad.

june 25

Catch a Little Big Movie

General George Armstrong Custer was one arrogant, vain, none-too-bright soldier (he graduated dead last in his class at West Point), and would have made for nothing more than an asterisk in American Civil War history if not for an event that happened on this day in 1876 at Little Big Horn, near what is now Billings, Montana.

The seminal event—forever after known as Custer's Last Stand—has been re-created in countless films. Errol Flynn portrayed a revamped, cleaned-up, and politically correct Custer in *They Died with Their Boots On* (1941), an entertaining whitewash that strays so far from the trail of truth it even has Custer as an advocate for the Indians! *Son of the Morning Star* (1991) is a little closer to the truth—and all the more boring because of it.

But by far the most entertaining version of Custer's Last Stand—if Custer's Last Stand can be considered as entertainment—is Arthur Penn's epic satire/homage to the Old West, **Little Big Man** (1970). Dustin Hoffman gives a chameleonlike performance as Jack Crabb, who is either the greatest liar in the world or the one man who was present at virtually every historic moment of the Wild West. During his adventures, Crabb is hired by General George Custer (Richard Mulligan, in a performance both frightening and funny) as a muleskinner. Not only is Jack responsible for Custer's calamitous decision to venture into the Little Big Horn—he's the sole white survivor! Directed by Arthur Penn (*Bonnie and Clyde*), *Little Big Man* is alternately funny, tragic, and action-packed—with a great supporting turn from Faye Dunaway as the not-so-prim-and-proper Mrs. Pendrake. Chief Dan George all but steals the movie as Jack's adoptive grandfather, Old Lodge Skins.

june 26

The Allure of Lorre

He planned, and studied, to be a psychiatrist. Instead, he ran away from home to become an actor. Good thing, too; imagine confessing your innermost thoughts, fears, and dreams to Peter Lorre.

He was born Laszlo Lowenstein on this day, 1904, in Hungary. Chaplin called him the greatest actor of the screen. Adolf Hitler agreed, extending a generous invitation to make films under the Third Reich, but Lorre declined, reportedly saying, "I'm afraid there's room for only one mass murderer of my ability and yours in Germany."

Peter Lorre had an otherworldly quality that was absolutely unique—an ability to tap into the creepiest corners of the human psyche (that psychiatric training came in handy) while projecting a childlike charm and vulnerability. He could play a sadistic murderer, a bewildered immigrant, or a cowering weasel—often all in the same part (check out his Raskolnikov in Von Sternberg's *Crime and Punishment*). Hitchcock used him to wonderful effect in two early films, *The Man Who Knew Too Much* (the actor's first film in English; he learned his lines phonetically) and *Secret Agent.* He was notorious for his scene-stealing ad-libs and on-set practical jokes. During the filming of *Casablanca,* he was seen exiting Ingrid Bergman's dressing room, zipping up his pants and saying "Thanks, Ingrid!" in front of a set full of visiting nuns. In later life, he was hobbled by ill health and obesity, and reportedly he was a morphine addict for much of his life.

His greatest role was as the tortured child killer in Fritz Lang's **M** (1930). It's an astonishing performance. Lorre creates a sense of dread as the murderer (he can be heard whistling Grieg's "Peer Gynt Suite" before he strikes). But when he's chased down and cornered by a makeshift tribunal of the city's criminals, he pathetically pleads that he cannot help what he does—and you believe him; miraculously, he turns from monster to victim in front of your eyes.

june 27

Write On

"Watch me run a fifty-yard dash with my legs cut off."
—Sidney Falco (Tony Curtis)

Today is National Columnists Day, a day that would be close to any gossip columnist's heart—assuming they had one. Observe this special day by starting a vicious rumor about someone, watch the sparks fly, and then settle in to watch a true master in action in **Sweet Smell of Success** (1957). Burt Lancaster delivers one of his best and bravest performances as Hunsucker—Big City King of the Newspaper Gossips, who wields the power to make or break a person like a dried-up twig between his fingers. Tony Curtis is Sidney Falco, the ambitious gossip-gatherer who helps Hunsucker do his dirty work—and rivals him in deviousness. "I'd hate to take a bite out of you," Lancaster tells him. "You're a cookie full of arsenic." This is a nasty piece of work about a nasty piece of business, black as the slippery and treacherous Manhattan avenues that Sidney haunts. A blistering screenplay by Clifford Odets and Ernest Lehman.

june 28

They Didn't Call Her Great for Nothing

Unlike most monarchs, Catherine the Great is remembered mostly for the number of lovers she had—but as to whether or not that's how she acquired her nickname is another matter. On this day in 1762, Catherine became the empress of Russia, after a military coup. She was thirty-three years old.

She was expected to provide an heir—but her husband, the infantile Peter, was impotent and never shared her bed. So, secretly encouraged by the dowager empress Elizabeth, she took on three lovers—each of whom she had a child with.

Commemorate the life of an amazing and amorous woman with **The Scarlet Empress** (1934). Marlene Dietrich is a far-fetched but fetching Catherine. Directed by the great Josef von Sternberg, *The Scarlet Empress* is a dizzying pastiche of costume drama, burlesque, romance, and spectacle. So rich in imagery that it borders on gaudy, the film is a bravura showcase for von Sternberg's skills as a director and Dietrich's imperious kitsch. She gets to dress up in male military drag, kill her idiotic husband, and lead an entire army into the palace. Now *that's* entertainment.

june 29

A Defective Movie

It was art vs. politics on this day in 1974. Twenty-five-year-old Soviet ballet dancer extraordinaire Mikhail Baryshnikov had just received a standing ovation after a performance while touring in Canada with the Kirov ballet. He exited into a mob of adoring fans at the rear of the theater, signing autographs, then suddenly sprinted to a car waiting two blocks away. The crowd gave chase, along with several Soviet police "bodyguards," but Baryshnikov made it successfully to the car, and was spirited away to a new life. He went on to become the most successful—and popular—dancer ever, eventually becoming artistic director of the American Ballet Theater. Along the way, he dabbled in acting, and became one of the few "athletes" to prove a more than capable thespian.

He made his acting debut in *The Turning Point* (1977) in a secondary juvenile role that allowed him to show his dancing skills along with his tentative but undeniable charm. His best role is in **White Nights** (1985). In a role created to mirror his own experiences, Baryshnikov plays a famous Russian ballet dancer (now there's a stretch!) now living in America, whose plane is forced to make a landing in the old homeland. The hapless dancer finds himself a prisoner in the country he abandoned ten years earlier. Gregory Hines makes for a pleasant screen partner in this fairly representative example of the very small subgenre known as "dancing buddy pictures." Cool dance sequences (a little classical ballet, a little tap, a splash of modern jazz), nice performances, and good direction by Taylor Hackford (*An Officer and a Gentleman*). Baryshnikov isn't called on to do much emoting, but the dancing is still breathtaking.

june 30

As Long as She Had Sufficient Time to Grieve . . .

On this day in 1975 Cher, divorced only four days earlier from her first husband, Sonny Bono, married rock star Gregg Allman. In retrospect, maybe she should have waited another day.

Exploitation rags across the country constantly blare the question, Will Cher ever find happiness with a man? At least in the movies there's a happy ending. **Moonstruck** (1987) is Cher's best film—an observant, funny, and unsentimental appraisal of sticky romance. Cher plays Loretta, a middle-aged widow in Brooklyn who agrees to marry her longtime suitor, Johnny (Danny Aiello). But things get complicated when she falls for Johnny's kid brother, Ronny (Nicolas Cage), an opera-loving, one-handed baker. Cher is luminous, delivering an unassuming performance that taps into her gift for underplayed sarcasm. Director Norman Jewison beautifully captures Italian-American nuances, and the script by John Patrick Shanley is both saucy and wise. Great support from Olympia Dukakis (as Cher's mom) and John Mahoney as her admirer. Cher and Dukakis each won Oscars for their performances. Warning: You'll have "That's Amore" in your head for the next three days.

july

july 1

Blame Canada

Today is Canada Day, formerly known as Dominion Day. Celebrate with a breakfast of Canadian bacon, and then sit back to enjoy that fine example of state-of-the-art animation, sophisticated wit, and tasteful restraint, **South Park** (1999), the outrageously in-your-face animated movie of the cable cult hit TV series. When South Park residents Cartman, Kyle, Stan, and Kenny ("Oh, my God, they've killed Kenny! You bastards!") get into trouble by sneaking into an R-rated movie, their parents declare war on Canada, and Satan and Saddam Hussein get into bed together. (Hey, it's that kind of movie.) Tasteless, offensive, gross, and out-and-out hilarious. This ain't your mommy and daddy's cartoons, kids. Then again, maybe it is.

july 2

Leave the Doors Open Tonight

Jim Morrison, a.k.a. the Lizard King, one of rock's true icons and lead singer for the Doors, spent his last night on earth in his Paris apartment this night in 1971, dying in his bathtub—bloated, bearded, and burned out at twenty-seven. His girlfriend, Pamela Courson, discovered his body early the next morning. For all intents and purposes, he was dead long before that; he just hadn't shucked off his mortal coil.

Was Morrison a visionary poet or a self-absorbed derivative hack? Critics and music fans argue over that question for endless hours. What just about everyone can agree on is that Morrison was a deeply charismatic presence whether onstage or off. He was dangerously volatile, darkly handsome, willfully self-destructive—a cross between Elvis Presley and Arthur Rimbaud. His lyrics were dark, too—but they could also be impenetrably sophomoric. But when he sang in that earth-rumbling, powerful, slurring baritone, he approached greatness.

Observe the anniversary of his passing through the Doors of earthly existence with **The Doors** (1987) an impressively mounted change of pace for maverick director Oliver Stone. In a piece of stunt casting that actually pays off, petulant screen hunk Val Kilmer scarily inhabits the Lizard King's skin in a virtuoso performance of self-destruction, seemingly conjuring and channeling Morrison's unpredictable and volatile spirit. He even sounds like Morrison. Meg Ryan plays against type as his drug-addled girlfriend, Pamela Courson.

july 3

Raid on Entebbe

In late June 1976, a group of PLO terrorists managed to hijack a French airliner with 258 passengers aboard, 103 of them Israeli citizens. They rerouted the plane to Uganda, where dictator Idi Amin welcomed them with open arms. Amin was a rabid anti-Semite, as well as being one of history's most vicious dictators. He was known to have executed well over 300,000 Ugandans—including his own wife and son.

Once safely at the Ugandan airport, the PLO terrorists demanded the release of fifty-two of their members being held in various countries. Israeli President Yitzhak Rabin held off on any kind of rescue attempt, until the terrorists surprised everyone by releasing the non-Jewish hostages. Then Rabin moved swiftly.

On this day in 1976, 3,200 Israeli soldiers boarded four C-130H cargo planes and lifted off for Uganda. When the planes touched down in Uganda, one of the most spectacular and successful hostage rescues ever attempted was executed with flawless precision. The assault teams stunned the surprised PLO, attacking in waves. They killed seven terrorists, losing only one of their own men. Within the hour, the hostages were free and heading home.

Raid on Entebbe (1976) recounts the events leading up to and including the rescue in one of the most historically accurate films ever made. An eclectic but effective cast includes Peter Finch, James Woods (in a rare sympathetic role), Sylvia Sidney, Charles Bronson, and, in a charismatic performance, Yaphet Kotto as Idi Amin. A visceral, straightforward account of the event which, not unpredictably, has precious little time for the Palestinian side of the story, and keeps the political issues suitably low-key. Directed by Irwin Kershner.

july 4

Happy Birthday, America . . .

. . . And happy anniversary to the Declaration of Independence, signed this day in 1776. For such a red-letter day in American history, the holiday has spawned little in the way of memorable movies.

Although not really about the Fourth of July per se, a suitable movie to celebrate the occasion would be *The Patriot* (1999). Mel Gibson stars as Benjamin Martin, a weary veteran of the French-Indian War who just wants to settle down and raise his family in peace, but who, along with his patriotic son Gabriel (Heath Ledger) gets caught up in the cause against the British. Gibson is impressive, and the battle sequences bring this entertaining history lesson to vivid life.

Depending on your preference, there are several other cinematic options. For sheer over-the-top, popcorn-consuming, FX-laden dumb entertainment, try *Independence Day* (1996). It's definitely a Fourth of July kinda movie.

For a more sobering take on the holiday, Oliver Stone's **Born on the Fourth of July** (1989) is perhaps his most mainstream and accomplished film, with Tom Cruise delivering a credible and affecting performance as real-life Vietnam vet Ron Kovick, a young idealist who went to Vietnam and returned a paraplegic. A movie that both questions the danger of myopic patriotism while fervently defending it, *Born on the Fourth of July* is compelling filmmaking.

A couple of musicals lend themselves to the occasion: *1776* (1972), based on the signing of the Declaration of Independence, is so stupifyingly hokey that it just might entertain you—for two and a half long hours. But for sheer patriotic vim and vigor, for pure, undiluted red-white-and-blue in black-and-white Hollywood hokum, it's tough to beat **Yankee Doodle Dandy** (1942), starring James Cagney in his Oscar-winning role as Broadway songwriter and hoofer George M. Cohan. Released right after the bombing of Pearl Harbor, *Yankee Doodle Dandy* was intended to fan the fires of patriotism and succeeded spectacularly, featuring such flag-wavers as "Over There," "You're a Grand Old Flag," and the title song.

In the mood for a little "payback" patriotism? Low-budget film guru Larry Cohen (Q) combined the Fourth of July with the slasher/horror genre with *Uncle Sam* (1996). A Desert Storm vet who was killed in battle rises from his grave after some teenagers burn an American flag over his gravesite on July fourth. He proceeds to systematically dispatch all the unpatriotic citizens in his hometown. Now *that's* patriotism!

july 5

Support Your Local Salvation Army

On this date in 1865, William Booth founded the Salvation Army in London, England. The organization went on to become one of the largest and most honorable charitable organizations in the world, and a boon to bargain-price garment-o-philes everywhere.

Make a charitable donation to your local chapter, and then enjoy a movie that takes its plot from the honored institution of the Salvation Army, **Guys and Dolls** (1958), based on the stories and characters of Damon Runyon. Marlon Brando (barely) makes his singing debut as big-time gambler and bon vivant Sky Masterson, slick operator of New York's "oldest-established permanent floating crap game." Frank Sinatra (who *should've* played Brando's part) gets stuck with being second banana Nathan Detroit, Masterson's perennially broke cohort and competitor. When pretty Salvation Army missionary Jean Simmons sets up shop in the neighborhood, Nathan wagers $1,000 that Sky can't seduce her, hoping to use the money to keep the crap game afloat. Sky takes him up on the offer, intrigued with both the wager and the woman (you ain't lived until you've heard Marlon musically mumble "Luck Be a Lady" through his nostrils). Soon enough the Sky is falling . . . in love. Lively choreography by Michael Kidd, a classic score by Frank Loesser ("Luck Be a Lady," "Guys and Dolls," "Sit Down, You're

Rockin' the Boat"), and crisp direction by Joe Mankiewicz keep things light and lively.

july 6

More Becomes Less

On this day at Tower Hill in London, Sir Thomas More was beheaded for refusing to agree to help his friend and king, Henry VIII, annul his marriage to Catherine of Aragon. Catherine had not produced a male heir and Henry was anxious to move on to more fertile pastures; his old friend stood in his way.

A brilliant lawyer, orator, and writer, Thomas More was an impressive, witty, and steadfast man when it came to law and ethics. Henry VIII recognized him as a brilliant negotiator, and More became lord chancellor of England, before falling out of the king's favor. Sir Thomas, torn between his vows to the Church and his duty to the State, could not in good conscience condone his king's decision, and paid the ultimate price on this day in 1535.

Commemorate the passing of a great man with a great movie, **A Man for All Seasons** (1966). An engrossing, literate script by Robert Bolt (based on his play) and a charismatic, underplayed, Oscar-winning performance by Paul Scofield as More combine to create one of the finest historical dramas on film. Great supporting performances by Orson Welles as the corpulent Cardinal Wolsey and Robert Shaw as a robust Henry VIII enhance this lovingly shaded, deeply absorbing historical movie. It's literate—perhaps *too* literate—but director Fred Zinnemann does a masterful job of expanding the stage play for the cinema, anticipating the grand Merchant-Ivory productions of a generation later. *A Man for All Seasons* is the kind of rich, involving historical drama that gives costume dramas a *good* name.

july 7

Just the Facts

Dum, da-dum-dum.

You don't even need the music—the theme to *Dragnet* instantly comes to mind. On this night in 1949, listeners all across the country heard that distinctive stinger for the first time when *Dragnet* debuted over the NBC Radio airwaves. As Sgt. Joe Friday, stolid actor, producer, writer, and director Jack Webb had definitely found his niche.

The show became a huge hit with its realistic yet noirish dramatization of the procedures and banalities of everyday police life. Webb's pacing, clipped narration, and dialogue was compelling and unmistakably unique. ("This is the city. Los Angeles, California. That's where I come in. I'm a cop. I carry a badge.") In 1951 *Dragnet* became a much-loved television series, and came back again in 1967. By 1968 the show had almost become a spoof of itself, and its own creator was not hip to it.

In addition to being a hit on radio and television, *Dragnet* made it to the big screen—twice. Jack Webb wrote, produced, and directed the first version, **Dragnet** (1954), where Joe Friday (Webb, of course) and partner Frank Smith (Ben Alexander) investigate a mob slaying in Friday's beloved Los Angeles. It's packed with Webb's patented directorial and acting oddities; his sanctimonious, metronomic monologues are literally spellbinding. The staccato dialogue, the choreographed exchange of looks, and compulsive head nodding—they don't make 'em like this anymore; in fact, nobody *ever* made 'em like this except Jack Webb.

Webb's creation was always ripe for satire. (Webb himself even participated in a hilarious "Dragnet" sketch with Johnny Carson on *The Tonight Show* in the 1970s.) In **Dragnet** (1987), Harry Morgan, who played Friday's second banana, Officer Bill Gannon, in the late '60s series, is now precinct captain, and Joe has left for that big police precinct in the sky. But he did leave behind a nephew, played by doughy Dan Aykroyd in what is arguably his best comedic film role. He has the Joe Friday mannerisms down—the ramrod stride that suggests a rigid stick up his ass, the clipped, monotonic dialogue, the droning but hypnotically passionate lectures on morality and procedure. But Aykroyd brings something more to the role than Webb could ever imagine (or probably approve of)—a teddy-bear likeability and pathos that is endearing, and all too rare in Aykroyd's screen career. The movie eventually falls into flailing anything-for-a-labored-laugh territory, and Tom Hanks in a secondary role as Friday's new partner is wasted. But for those who remember the original *Dragnet,* it's a sentimental favorite, and an oddly affecting one. And those are just the facts, ma'am.

july 8

Alien Dummies Invade Roswell

On this day in 1947, the headline of the *Roswell Daily Record* in Roswell, New Mexico, proclaimed, "RAAF Captures Flying Saucer on Ranch in Roswell!" Witnesses claimed to have seen pieces of the strange aircraft, and the bodies of aliens being retrieved from the site by officers from the nearby Roswell Army Air Field. Within days the story was making headlines worldwide, and it has served as grist for the mill for UFOlogists and government conspiracy theorists ever since. Fifty years later, on June 24, 1997, the air force published "The Roswell Report: Case Closed," which claims that the bodies were "anthropomorphic test dummies that were carried aloft by U.S. Air Force high-altitude balloons for scientific research." Those so-called official tests did not commence until 1953—six full years after the sightings—but no matter. The alien was out of the bag.

Commemorate the first public announcement that we are not alone in the universe with the delightful **Men in Black** (1997). Will Smith and Tommy Lee Jones are the title characters, government agents who spend their professional lives weeding out the illegal aliens who are living among us. As in, extraterrestrial aliens. You didn't know they've been living among us for years, cleverly disguised as humanoids? How else could you account for the popularity of Sylvester Stallone and Al Roker? Director Barry Sonnenfeld keeps the laughs, action, and knock-out special effects coming. A fun, exhilarating movie, and the one in which Will Smith proved his box office power. Watch it with your favorite alien.

For a more spiritually attuned take on extraterrestrial visitations, **Close Encounters of the Third Kind** (1977) still casts a spell that is simultaneously scary and awe-inspiring. Richard Dreyfuss plays Roy, an average guy in Muncie, Indiana, who just happens to see a genuine UFO and refuses to be persuaded otherwise by doubtful family members and government representatives. Roy becomes obsessed with the experience, and eventually finds he is not the only one. Steven Spielberg's fantasy masterpiece has elements of humor, drama, science fiction, and suspense, but the overall effect is of childlike wonder and awe.

By the way, see if you can catch the continuity errors: During Dreyfuss's climactic car trip to Devil's Tower, the license plate number on his station wagon keeps changing. And during the TV news report that Dreyfuss watches, the correspondent refers to ABC anchorman Howard K. Smith as "Walter." Apparently Walter Cronkite was supposed to provide a cameo but got abducted by aliens that day.

july 9

Little Big Movie

He began to make a splash in *Splash!* After *Big* he became Very Big. With *Forrest Gump,* he was nearly made an unofficial saint.

OK—so maybe he hasn't quite been papally anointed, but if any actor were to be, it would probably be Tom Hanks, who was born this day in 1956 in the town of Concord, California.

He came from a broken home, and a constantly evolving family. Hanks knocked around community theater and did some TV (a memorable bit as a stoned-out college student in an episode of *Taxi* and costarring in the short-lived series *Bosom Buddies*) before breaking into movies.

There is something innately decent and likeable about Hanks, and it comes out in *Nothing in Common* (1986), in which he plays Jackie Gleason's son. After playing a businessman who falls in love with mermaid Daryl Hannah in Ron Howard's charmer *Splash!* (1984), his career took off. As of this writing, he's won two Best Actor Oscars—one for his brave portrayal of a gay lawyer who gets fired because he has AIDS in *Philadelphia* (1993), and one, most memorably, for his savantlike, saintly title character in *Forrest Gump* (1994).

In *Cast Away* (2000), he morphs from paunchy FedEx employee Chuck Noland into a modern-day Robinson Crusoe—losing fifty pounds in the process (Hanks had to take five months off to lose the weight and grow his hair and beard before returning to filming.)

And then there's *Forrest Gump*. Indelible as Hanks's performance is, it's a one-note samba. And the movie, while clever, is facile and downright offensive to anyone who was a leftist or liberal in the '60s; literally all the activists against the war in Vietnam are depicted as either drug-addled dimwits or misogynistic bullies.

Instead, why not savor Hanks's wonderfully inventive, very funny, and ultimately touching portrayal of Josh Baskin, a little boy who wishes he were big, and gets his wish, in **Big** (1988). Penny Marshall established herself as a major director with this charmer, which was a huge hit with audiences and solidified Hanks's box office clout. Hanks delightfully inhabits the part of the guileless Josh; his open, optimistic traits have seldom been so endearing, and he was still young enough to pull it off. Among his other gifts, Hanks seems to have a direct hot line to the child in most of us—in a Big way.

Steve Uhler

july 10

Scopes This Film Out

It was dubbed "the trial of the century," and in some places it's still going on. On this day in 1925 in Dayton, Tennessee, John Thomas Scopes, a young high school science teacher, was put on trial for the crime of teaching the theory of evolution. A recently passed state law had made it a misdemeanor to "teach any theory that denies the story of the Divine Creation of man as taught in the Bible, and to teach instead that man was descended from a lower order of animals." William Jennings Bryan, a high-profile, three-time Democratic presidential candidate and fundamentalist leader, offered to assist the prosecution. Days later, brilliant liberal lawyer and orator Clarence Darrow agreed to join the ACLU in the defense—and the stage was set for one of the most important, exciting, and thought-provoking trials of the twentieth century.

Relive the "Scopes monkey trial" with what is arguably the greatest courtroom drama ever made, **Inherit the Wind** (1960). Fredric March and Spencer Tracy give two of the finest performances of their careers as Bryan and Darrow, and the atmosphere is absolutely electric when they're sharing the screen. Tracy's climactic, passionate grilling of March on the witness stand is riveting—it is perhaps Tracy's most intense moment ever onscreen. He was never better—which means this is one of the greatest performances ever captured on celluloid, period. Stanley Kramer, in an uncharacteristically understated production, directed this enthralling, intelligent, and still-topical look at the separation of Church and State.

july 11

Saving Public Ryan

"What's before me is the fact that death is a fine, long sleep. I'm damn tired—and it can't come soon enough for me."

—Larry Slade (Robert Ryan) in The Iceman Cometh

Let us now praise neglected actors—those actors who are never selected as one of the Top 100 stars of all time, but who quietly build a unique, irreplaceable niche for themselves in the pantheon of players and the collective consciousness of film buffs everywhere.

Robert Ryan, who died on this date in 1973, at age sixty-four from cancer, was one of the most versatile and charismatic players ever to grace the big screen. Whether playing a sociopathological heel, a western bad guy, or a tortured antihero, Ryan's leathery, world-weary face burrowed its way into the audience's subconscious like no other actor before or since. He could convey seething hatred, dissipated dignity, or haggard romance (though he was almost always more likely to be a threat to women he shared scenes with). Early on, Hollywood recognized the anger Ryan could make seethe beneath the chiseled brow. He was cast as a psychotic but calculating anti-Semite in *Crossfire* (1947). As the small-town boss in *Bad Day at Black Rock* (1954) he was vacuous greed and evil on spindly legs, and his sadistic seaman Claggart in *Billy Budd* (1962) is one of the most complex screen villains ever. As he aged, Ryan's haggard features suggested a fallen idealist; his world-weary bounty hunter Deke Thornton in Sam Peckinpah's *Wild Bunch* (1969) was a logical extension of Randolph Scott's over-the-hill character in Peckinpah's earlier *Ride the Wild Country* (1961).

By the time he filmed **The Iceman Cometh** (1973) for the American Film Theater, Ryan was a lion in winter. He knew he was dying of cancer—but he summoned all his history and artistry for his farewell role, and he's a revelation in it. As Larry Slade, retired dreamer, third class, he brings an absolutely mesmerizing dimension to the character; it's as if you're watching an actor and a fictional character literally merge into one being. Lee Marvin is Hickey—the Iceman of the title—who dominates the action (or nonaction, as the case may be—the entire film takes place in a bar) by pretty much pissing on everyone's parade, including Ryan's Larry Slade. Marvin is good in the lead role (as is an impossibly young Jeff Bridges as Larry's naïve companion) but it's Robert Ryan's riveting, affecting portrayal of a weathered but upright man stoically facing the inevitable that makes this movie really great.

july 12

Give for the Cos

His career wasn't always made of Jell-O. Comedian and cultural icon Bill Cosby was born this date in Philadelphia in 1937. He was a high school dropout—joining the navy soon afterward. Upon his release, he returned to school, earned a diploma, and was awarded a football scholarship at Temple State University in Massachusetts. He went on to become a phenomenally popular stand-up comedian in the early '60s with his gentle, all-embracing humor in which he often described his childhood—which he shared with the likes of "Fat Albert" and Cosby's little brother, Russell. In 1965, Cosby showed his dramatic ability in his role as secret agent Alexander Scott, memorably partnered with Kelly Robinson (Robert Culp) in the wittiest and best-written American TV spy series ever, *I Spy* (1965–67). Cosby won two consecutive Emmies for his work in the series. He later went on to create and star in the most successful TV sitcom ever, *The Cosby Show* (1984–92). He remains one of the wealthiest entertainers in history.

For all his successes and accolades, Bill Cosby has not made much impact on Hollywood. His acting roles tend to be either bland or sugar-coated. For a while in the early '70s he bordered on pushing the envelope (*Hickey and Boggs* [1972] with old costar Culp; *Uptown Saturday Night* [1974]; *Mother, Jugs and Speed* [1976]; and paired with Richard Pryor in a lackluster segment of *California Suite* [1978]) before retiring to the comfort of his own cultivated, curmudgeonly character. So it should be no surprise that his best cinematic legacy—so far—is the one-man show of Cosby in concert, **Bill Cosby—Himself** (1982). Compared to footage from his early television appearances in the '60s, this is pretty tame, tepid stuff. It was released at a time when Richard Pryor was making his brilliant in-concert films. Cosby was considered to be passé, and his low-key film suffered in comparison to Pryor's incendiary brilliance. But *Bill Cosby—Himself* does manage to capture the apparent intimacy and charisma that have always made Cosby so ingratiating.

july 13

An Af-Fordable Evening In

When failing in his initial efforts to make a living as an actor in movies, Harrison Ford decided to chuck it all and go back to his first vocation, carpentry—designing and constructing countless beds, tables, cabinets, and patios for Hollywood's biggest stars and moguls. When one of his clients, a young up-and-coming director named George Lucas, invited him to audition for a small part in a little film he was planning called *American Graffiti,* Ford declined, telling him he could make more money as a carpenter. When Lucas told him he'd also toss in all the donuts he could eat, Ford took the part. Soon after, Lucas cast him as cocky, swashbuckling pilot Han Solo in *Star Wars,* and Harrison Ford's ascent to being the most popular actor of his generation took off at warp speed.

He was born this day in 1942 in Chicago, Illinois. No doubt you've seen his signature roles countless times: Han Solo in the *Star Wars* trilogy, Indiana Jones, CIA operative Jack Ryan, and especially his Gary Cooperish portrait of a modern cop, John Book, living among the Amish in Peter Weir's exquisite *Witness* (1985). (But perhaps you've missed some of his smaller roles for which he refused screen credit: a captain who gives Martin Sheen his assignment in *Apocalypse Now,* a highway patrolman in *More American Graffiti,* and, with his back to the camera, the science teacher in *E.T.*)

Ford knows what his audience expects of him, and seldom plays outside the perimeters of his niche. But his most daring performance—and in many ways his most atypical—is in Peter Weir's thinking man's adventure, **The Mosquito Coast** (1986). Ford plays idealistic inventor Allie Fox, who becomes disenchanted with modern life in America and takes his wife and family to the jungles of Central America, where he begins to become unhinged. Ford's gradual disintegration from enthusiastic utopian dreamer to mentally unbalanced villain is an astonishing turn, and he never attempted another part like it. And that's a shame. Based on the novel *River of No Return* by Paul Theroux, the film also features the late River Phoenix as Fox's sensitive yet resourceful son. In recent years, Ford has expressed a reluctance—a refusal, in fact—to undertake roles outside the zone which he perceives his audience wants to see him in, and that's too bad. *The Mosquito Coast* is the revelation of a superb actor at the peak of his commitment to his art.

july 14

Celebrate with a Woody

> *"I hate a song that makes you think you're not any good. I hate a song that makes you think you are just born to lose. No good to nobody. No good for nothing. Because you are either too old or too young or too fat or too slim or too ugly or too this or too that.*
>
> *"I am out to sing songs that will prove to you that this is your world and that if it has hit you pretty hard and knocked you for a dozen loops, no matter how hard it's run you down or rolled over you, no matter what color, what size you are, how you are built, I am out to sing the songs that make you take pride in yourself and your work."*
>
> *—Woody Guthrie, in an interview on New York radio station WNEW, Dec. 3, 1944*

If Robert Frost was our country's poet laureate, and John Steinbeck the "voice of the common man," then Woody Guthrie was our Holy Troubadour. He was born this day in 1912 in Okemah, Oklahoma, which he described as "one of the singiest, square dancingest, drinkingest, yellingest, preachingest, walkingest, talkingest, laughingest, cryingest, shootingest, fistfightingest, bleedingest, gamblingest, gun, club and razor carryingest of our ranch towns and farm towns."

Guthrie gave us some of our greatest songs—truly songs both of and for the comman man: the heart-wrenching "Deportee," inspired by a real-life plane crash; "Do-Re-Mi," which captured the plight of the Oakie immigrant with humor and heart; and, of course, the song many believe should be our national anthem (though Woody himself wouldn't have wanted that), "This Land Is Your Land."

His life was, in a sense, the Great American Life, rich in experience, adventure, and tragedy; fun and unbridled; filled with ceaseless creativity. His childhood was haunted by a series of tragic personal losses: first the death of his sister Clara by fire, followed by financial ruin and the institutionalization of his mother; later in life, he lost a daughter to death by burning, too. But his strength and resiliency were at the core of the man, and they come through time and again in his art—an art which has the uncanny ability to give others strength. And if there's a more noble existence or legacy for any artist, I'd like to know what it is.

Hal Ashby's **Bound for Glory** (1976) is not the movie about Woody Guthrie most people would expect, which may be one reason it failed initially at the box office. David Carradine seems, at first blush, a strange choice to play the title role—but he begins to grow on you through the film. The story centers on the easy-going Guthrie's life in Oklahoma and Texas during the Depression years, and his political and activist awakenings. The feeling of the times is brought vividly to life, and Haskell Wexler's breathtaking, seemingly leisurely cinematography is the icing on the cake.

july 15

Death of America's First Juvenile Delinquent

"¿Quién es?"

Those were the last words uttered by notorious outlaw Billy the Kid, just before Sheriff Pat Garrett shot him through the heart on this night in 1881 in Fort Sumner, New Mexico. As Billy's brief, stormy life ended, his legend began.

The story of Billy the Kid has been told countless times in movies, most of them total fiction. One of the best—and most underrated—is **The Left-Handed Gun** (1958), starring Paul Newman (doing his best James Dean impression) as the sensitive, not-too-bright outlaw. Directed with inventiveness and style by Arthur Penn (who would later go on to helm such masterpieces as *Bonnie and Clyde* [1967] and *Little Big Man* [1972]), *The Left-Handed Gun* is an intriguing, symbol-laden character study of the prototypical juvenile delinquent—misunderstood, in need of parental guidance, unable to channel his violent tendencies. Newman plays Billy as a simpleton, more or less, amiable but dangerous. And Billy's legendary escape from Lincoln County Jail is faithfully reproduced exactly as it happened, for once. Based on an original teleplay by Gore Vidal.

For another take on the Billy the Kid saga, watch the restored version of Sam Peckinpah's flawed but fascinating **Pat Garrett and Billy the Kid** (1973), starring James Coburn as the taciturn outlaw-turned-lawman Pat Garrett and Kris Kristofferson as an overage, lethargically charismatic Billy. Like much of Peckinpah's work, *Pat Garrett and Billy the Kid* is at heart an elegy for the passing of the Old West and the betrayal of friendship justified by fuzzy ethics. When someone asks Garrett how it feels to be hunting down his old saddle pal Billy, Garrett replies, "It feels like times have changed"; the character is almost a reprise of Robert Ryan's bounty hunter in *The Wild Bunch* (1969). Speaking of "changin' times," Bob Dylan appears in his acting debut as the enigmatic "Alias" (When someone asks him, "Alias what?" Dylan responds, "Alias anything you please"). While his presence generates nothing spectacular, Dylan did project a certain beguiling, photogenic charm in those days. *Pat Garrett and Billy the Kid* failed miserably when it was released (in an edited form that Peckinpah denounced), but now stands, in its restored version, as one of the director's most mature, complex works.

july 16

End of a Dynasty

In one of the most notorious political executions in modern history, the former czar of Russia, Nicholas II, and his family were executed by the Bolsheviks under the order of Vladimir Lenin this day in 1918. The royal family had been living as prisoners under armed guard in Ekaterinburg since their overthrow fourteen months before, with their ultimate fate left to be determined by their successors in Moscow. Those successors realized the potential of the idea of a living, exiled aristocracy; alive, Nicholas was the most serious threat to the legitimacy of the new Bolshevik regime.

On this night, Czar Nicholas, his wife, Alexandra, their three daughters, and their son, Alexi, were led downstairs into a small cellar, where a firing squad lay in wait. The entire family was summarily shot and bayoneted by at least twelve gunmen. It was the end of the Romanov dynasty in Russia.

For years afterward there were wistful rumors that some members of the family escaped—most famously, daughter Anastasia, whose name would be forever linked with royalty, romance, and mystery. On February 17, 1920, a young woman named Anna Anderson was placed in a sanitarium after attempting to jump off Bendler Bridge in Berlin. She soon claimed to be Anastasia, the only survivor of the massacre. She was the right age and bore remarkable physical similarities to the czarina. Never mind that she didn't speak a word of Russian (she claimed the trauma of the events had made her lose her memory). After she had lived to a ripe old age and passed away, postmortem DNA testing and the later discovery of the Romanov family's gravesite seemed to put the riddle to rest. Still, the legend lives on.

The Romanovs' story has served as inspiration for several movies. One of the earliest, *Rasputin and the Empress* (1933), had the distinction of being the only film ever to costar Ethel, John, and Lionel Barrymore. Unfortunately, that was about its only distinction; the studio's legal department insisted on changing the names and actions of virtually everyone involved—a bad sign in any "history" movie. Lionel makes a fine, malignant Rasputin, though.

Ingrid Bergman, in her first role in an American movie after a four-year exile in Italy, gives a refined and suitably regal performance in *Anastasia* (1956), based on the successful stage play of the same title. Far more of a romance than a mystery, it was inspired by the story of Anna Anderson. Yul Brynner plays a Russian con artist who promotes the theory that Bergman is indeed the Russian princess.

Nicholas and Alexandra (1971) is that rare accomplishment, an epic with heart, a mammoth-scale romance. Czarist Russia is splendidly depicted, with gorgeous costumes and opulent palaces. The first part of the movie is an affecting love story set against a collapsing dynasty; the twist is that the protagonists *are* the dynasty. Michael Jayston and Janet Suzman give excellent performances as the czar (portrayed here as a well-meaning naïf who was in over his head) and his loyal, vivacious wife. An excellent script by James Goldman. Several of the sequences are based on existing photographs and film clips of the royal family. Tom Baker, better known as "Dr. Who," plays Rasputin.

july 17

And He Never Once Said "You Dirty Rat"

Will Rogers once described his friend James Cagney by saying, "Every time I see him work, it's like a bunch of firecrackers going off all at once."

It's about as succinct a description as can be applied to a movie star whose style was so unique that real-life gangsters copied him. Cagney was more than a "personality"; he was a veritable force of nature, and an American icon during his own lifetime. The public went to a Cagney picture knowing exactly what they'd get. On-screen, he was electrifying—a strutting, cocky, buoyantly confident everyman with, as he used to describe himself, "a touch of the street." He was born on this day in 1899 in New York City's East Side.

Cagney literally blasted his way into stardom in one of the great gangster movies, 1931's *Public Enemy.* He was originally cast for a supporting role, but director William Wellman recognized star power when he saw it and immediately recast the picture with Cagney as Chicago street punk Tom Powers, who rises from petty theft to big-time bootlegger to cold-blooded murderer. Cagney gives a cathartic, hyperkinetic performance. It was such a powerful portrayal that actual mobsters modeled themselves after Cagney, a backhanded compliment if ever there was one.

Cagney further refined and perfected his screen persona in **Angels with Dirty Faces** (1938), the story of two childhood friends, Rocky Sullivan (Cagney) and Jerry Connelly (real-life pal Pat O'Brien), who grow up to become a crook and a priest, respectively. Jerry tries to keep the neighborhood kids in line, but successful, high-living Rocky is their hero.

When Rocky is condemned to the electric chair, Jerry begs him to make the boys lose their respect for him by "turning yellow" on his way to the execution chamber. As he's led away, Rocky pretends (or does he?) to break down, his voice whimpering, crying, screaming, animalistic. It's one of the most harrowing slices of screen acting ever. Cagney lost five pounds in one day shooting that last scene.

Did Rocky really "die yellow"? Cagney himself was cagey when asked the question. "I played it with deliberate ambiguity so the spectator could make the choice," he said. "You have to decide."

july 18

A Glory-ous Day

The Fifty-fourth Massachusetts Voluntary Infantry wasn't the first black regiment in the Civil War, but it was by far the most famous.

As the sun was setting this day in 1863 in Charleston, South Carolina, the Fifty-fourth made history by attacking a nearly impenetrable Southern stronghold, Fort Wagner, which guarded the approach to Charleston Harbor. It was a virtually impossible assignment. The soldiers had to approach the fort along several hundred yards of narrow, exposed beach. Musket fire and exploding shells hampered the assault, and the regiment suffered an overwhelming 50 percent casualties. But the soldiers persevered.

During the Civil War some in the North quietly questioned whether or not the black man would prove himself a worthy soldier. The events of this day settled that. Fighting for the Union helped former slaves achieve dignity, respect, and political rights after the war.

Glory (1989) re-creates that battle, and more than lives up to its title. A few fictitious incidents aside, it does an admirable job of integrating historical fact with a spellbinding storyline. Matthew Broderick gives a convincingly mature performance as real-life hero Col. Robert Gould Shaw, who is assigned the unenviable task of making a disciplined fighting unit out of his charges. Strong supporting performances from Denzel Washington as Trip, a runaway slave (Washington won Best Supporting Actor that year), and Morgan Freeman.

Inspiring and patriotic in the best sense of the word, *Glory* is the perfect antidote to the magnolia-scented romantic fiction of *Gone With the Wind.* A masterful marriage of history, film, and compelling entertainment.

july 19

The Chairman's Child Bride

When Ava Gardner first heard that her ex-husband Frank Sinatra had just married short-haired, flat-chested, nineteen-year-old Mia Farrow on this day in 1966, she remarked, "I always knew Frank would end up in bed with a boy someday."

It was a marriage few expected to last—and it didn't, not for long. It was already coming apart in 1968; Farrow had realized she was looking at Sinatra as a father figure, and as for Frank, well . . . Frank was Frank, daddy-o. He didn't like the little missus making movies, and he didn't want her to make one movie in particular.

Watch the movie that signaled the end for Mr. and Mrs. Frank Sinatra: **Rosemary's Baby** (1968), Roman Polanski's creepy thriller about a woman (Farrow) whose husband (John Cassavetes) makes an unholy alliance for his wife to give birth to . . . could it be Satan? The atmosphere (much of it filmed in the Dakota apartment building on New York's Upper West Side) is suitably unsettling. And there's an explicit scene or two where you can imagine Uncle Frank drawing the line. Farrow delivers a compellingly wan performance in the movie (largely enhanced by her pale, gaunt, waiflike features); you can see the life being sucked out of her even as she finds endless fascination in what it's like to be pregnant. A genuinely frightening film.

july 20

Moon 'Em

He was supposed to say, "That's one small step for *a* man, one giant leap for mankind." Instead, it actually came out, "That's one small step for man, one giant leap for mankind." But who could blame Neil Armstrong for blowing his line? He was the first human on the moon, and the pressure was on (or off, as it were). And it happened on this day in 1969.

But did man *really* land on the moon? Or was it all a fake to fool the gullible American public? In the February 1997 issue of *Fortean Times* magazine, a panel of photographic experts were invited to examine the "lunar landing" photos. They concluded that there were numerous anomalies and discrepancies in the photos—variations in "light sources," discrepancies in scale, long and short shadows appearing in the same photograph, Lee Harvey Oswald crouching behind a rock. . . . (OK, so I made that last one up.)

That's the premise of the kitschy, low-budget but enjoyable "what if?" B movie **Capricorn One** (1977). Three astronauts (Sam Waterston, James Brolin, and O. J. Simpson) are about to be blasted off to the moon when, at the last moment, they're shuttled off to a nearby "lunar landscape"—a movie set—and photographed "walking on the moon." The broadcast is watched by the world. But things go wrong, and they find themselves being hunted down by government agents who want to cover up the cover-up. Elliott Gould plays a journalist who finds out about the hoax. Plus, Telly Savalas saves the day as a crop-duster pilot. Hell, I'd believe man walked on the moon before I'd believe Telly Savalas as a crop-dusting pilot.

For a more down-to-earth change of pace, enjoy *The Dish* (2000)—a charming and funny sleeper from down under, based on the true story of a small Australian town that enjoys its moment in the world's spotlight when its satellite dish is selected to beam the live TV images of the astronauts landing on the moon. A feel-good movie that is both amusing and inspiring. Sam Neill stars.

july 21

Spend an Evening at Home with Papa

To a generation of readers he was "Papa" Hemingway. One of the most popular—and most filmed—authors of the twentieth century was born this day in 1899, in Oak Park, Illinois.

Many of Hemingway's bestsellers were adapted into motion pictures—perhaps more so than any other contemporary writer: *The Old Man and the Sea* (1958), *For Whom the Bell Tolls* (1943), *A Farewell to Arms* (1932), *The Sun Also Rises* (1957), *The Snows of Kilimanjaro* (1952), and *The Killers* (1946 and 1964) included.

For my money, the best of the lot—and the one that plays best on a small screen—is **The Old Man and the Sea** (1958), starring Spencer Tracy in a tour-de-force performance as the old Mexican fisherman who yearns to land a giant marlin. On the big screen, the movie looked unconvincing, the endless shots of the fisherman in his small boat too intimate for the large screen and the use of rear-projection distracting and obvious. Television reduces the tale to what it rightly is—a metaphorical short story. And it may be just a short story, but Tracy's typically great performance lends it an austerity and class that make it appear positively mythic. It's not hard to imagine Tracy's aging fisherman could well be his beloved character Emmanuel from *Captains Courageous* a few years down the line. Look for a quick glimpse of Hemingway himself in a bar scene near the end.

july 22

Care for Fava Beans and a Nice Chianti with That?

Twenty-two-year-old Tracy Edwards was lucky—he got away. When he flagged down two Milwaukee police officers on this day in 1988, the handcuffs were still dangling from his wrists. He said he had been sexually molested, and directed the officers to the nearby Oxford Apartments. The cops found more than they bargained for when they entered the home of Jeffrey Dahmer, a thirty-one-year-old man who had been accused of sexually molesting another man. While interrogating the nonplussed suspect, they found a collection of severed heads and body parts preserved in formaldehyde and in the refrigerator, along with photos of victims at various stages of their death. Dahmer tried to make a break for it but was subdued and arrested, and he eventually confessed to murdering at least thirteen people. Most of his victims were young gay African Americans he had lured to his home by promising to pay them for posing for nude photos. Once there, he would drug and strangle them and then mutilate and occasionally cannibalize their bodies. He was found guilty on February 12, 1992, and sentenced to fifteen consecutive life sentences. Dahmer himself was beaten to death by another inmate two years later.

Skip dinner tonight and watch **The Silence of the Lambs** (1990), Jonathan Demme's brilliantly creepy thriller about a serial killer who is torturing young women and skinning them for reasons that are stumping the FBI. Jody Foster gives a sterling performance as FBI agent Clarice Starling, who is assigned to the case. She seeks the aid of notorious locked-up serial killer Hannibal "the Cannibal" Lechter, a brilliantly insightful psychologist who has a fondness for eating his victims and washing them down with a nice Chianti. Anthony Hopkins deservedly won an Academy Award for his layered performance—showy yet underplayed, serious yet funny, animalistic yet fiercely and cruelly intelligent. And Foster is every inch his equal as the vulnerable but determined FBI trainee. All in all, an excellent meal.

july 23

Noir Tonight, Babe, I Have a Headache

He helped define the American detective novel by inventing the quintessential iconoclastic private eye, Phillip Marlowe (played on-screen by everyone from Dick Powell to Humphrey Bogart to Elliott Gould to Paul Newman). He also helped script some of Hollywood's darkest film noirs. Raymond Chandler was born in Chicago on this day in 1888, the son of a violent, abusive, alcoholic father and a self-sacrificing Irish mother; the two extremes coursed through his veins, life, and work like a river.

Raise a shotglass in his honor and watch **Double Indemnity** (1944), his first and best work for the screen. Based on James M. Cain's novella, Chandler's contentious collaboration with director and writer Billy Wilder resulted in what is arguably the best film noir ever—bleak, black, and gloriously seedy. The dialogue is so sharp it can cut your earlobes just listening. Fred MacMurray delivers an astonishing performance as not-so-scrupulous insurance salesman Walter Neff, who falls for married woman Phyllis Dietrichson (Barbara Stanwyck in full viper mode). Together they concoct a seemingly foolproof scheme to kill her husband and collect on the insurance. MacMurray was reluctant to take the role of the morally bankrupt murderer, feeling it would destroy his image. It was the best part he ever played. By the way, Wilder originally had an additional twenty minutes at the end, featuring MacMurray going to the gas chamber, but left it out of the final edit.

july 24

Was He Ever Really There to Start With?

Peter Sellers disappeared so deeply into his characters that when asked by reporters what the real Peter Sellers was like, he'd reply that he had no idea. But by most accounts he was a deeply complex, disturbed, and vexing human being. He died on this day in 1980, at age fifty-five, while recovering from heart surgery.

He was arguably the greatest screen chameleon since Lon Chaney, who was widely known for his ability to disappear into a role; I'd argue Sellers was even better. His gallery of great performances is awesome: His early Ealing comedies like *The Ladykillers* (1955) and *The Mouse That Roared* (1959) set the groundwork for his formidable talents. The influence of his reluctant mentor Alec Guinness is very much in evidence in Sellers's early roles, and adds a depth and humanity to them which would be noticeably absent later on. For Stanley Kubrick, Sellers did the best work of his career as three separate characters in *Dr. Strangelove* (1964), and as smarmy, chameleon-like Claire Quilty in *Lolita* (1962). And there was, of course, his immortal Inspector Clouseau of the *Pink Panther* film series (so immortal they kept putting together movies made from his old outtakes after he was dead).

But the role Sellers most fought for—and most wanted to be remembered for—is as "Chance," in Jerzy Kosinski's cult novel, **Being There** (1979)—and it turned out to be an apropos swan song. As Chauncy Gardiner—"Chance"—Sellers creates a total innocent, an absolutely undistilled product of the TV culture from which he was never weened as an adult. Sellers is funny and touching, like a cross between Stan Laurel and Alec Guinness, underplaying so superbly he seems to disappear sometimes. Shirley MacLaine is the senator's wife who finds herself in love with Chauncy, and Melvyn Douglas gave one of his last great performances as the dying politico.

july 25

It's the Bomb

On this day in 1946, at a fashion show in Paris, France, the first bikini was modeled. Civilization has been tumbling ever since.

The then-scandalous two-piece bathing suit was actually named after the site of the early A-bomb tests, the Bikini Islands. I say, who cares? Let's all watch **Bikini Beach Party** (1964), arguably the best of the popular *Beach Party* movies. During the '60s, AIP Pictures, a highly cost effective little B studio that could, owned a veritable franchise on clean juvenile flicks with the *Beach Party* series—invariably starring Frankie Avalon (the most East

Coast Italian-looking surfer in the history of California!) and Annette Funicello (who actually had it stipulated in her contract that she would not appear in a bikini for the entire series—and she never did). The usual gang of *Beach Party* eccentrics is here, including Harvey Lembeck, Don Rickles, and the immortal teen go-go dancer, Donna Loren.

In this installment, Frankie plays two roles—one, his usual surfer boy and the other, a member of the Potato Bugs, a takeoff on the then-prominent British Invasion. Look for a cameo on Boris Karloff in one of his last screen appearances.

july 26

Bad, Bad Pee-wee

It was a dark theater—and a dark day—for comedian Paul Ruebens when he was arrested in an adult cinema in Florida for indecent exposure on this date in 1991.

Ruebens was known and beloved by millions of fans, both children and indulgent adults, as his character, Pee-wee Herman, the child-man who came across like the product of a truly unholy alliance between Jerry Lewis and Pinky Lee. He had scored a tremendous success with the popular, subversive character, making two movies and starring in one of the hippest, most creative "kid's" shows ever, *Pee-wee's Playhouse* on CBS TV.

But after his mug shot was plastered across every newspaper in the country, CBS pulled the plug and Pee-wee Herman was expediently put into the dustbin (except for one memorable appearance on the MTV Awards after the scandal, when Ruebens came out as Pee-wee and asked the audience, "Heard any good jokes lately?"). Since then, Ruebens has kept a fairly low profile; if he's been able to come up with another character as strong as Pee-wee, we haven't seen it. Yet.

Meanwhile, give the guy a break and enjoy one of the most inventive, surrealistically sunny comedies of the '80s, **Pee-wee's Big Adventure**

(1985). Directed and cowritten by Tim Burton (his first film), *Pee-wee's Big Adventure* follows Pee-wee as he journeys across America searching for his treasured stolen bicycle. A series of inventive vignettes strung together make up the engaging and surreally whimsical narrative, including Pee-wee's classic dance to "Tequilla" at a biker bar, his frustrated search for the basement of the Alamo, his brief time on the road with spooky "Large Marge," and his brave heroics in a burning pet store. Exhilarating, inventive, and endearing, this comedy will have you irritating your friends for days by asking, "I know you are but what am I?"

july 27

Gotta Gogh Now

"This misery will never end."

—Vincent Van Gogh, July 23, 1890

He had been a schoolteacher, a bookseller, a theologian, and a minister before taking up painting late in life—and sold only one single painting during his lifetime. He was tortured for years by crippling, unrelenting depression, finally being confined in a mental hospital. Upon release, he painted one last masterpiece, *Cornfield with Crows.* Then, on this day in 1890, Vincent Van Gogh put a gun to his heart and pulled the trigger. He missed the vital organ, but died two days later of the gunshot wound.

Remember the artist and his work with **Lust for Life** (1956). Kirk Douglas delivers an atypically restrained performance as the tortured artist. Vincente Minnelli did an inventive job of avoiding the clichés that must have been tempting, choosing instead to focus on the artist's vision. Extraordinary re-creations and beautifully shot location photography (mostly shot on the exact locations where they occurred; the trains, coaches, asylum, and houses are the same ones Van Gogh occupied). Minnelli chooses to "paint" his scenes with the same colors Van Gogh uses in his paintings, and the effect is extraordinary.

Anthony Quinn won an Academy Award for his fiery, life-ingesting portrait of Van Gogh's friend and fellow artist, Paul Gauguin. *Lust for Life* is far from a depressing autopsy of Van Gogh's life; it's a vibrant celebration of it.

july 28

An Undercover Story

On this day in 1982, one of the greatest undercover scams in the history of the FBI came to an end. Three agents from the New York office of the FBI walked into the Motion Lounge in Brooklyn and told the proprietor, Dominick "Sonny Black" Napolitano, that his good friend and "business associate," Donnie Brasco, was really an undercover agent working for the FBI, and that Napolitano and his entire organization had been under surveillance for years.

"Donnie Brasco" was, in real life, FBI officer Joe Pistone, who had been working undercover for the past six years, incredibly gaining access to the Mob, and gathering evidence all the while. It was a dangerous assignment, to say the least. As a result of his penetration of the Mob, Pistone was given the Attorney General's Distinguished Service Award as outstanding agent in the FBI in 1982. What Sonny Black got was a bullet through the head and his hands chopped off by his disappointed business associates.

The whole incredible story is recounted in the absorbing real-life crime drama, **Donnie Brasco** (1997). Johnny Depp plays Pistone, a.k.a. Donnie Brasco, a man who is increasingly being torn between two conflicting lives as FBI agent and member of the Mob. But the movie really belongs to Al Pacino, who delivers a mesmerizing turn as aging, low-level wiseguy Lefty Ruggiero, who is taken in by the young undercover agent and allows him entry into "the family." Pistone begins to admire and respect his new mentor, and the two develop a friendship that puts everyone's lives in jeopardy. It's amazing to watch Pacino—the Mafia kingpin of all time as Michael Corleone in the *Godfather* saga—play a "made man" who exists by hanging on to the bottom rung of the ladder. His performance is proud, funny, seasoned, and tinged with pathos. In Mobspeak, Donnie Brasco was a "fugazi" (a fake)—but *Donnie Brasco* is no fugazi. Great supporting turns from Michael Madsen as Sonny Black and Anne Heche as Depp's understandably stressed wife.

july 29

The Magnificent Tarkington

One of America's most revered authors, Booth Tarkington, was born this day in 1869. During his youthful travels, he met up with a feckless, wanderlust-driven inventor and salesman named George Welles, who had invented and perfected the modern army mess kit and was currently applying kerosene headlamps to horseless carriages. The inventor would serve as the inspiration for the character of Eugene Morgan in Tarkington's Pulitzer Prize–winning masterpiece of small-town America, *The Magnificent Ambersons.*

Years later, George Welles's real-life son, a creative upstart prodigy named Orson, filmed the story as his follow-up to *Citizen Kane.* Unfortunately, there was a changeover in management at his studio, RKO, and the film was taken away from him after completion. Half of the film was literally chopped away and discarded, and a fake Hollywood-style happy ending was hastily filmed and tacked on before the film was released on the lower half of a double bill with a Lupe Velez comedy, *Mexican Spitfire Sees a Ghost.* The debacle effectively ended Orson Welles's Hollywood career just as it was gaining momentum. Today, however, *The Magnificent Ambersons* is recognized as being Orson Welles's greatest achievement, even in its truncated form.

It's astonishing that Welles, only twenty-six years old at the time, could have conceived and produced a work of such elegiac and mournful beauty. **The Magnificent Ambersons** (1942) chronicles the decline of a well-to-do family in a small midwestern town at the turn of the century. After his father's death, George Amberson Minnifer (Tim Holt) selfishly prevents his mother (Dolores Costello) from seeing the one man who has always loved her, Eugene Morgan (Joseph Cotton), inventor of the Morgan automobile. George wants to stick to the safety and comfort of the old days, while Morgan represents the inevitable progress of the coming automobile revolution. Even in its truncated form, this is still a spellbinding picture suffused in light and darkness. Welles restrains from the showy style of *Citizen Kane* in favor of an elegant, melancholy depth which envelopes the viewer like a shroud. There are bravura set-pieces to be sure: The final, elegant Amberson ball, the ride through the snowfields which looks like a Currier and Ives print come to life, and the entire opening sequence are marvelously inventive and fresh. Stanley Cortez's masterfully moody cinematography is a textbook example of the art of black-and-white photography, so rich that you feel you can step into it.

july 30

A Very Long Lunch

On this day in 1975, Jimmy Hoffa went out to lunch with an Eastern Teamster official and a Detroit mobster—and never came back. Hoffa had ruled the powerful Teamsters Union from 1957 to 1967, turning it into the world's most powerful union. It was also the richest and most corrupt union ever, raising the ire of then-Attorney General Bobby Kennedy. Kennedy and Jimmy Hoffa became bitter enemies. In 1967, Hoffa was convicted of jury tampering and sent to federal prison. He was released in 1971, and immediately began his crusade to regain power and control. He almost made it.

As of this printing, Jimmy Hoffa is still officially out to lunch—and is not likely to be picking up the check anytime soon—but his story is convincingly told in **Hoffa** (1992). Jack Nicholson gives a daring performance as union boss Jimmy Hoffa, who started out as a prewar trucker and then gets involved with the unions—and soon finds himself committing arson and racketeering. Danny DeVito (who also produced and directed) costars as his long-time friend Bobby Ciaro. A sharp script rich in ambiguities by David Mamet.

july 31

The Name's Bond . . . Um . . . Timothy Bond

Amidst much media hoopla (and audience apathy), Sir James Bond the Fourth made his official debut in theaters across America this day, as British actor Timothy Dalton took over the part that had previously been portrayed by Sean Connery, George Lazenby, and Roger Moore. The producers had originally wanted actor Pierce Brosnan when Moore retired from the part, but gave it to Dalton when Brosnan was unavailable due to a contractual obligation to his television network.

So Dalton took the role. He lasted for only two movies (the last being *License to Kill* [1989]) before passing the torch to Brosnan. Audiences and critics disagree on the merits of Dalton's short-lived association with the role; my own personal take on it is that the world was not ready for a Bond named Timothy.

Today is the anniversary of the release of **The Living Daylights** (1987), the official debut of the Man-Who-Would-Be-Bond-but-Only-for-a-Little-While, which occurred this day in 1987, at 1,725 theaters across the U.S.A.

If you haven't seen this Bond, check it out. It marks a welcome return to form for the series after the long, long stretch that was Roger Moore's interpretation. Dalton was an ideal Bond—and brought a much-needed gravity—to the role. Better-than-average Bond—which means better-than-average movie. Enjoy with a martini—you know: shaken, not stirred.

august

august 1

A Movie That's Right on Targets

On this day in 1966, twenty-five-year-old honor student Charles Whitman, after murdering his wife and mother the previous night, climbed atop the twenty-seven-story-high University of Texas tower in Austin and began firing. He shot fifty-six people, killing sixteen and wounding forty, before he himself was shot by police. At the time it was an unprecedented act; in retrospect, it is a sad template and harbinger of things which were to come. Charles Whitman was one of the first to "go postal."

Peter Bogdanovich used Whitman's shooting spree as the inspiration for his breakthrough debut movie, **Targets** (1967). In 1967, Bogdanovich was a fresh-scrubbed film school graduate, and *Targets* was his first full-feature production, financed by indie icon Roger Corman. Although budgeted and shot on the proverbial shoestring, film icon Boris Karloff was sufficiently impressed with the fledgling director's story that he signed on. And lucky for us, too; Karloff gave his last great performance in the elegiac, beneficent role of Byron Orlok, a retired old-time horror film actor, very much based on himself. The story (by Bogdanovich) centers on a psychopathic sniper (Tim O'Kelly is the Charles Whitman stand-in) who goes on a rampage, eventually ending up at a drive-in theater, where he takes a perch atop the screen and begins firing. Orlock confronts him both on the screen and in person. By far Bogdanovich's most audacious creation, *Targets* is a fascinating and all-too-relevant examination of violence in American culture.

august 2

Now *That's* What I Call Effective Campaigning

In 1943, the Japanese were beginning to withdraw farther west in the South Pacific among the Solomon Islands, preparing for an inevitable U.S. invasion. A squadron of poorly armed PT boats was assigned to hunt down and sink Japanese supply ships, a mission that was easier said than done. U.S. PT boats were nimble, but notoriously unreliable when it came to firepower.

One of the boats, PT *109,* was under the command of Lt. John F. Kennedy, the twenty-eight-year-old son of millionaire Joseph Kennedy. The younger Kennedy, who had suffered for years from Addison's disease, had lied about his past medical records in order to get the assignment.

It was on this night in 1943, in the darkness shortly after midnight, that one of *109*'s crew saw a huge black shape looming dead ahead, and shouted a warning, but it was too late. A Japanese destroyer rammed PT *109,* slicing it in half in an explosion of fire, instantly killing two crew members. Eleven survived, clinging to what was left of the boat. Lt. Kennedy, realizing they'd be sitting ducks after sunup, ordered his men to swim toward the nearby island of Plum Pudding, a speck in the distance. It was a torturous task—Kennedy, using a life jacket clenched in his teeth, dragged one of his crew members for four hours. Eventually they reached the island. Kennedy's unquestioned bravery and leadership earned him the U.S. Navy Medal for Heroism, and no doubt helped him win the presidency seventeen years later.

Commemorate the anniversary of his shining hour by watching **PT 109** (1963), filmed during the time JFK was in office and released five months before his assassination. Reportedly, Kennedy himself selected buttoned-down leading man Cliff Robertson to portray him (the runner-up was a young up-and-coming player named Warren Beatty, who undoubtedly had more in common with JFK than Robertson did). Though the film does portray Kennedy in an understandably glowing, heroic light, PT 109 takes relatively few liberties with the facts. And those are impressive enough.

august 3

One Last Obscene Act

> *"I'm sorry if I'm not funny tonight, but I'm not a comedian. I'm Lenny Bruce."*
>
> *—Lenny Bruce*

Lenny Bruce used his outrageous and controversial humor to jolt a complacent America into an awareness of who we really were and where we *really* lived. As a performer and an artist, Bruce was compulsively, ruthlessly honest—and brilliantly funny. In his glorious early days on the West Coast 1950s nightclub scene, he was to comedy what Charlie Parker was to jazz—a revolutionary artist going out on wild, improvised flights of invention and brilliance.

Labeled as a "sick comedian" by *Time* magazine, Lenny insisted it was society that was sick, not him; he was a surgeon wielding the scalpel. His humor was a heady mix of social commentary and improvised stream of consciousness, miles ahead of Mort Sahl's topical cerebralism, Redd Foxx's raunchy sex jokes, and Lord Buckley's hipster posing. Lenny was a hero to young beats, liberals, and leftists—and a dangerous threat to the powers-that-were.

By the '60s, his endless arrests and trials on obscenity charges had worn him down, drained him of all his money, and made him virtually unemployable—club owners risked being shut down if they booked "Dirty Lenny." On this day in 1966 police found him in the bathroom of his apartment, dead of an overdose of heroin.

His life story served as the basis for Bob Fosse's ambitious *Lenny* (1974), starring a woefully miscast Dustin Hoffman in the title role. *Lenny* is a noble effort, undermined by a disappointing script and its central performance. The real Lenny's voice was a versatile, seductive, and playful instrument; Hoffman's pinched nasal whine strangles any comedic possibilities.

Bruce himself actually wrote and starred in a cheesy low-budget movie, *Dance Hall Racket* (1952), playing a young hood; if it was meant to be a parody, the joke didn't come off. Aside from the novelty of seeing Lenny Bruce "act," it's a bargain-basement bore. *The Lenny Bruce Performance Film* (1967) features the sadly dissipated comic in one of his last shows, at the dreary Basin Street West Club in San Francisco. He's obsessed with his legal trials—literally reading court transcripts verbatim onstage—and remains stubbornly unfunny. It's a depressing, disquieting swan song.

The best way to see Lenny Bruce in his subversive glory is in **Lenny Bruce Without Tears** (1972), which pieces together rare footage of Bruce—in performance on *The Steve Allen Show* and in interviews, newsreels, and recordings. It's a little heavy-handed in places, but Bruce is truly marvelous. Except for the last image of Lenny, facedown on the bathroom floor, nude, with a towel tied around his arm and a syringe on the floor. That's obscenity.

august 4

Look into This Special Diary

On this day in 1944, after nearly two years in hiding, fifteen-year-old Anne Frank was arrested by the Nazis.

Born in Germany in 1929, young Anne Frank and her family fled to Amsterdam in 1933 to escape the Nazis. She began keeping her diary in 1942 when she was just thirteen years old. In Amsterdam, they hid in a sealed-off section of a warehouse with another family. They stayed there for nearly two years.

Anne Frank, who famously wrote that deep down, she believed all people were good, was arrested by the Nazis this day in 1944, along with the rest of her family. They were immediately sent to Auschwitz. Later, Anne and her sister were transferred to Bergen-Belsen, where they both contracted typhus. Anne Frank died only weeks before the war ended.

Like *Schindler's List* and *Shoah,* **The Diary of Anne Frank** (1959) is a challenge to sit through, and not simply because of the subject matter. We know the ending all too well—just as we think we can imagine what led up to it. Since it was based on a stage play, and most of the drama takes place within four attic walls, it's a claustrophobic film. As the young Anne, Millie Perkins is a cypher, but it's tough to know whether it was the actress or the direction. And Richard Beymer was never a convincing juvenile lead (see *West Side Story* for further proof—he projects all the chemistry of a potato). Still, an impressive, austere, and affecting film. Shelley Winters, continuing in her admirable series of nonglamorous roles, received a Best Supporting Actress Oscar for her portrayal of Mrs. Van Daan.

august 5

"Arf!" Goes Sandy

Little Orphan Annie, Harold Gray's comic strip about the adventures of a "poor little rich girl" and her loyal dog, Sandy, debuted in newspapers across the U.S.A. this day in 1924, and immediately struck a chord with readers. Throughout the coming Depression, *Little Orphan Annie* was the single most popular comic strip in the world. She became a symbol of America's self-image in the '30s—tenacious, resilient, and optimistic in the face of unrelenting adversity. She was to comics what Shirley Temple was to movies in the '30s.

Celebrate Annie's birthday with **Annie** (1981)—the only musical ever directed by John Huston. Based on the wildly successful Broadway musical of the same name, *Annie* was an attempt to bring back the big-budget Hollywood musical (it cost $60 million to make). But a lot had changed between the '30s and the '80s—not the least of which was the public's taste in musicals—and the film was a commercial flop. The story recounts how poor Annie (Aileen Quinn) runs away from her hard life at an orphanage run by dastardly Miss Hanigan (Carol Burnett). She ends up in the streets of New York City, and into the arms of big-hearted billionaire Oliver Warbucks (a dome-pated Albert Finney). A sunny tip of the hat to another time and place where the sun will always come out tomorrow. Bet your bottom dollar on tomorrow. . . .

august 6

Those Who Do Not Remember the Past . . .

It's still incomprehensible—a surreal image of such shocking repercussions that most of us simply cannot imagine it and quickly shut it out of our minds. But on this day in 1945, at precisely 8:15 A.M., the *Enola Gay* carried out its unprecedented mission by dropping an atomic bomb on the Japanese city of Hiroshima, killing seventy-five-thousand people.

Remember this day with Alain Resnais's **Hiroshima, Mon Amour** (1959)—a stunning, unforgettable film about the doomed love between a Frenchwoman and a Japanese architect in 1950s Hiroshima, who are both united and repelled by memories of their past, including the woman's long-ago scandalous affair with a German soldier and her vivid memories of nuclear horror. Alain Resnais' first full-length film, *Hiroshima, Mon Amour* is a melancholy examination of the relationship between world calamities and personal histories, between the past and the present. Quite simply, an unforgettable film. Screenplay by Marguerite Duras.

august 7

We're Giving You One Last Chance

Time Warner wasn't going to take it anymore. Throughout New York City, too many people were picking up their cable broadcasts illegally, and it was time for action. This was the final day of amnesty for illegal Manhattan cable box users in 1991. Time Warner announced that, effective the next day, it would prosecute "cable pirates."

Observe the anniversary with **The Cable Guy** (1996), a twisted and somewhat nasty little comedy starring Jim Carrey as Chip Douglas, a lisping cable installer from hell, and Matthew Broderick as his hapless victim, Steve Kovaks. Carrey, then at the height of his popularity, took on the decidedly bizarre role as a change of pace. It was certainly that. As the deluded and disturbed title character, he's sometimes hilarious (as when he's crooning a karaoke rendition of "Somebody to Love") and occasionally out-and-out creepy. He's actually outacted by Broderick as the put-upon mensch that the audience can't help but identify with. Directed by Ben Stiller.

august 8

Dustin Time

For a geeky-looking guy with bad acne, the most adenoidal voice in movies, and a well-deserved reputation as one of the most difficult actors in Hollywood, Dustin Hoffman has succeeded admirably. He was born this day in 1937 in Los Angeles; it's one of the rare instances when he didn't demand a retake.

From *The Graduate* (1967) through *Midnight Cowboy* (1968), *Rain Man* (1988), and *Tootsie* (1982) he has created one of the most diverse and memorable gallery of characters in film—and they're all great movies with which to celebrate his birthday. But one of his finest performances is seldom seen. In **Straight Time** (1977), Hoffman delivers an unflinching, galvanizing performance as recently paroled convict Max Dembo. Torn between an uncaring criminal system and his own pathological tendencies toward self-destruction, Max cannot adjust to life on the outside. He teams up with old partner Harry Dean Stanton and unreliable young strung-out junkie Gary Busey to pull a jewelry store heist. Hoffman was originally slated to direct, but became overwhelmed trying to direct himself, and turned over directorial duties to trusted friend Ulu Grosbard halfway through production. A searing, intelligent, and totally unsentimental examination of a compulsive criminal, with Hoffman delivering an absolutely riveting performance. Not to be missed.

august 9

A Lame Dick

It was the first and only time a U.S. president stepped down from office. On this day in 1974, as the rising tide of the Watergate scandal threatened to take the presidency to the impeachment level, President Richard M. Nixon went on national television and resigned. Vice President Gerald Ford took office the next day, and promptly pardoned Nixon for any possible crimes he may have committed as president.

Observe the anniversary with **Nixon** (1995), Oliver Stone's fascinating and controversial look at the most complex, contrarian personality ever to occupy the Oval Office. Stone's cinematic character study is a journey into the dark machinations of a compulsively driven man—and it's one of the few instances where Stone's schizoid method of filmmaking suits his subject. Anthony Hopkins may not look much like Richard Nixon—in fact, he looks more like Herbert Hoover—but he delivers a masterful and insightful performance as the complicated overachiever driven to succeed at any cost. A fabulous supporting cast includes Paul Sorvino as Henry Kissinger, Bob Hoskins as J. Edgar Hoover, and Joan Allen in a shattering turn as Pat Nixon. Using different film stocks and cinematic styles, Stone weaves a complex tapestry of guilt, paranoia, despair, sex, lies, and audiotape. A rich, rewarding study of one of the twentieth century's most fascinating enigmas.

august 10

Whew! Another Close One!

It was an uncanny sight—and a scary one. On this day in 1966, a meteor streaked across the skies over the U.S. in broad daylight—the only known case of a meteor entering the earth's atmosphere and leaving it again. Another close call.

But what if . . . ? What if it *had* hit the earth? What if a *huge* meteor were set on a crash course with the planet, with precious little we could do about it? That's the premise of **Deep Impact** (1998), which chronicles the final days and hours of an inevitable catastrophe. A refreshing change of pace in the "disaster epic" genre, the film concentrates as much on human relationships as it does on special effects, and director Mimi Leder delivers the goods in both departments. Morgan Freeman is the president of the United States, Robert Duvall a space cowboy sent up to nuke the meteor, and Téa Leoni is a career-conscious news broadcaster who decides to reunite with her estranged father (Maximilian Schell) before the Big One hits. Feel free to fast-forward to the good parts. And keep checking the skies.

august 11

Only Kidding!

On this day in 1984, President Ronald Reagan jokingly orders a nuclear strike on Russia while testing a microphone before a speech. He didn't realize the microphone was on, and the faux pas was picked up on live television. Oooops.

Commemorate the close call with Stanley Kubrick's dark cautionary comedy, **Dr. Strangelove** (1963). Perhaps Kubrick's most accessible film—and certainly his most commercially successful. Peter Sellers is absolutely brilliant in three different roles: as an RAF captain trying to convince General Jack D. Ripper (Sterling Hayden) to recall the nuclear bombs he has ordered to be dropped on Russia; as the harried, ineffectual president of the United States, Merkin Muffley; and as the title character, wheelchair-bound former Nazi scientist Dr. Strangelove. George C. Scott gives one of his most brilliant performances as the gung-ho military advisor Buck Turgidson, and Sterling Hayden is frighteningly effective as the loony general obsessed with his "precious bodily fluids" who pushes the button. A brilliant script by Kubrick and Terry Southern ("Gentlemen! Gentlemen! You can't fight in here—this is the War Room!"). Keep a sharp eye on actor Peter Bull (the Russian diplomat) during Strangelove's tirade in the War Room toward the end; Bull breaks character, cracking up at Sellers's performance. The film originally ended with an epic pie fight, but Kubrick wisely cut the segment out. A pie fight after Armageddon might have been a little anticlimactic.

august 12

Ready When You Are, C.B.

Cecil B. DeMille, the director whose name became synonymous with bigger-than-life spectacle and showmanship on the screen, was born this day in 1881 in Ashfield, Massachusetts. In 1913 he went into partnership with Jesse Lasky and glove salesman Samuel Goldfish—who later modified his last name to Goldwyn—to produce and direct motion pictures. His first effort, *The Squaw Man* (1914) was a huge sensation. It was filmed in a deserted hamlet in California called "Hollywoodland."

DeMille thrived in the sunny climate, and turned out hit film after hit film. The trick up his sleeve was positioning his films as "moral lessons" while inserting all manner of scintillating, titillating footage designed to appeal to prurient tastes. He literally created a cottage industry in the '20s of deeply "moral" movies featuring plenty of exposed skin and violence, including *King of Kings, The Ten Commandments, Cleopatra,* and others.

He continued to thrive into the sound era, producing vulgar but wonderfully entertaining movies. Celebrate the birth of "the Greatest Showman on Earth" with his remake of his own movie, **The Ten Commandments** (1956), his final bow as director and a movie so over-the-top, pompous, and vulgar that it deserves a prime corner in the Kitsch Hall of Fame. Charlton Heston heads an all-star cast as Moses—and what a holy beefcake he was. Yul Brynner is the pharaoh, and luscious Anne Baxter (sporting a fetching 1950s hairdo) is there to tempt everyone. The effects, so applauded in the '50s, are quaint now, and the acting and script laughable. In short, this is one fun, cheesy epic. DeMille obviously cared about the virtuous significance of this deeply moral movie; perhaps that's why he spent three weeks filming the orgy sequence alone. Hubba hubba.

august 13

The First New York World's Fare

On this date in 1907, the first official U.S. taxicab took to the streets in New York City. The driver, who didn't speak English, managed to mow down three pedestrians his first day on the job. (OK, so I made that second sentence up.)

Observe the occasion with—what else?—**Taxi Driver** (1976), Martin Scorsese's brutally brilliant vision of a Manhattan cab driver's alienation, isolation, and eventual breakdown. Robert DeNiro gives the most lauded (and parodied) performance of his career as Travis Bickle, the troubled Vietnam vet who makes his living driving a taxicab through the bowels of lower Manhattan in the steamy predawn hours.

For a more enjoyable ride, you can get five times the mileage with the enchanting and offbeat omnibus (omnitaxi?), **Night on Earth** (1991). Maverick director Jim Jarmusch came up with this inventive anthology of five stories, all of which happen in various taxicabs simultaneously, but in different time zones around the world during one night on earth. The five tales are told separately, but all weave together in the whimsical, wistful fabric of the movie. Highlights include Roberto Benigni's absolutely hilarious, lengthy vignette about a talkative Italian cab driver confessing his increasingly kinky carnal sins to a priest in the backseat, and Matti Pellonpää's woeful monologue. It's been said that Jarmusch catches moments that other filmmakers don't even notice, and this small but rare gem is proof. Once more around the block, driver. And take it slow.

august 14

Have a Wild and Crazy Time

"Sex is one of the most beautiful, natural things money can buy."

—Steve Martin

On this day in 1945, Steve Martin was born in San Antonio, Texas—"a poor, black child," according to his first movie.

When his family moved to California, he began his show business career demonstrating magic tricks at the Magic Castle store in Disneyland. In 1968 he was hired as a writer on *The Smothers Brothers Comedy Hour,* where he made his first tentative on-camera appearance. He became a star by taking his stand-up act on the road as an opening act for rock 'n' roll groups such as the Eagles ("Well, excuuuuuuse me!"), and became a huge hit on the college circuit. After hosting *Saturday Night Live* in 1976 his popularity went through the roof.

He went on to star in—and often write—a series of successful comedies, including *The Jerk* (his 1979 debut, and, laugh-for-laugh, one of his funniest), the inventive *Dead Men Don't Wear Plaid* (1982), and *The Man with Two Brains* (1983). Martin has been adventurous in his film career, tackling such offbeat projects as *Pennies from Heaven* (1981) and *The Spanish Prisoner* (1997). His best film is **Roxanne** (1987), an inspired comic updating of *Cyrano de Bergerac*. Martin plays Charlie "C. D." Bales, a small-town fire chief whose prominent proboscis has circumvented his romantic life, until he meets beautiful astronomy student Roxanne (Daryl Hannah). Romantic, funny, touching—*Roxanne* is breathlessly sunny and a great date film. Martin delivers one of his most affecting and balanced performances, perfectly poised between clown and noble dreamer.

august 15

Peace, Bro—and Pass the Umbrella

To some it was three days of Love, Peace, and Music. To others it was an interminable weekend of pouring rain, thunderstorms, bad acid, rivers of mud, and no toilets. The Woodstock Music Festival kicked off this day in 1969, and it was both a beginning and an end.

Relive the festival in the comfort of your own home—no rain!—with **Woodstock** (1970). Aside from a few acts (Santana, the Who, Sly and the Family Stone, Jimi Hendrix) the music wasn't that great (coulda been the purple acid, man). But as a document and stunningly effective evocation of the times, *Woodstock* is compelling entertainment. Utilizing then-revolutionary multiple screen images, director Michael Wadleigh captures all the innocence, naïveté, music, and mud. The backstage moments are infinitely more entertaining and revealing than the performances. My favorite is the poor love-struck sixteen-year-old blond boy, moon-eyed for his female companion, whom he just met. Infinitely wiser than his years, he only "wants to maintain." Here's hoping he got laid and grew up to be a therapist.

A fascinating time capsule in many ways.

august 16

Elvis Has Left the Building

The King passed away this day in 1977—although John Lennon, never one to mince words, claimed that "Elvis died the day he went in the army."

Commemorate his life and passing with **This Is Elvis** (1981), an absorbing hybrid of documentary and screen bio, "narrated" from beyond the grave by "E" hisself (actually, the voice of an Elvis impersonator). Some of the film is fuzzy, hampered by a few awkward "fictitious re-creations," and some of Elvis's more unsavory aspects are glossed over. But the real-life great moments are all here: his initial, cathartic TV appearances with Milton Berle, Steve Allen, and above-the-waist-only Ed Sullivan; rare footage of his barnstorming days in the South; his early singing and screen career; his hysteria-inducing induction into the army; his one-time-only duet with Frank Sinatra after his release from the army; the movies; the glorious 1968 NBC-TV "comeback special"; plenty of backstage rehearsal footage; and the long, sad, slow decline. The final footage of a bloated, perspiring Elvis is heartbreaking and difficult to watch, especially when juxtaposed against the inevitable montage of shots from his glory days. And, tacky as it is, the home movie montage set to "You Were Always on My Mind" is heartbreaking. But the great stuff is here, too—the King in his glory days. The King is dead. Long live the King.

august 17

A Cry in the Dark

"A dingo took my baby!"

Lindy Chamberlain screamed out those words in a camping ground near Ayers Rock, Australia, on this night in 1980, when she discovered that her nine-week-old baby, Azaria, had been taken from their tent. Chamberlain had left her sleeping four-year-old son, Reagan, and Azaria in the tent only moments before, when her husband, Michael, was sure he heard Azaria cry out. As she approached the tent, Lindy saw a large dingo coming out, dragging something in its teeth. When she inspected the tent, her baby was missing. Searching for their child in the dark, the couple found a bloody baby suit. When they appeared on Australian television with their story, they used the opportunity to extol their faith as Seventh-Day Adventists, which didn't go down well with the public, who mistook Lindy's faith for unrepentant guilt. The couple were put on trial for murder.

The whole incredible story is recounted in **A Cry in the Dark** (1988). Meryl Streep adds an Australian accent to her impressive gallery of dialects as Lindy Chamberlain in the wrenching true-life drama. Director Fred Schepisi's riveting reconstruction of events eerily anticipates elements of the JonBénet Ramsey murder case and subsequent trial by media. Streep gives one of her most impassioned—and underrated—performances as the traumatized and persecuted Lindy, and Sam Neill does excellent work as her husband, Michael.

In real life, Lindy currently lives with her second husband in Seattle, Washington, running a publishing house specializing in health books.

august 18

This Book Is Awful . . . and Such Small Portions!

Several years after it was quietly published in France, the *New York Times* finally got around to reviewing a little book called *Lolita,* by Vladimir Nabokov, on this day in 1956. The reviewer lambasted the story as "dull, dull, dull . . . and repulsive." Well, tell us what you really think.

They said it could never be filmed—but leave it to maverick director Stanley Kubrick to break the rules. **Lolita** (1962) is brilliantly perverse, darkly comic, and still shockingly risqué—it really is amazing that a comedy about a man in love with his thirteen-year-old step-daughter managed to get filmed at all. James Mason is disturbingly effective as college professor Humbert Humbert, who rents a room from lonely widow Charlotte Haze (a knockout performance by Shelley Winters) and finds himself irresistibly attracted to her daughter, Lolita (Sue Lyon, only fourteen at the time of the filming). Kubrick managed the impossible—capturing the author's dark, provocative humor and making it palatable to audiences. Peter Sellers delivers the best performance of his career as the slimy and manipulative Claire Quilty, Humbert's nemesis and rival for Lolita's schoolgirl affections. Sellers appears sporadically throughout the movie—each time in a different disguise and persona to torture Humbert—and sparks fly whenever he's onscreen. The opening sequence is probably Sellers's best ten minutes on film—a dazzling one-man show of breathtaking comedic invention mixed with superior acting. Watch for Sellers's improvised joke about Kubrick's previous movie, *Spartacus.*

august 19

Teeth Together, Lips Apart

On this day in 1888, the first-ever beauty contest was held in Spa, Belgium. It was won by an eighteen-year-old West Indian girl. Legend has it she had the edge in the belly dancing competition.

Depending on your point of view, beauty pageants are a wonderfully wholesome, albeit tacky, competition, an insulting denigration of womanhood, or both. Whichever way you look at it, you'll find something to like in Michael Ritchie's wonderfully off-the-wall **Smile** (1974), a satirical look at small-town America beauty pageants, spotlighting Santa Rosa's Young American Miss competition. Ritchie exposes the shallow, backbiting competitiveness of his characters, but develops a fondness for them along the way. He satirizes the meat-market mentality and hypocrisy of the pageants while winkingly enjoying the whole fiasco. With Bruce Dern, Barbara Feldon (Agent 99 from *Get Smart!*), and a young and nubile Melanie Griffith.

august 20

Give 'Em Enough Rope . . .

The two spoiled, rich, and unquestionably disturbed young men thought it might be fun to commit a murder—just for kicks.

On Wednesday, May 21, 1924, Nathan Leopold (son of a millionaire shipping magnate) and Richard Loeb (son of the vice president of Sears Roebuck) kidnapped and murdered fourteen-year-old Bobby Franks near Chicago. They wanted to see how the victim would react, and were looking forward to playing games with "simple-minded cops." But the law caught up with them in short order, and each ratted out the other. The resulting trial was a sensation. Renowned lawyer Clarence Darrow pleaded for mercy on their behalf, claiming that, among other things, their privileged status prevented them from having a sense of right and wrong. His passionate pleading saved them from the death penalty.

On this day in 1924, Leopold and Loeb were sentenced to life imprisonment. Leopold, the mastermind, was killed in prison not long after, stabbed to death by an inmate who said he had made advances to him; Loeb was paroled in 1958, married, and moved to Florida, where he ran a flower business until he died in 1971.

The crime and subsequent trial inspired several movies. **Compulsion** (1959), is an outstanding and thought-provoking treatment of the story. The film is divided into three sections: The first section establishes the two main characters, Judd and Artie (Bradford Dillman and Dean Stockwell), two "dangerously close" friends who are rich and bored, examining their friendship and then depicting the kidnapping and murder of a young boy. The second third covers the police investigation, and the final segment re-creates the trial. Orson Welles gives the performance of his career as the Clarence Darrow–inspired defense attorney. His summation speech is probably the finest acting Welles ever did on-screen—subdued, articulate, and passionate. No matter your stand on capital punishment, you will be moved.

Make it a double bill with **Rope,** Hitchcock's experimental film which was also inspired by the murder. James Stewart plays a college professor who is invited by two favored students (Farley Granger and John Dall) to a dinner party. Little does he realize they've murdered an old schoolmate, and the body is hidden in a chest in the center of the room. The movie is a long, sustained cat-and-mouse game, with Stewart and his two protégés bandying Nietzschean philosophy over the hidden corpse. Typically, and perversely, Hitchcock manipulates the audience to side with the murderers, hoping they won't get caught. Hitchcock audaciously filmed the movie entirely on one set—and in one seemingly continuous shot—no breaks. (Actually, the film stock had to be changed every ten minutes—see if you can detect Hitchcock's tricks to disguise the changes.) A fascinating cinematic experiment, and one of Hitch's most inventive, if stilted, films.

august 21

Get Lei'd Tonight

On this day in 1959, amidst much ukulele playing, Hawaii was admitted as the fiftieth state. If you can't afford to fly there to celebrate, watch **Hawaii** (1966), the epic screen adaptation of James Michener's sprawling historical novel of white settlers who came to the islands in the 1800s. Max Von Sydow is typically humorless and dour as a missionary, and Julie Andrews plays his neglected, much-suffering wife. The dramatic charge is provided by Richard Harris as the bellowing ship captain who falls in love with Andrews.

If you're looking for something a little lighter (a lot lighter—so light it floats away) indulge your taste for paradise in **Blue Hawaii** (1961), Elvis's first cinematic sojourn to the fiftieth state (he would return in *Paradise, Hawaiian Style*). He plays a returning GI who decides against his family's pineapple business to run a touring service. Naturally, his clients are mostly beautiful girls. Some guys have all the luck.

august 22

Attica! Attica!

It was a typically hot, humid morning in New York City and tempers were short—the kind of day they call a Dog Day. On this day in 1972, a bank robbery in Brooklyn went hopelessly wrong. A young bisexual man was desperate to raise money for a sex change operation for his lover, so he and an accomplice walked into a bank, pulled out their firearms, and took everybody hostage. From there just about everything that could go wrong in the hapless robber's poorly planned scheme did. The event became a media circus—and even a pizza delivery boy got his moment in the spotlight.

The event is re-created in vivid detail in Sidney Lumet's sizzling **Dog Day Afternoon** (1975). Al Pacino gives one of his greatest performances as Sonny, the doe-eyed, inept would-be bank robber with a soft heart who's in way over his head. Lumet delivers a taut thriller with heart, laughs, and suspense. Charles Durning is the cop who tries to reason with Sonny, and John Cazale (who played Pacino's brother Fredo in *The Godfather*) gives a great performance as Sal, Sonny's none-too-bright accomplice. One of the best "New Yawk" movies ever.

august 23

He Was Hot, He Was Sexy, He Was Dead

Rudolph Valentino was the first heartthrob of Hollywood, the prototypical matinee idol, the ultimate "Latin lover" for whom women melted like Creamsicles in the sun. When he died this day in 1926 of peritonitis, the female population of America went into mourning. Suicide attempts from grieving women were reported all across the country. He was probably the first example of America's curious ongoing fascination with dead celebrities. One hundred thousand mourners showed up at his funeral, and actress Pola

Negri, who apparently never did anything in moderation, sent four thousand roses. For years afterward, a mysterious "Lady in Red" came on the anniversary of his death to bestow long-stemmed roses by his crypt.

He was the subject of two screen biographies, including Ken Russell's visually stunning but dramatically uninspiring 1977 *Valentino,* starring a badly miscast Rudolf Nureyev, a severe case of stunt casting if there ever was one. See what all the fuss was about by watching the real thing in action in **Son of the Sheik** (1925), the hugely successful follow-up to Valentino's earlier hit, *The Sheik.* By the time he had make *Son of the Sheik,* he was near the end. The press had dubbed him "the Pink Powder Puff" and, had he lived, he may well have become a victim of scandal due to his off-camera lifestyle. Like James Dean some thirty years later, it could be argued that he died at the perfect moment—and left a good-looking corpse.

august 24

The Big Boom

On this day in A.D. 79 in southern Italy, Mt. Vesuvius erupted, burying the entire nearby city of Pompeii. About half of the populace escaped toward the sea, but more than two thousand were buried under seven feet of lava and volcanic ash. When the site of the ancient city was excavated seventeen hundred years later, archeologists found a perfectly preserved picture of the everyday life of an ancient civilization.

Commemorate the eventful day with **The Last Days of Pompeii** (1935), a big-budget, old-fashioned epic that's an entertaining cross between a sword 'n' sandals cheesefest and an Irwin Allen film. Their age aside, the special effects still look great. Based on Lord Lytton's book of the same title.

august 25

The Man Who Would Be Bond

He worked as a bricklayer, lifeguard, coffin polisher, and male model before being selected by producer Albert "Cubby" Broccoli to play secret agent James Bond in the first 007 adventure, *Dr. No* (1962). With its huge success (helped in no small way by being President Kennedy's favorite film) the hunky Scotsman became an overnight star—the personification of the suave, lady-killing secret agent who preferred his martinis shaken, not stirred. In the public's mind, he *was* James Bond—virile, charming, sophisticated, and deadly—and his portrayal of 007 is still the standard by which all others are measured and invariably fall short. Sean Connery was born this day in 1930 in Edinburgh, Scotland, the son of a charwoman and a truck driver.

In 1971, frustrated at being typecast, he walked away from the role that made him an international superstar, and the general consensus at the time was that he had made a huge blunder. But against all odds he managed to shake off his old image and become one of the most popular film superstars ever, improving with age like a vintage Merlot. His banner year was 1975, when he made three of his best movies: *Robin and Marion, The Wind and the Lion,* and, best of all, **The Man Who Would Be King** (1975).

John Huston had long wanted to film the Rudyard Kipling story about two cocky English sergeants-of-fortune who find themselves leaders of a kingdom in Karafistan. (The project was originally planned for Humphrey Bogart and Clark Gable.) Sean Connery is marvelous as the proud but not-too-bright Danny Dravot, and Michael Caine is perfect as Peachy Carnehan, his best friend and partner in con. Together, they generate an extraordinary chemistry on-screen. Through a fluke of fate, Danny comes to be regarded as a god by the locals and is crowned king, to the escalating consternation of his friend, Peachy. "He can break wind at both ends, simultaneous, which I'm willing to bet is more than any god can do," comments Peachy ruefully. But Connery is immensely endearing as the title character, a not-too-bright small-time con artist elevated to the status of royalty. "If a king can't sing," he decrees, "it ain't worth being king." *The Man Who Would Be King* is packed with adventure, laughs, derring-do, and derring-dumb. It's far too enjoyable to be considered a rumination of how absolute power corrupts, but the lesson is not lost on our heroes. With Christopher Plummer in a wraparound role as Kipling.

august 26

A Mutiny Against Injustice

The U.S. Navy brig *Washington* seized the Cuban slave ship *Amistad* off the coast of Long Island, New York, on this day in 1839—starting one of the most complex and historic court battles in American history.

Two months earlier, the Africans who were crammed like sardines aboard the *Amistad*—"cargo" slated to be sold as slaves—had seized control of the ship in a bloody coup, rebelling against the inhumane conditions in which they were kept. The uprising was spearheaded by Sengbe Pieh, a Membe African known as Cinque, who managed to free himself and the other slaves. They seized their opportunity in the midst of a violent storm at sea on July 2, using sugar cane knives to kill the captain, and took over the ship.

Cinque demanded that two surviving crew members who had purchased the slaves, José Ruiz and Pedro Montes, sail the *Amistad* back to Africa—but at night Ruiz and Montes steered the vessel toward America. On this day the ship was spotted and escorted to New London, Connecticut. Ruiz and Montes were freed, but the Africans were imprisoned pending an investigation of the revolt.

The story and resulting trial are recounted in Steven Spielberg's impressive and moving **Amistad** (1997). The opening mutiny scene is not for the squeamish, and a flashback depicting life aboard the vessel is emotionally wrenching. But for the most part, the film is an elaborately produced courtroom drama. As both an actor and a lawyer, Matthew McConaughey is in over his head as a young attorney who initially defends the fifty-three slaves, but Anthony Hopkins steals the movie in a fabulous performance as former president John Quincy Adams, who becomes an advocate for the slaves. Djimon Hounsou is a magnificent Cinque. An absorbing, if overlong, account of one of the most fascinating events in U.S. legal history.

august 27

Have a Blast

On this day in 1883, the volcano on the island of Krakatoa, west of Java, exploded with a force of 1,300 megatons. It remains the world's most spectacular recorded natural disaster. The blast virtually blew up two-thirds of the island, causing 120-foot tidal waves that killed over thirty-two thousand people on the nearby populated islands. It could be heard from one thousand miles away, and the resulting ash and smoke blanketed the atmosphere, turning the sunsets scarlet red and lowering the temperature around the entire planet.

Hollywood may know how to market but it apparently has no sense of direction; thus, the mistitled **Krakatoa, East of Java** (1968), a precursor to all megabudget, FX-laden disaster movies to follow. It features an all-B-movie-star cast—Brian Keith as a deep-sea diver who has become addicted to laudenum, John Leyton as a bathosphere specialist who suffers from claustrophobia, Sal Mineo as an Italian balloonist, and more! Not only do you get the explosion—the filmmakers have also tossed in a mutiny, a sunken treasure, a newfangled diving bell, and other smoke and mirrors. Big and dumb—but you get a lot of bang for your buck. And the big bang at the end sounds good through the stereo speakers. Nice rumble. Turn up the bass.

august 28

Here's to You, Mr. Robinson

A red-letter day for African Americans in the sports world. On this day in 1945, Jackie Robinson was signed by Branch Rickey to the Brooklyn Dodgers, thus becoming the first black player in major league baseball. The first time he went on the field, there were catcalls, boos, and epithets. By the time he left, there were cheers.

Celebrate the breakthrough with **The Jackie Robinson Story** (1950), starring none other than Jackie Robinson himself. The film covers the period from when he played at UCLA to his breakthrough as the first black American to play in the majors. While he was certainly a better ballplayer than an actor, Robinson acquitted himself nicely as, well, himself. For the time in which this film was produced (the early '50s), it's quite frank in its presentation of the barriers he came up against both professionally and personally—although the Hollywood homogenization machine did clean things up quite a bit. A young Ruby Dee costars as his wife.

august 29

Re-Cycle

On this day in 1885, Gottlieb Daimler patented a motorized bicycle—the world's first motorcycle. His invention didn't really catch on until after 1910, but it was used heavily by the armed forces in World War I. Popularity sagged during the '30s, but roared back with a vengeance after World War II. Moviegoers got their first real biker movie with 1954's *The Wild One* with Marlon Brando as the leather-jacketed, hog-riding rebel. Steve McQueen, a motorcycle enthusiast, did his own stunts for *The Great Escape* (1963). Roger Corman and AIP Studios produced a series of B biker flicks in the

'60s, including such tempting titles as *Hells Angels on Wheels, The Wild Angels,* and more.

But the ultimate biker movie is **Easy Rider** (1969). Ex-AIP regulars Dennis Hopper and Peter Fonda concocted the idea of filming what was originally conceived to be "a Western with motorcycles instead of horses." With Terry Southern cowriting, Peter Fonda producing and costarring, and Dennis Hopper directing and costarring, they managed to conjure up one of the most influential and culturally important films of the '60s—not to mention one of the most drug-influenced. Fonda and Hopper are Captain America and Wyatt, two loners who score a major drug sale (look for producer Phil Spector in his first—and so far only—acting job as the buyer in the opening sequence) and decide to go "looking for America," cruising the highways and back roads on their bikes.

Along the way they meet up with George Hanson, a ne'er-do-well ACLU lawyer in the deep South, sleeping off a bender in a jail cell. Jack Nicholson became an overnight star for his movie-stealing turn as the lawyer who decides to join the duo, donning a football helmet, taking his first hit of pot (no stand-ins were used for this scene), and jabbering about Venusions among us.

august 30

A Wighter Shade of Sale

Woodstock may have become the iconic rock festival, and the Monterey Pop Festival of 1967 may have had better music, but for sheer lunacy, you can't top the Isle of Wight Festival, which took place on this small island off the coast of England, kicking off this day in 1970.

It was almost a disaster from the start, but a fabulously entertaining one. Nearly 600,000 people invaded the small island (accessible only by boat) to attend the concert—but only about one in ten of them had tickets. A radical, disorganized, and fairly zoned-out bunch of hippies—mostly Americans—

began protesting outside the grounds for a "free concert," chanting "The fence must die!" The event organizers tried to keep them out, and the resulting and escalating confrontations were both comical and frightening. And it's all captured in **Message to Love: The Isle of Wight Festival** (1996). Filmmaker Murray Lesser was on hand to record the concert, but ended up with much more. What he caught on film was both funny and disheartening. The festival was called "the last Great Event" (mostly by the producer), but there's a case for that. You can literally see the hippie dream coming apart at the seams, and it's even more discouraging to find that most of the troublemakers were Americans. The young space case who admits to feeding LSD to his five-year-old son is still shocking, an unforgettable segment.

Musically, the performances are spotty, but fascinating—much better than in *Woodstock.* The impending break-ins through the fences were nerve-wracking on the performers. A drunken Kris Kristofferson looks over his shoulder and says, "I think they're gonna shoot us" to a bandmate, before stumbling offstage in midsong; a shaken and fragile-looking Joni Mitchell admonishes the crowd to "stop acting like tourists" before going into a spacey story about Native Americans. Of more historical interest, the movie contains Jimi Hendrix playing his next-to-last live gig ever (he would be dead within two weeks) and one of the last performances by the Doors—led by somnambulistic shaman Jim Morrison in magnificent voice.

Remember: *"The fence must die!"*

august 31

A Ripping Yarn

He was the first serial killer to capture the attention of the public, and his name is synonymous with unsolvable crimes and unspeakable evil. On this day in the Whitechapel district of London in 1888, Jack the Ripper claimed his first official victim, a prostitute named Polly Nichols. She was discovered by a laborer on his way to work early in the morning, her throat slashed so deeply that it had severed her spinal column. In the next few months, "the Ripper" would dispatch at least four more victims, each murder more grisly than the last. Then, as suddenly as they began, the murders ceased—and amateur sleuths have been speculating ever since on the identity of the villain the press dubbed "Saucy Jack."

Jack the Ripper has inspired numerous movies, starting with Alfred Hitchcock's early masterpiece, *The Lodger* (1926). Others include Klaus Kinski playing the lead role in *Jack the Ripper* (a.k.a. *The Web*) (1976), and *Jack the Ripper* (1988), an intriguing two-part TV miniseries starring Michael Caine as Frederick Abberline, the alcoholic Scotland Yard inspector in charge of the perplexing case.

But the most inventive appearance of Jack in film is in Nicholas Meyer's remarkably inventive romance-suspense-sci-fi-fantasy-comedy, **Time After Time** (1979). Malcolm McDowell gives an unexpectedly charming performance as H. G. Wells, who, in one of the screenplay's clever conceits, has not only written about, but actually constructed a time-travel machine in 1870s London. He believes the future will be a crime-free Utopia, and plans to visit. At a dinner party he unveils his invention to a group of his skeptical friends and colleagues, including a good doctor who, unbeknownst to Wells, is really Jack the Ripper (a marvelous performance of pure evil by David Warner). The evil doctor absconds with Wells's time machine and winds up in 1970s-era San Francisco. "Back home I was a freak," he gloats. "Here, I'm an amateur."

The horrified Wells chases after him, terrified of what he has unleashed on his "utopian" future. Arriving in "modern-day" San Francisco, the befuddled author finds it a far cry from the Utopia he imagined. But he teams up with Amy Robbins (Mary Steenburgen), a pretty bank teller who's smitten with the odd little man, and romance blossoms.

A terrific blend of sci-fi, romance, comedy, and suspense, *Time After Time* boasts one of the most inventive screenplays of the '70s, and delightful performances. If you detect a little chemistry between McDowell and Steenburgen, you're right; they were married shortly thereafter (too bad it didn't last).

september

september 1

Come Out Swinging

On this day, Edgar Rice Burroughs, the author who created the vine-swinging, chest-thumping Tarzan of the Apes, was born in 1875. The tale of the young English orphan who is raised by apes in the African jungle started as nothing more than a pulp story—one of many that Burroughs cranked out during his lifetime—but went on to achieve mythic status via sequels, comic strips, and movies.

Countless film versions have been made, with over a dozen actors portraying the Ape Man over the years, starting with Elmo Lincoln as early as 1912. *Greystoke: The Legend of Tarzan, Lord of the Apes* (1984) has the dubious distinction of having the longest title and sticking closest to the original story—although half of the movie takes place back in England, and the character is never once referred to as "Tarzan." Bo Derek stars in a wonderfully campy version (no, not *that* campy; she plays Jane) in 1981's *Tarzan, the Ape Man,* which focuses more on Derek's clinging loincloth (which displays much more loin than cloth) than on the title character; and Disney produced an impressive and very entertaining animated version in 1998. But the best movie version is still **Tarzan, the Ape Man** (1932) starring the quintessential movie Tarzan, Johnny Weissmuller, who couldn't act worth a damn but didn't need to. A surprisingly adult movie, *Tarzan* features shockingly graphic violence for its day, and a still eyebrow-raising nude swimming sequence with Maureen O'Sullivan, the sexiest Jane ever. The film was a smashing success, inspiring thousands of young boys all across America to break their necks while attempting to swing by rope from tree to tree.

september 2

That's News to You

It was a big day for network news today in 1963. The two major networks, CBS and NBC, expanded their evening news reports from fifteen minutes to a full half hour. Until this day, the evening news consisted of a single camera pointed at an anchorman reading the day's top stories behind a desk from a sheaf of papers held in his hands.

To justify the expansion, the networks began to rely more and more on videotape reports and remotes, adding correspondents, flashier graphics, more in-depth interviews, and live satellite feeds, and replacing bona fide news journalists with generic TV "personalities." The fine line between news and entertainment—and, more importantly, between reporting the news and creating the news—became increasingly blurred as the warring networks battled for ratings and viewers.

Celebrate this turning point in media manipulation with a double bill of two excellent exposés of network news. **Broadcast News** (1987) stars Holly Hunter as overachieving Washington bureau news producer Jane Craig, who begins an affair with vacuous but ambitious reporter Tom Grunnick (William Hurt), who has his eyes set on the coveted anchor chair for the evening news. Tom has the looks, style, and charisma for the job—it's just that he cannot grasp the concept of facts or news. Also in love with Jane is reporter Aaron Altman (the magnificently funny and neurotic Albert Brooks), who has the conscientiousness, knowledge, and brains for the job—but unfortunately breaks out in a cold sweat when presented with his once-in-a-lifetime opportunity. Writer-director James Brooks has fashioned an on-target, hilarious, and insightful exposé on how network news really operates, with three top-drawer performances.

Follow up the lead story with Paddy Chayevsky's scathing indictment of television news—and television in general—**Network** (1976). Washed-up news anchorman Peter Finch goes ballistic, live on-the-air, ranting about how the system *really* works—and the ratings go through the roof. The corporation recognizes a gold mine when it sees one, even an unstable one, and begins to exploit the situation to boost ratings and profits. Finch's performance—his last—galvanized a nation to go to their windows and shout, "I'm mad as hell and I'm not going to take it anymore!" Then they returned to their televisions and switched channels.

september 3

Extra! Extra!

On this day in 1833, the *New York Sun* rolled off the presses and published its first edition—becoming the first daily newspaper in America. Commemorate the watermark event with Howard Hawks's comedy classic, **His Girl Friday** (1939), one of the all-time great screwball comedies, a remake of the classic Ben Hecht–Charles MacArthur stage play, *The Front Page.* Cary Grant gives one of his finest, funniest performances as manipulative and merciless editor Walter Burns, who will stop at nothing to get a story, best the competition and, incidentally, win back the affections of his ex-wife, Hildy (the fabulously saucy Rosalind Russell). Hawks had the inspiration to switch the dynamics of the original stage play by making Hildy Johnson, previously a male role, into a woman recently divorced from editor Walter Burns. One of the funniest—and fastest—talkies ever made; you simply can't get all the jokes with one viewing.

september 4

Have a Night In, on the Town

On this day in 1609, navigator Henry Hudson stumbled upon a tiny island between what is now New York and New Jersey. It would come to be called Manhattan.

Next to Hollywood itself, no location has served for the inspiration, heart, soul, and setting of so many memorable movies. A dazzling celebration of Manhattan, **On the Town** (1949) was the first musical to step out of a Hollywood soundstage and into the real world. Gene Kelly, Frank Sinatra, and Jules Munshin play three carefree sailors who find romance and adventure on a twenty-four-hour leave in the Big Apple. Director Stanley Donen revolutionized the genre by having the stars sing and dance at actual Manhattan landmarks—on a carriage through Central Park, from the Statue of Liberty, on a Fifth Avenue bus, from atop the Empire State Building, and more. Manhattan never looked more colorful or alive with possibilities. Includes the classic songs "New York, New York" and "Come Up to My Place."

And if you want to see Manhattan in glorious black and white, savor the view from what is arguably Woody Allen's finest film, **Manhattan** (1979). Woody was at the peak of his form, starring as an angst-consumed TV writer who's having guilt pangs and qualms about his relationship with a high school student (an affecting Mariel Hemingway)—an ironic foreshadowing of real life to come. Allen's valentine to the limitless romance that permeates and envelopes the city is perhaps his most astute blending of the comic and the profound. Gordon Willis's rapturous cinematography is sumptuous—virtually every exterior shot is picture-postcard perfection.

september 5

You Can See the Doctor Now

Author Boris Pasternak's popular historical novel of love, loyalty, and sacrifice during the Russian revolution, *Doctor Zhivago,* was published in the U.S. on this day in 1958 and promptly became a gargantuan bestseller among romantics and historians alike.

Director David Lean was an ideal choice for the screen adaptation of **Doctor Zhivago** (1965); his gift for literate, sweeping, and intelligent epics (*The Bridge on the River Kwai* [1957], *Lawrence of Arabia* [1962]) was well established. In *Zhivago,* Lean does a magnificent job of creating both a spellbinding saga and a fascinating look at one of the most important times in the history of humanity. Omar Sharif—who became a star largely due to his role in Lean's *Lawrence of Arabia* two years before—is noble and handsome as the suffering, self-sacrificing title character, supported by a prestigious ensemble cast including Alec Guinness, Julie Christie, Geraldine Chaplin, Ralph Richardson, and Rod Steiger. A lush, lavish, epic romance—and if you're not humming "Lara's Theme" after the movie's over there's something seriously wrong.

september 6

Trekker Treat

At 9 P.M. on this night in 1966, *Star Trek* premiered on NBC and boldly went where many a TV series had gone before—straight to the bottom of the ratings.

For a TV series that was a ratings bomb during its initial three-year run, *Star Trek* certainly left a cultural legacy. By far the most successful TV franchise ever, what started as a tepidly popular show with a devoted "cult" following evolved into a success as reruns with an increasingly mainstream audience and, eventually, a stream of motion pictures. Its reach and influence are remarkable: It has spawned seven major motion pictures with the original cast, four spin-off TV series (*Deep Space Nine, Star Trek: The Next Generation, Voyager,* and *Enterprise*), three additional motion pictures with the *Next Generation* cast, one animated cartoon series, and a veritable lexicon of phrases that have entered the cultural vernacular ("He's dead, Jim"; "Beam me up, Scotty"; "Live long and prosper").

Celebrate the phenomenon of Trekdom with **Galaxy Quest** (1999), a winking and enormously good-natured homage packed with enough clever conceits and fun performances for three *Star Trek* movies and a *Star Wars Episode One: The Phantom Menace,* to boot. In his best screen role yet, Tim Allen stars as has-been actor Jason Nesmith, who starred as Commander Peter Quincy Taggart of the starship *Protector* in the long-defunct cult TV series, *Galaxy Quest.* Twenty years after the show was cancelled, he and his old TV crew are reduced to making a living by donning their old uniforms at sci-fi conventions and hardware store grand openings. Meanwhile, a group of real aliens have been receiving television transmissions of the long-defunct series and mistake the episodes for "historical documents." (They also believe the *Gilligan's Island* crew is still marooned after that three-hour tour!) The aliens transport Allen and his crew (including a delightful Sigourney Weaver, a self-parodying Alan Rickman, and a hysterical Sam Rockwell as "Panicky Guy") to their real-life spaceship to help save their race, under attack by one nasty-looking alien from another galaxy.

Packed with affectionate in-jokes and lots of heart, *Galaxy Quest* delivers the goods in this dead-on parody of the Star Trek phenomenon. Set your phasers on fun.

september 7

Bad Day for the James Boys

He was the first American outlaw to be embraced by the public as a hero, and he was elevated to legend status in his own lifetime. Never mind that in real life he was as likely to shoot a man as to help him, and that he rode with the notorious Quantrill's Raiders, one of the deadliest rebel terrorist groups of the Civil War. In reel life, he's inspired more movies than any other outlaw, a mythical Robin Hood of the Old West.

But at two P.M. on this day in 1876, Jesse James's luck took a turn for the worse, when he attempted to rob a bank in Northfield, Minnesota, along with his brother Frank, the Younger brothers, Bill Chadwell, Clell Miller, and Charlie Pitts. The gang was hundreds of miles from their familiar home turf, and had no idea how tenaciously the citizenry of Northfield would defend their town from the notorious James Gang. By the end of the day, Chadwell, Pitts, and Miller were dead, the Youngers were shot to pieces, and only Jesse and Frank managed to escape. To add insult to injury, the entire take was a measly twenty-six dollars.

The pivotal event is depicted in several movies about the renowned outlaw. *Jesse James* (1939), starring Tyrone Power as a sanitized and saintly Jesse and a laconic Henry Fonda as brother Frank, was filmed on location at many of the actual places the Jameses frequented. An early Technicolor movie, it's still gorgeous to look at, and the legendary Northfield Raid is a highlight.

But the best re-creation of the infamous robbery is in director Walter Hill's **The Long Riders** (1980), a minor western masterpiece. Boasting some of the best stunt casting in Hollywood history, real-life siblings James and Stacy Keach play Jesse and Frank James, with the Carradine brothers—David, Keith, and Robert—as the Youngers, plus Nicholas and Christopher Guest as Bob and Charlie Ford. The Northfield Raid is the highlight of the movie—a slow-motion ballet of carnage and confusion. Simultaneously elegiac and gritty, mythical and realistic, *The Long Riders* will make you want to get on the nearest horse and follow the sun. An excellent, evocative music score by Ry Cooder (*The Buena Vista Social Club,* 1999) adds to the mythos.

september 8

A Fragile Revolutionary Gives Up the Fight

On this day in 1979, at age forty-one, troubled actress Jean Seberg committed suicide with an overdose of barbiturates. She had recently suffered from a nervous breakdown following a miscarriage, and had been hounded and vilified by the American press and government agencies for her support of the Black Panthers.

The tragedy of Jean Seberg is that she never got to find out who Jean Seberg was. She was a star before she was an actress. At seventeen years old, she was selected from over eighty thousand applicants by director Otto Preminger to play Joan of Arc in *Saint Joan* (1957). The film was a flop, but Seberg's unique quality of rebelliousness mixed with innocence struck a chord. She moved to France to play an American beatnik in Jean-Luc Goddard's first film, *Breathless* (1960). Her best performance was in Robert Rosen's *Lillith* (1964), as a schizophrenic patient who seduces her therapist, played by a young up-and-coming Warren Beatty. Her image as being unstable, sensitive, and seductive strangely foreshadowed her future private life.

Explore the fragile actress's life with the fascinating **From the Journals of Jean Seberg** (1995), director Mark Rappaport's brilliant pastiche of documentary and what could be described as cinematic impressionism. Mary Beth Hurt narrates as Seberg from beyond the grave, recounting everything from her Midwest school days through her movie successes, her hellish marriage to Romain Gary, her involvement with the Black Panthers, and her suicide. Interspersed with remarkable footage of the real Seberg, *From the Journals,* becomes much more than a documentary or film bio.

september 9

Bowl Yourself Over

On this day in 1895, the American Bowling Congress, the first official bowling organization, was started in the United States, and the sport of bowling became an accepted institution. Originally a pastime of the aristocracy, in America the sport was embraced by the working class. Celebrate the sport with the Farrelly Brothers' first big box office hit, the boisterously entertaining **Kingpin** (1996). Woody Harrelson plays professional bowler Roy Munson, who finds himself up against "Big Ern" McCracken (Bill Murray). After angry competitors cut off his bowling hand, Munson's career is in the gutter—until, seventeen years later, he meets Ishmael (Randy Quaid), a not-too-bright Amish man with a killer bowling technique. Together, they become the hustlers of bowling. Packed with great (and occasionally tasteless) gags and a lot of heart, *Kingpin* will make you want to head to the nearest bowling alley.

Make it a double feature with **The Big Lebowski,** also produced by a pair of brothers, Joel and Ethan Cohen. The magnificent Jeff Bridges stars as Dude, the ultimate California slacker, whose only passion—other than zoning out—is bowling. John Goodman (in a scene-stealing performance as a slightly psycho Vietnam vet) and Steve Buscemi play his bowling buddies. Surreal, deadpan, and original, *The Big Lebowski* is a solid strike, with laughs to spare.

september 10

A Long Shot

They don't make politicians like Huey Long anymore; there are laws now. The autocratic Long served as governor of Louisiana—some would say dictator of Louisiana—from 1929 through 1932, and was then elected to the U.S. Senate. He was gunned down this day in 1935 by the son-in-law of a political opponent.

He was a powerful man, and a compelling genuine American character. His record for civic improvements and social benefits was amazing—but his uncontrollable lust for power was his undoing. **All the King's Men** (1949) is the thinly fictionalized story of his meteoric rise and fall, based on Robert Penn Warren's Pulitzer Prize–winning novel. In an Oscar-winning performance, Broderick Crawford literally commands the screen in the best part of his career as the bullheaded Southern demagogue Willie Stark, who starts out with an honorable sense of purpose and a disarming honesty, only to succumb to greed, corruption, and temptation. Directed by Robert Rosen, *All the King's Men* is grim, graphic, and compelling. Academy Award winner for Best Picture 1949.

september 11

Five Films in One

Few stories of the rise to success are as circuitous or compelling as that of William Sidney Porter, born this day in 1862.

An aimless but amiable drifter, he spent his early years in Austin, Texas—eventually getting a job as bank cashier at the National Bank, marrying, and having a son. Things were going fine until there was a small discrepancy in the bank's books, and Porter was charged with embezzling. A warrant was issued for his arrest, and he skipped town to Honduras rather than stand trial. Upon receiving word that his wife was dying, he returned to Austin in 1897 and, after her death, turned himself in to the authorities. He served three years at the federal penitentiary in Columbus, Ohio, and was by all accounts a model prisoner. During his incarceration, he began writing to pass the time—short stories with unique twist endings that became his trademark. After his release from prison, he took the nom de plume O. Henry, moved to New York, and became one of the most successful and popular short story writers in American history.

His stories have served as the basis of several movies, but the film that best captures the flavor of his style is the delightful **O. Henry's Full House** (1952), an omnibus of five vignettes adapted from his works with a wonderfully eccentric cast including Charles Laughton, Marilyn Monroe, Richard Widmark, Fred Allen, and Oscar Levant. Two of O. Henry's most famous and affecting stories are included: "The Gift of the Magi," about a poor young couple's Christmas presents for one another, and "The Ransom of Red Chief," where a couple of kidnappers (Fred Allen and Oscar Levant) offer to pay a ransom to the parents to take the obnoxious child they've kidnapped off their hands. The first episode ("The Cop and the Anthem"), in which Laughton plays a dignified bum trying to get himself jailed for the winter, is both amusing and wistful (look for a brief role by Marilyn Monroe as a streetwalker). O. Henry's recurring motif of the redeeming power of love permeates the film like a benign aura. An uplifting break from the usual fare and highly recommended. The stories are introduced by on-screen narrator John Steinbeck in an extremely rare film appearance.

september 12

Here They Come . . .

It was a Monday night and the time was 7:30—not too late for the preteens to watch. That pre-fab four from the '60s, the Monkees, made their premiere on NBC this night in 1966. The series, which tried to emulate the feel of the Beatles' *Hard Day's Night,* cast four unknown young actors to portray a rock band and was an immediate hit with young viewers. Surprisingly, the series actually won an Emmy for Best Comedy Series after its first season.

Commemorate this landmark occasion in pop culture by watching the Monkees' cult film, **Head** (1968), made just after their show had been canceled. It was too far-out for their teenage fans, and no self-respecting leftist radical college student of the time would be caught dead in the theater watching a Monkees movie, so it bombed at the box office. Too bad, because *Head* is really an eccentrically bizarre and inventive trip, infinitely more inventive and outré than the Beatles' cinematic efforts. A true pop cinema oddity, it was written by Jack Nicholson (yes, that Jack Nicholson), directed by Bob Rafelson, and features appearances by such pop culture icons as Frank Zappa, Annette Funicello, Sonny Liston, Dennis Hopper, Jack Nicholson, Timothy Carey, and Victor Mature (as "the Big Vic"). A free-association mix of comedy, music, and some actual subversive satire, *Head* still has a refreshingly avant-garde feel to it. (By the way, the reason they named it *Head* is that, in the event there was a sequel, it could be publicized as being "from the folks who gave you *Head.*" Not surprisingly, there was no sequel.)

september 13

A Bad Rap

One of rap music's most eloquent artists—and a promising actor—died this day in 1996 as the result of four gunshot wounds received on September 7. He had been riding in a car driven by controversial record label owner Suge Knight, in Las Vegas, when he was attacked. The killers were never caught. He had survived a previous attempt on his life only months earlier. In death, as in life, Tupac Shakur became a lightning rod for both criticism and support of his chosen art.

As an actor, Tupac had charisma and an amiable, sensitive face that the camera loved—capable of projecting anger, strength, and, most poignantly, vulnerability. He was born in 1971 to Alfani Shakur, a member of the Black Panther party, while she was serving a sentence in jail. His name derived from "Tupac Amaru" (an Incan phrase meaning "shining serpent") and "Shakur" (derived from Arabic, "thankful to God"). It was a dichotomous name that seemed to haunt the artist.

In his short career as an actor, he gave his finest performance in **Gridlock'd** (1996) as Spoon, a junkie and sometimes-musician with bug-eyed Stretch (Tim Roth) and their singer, Cookie (Thandie Newton). When Cookie OD's and goes into a coma, Spoon and Stretch decide to kick the habit and get clean—but find themselves endlessly shuffled around within a social system that's supposed to help them. The two also find themselves the prime suspects in their ex-dealer's murder. A bracing mix of comedy, drama, and social commentary.

september 14

A Head Trip Not for the Squeamish

He was only trying to help—but with help like this, who needs a Good Samaritan?

On this day in 1936, in an attempt to relieve the symptoms of an elderly patient's depression and anxiety, psychosurgery advocate Walter Freeman oversaw the first prefrontal lobotomy in Washington, D.C. During the operation, nerve pathways to the frontal lobe of the patient's brain were severed, in a blind attempt to balance the two sides.

Within the next twenty years over forty thousand people would undergo the "treatment." By 1945, Freeman refined the procedure with the "ice pick lobotomy," where an ice pick–like instrument was drilled into the brain through the tear duct, and rotated on a fifty-degree arc. Thankfully, the practice was discredited by the early '60s.

The practice and malpractice of prefrontal lobotomies (and electroshock therapy) is addressed with compassion, honesty, and surprising humor in the vastly entertaining **One Flew over the Cuckoo's Nest** (1975). Jack Nicholson gives one of his greatest performances as Randall McMurphy, a small-time crook who fakes insanity to get out of work detail by being sent to a mental hospital. Once there, he acts as a catalyst for his fellow patients (including Danny DeVito, in his first substantial film role, and his future *Taxi* costar, Christopher Lloyd) and rebels against the abusive head nurse, Nurse Ratchet (Louise Fletcher). Funny, touching, and brilliantly written. A clean sweep at the 1975 Oscars, capturing Best Picture, Best Director (Milos Forman), Best Screenplay, Best Actor (Nicholson's first win), and Best Actress.

september 15

Space Out with a Dysfunctional Family Other than Your Own

Lost in Space fans may not be as ubiquitous as *Star Trek* fans; they seem to stay incognito.

The sci-fi/fantasy series premiered on ABC-TV on this evening in 1966. Created by '60s pop culture sultan Irwin Allen (*Voyage to the Bottom of the Sea* and *The Time Tunnel*), *Lost In Space* chronicled the adventures of the Robinson family, who got lost in space due to the machinations of evil stowaway and enemy agent Dr. Smith (memorably essayed by Jonathan Harris). Whatever pretensions or possibilities for literate story lines the creators had soon got lost, too; by the middle of its first season, the show had turned to low camp. The doctor was reduced to over-the-top comic relief against the robot and costar Billy Mumy, and the story lines were bursting at the seams with rubber-suited monsters and walking carrots.

Commemorate the premiere of the original with the big-screen version, **Lost in Space** (1998). Like leftover pizza, the movie actually improves the second time around and reheated. On the big screen, it was a disappointment for many; but transferred to TV-size it proves more amiably entertaining than the series that inspired it. Gary Oldman is about as light on his feet as he is capable of being as treacherous Dr. Smith. The effects are suitably impressive, and while it's no *Armageddon,* is that a bad thing? Many of the original TV cast members (June Lockhart, Bill Mumy, Angela Cartwright, Marta Kristin, and Mark Goddard) appear in cameos for knowing (and aging) fans.

september 16

Stampede!

It was a human stampede quite unlike any other in history. On this day in 1893 the Great Oklahoma Land Run occurred. More than 100,000 hopeful pioneers from all over the country came to stake out their part of the American dream. When the starting gun fired, it was every man and woman for themselves—and the massive surge of humanity was unbelievable. Those who jumped the gun were labeled as "sooners," which gave rise to the state's nickname—the Sooner State.

The event is re-created in several movies, including both versions of Edna Ferber's epic Oklahoma tale, *Cimarron* (1935 and 1960) But the best version is director Ron Howard's impressively sweeping drama, **Far and Away** (1992). Tom Cruise and Nicole Kidman star in this old-fashioned romance about a young Irish immigrant couple (one working class, one well-to-do) who come to America to make their fortune. The film covers their journey from Ireland to the new land, and climaxes with the Oklahoma Land Run.

september 17

Have a Hank-erin' for Some Country Music?

Hank Williams was America's poet laureate of the honky-tonks, and by far country music's biggest influence, if not its biggest star. His songs are simple three-chord affairs, but their virtuoso shading and colors are endless—from the wistful and piercing imagery of "I'm So Lonesome I Could Cry" and "I Saw the Light" to the rowdy good-times feel of "Honky Tonkin'" and "Hey, Good-Lookin'." He had trouble handling fame, though, and became addicted to alcohol and painkillers to ease the spinal pain from which he suffered all his life. On his way to a gig on January 1, 1953, he died, at twenty-nine, of a heart ailment, looking three times his age.

But before he left this world he changed country music forever, and became the original "outlaw" troubadour along the way, inspiring such future singer-songwriters as Willie Nelson, Johnny Cash, and Merle Haggard.

He was born this day in 1923. His story is told—in a somewhat sanitized Hollywood version—in **Your Cheatin' Heart** (1964). George Hamilton (yes, that George Hamilton, master of the ageless tan) had the best film role of his career as the carousing singer. The movie glosses over Hank's drug addictions and infidelities, but does a splendid job of capturing the raw and infectious energy the young newcomer had. Susan Oliver is outstanding as Hank's put-upon wife. The songs—classics all—are performed by Hank's real-life son, Hank Williams, Jr.

september 18

'Scuse Me While I Catch This Movie

On this morning in 1970, twenty-seven-year-old rock star Jimi Hendrix was found dead in his London apartment by his girlfriend, Monika Danneman. Two days earlier, Hendrix had played what was destined to be his last public performance, at Ronnie Scott's in London, backing up Eric Burdon and War. The visionary guitarist was looking forward to recording an album with Miles Davis and Gil Evans, but it was not to be.

Jimi Hendrix (1973) is an extraordinary compilation featuring some of his best-known performances—with footage from the Monterey Pop Festival, the Isle of Wight, Woodstock, and a live appearance on British TV; his in-your-face incendiary version of "The Star Spangled Banner"; plus rare footage of Jimi at Fillmore East with his Band of Gypsies. Interspersed between the clips are interviews with his dad, three of his girlfriends, Little Richard, Eric Clapton, and Pete Townshend of the Who. The clips and story are presented chronologically—so you see the short but fiery arc of Hendrix's short musical life, evolving from a nervous, eager-to-please showman to a withdrawn, drug-addled, and coddled celebrity. An insightful and enlightening documentary, packed with incendiary performances.

september 19

The First Films Protected by the U.S. Government

On this day in 1989, the Library of Congress posted a list of twenty-five American films to be placed on the National Film Registry as "culturally, historically, or aesthetically significant"—thus ensuring their perpetuity. Other lists followed in later years, but these were the first to be saved from possible extinction. Take your pick and enjoy; it's Reader's Choice tonight, and you can't go wrong with any of them.

Here's the complete list, in alphabetical order:

The Best Years of Our Lives
Casablanca
Citizen Kane
The Crowd
Dr. Strangelove
The General
Gone With the Wind
The Grapes of Wrath
High Noon
Intolerance
The Learning Tree
The Maltese Falcon
Mr. Smith Goes to Washington
Modern Times
Nanook of the North
On the Waterfront
The Searchers
Singin' in the Rain
Snow White and the Seven Dwarfs
Some Like It Hot
Star Wars
Sunrise
Sunset Boulevard
Vertigo
The Wizard of Oz

september 20

Cannes Do

The very first ever Cannes Film Festival kicked off this day in 1946 on the French Riviera. It would go on to become the most prestigious—and media-hyped—film festival in the world. But the first festival was fairly low-key, handing out a mere four awards. It would grow to become the most influential showplace for new talent, until Robert Redford's Sundance Film Festival came along in the early 1970s.

The only American film to be honored at the first Cannes festival was Billy Wilder's now-classic portrait of an alcoholic's trial by fire, **The Lost Weekend** (1945), for which Ray Milland won the Best Actor award at Cannes. The film still holds up as a harrowing depiction of alcoholism. The film takes place over a single weekend in the life of an alcoholic writer (Milland) who cannot accept the fact that he's an addict. Standout sequences include Milland's desperate search for liquor on a holiday when bars and stores are closed, and his hallucinatory withdrawals. Milland's remarkably brave, soul-bearing performance is one of the cinema's most affecting portrayals. A sobering film, no pun intended. In addition to being honored at Cannes, Milland won Best Actor at that year's Academy Awards ceremony. The film also took Best Picture and Best Director.

september 21

King for a Day

The most popular author of the last fifty years, and the most successful writer ever, Stephen King's specialty is scaring the bejeezus out of readers and making money hand over fist (not necessarily in that order). He was born on this day in 1947 in Portland, Maine—the state that's the setting for most of his novels.

King's bestsellers have been embraced by Hollywood—you may more accurately say "smothered by Hollywood"—usually with disappointing results. *Carrie* (1976) was his first Hollywood smash, followed by such varied successes as *Cujo* (1983), *Christine* (1984), *Misery* (1990), and Stanley Kubrick's controversial version of *The Shining* (1980). Kubrick radically rewrote King's material, much to the author's consternation.

But the best adaptation of a Stephen King story is not one of his horror tales. It's writer/director Frank Darabont's film of one of King's short stories. **The Shawshank Redemption** (1994) stars Morgan Freeman as Ellis "Red" Redding, an inmate at Maine's Shawshank State Prison. Tim Robbins is new inmate Andy Dufresne, a low-key banker convicted of murder. Andy's indomitable will earns Red's friendship and gradually transforms the entire prison. A surprising film that is alternately dark and inspiring, gritty and uplifting, and finally emotionally satisfying.

september 22

The Man You Love to Hate

He was the first film director to earn a reputation for extravagance, both artistically and financially, sixty years before James Cameron. As an actor, he was known and loathed the world over as "the man you love to hate."

Erich von Stroheim, born this day in Vienna, began his career as an extra for D. W. Griffith, and found himself cast as a despicable Hun in several World War I dramas. Audiences hissed when he threw a live baby out the window in *Hearts of the World,* and he was once stoned in the street after leaving a theater that showed the film.

After the war, when casting calls for vicious Huns dwindled, he managed to convince Universal Studios to let him direct a scandalous story of romantic deception, *Blind Husbands* (1919), in which he played an Austrian officer who seduces the naïve wife of an American tourist in the Alps. The film was a sensation, and Stroheim became the hottest director in town. His extravagances and quest for "realism" in his films bordered on madness and became the stuff of legend. He filmed real orgies (knowing full well they'd be censored) for *The Merry Widow.* He insisted that extras playing Prussian soldiers wear silk monogramed underwear under their uniforms—even though it would never be seen on the screen. He had an exact replica of Monte Carlo built for his film *Foolish Wives.* Studio publicists began issuing press releases spelling his name "von $troheim."

His greatest achievement—and grandest folly—was **Greed** (1924), his epic film adaptation of Frank Norris's realistic novel, *McTeague,* the story of the effects of money on a young struggling dentist and his wife in San Francisco. Stroheim filmed virtually every page of the novel exactly as written, in the actual locations described in the book, including the Sierras, San Francisco, and Death Valley. The final film ran eight hours, and was shown only once, at a preview for the press (several critics lucky enough to see it pronounced it the greatest film ever made). His new studio, MGM, insisted he edit the film to a more manageable length; he submitted a four-hour version. Told it was still too long, he defiantly refused to cut any more. It was taken out of his hands and edited by a man who, von Stroheim said, "had nothing on his mind but his hat." It was finally released in a butchered 140-minute version, a shadow of its former self. Still, *Greed* is an amazing film, painfully detailed and realistic, more cynical than a dozen Tarantino films, and a testament to Stroheim's phenomenal talent and iron will. A film unlike any other, and a true masterpiece of cinematic art.

september 23

Slip Yourself a Mickey

At one time, Mickey Rooney was the most popular box office star in America—outdrawing Gable, Cooper, and Hope and Crosby. During the early 1940s his Andy Hardy series literally paid MGM's bills, and his musicals with Judy Garland were phenomenally successful. A human dynamo,

Rooney has spent virtually his entire life before a motion picture camera (he made his debut at age six). He was born Joe Yule this day in 1920.

One of the amazing things about Rooney, other than the sheer force of his energy and his longevity, is his versatility as an actor. Consider the gamut of his astonishing range: a tough punk kid won over by Spencer Tracy in *Boys Town* (1938); a remarkably effective Puck in Shakespeare's *A Midsummer Night's Dream* (1935); his American everyboy in *The Human Comedy* (1943); the jockey in *National Velvet* (1944); the working stiff in over his head in *Quicksand* (1949); the retired jockey in *The Black Stallion* (1986).

But the Mickey that America embraced is the pint-sized dynamo who—figuratively, anyway—carried the country through the war years on the homefront. Catch what may be his finest performance in **The Human Comedy** (1943). Mickey plays a sensitive small-town teenager during the war who gets a job delivering telegrams. Frank Morgan (best remembered as the Wizard in *The Wizard of Oz*) is terrific as his kind-hearted, flask-tipping boss. A true slice of all-American pie—a little sugary but, in the end, unforgettable and very moving. As the young boy who becomes a young man through the course of the story, Rooney runs the gamut from comedy schtick to heartbreaking drama; it's a bravura performance in an unjustly forgotten film.

september 24

Tonight, Tonight

On this night in 1954, NBC Television premiered a unique late-night talk show, live from New York City, and dubbed it *The Tonight Show*. It was originally a two-hour live broadcast five nights a week, hosted by comedian Steve Allen. "You might as well know now," he commented during his opening remarks, "this show's gonna go on forever." He had no idea how prophetic those words were.

Over the next forty-five years, *The Tonight Show* went through a series of hosts (Steve Allen, Ernie Kovacs, Jack Paar, Johnny Carson [the longest, clocking in at twenty years], and, as of this edition, Jay Leno) to become an American institution, a siren song for insomniacs. Its power still exudes a dominant influence on our culture.

Martin Scorsese's **The King of Comedy** (1982) is an apt homage to its inspiration and lineage. *The Tonight Show* becomes *The Jerry Langford Show,* hosted by the fictitious Jerry Langford (played by Jerry Lewis in a startlingly good performance). Obsessive fan and stand-up comic (though he's never performed in front of a live audience) Rupert Pupkin (Robert DeNiro) imagines himself on the show, pals with the host, basking in the limelight of celebrity. When he's rebuffed by Langford, the already unhinged Pupkin finally goes even further over the deep end and, with the help of fellow psychotic Sandra Bernhard, kidnaps Langford, demanding the opening monologue spot on the show as ransom. Funny, disturbing, provocative, and dark, *The King of Comedy* captures the zeitgeist of *The Tonight Show* so effectively it's scary. Packed with in-jokes: real *Tonight Show* director Fred DeCordova plays the show's producer, and Scorsese himself contributes a winking cameo as the director. (Carson was approached to play himself but wisely declined.)

september 25

Biko Lives

On this day in 1977, fifteen thousand mourners attended the funeral of black South African activist and martyr Steven Biko. The police—who had taken the activist into custody weeks before—claimed he had died from a hunger strike. The ugly truth was revealed later: he was tortured to death.

Commemorate his life with **Cry Freedom** (1987), director Richard Attenborough's passionate and provocative story of friendship and honor. South African journalist Donald Woods (Kevin Kline), editor of the *Daily Dispatch,* writes a critical editorial of Biko, and is challenged to meet him. When he does, he is won over by the man's passion, articulateness, and sincerity, and the two begin a tentative but loyal friendship. When Biko is murdered, Woods applies pressure to investigate the case and finds his own life, and his family's, endangered. Denzel Washington gives a great performance as Biko, putting a human face on an icon—much as he would do years later portraying Malcolm X. Attenborough's film is a passionate, powerful work of conviction and anger.

september 26

Let's Do the Time Warp Again

The Granddaddy of All Cult Movies premiered with little fanfare and a very small audience this day at L.A.'s Westwood Theater in 1975.

The Rocky Horror Picture Show (1975) began its strange life as a stage musical written by Richard O'Brien and produced in London. American pop producer Lou Adler saw it and brought it to L.A., where it started playing to sell-out houses, eventually spawning several touring companies. The next logical step was a movie.

The audience at the Westwood premiere collectively scratched their heads, many leaving halfway through the screening. They had come expecting an innocuous sci-fi parody, and ended up with more than they bargained for—a campy, kitschy orgy of hedonistic self-indulgence and transvestitism. Most were perplexed, a few were offended . . . but a very few liked what they saw.

A couple of years later, the film began showing at midnight performances in small art theaters scattered across the country, most famously at the Waverly Theater in New York's Greenwich Village. A curious event began to happen: Die-hard fans were seeing the picture over and over, bringing in their uninitiated friends, dressing up in costume as their favorite characters, and talking back to the screen in what gradually became a rite of passage. It went from a local ritual to a nationwide phenomenon that still endures.

Gather a bunch of your strangest friends and celebrate the anniversary of the premiere of one of Hollywood's strangest success stories with *The Rocky Horror Picture Show.* The DVD version even cues you on what to say and when to toss your rice. If you've never seen it . . . well, don't dream it, be it.

september 27

Never Say Never Again

On this day, after over a decade of saying "never again," Sean Connery returned in front of the cameras to the role that made him famous, as agent 007 in *Never Say Never Again.*

The role of James Bond made Connery an overnight international star in 1963 when he appeared in the first 007 adventure, *Dr. No.* The right film for the right time, it struck a chord with audiences. It was soon followed by the even more successful *From Russia with Love.* By the time *Goldfinger* was released, the whole country was on a secret agent kick, with countless film imitations and TV shows like *The Man from U.N.C.L.E.* and *I Spy.*

But after 1966's *Thunderball,* Connery was wary of typecasting and vowed never to play the part again. A series of actors followed, but none had that special savoir-faire. Connery went on to surprise critics and audiences with fine performances in other films.

But in 1982 they made him an offer he didn't refuse, and, twelve years after saying "never again," he donned the tuxedo one more time. Basically a revamped version of *Thunderball,* **Never Say Never Again** (1982) is a welcome return to basics, with Bond a little older, a little slower, a little stiffer. Connery takes fun pokes at his old image while still living up to it ("I hope this is a return to more gratuitous sex and violence," comments Q). Klaus Maria Brandauer makes a more subtle and human nemesis than Bond's usual villains (he has feelings and a sense of humor), and Max von Sydow adds another spoonful of prestige to the mix. There's less reliance on gadgets and gimmicks, and Bond is as smooth as ever. It's good to have him back.

september 28

"Say It Ain't So, Joe"

It was baseball's first black eye, and America's first sports scandal. On this day in 1920, eight stars of the Chicago White Sox, including "Shoeless" Joe Jackson, were charged by a grand jury with conspiring with a gambling consortium to throw the 1919 World Series. Dubbed "the Black Sox Scandal," it tainted the great American pastime overnight, and heroes were turned into heels.

John Sayles's intelligent and insightful **Eight Men Out** (1988) recounts the sad story in a compelling, multilayered narrative, rich in period detail. Sayles's films are often about frailties that lie beneath the surface, and *Eight Men Out* does an admirable job of revealing the factors that led to the first sports scandal. As in his other films (*Return of the Secaucus Seven; Matewan*), Sayles doesn't focus on just one protagonist; he tells an ensemble story from various perspectives and viewpoints. His ability to weave together so many stories and characters is reminiscent of Robert Altman at his best. Each of the underpaid and underappreciated players of the Chicago White Sox has a different reason for succumbing to temptation, and Sayles allows us to feel sympathy for them while still condemning their actions. A uniformly excellent cast, with standout performances from John Cusack, D. B. Sweeny, and David Strathairn.

september 29

My, How You've Grown

Happy birthday today to the United States Army. It was on this day in 1789 that Congress voted to create and maintain a uniform U.S. Army with a permanent strength of one thousand enlisted men and officers.

There are countless movies depicting army life in both wartime and peacetime, but one of the finest is **A Walk in the Sun** (1946), directed by Lewis Milestone, who fifteen years earlier had directed the greatest antiwar film ever made, *All Quiet on the Western Front. A Walk in the Sun* may be a contender for "greatest war film ever made." The film follows the exploits of a lone army patrol on a single day during the Salerno landings of 1943. A masterful and suspenseful character study, and a celebration of the resourceful foot soldier.

And let's not forget our female contingent. **Private Benjamin** (1980) stars Goldie Hawn as a spoiled New York Jewish American princess who impulsively enlists in the U.S. Army after her husband (Albert Brooks) dies of a heart attack on their wedding night. Probably Goldie's best movie role—funny, flighty, and surprisingly touching.

september 30

Make the Dean's List

"That guy up ahead has got to see us."

Those were the last lines delivered by James Dean, uttered on this date as he sped his new car northward on Highway 466, near the junction of Highway 41 just outside the small town of Cholame, California. He was in a hurry to get to Salinas to drive his new car, a Porsche Spyder dubbed "Li'l Bastard," in the races that weekend. He'd already been pulled over earlier that day by a highway patrolman who clocked his speed at 75 mph and gave the young actor a stern warning. At approximately 5:45 P.M. Donald Turnupseed was negotiating a left turn onto the highway, the setting sun blocking his view of oncoming traffic. Dean tried to swerve and avoid the car, to no avail. When it was over, Turnipseed was dazed but unhurt, and Dean's traveling companion, Rolf Wutherich, suffered only a bruise on his forehead, having been thrown clear of the car. Dean was not so lucky; he was impaled on his steering column, his head nearly severed from his body. It was the end of his life, and the beginning of his legacy and legend.

A lot of people think James Dean made only three pictures before his tragic death at twenty-four—*East of Eden, Rebel Without a Cause,* and *Giant.* But before he graduated to star billing, he appeared very briefly in three other Hollywood picks: as a teenage wiseass badgering soda jerk Charles Coburn in *In the Good Old Summertime* (1952), appearing as an extra in the World War II action flick *Fixed Bayonets* (1951), and as a ringside boxing attendant in, of all things, a Martin and Lewis comedy, *Sailor Beware* (1951).

But of the three features he made, the one that really made him into an enduring icon (released only twenty-seven days after his death) was his penultimate film, **Rebel Without a Cause** (1955). Director Nicholas Ray began filming in black and white—but when the studio execs got sight of the exciting dailies (combined with glowing press on Dean's just-released starring role in *East of Eden* [1955]), they decided to shoot in Technicolor. Ray took full advantage of the spectrum, saturating his images in increasingly bold and vibrant colors—culminating in the iconic red jacket that Dean wears late in the film.

Dean's portrayal of disturbed teen Jim Stark (he was twenty-four at the time) set the tone for succeeding generations of sensitive-yet-volatile youth. Perhaps more effectively than any other actor, Jimmy Dean knew instinctively how to milk the method. His performance as Jim Stark is at once angry and wounded, and his body language often evokes a marionette being dangled by invisible strings. Dig how he soothes his fevered brow with a cold bottle of milk from the fridge, or the resigned release of air from his body—like a punctured tire—when he realizes he's going to have to fight. Dean's method acting caused numerous on-set problems; the scene where he bangs his fist into a solid oak desk wasn't faked. Immediately after filming, the actor was rushed to the hospital with two broken fingers. The motives behind the rebelliousness of him and his fellow wounded teens (Natalie Wood and Sal Mineo) appear hopelessly anachronistic now, almost quaint—but Dean's performance is endlessly insinuating and inventive. Keep an eye out for a young Dennis Hopper as a gang member named "Goon."

october

october 1

A Movie That Plays Hardball

"I see great things in baseball. It's our game.
The American game.
It will repair our losses and be a blessing to us."

—*Walt Whitman*

The very first officially sanctioned World Series baseball game occurred on this day in 1903 between the National League Pittsburgh Pirates and the American League Boston Pilgrims (now Boston Red Sox). When it was over on October 13, the Pirates had won the series five games to three.

No filmmaker understands the nearly mystical allure baseball holds for the American psyche like Ron Shelton does. He wrote and directed *Cobb* (1994), the exposé-bio of baseball's first superstar. He followed it up with the witty and game-savvy **Bull Durham** (1988). Kevin Costner plays Crash Davis, a minor-league catcher demoted to coaching a promising but raw new pitcher, Nuke LaLoosh (Tim Robbins in his breakthrough role). Susan Sarandon is sexy and sassy as Annie, who selects one player each new season for some very unorthodox private lessons (including tying Nuke down to the bedposts and reading him poetry). *Bull Durham* is a homage to the undefinable Zen-like magic of the game, with all its superstitions, talismans, and traditions.

If you've already seen *Bull Durham,* here are some other suggestions waiting in the bullpen: Robert Redford's elegiac, *The Natural* (1984); Kevin Costner (again) in the male-weepie *Field of Dreams* (1989); *Major League* (1989); Albert Brooks as *The Scout* (1994); and, if you've got a whole day to kill, Ken Burns's fascinating and exhaustive PBS documentary, *Baseball* (1997).

october 2

Hello, I Must Be Going

"Remember, men, we're fighting for this woman's honor, which is probably more than she ever did for it."

—Groucho Marx, in Duck Soup

Julius Henry Marx was born on this day in 1890 in New York City. With his brothers, Arthur, Leonard, and Herbert (better known as Harpo, Chico, and Zeppo), he formed one of the most legendary comedy acts of all time: the Marx Brothers. With his leering eyes and hyperactive brows, demented gait, quicksilver wit, and lightning-fast ad-libs, Groucho earned himself a place among the immortals—although he once said he wouldn't want to be in any club that would have him as a member.

Celebrate the loony glory of movie Marxism with **Duck Soup** (1933), the Marxes' most anarchic, joyous, undisciplined, anything-goes film. Groucho is Rufus T. Firefly, flighty president of Freedonia. All the elements for Marxian mayhem are in place: looney lampoonery, Harpo's horn, Chico's puns, and, of course, the great grande dame Margaret Dumont. But it's Groucho's finest, funniest hour—a devastating satire of war, politics, and patriotism. *Duck Soup* is brimming with classic bits, including Harpo's masterful "mirror" sequence, which he re-created twenty-three years later with Lucille Ball on *I Love Lucy.* Groucho's character and timing are perfection. Future Marx Brothers excursions would be made at MGM, and though the budgets were more lavish, the plots were watered down with extraneous romantic subplots and musical interludes. *Duck Soup* is pure, undistilled Marxism—and all the funnier for it.

october 3

Hur Finest Moment

One of the great movie action sequences of all time commenced filming on this day in 1925 at MGM's studio in Culver City after months of preparation and delays: the famous "chariot race" sequence in *Ben-Hur.* The film was slated to be the biggest feature made up until that time—with a massive set of Rome's Circus Maximus constructed out of plaster. It lived up to its expectations.

In addition to stars Ramon Novarro and Francis X. Bushman, ten stuntmen, forty-eight horses, and a dozen chariots, the gallery was packed with a few well-known celebrities appearing as extras. Among the observing throng: Charlie Chaplin, Mary Pickford, Douglas Fairbanks, Lillian Gish, Harold Lloyd, and John and Lionel Barrymore.

The final sequence took days to shoot, with director Fred Niblo shooting from a variety of angles—ground level, underground level, from high atop the stands, and in a jeep tracking alongside the action. The hoopla was well worth it: The sequence became the highlight of the movie, which went on to become the biggest film of 1926 (not to mention the most expensive movie ever made up until that time, at a cost of—gasp!—$4,000,000).

The film was remade by director William Wyler in 1959. Wyler was familiar with how to film the chariot race sequence, having served as assistant director in the original version. Seek out the original **Ben-Hur** (1926). One of the great silent films ever; the chariot races and battle sequences are still impressively spectacular. The reconstructed version of the original silent film (overseen by esteemed British film historian Kevin Brownlow) features a stirring score by Carl Davis and several carefully restored original Technicolor sequences.

october 4

The Great Stone Face

Joseph Frank Keaton came from a traveling vaudeville family. By the age of two, he was performing onstage with his mother and father. One day the toddler tumbled down a flight of stairs, to emerge unscathed but befuddled at the bottom. Frequent house guest Harry Houdini picked him up, brushed him off, and commented, "That was some buster you took there!" From that day on, the nickname stuck . . . as did the youngster's uncanny ability to use his body to seemingly defy the laws of physics. That initial tumble down the steps was a metaphor for his life in more ways than one.

Buster Keaton—born this day in 1895 in Piqua, Kansas—was the silent screen's most inventive, surreal, avant-garde clown. His contemporaries Chaplin and Lloyd were more popular, but Keaton was decades ahead of his time. Whereas Chaplin's films now appear positively Victorian in both their sentimentalities and their execution, Keaton's films are still fiercely inventive and fresh. As an athlete and stuntman, he was without peer. As a director, he was visionary, using the camera like no one else before to actually participate in the gags.

Nowhere is Keaton's genius more evident than in the dizzyingly inventive **Sherlock Junior** (1924), his slightly surreal homage to the art of motion pictures. Keaton plays a young movie projectionist who is studying to be a detective. One day he falls asleep while projecting a movie, and his dream self leaves his body and literally projects himself into the film. Once there, he is buffeted around by the events happening in the movie-within-a-movie around him. (Woody Allen paid homage to this film in *Purple Rose of Cairo* [1985].) Most silent films become, in the hindsight of nearly a century, mere historical curiosities. But Keaton's surreal masterpiece still seems light years ahead of its time in its sensibilities. The movie is capped off with an incredible chase sequence featuring, among other things, Keaton riding on the handlebars of a driverless motorcycle. A stunningly original work.

october 5

And Now for Something Completely Different . . .

In not-so-merry Old England in 1969, BBC Television was losing its audience—which is an impressive and discouraging feat when you're the only broadcaster in the country. Their Sunday night religious show was pulling in abysmal ratings—and they decided to try something completely different. So they hired on a group of comedy writers—John Cleese and Graham Chapman (who had worked and written for Peter Sellers), Eric Idle, Michael Palin, Terry Jones, and one American, Terry Gilliam—to write and appear in a weekly series of comedy sketches. They called themselves Monty Python's Flying Circus. When the BBC said they didn't like the name, the group threatened to change their name every week. The BBC backed down, and the moniker stayed.

Monty Python's Flying Circus premiered at 10:55 P.M. this night in 1969, starting with John Cleese looking into the camera and saying, "And now for something completely different." And it was. The anarchic series became a cult sensation in England, then went on to become a national sensation. Reruns began airing on PBS in the States in 1974, and the members found themselves at the vanguard of a surreal new style of comedy.

They made several forays into movies. Their first, *And Now for Something Completely Different* (1971), is a film version of some of their most popular TV sketches (including such classics as the Dead Parrot sketch, the

Ministry of Silly Walks, and the Argument Clinic). They followed up with *Monty Python and the Holy Grail* (1974), a King Arthur spoof that proved a surprising international hit.

But the third time was the charm—**Monty Python's Life of Brian** (1979). The group had long wanted to film a spoof on the life of Jesus, to be called *Jesus Christ: Lust for Glory,* but more pragmatic heads prevailed. Finally they came up with the idea of telling the story of one of Jesus' contemporaries, Brian, who gets mistaken for the Messiah.

Life of Brian is audacious, inventive, cheeky, provocative, silly, and immensely fun. It's also Monty Python's most sustained film. Look for a quickie appearance by ex-Beatle George Harrison (who financed the film) as a reporter.

october 6

You Ain't Heard Nothin' Yet

On this day, the golden era of silent film was effectively ended: *The Jazz Singer,* generally regarded as the first successful "talkie," premiered this date at the Warner Theater in New York . . . and movies would never be the same. Fact is, *The Jazz Singer* is mostly a silent film, with brief recorded songs and intros, by star Al Jolson. His most famous catchphrase, "You ain't heard nothin' yet," was one of the recorded lines—and it was true in more ways than one.

The transition from silent movies to talkies was a rocky road for film studios. Their first efforts were often as clumsy as a toddler's first tentative steps. Cameras had to be in insulated boxes; microphones had to be strategically placed in flower vases and telephone receivers; and actors' voices sometimes didn't match their screen images.

The Jazz Singer is a movie milestone—but it's a lousy movie. Instead, celebrate the birth of the talkies with the musical comedy that celebrates the birth of talkies like no other movie, **Singin' in the Rain** (1952). Gene Kelly plays a silent screen idol who has to cope with the advent of talkies. A book could be written about how *Singin' in the Rain* is the greatest movie musical ever (and for my money, it is), but it's also the sharpest satire of the early days of Hollywood ever put on film. Donald O'Connor was one of the few hoofers who could keep up with Kelly, and in some ways outdo him; his "Make 'Em Laugh" solo dance is the highlight of the picture. Gene Kelly's solo sequence of the title song alone is worth the price of the film.

october 7

A Poe Excuse for a Movie

On October 3, 1849, in Baltimore, Maryland, a courier delivered the following note to Dr. J. E. Snodgrass:

"Dear Sir—There is a gentleman, rather the worse for wear, who goes by the cognomen of Edgar A. Poe, and who appears in great distress, and says he is acquainted with you, and I assure you, he is in need of immediate assistance. Yours in haste, Jos. W. Walker."

The good doctor arrived to find Poe suffering from a raging fever, alternating between consciousness and delirium. He had been found facedown in the gutter, penniless and either drunk or in an opium-induced stupor. He never recovered. On this day in 1849, at around 5:30 P.M., he suddenly gasped, "God help my poor soul!" and died.

The man credited with inventing the modern detective story left one mystery unsolved—his own death. No one knows where or how he spent his last few days. He left behind a wealth of masterfully constructed poems and short stories, many of which served as the basis for movies. He was obsessed with death, disease, and decay.

His tales do not easily lend themselves to cinema in a linear sense—they create more of a mood than a narrative—but they have served as inspiration for some memorably macabre movies. B-movie mogul Roger Corman directed a series of low-budget but critically acclaimed treatments of Poe's tales, including "Masque of the Red Death," "Tales of Terror," "The Pit and the Pendulum," "Fall of the House of Usher," and a parody of "The Raven," with old pros Karloff, Lorre, and Price sending up the horror genre.

But the best "Poe-Man's Film Festival" is a double bill of two great Poe-inspired films from the golden age of Universal Studios, *The Black Cat* and *The Raven*—both starring the two "Titans of Terror" of the '30s, Bela Lugosi and Boris Karloff.

Both films borrow liberally from Poe's motifs. The best of the two is **The Black Cat** (1934), a gothic-art deco masterpiece directed by the resourceful and creative Edgar G. Ulmer (who went on to direct the noir classic *Detour*). For once, Lugosi plays a hero—or at least as close to a hero as he ever came—as Dr. Vitus Verdegast, a tortured exile who returns to his war-torn European homeland to exact revenge on his traitorous former friend, Poelzig (Boris Karloff). Little does Verdegast know that his black magic-practicing old friend has murdered Verdegast's ex-wife . . . and married his daughter. This surrealistic thriller touches on some very perverse themes for its day. Then, settle back for **The Raven** (1935). Lugosi is back in his evil mad scientist mode as Dr. Volin, a renowned plastic surgeon who is obsessed with the works of Poe—particularly his torture devices. Karloff plays a murderer on the lam who enlists Lugosi's aid in getting a new face—and comes to regret it. Poe choice.

october 8

Coffee, Tea, or Popcorn?

On this day in 1943, the very first in-flight movies premiered in the sky: a newsreel and two shorts (including a Bugs Bunny cartoon) were screened on a transcontinental air transport flight. Commemorate the occasion with **Airplane** (1980)—the high-flying comedy from the Zucker Brothers, who would later go on to create the Police Squad series. The gags come fast and furious—and even if half of them fall flat, that still leaves a sizable portion of hilarious zingers. Robert Hayes and Julie Haggerty play a pair of star-crossed lovers who reunite on an air flight. But plot is virtually expendable in this uproarious send-up of every airline-related disaster movie ever made. The cleverest conceit of the movie is in the casting; old familiar '50s B-movie veterans like Lloyd Bridges, Robert Stack, and Leslie Nielson lampoon their former stalwart screen images to hilarious effect. And the dialogue, both sophomoric and sophisticated, has worked its way into the vernacular. "We have clearance, Clarence." "Roger, Roger. What's our vector, Victor?"

october 9

Rebel with a Cause

> *"At the risk of seeming ridiculous, let me say that the true revolutionary is guided by great feelings of love. It is impossible to think of a great revolutionary as lacking this quality."*
>
> *—Che Guevara, 1965*

After attempting to spearhead an uprising against the Bolivian government, Che Guevara, the idealistic Cuban revolutionary who became a symbol to a generation, was executed this day in Bolivia. He was a student who became a doctor—a doctor who became a revolutionary—a revolutionary who became a martyr—and a martyr who became an icon. It was rare to go into any American college dorm in the late '60s without finding his photo adorning a wall; he is still regarded as a god among countless social reformers and activists.

Born in Rosario, Argentina, Ernesto Che Guevara was restless. He fought against the Peron regime in his native country while he studied to become a doctor. As a physician he traveled extensively, until in Mexico he met Fidel Castro, who convinced Guevara to join him for the revolution in Cuba.

From 1955 to 1959, Guevara became one of the most cunning guerilla leaders of the revolution there, and was appointed by Castro to numerous government positions. Having achieved his goal to bring socialism to Cuba, Che left Castro to spark similar movements in other oppressed areas. He went to Africa in 1965, and in 1966, disguised as a bald, middle-aged businessman, he went to lead a failed revolution in Bolivia. On this day in 1966 he was captured and executed.

For sheer camp value, it's tough to top Jack Palance cast as Fidel Castro in **Che!** (1969)—a highly fictionalized account of the revolutionary's short and eventful life. Omar Sharif is almost as ludicrously miscast as Che.

The spirit of Che Guevara is best represented on film through his exchange of ideas with Eva Perón, beloved first lady of Che's native Argentina. Though the two historic figures never met in real life, that didn't stop composers Andrew Lloyd Webber and Tim Rice from concocting such a meeting in their stage musical *Evita.* Mandy Patinkin played the role in his first major Broadway role, but the part of Che was essayed (not quite so effectively) by Antonio Banderas in the 1996 movie version.

october 10

A Wooden Heart

There are bad movies and there are really great bad movies—movies so bad they transcend their own ineptitude to become something . . . well, something. The patron saint of bad movies is Ed Wood, the cross-dressing, literately-challenged creator of such camp classics as *Glen or Glenda?* (1952; starring Wood himself as a cross-dressing man exceedingly fond of angora sweaters), *Bride of the Monster* (1955; featuring an unforgettable battle between seventy-year-old Bela Lugosi and a rubber octopus), and his magnum opus, the immortal *Plan 9 from Outer Space* (1956), often awarded the dubious honor as the worst film of all time.

It's easy to make fun of Wood's incredibly inept cinematic oeuvre. But what endears Wood to so many fans is the unquestionable passion that emanates from his movies like limburger cheese. He tried, he really tried.

Celebrate Ed's birthday today (born 1922) by watching any of his, ahem, "classics," if you can force yourself to sit through one. Or, better yet, savor **Ed Wood** (1994), maverick director Tim Burton's loving homage to the master of cinematic ineptitude. Johnny Depp is both charming and bizarre as Wood, perennially hopeful, full of dreams, and in blissful denial of his failings as a filmmaker. Martin Landau won an Oscar for his sympathetic portrayal of over-the-hill, morphine-addicted horror icon, Bela Lugosi. Bill Murray is a hoot as "Bunny" Breckinridge, the flamboyantly fey member of Wood's oddball group of thespians, sort of a bargain-basement Mercury Theater. And the amazing Vincent D'Onofrio contributes an uncannily dead-on appearance as Orson Welles (who, incidently, died this day in 1985). Burton obviously loves and respects his subject matter, and this is arguably his finest, most endearing film—funny, touching, and sunny—worth a dozen of Burton's far less successful *Mars Attacks.* It has heart. And, if nothing else, Wood had heart.

october 11

The Most Offensive Movie Ever?

Today marks the anniversary of the opening of the film marketed as "the motion picture with something to offend everyone," Tony Richardson's **The Loved One** (1965). Written by Christopher Isherwood and Terry Southern, and based on Evelyn Waugh's satirical novel of the funeral business in Southern California, this one-of-a-kind movie truly does have something to offend everyone. Robert Morse stars as an Englishman transplanted to California, and the film features one of the most eccentric supporting casts ever assembled, including Jonathan Winters, Liberace, Sir John Gielgud, Robert Morley, James Coburn, Paul Williams, and, most memorably, Rod Steiger as the fey, overly enthusiastic mortician, Mr. Joyboy. Though not for everyone's taste—imagine David Lynch meets Mel Brooks (and they did, in *The Elephant Man,* but that's another story)—*The Loved One* still maintains the power to shock and offend, and was a precursor to many midnight cult movies. The scene where Mr. Joyboy's supremely obese mother rolls around in orgasmic ecstasy under a refrigerator full of food as she stuffs herself is not easily forgotten. The truth is that the offensive sensibilities of the film lie mostly in the film's truly morbid but unblinking obsession with death—the most taboo subject of all.

october 12

A Vicious Crime

Sid Vicious and Nancy Spungen were a punk Romeo and Juliet, star-crossed lovers united in mutual rebellion and, eventually, death. He was the notorious bass player for the Sex Pistols, and she was a suicidal middle-class runaway from Philadelphia who wanted to be somebody. They were rebels united in mutual self-annihilation. Together, they thumbed their nose at the outside world while shutting it out. They had recently left London to come to New York City to kick their respective heroin habits. But on this night in 1978, it all came crumbling down.

Vicious woke up in their room in the fashionably dilapidated Chelsea Hotel and found his girlfriend's body, dressed in black bra and panties, with a five-inch knife driven into her side and blood all around. He couldn't remember a thing. "I did it because I'm a dirty dog," he sneered as police arrested him for second-degree murder. Within a few months, Vicious would join his beloved, a suicide.

The whole sordid tale is graphically told in **Sid and Nancy** (1986)—the birth of punk rock with Johnny Rotten and the Sex Pistols, the fateful meeting of the two lovers, the fights, the mind-frying drugs, the scoring, the whole *dolce vita.* Gary Oldman is positively spooky as the cadaverous Vicious, and Chloe Webb makes for a crazed, ambitious, loony, vulnerable Nancy. It's a dark tale, but leavened by healthy doses of knowing, sometimes endearing humor. When all is said and done, it's ultimately a love story, a postapocalyptic *Romeo and Juliet* for the end of Western civilization, and not an unaffecting one. And, in a piece of prophetic casting, look for a young Courtney Love in a small role.

october 13

Simon Says Happy Birthday

Singer-songwriter Paul Simon was born this day in Newark, New Jersey, in 1941. As a teen, he fell in love with the popular doo-wop music of the day. His neighbor, Art Garfunkel, shared his enthusiasm, and the two formed a duo, Tom and Jerry, which had a regional East Coast hit with "Hey, Schoolgirl" in 1959.

When folk music became commercially viable in the early '60s, Simon and Garfunkel started writing and performing in its style. The duo started using their real names and recorded an all-acoustic album in 1964 for Columbia, *Wednesday Morning, 3 A.M.,* which stiffed.

Simon moved to London, England, and was in the process of recording a solo album when he received word that, back in the States, Columbia had taken one of the cuts from their album, a song called "The Sounds of Silence," and added electric guitar, bass, and drums. They released it as a single that went straight to #1 on the charts. Simon headed back home, and Simon and Garfunkel became one of the biggest hit-makers of the '60s, before splitting up in 1970. Simon went on to a successful career as a solo artist.

In 1980, Paul Simon wrote, starred in, and composed the music for a modest, semiautobiographical film, **One Trick Pony** (1980). The film chronicles the story of Jonah Levin (Simon), a folk-rock star of the '60s who, twenty years later, is now struggling to make a living on the road with his band, his glory days well behind him. On top of trying to keep his muse and music alive, he's also trying to reconcile with his wife and son. *One Trick Pony* may be a one-trick film, but it's a good one. Simon is quietly likable as Jonah, and the script is wise, understated, funny, and on-target. Nice supporting turns from Rip Torn as a record industry bigwig who offers Jonah a comeback chance, and Lou Reed as a prissy record producer who is overly fond of treacly strings. Cameos from the B-52s, Sam and Dave, Tiny Tim, and the Lovin' Spoonful. And the Simon-scored music is some of his finest, including "Late in the Evening" and "Ace in the Hole."

october 14

Watch at the Speed of Sound

The nay-sayers said it couldn't be done—flying faster than the speed of sound. It just wasn't possible. But on this day in 1947, test pilot Chuck Yeager proved them wrong. Piloting a Bell X-1 rocket plane named *Glamorous Glennis* (after Yeager's wife), he hit a speed of 700 mph, or Mach 1.06, broke the sound barrier, and ushered in what would soon be dubbed the "Space Age."

That landmark event, and the subsequent dawn of the U.S. space program, is vividly brought to life in Philip Kaufman's fabulous film, **The Right Stuff** (1983). This cocky and entertaining history of the U.S. space program takes us from Yeager's history-making flight through John Glenn's orbiting of the earth in *Friendship 7*. Playwright and occasional actor Sam Shepard plays Yeager as a low-key, no-frills man's man, stoic and vaguely mystical. Based on the original book by Tom Wolfe. As both history and a satirical exposé of the media circus surrounding America's space race, *The Right Stuff* lives up to its title.

october 15

On Second Thought, Skip That Trip to Bermuda

It wasn't the first time something weird happened in the area known as "the Bermuda Triangle." On this day in 1976, the 590-foot cargo ship *Sylvia L. Ossa* disappeared with a crew of thirty-seven in the waters between Bermuda and Puerto Rico. Over the years, hundreds of ships, planes, and men have disappeared in the area, seemingly without a trace.

Strange incidents in the triangle have been reported back as far as when Christopher Columbus wrote in his captain's log about seeing a meteor fall from the night sky, and his compass acting strangely. In 1872, the ship *Mary Celeste* was found floating abandoned, with no sign or clue of her captain and crew. There's the notorious story of "Flight 19"—wherein five navy Avengers on a training mission disappeared, as did the rescue plane that was sent to search for them. Three years later, a DC-3 disappeared with thirty-two passengers. The term *Bermuda Triangle* was first coined in an article which appeared in *Argosy* magazine in 1964; it was followed by a best-selling exploitation book by author Charles Berlitz—a wildly inaccurate tome called *The Bermuda Triangle.*

Explore the unexplained phenomena with the intriguing, if totally unbalanced, biased, and inane pseudodocumentary **The Bermuda Triangle** (1978). Rife with farfetched theories about alien abductions, badly reenacted vignettes, and wildly off-the-wall testimony from "experts," the movie nonetheless does raise some interesting questions about the area. But anyone who's ever seen *Close Encounters of the Third Kind* knows what *really* happened to all those missing ships and planes.

october 16

Catch This Bus

It was at once inspiring and disconcerting, a bringing together and a dividing apart. On this day in 1995, the first Million Man March took place in Washington, D.C., to show solidarity among African American men. The march was organized by controversial Nation of Islam leader Louis Farrakhan. While some saw it as a positive, proactive symbol of black American pride and unity, others viewed it as an assault on white, Jewish, and/or female America. Many women's groups were incensed that Farrakhan's march was intended for men only.

A black and white issue that was anything but black and white, the controversial march divided African Americans as much as anyone else. It was lightning in a bottle, and Spike Lee got it just right with his underrated **Get On the Bus** (1998). Several black men, including a light-skinned African actor, a dutiful father literally handcuffed to his law-breaking son, and an old-timer activist, are uncomfortably gathered together on a cross-country bus (driven by Richard Belzer) to attend the march. Lee sometimes lapses into pedantic talky dialogue, and the bus sputters and runs out of gas in more ways than one, but for the most part *Get On the Bus* is a trip worth taking.

october 17

Pop Culture Quiz

It was the beginning of the end of innocence for the new medium of television. On this day in 1960, quiz show contestant Charles Van Doren was arrested with thirteen others, including producers Daniel Enright and Al Freedman, for perjury. He had previously testified in front of a grand jury that he was not provided with answers to the questions he was asked on the game show. The truth was different.

Two years earlier, Herb Stemple, an angry, former contestant on the popular quiz show *Twenty-One,* barged into the D.A.'s office in New York City. He alleged that the show's producer, Daniel Enright, had bribed him to throw the December fifth show to new contestant Charles Van Doren, a thirty-three-year-old assistant professor at Columbia University. Stemple had won several thousand dollars in previous weeks on the show—but was informed by the producer that the public wanted "new blood, fresh faces," and he was elbowed aside. The only snag was that the stubborn Stemple refused to go quietly, and started a scandal that rippled throughout the infant industry.

Robert Redford's **Quiz Show** (1994) effectively re-creates the times and the story. In one of the best showcase performances of his impressively eclectic career, John Turturro is both contemptible and pitiable as the snubbed Stemple. Ralph Fiennes makes for a memorably enigmatic, complex, and ambiguous Charles Van Doren, and Paul Scofield brings quiet dignity and heartbreak to the role of Van Doren's disgraced father.

october 18

A Trial to Sit Through

In 1945, the eyes of the world were on Nuremberg on this day, where the international trials to determine the innocence or guilt of Nazi officers accused of atrocities committed under the Third Reich of World War II officially got under way. Were the Nazi officers responsible for their reprehensible actions or were they merely "following orders"?

Commemorate the proceedings with Stanley Kramer's riveting **Judgment at Nuremberg** (1961), with an all-star cast of exceptional performers. Spencer Tracy took on one of his last great performances as the American judge sent to preside over the proceedings. Maximilian Schell won a well-deserved Oscar for his fiery, mesmerizing turn as the German defense attorney, and Montgomery Clift delivers a brief but intense performance as a confused victim of Nazi sterilization. And July Garland is stunning in her brief role as a German hausfrau who finds herself compelled to testify. The courtroom sequences are absolutely riveting, and Tracy, as always, grounds the movie with his humanity and quiet authority. Look for a young William Shatner in the background as an officer observing the proceedings. Thought-provoking, historically vital, and ultimately inspiring.

october 19

You Can Call Him Al

"You can get much further with a kind word and a gun than you can with a gun alone."

—Al Capone

Prohibition was the best thing that ever happened to Italian immigrant Alphonse Capone. Within ten years of getting his first job as a dishwasher in Chicago, he had risen to literally rule the city. He commanded a private army, was chauffeured around town in a bulletproof car, gave thousand-dollar tips, and held just about every Chicago cop in his well-lined pocket. His links to gangland killings were notorious—the most famous being the St. Valentine's Day Massacre of 1929 (the same one witnessed by Tony Curtis and Jack Lemmon in *Some Like It Hot*). The law finally found a way to get Capone on this day in 1931, when he was found guilty of tax evasion.

Capone figures in countless movies. Rod Steiger—complete with a ridiculous large facial scar—starred in 1959's *Al Capone.* Steiger is great, but the B budget and the fictitious (and somewhat unsavory) love story hamper its impact. The best version by far is Robert DeNiro's turn as Capone in Brian DePalma's best film, **The Untouchables** (1987). Kevin Costner stars as G-man Eliot Ness, and Sean Connery got a well-deserved Best Supporting Actor Oscar for his role as Ness's mentor, Malone. The film plays fast and loose with facts (the real-life Ness was an alcoholic, and he didn't kill Frank Nitti), but it's grandly entertaining and action-packed. With a sharp, literate script by David Mamet, full of action and suspense, and a great score by Ennio Morricone.

october 20

Birth of a Vampire

"To die—to be truly dead—that must be glorious."

—Bela Lugosi as Dracula

To generations of horror buffs, Bela Lugosi didn't just play Dracula, he *was* Dracula. The horror icon was born this day in Lugos, Hungary—just a few miles from Transylvania—in 1882. After performing Shakespeare in his native country, he moved to America, where his distinctive accent helped earn him the lead in the Broadway play *Dracula* in 1928. Reportedly, female audience members fainted, not so much from fright as from a hormonal boost generated by his Continental looks and manners. When it came time for the film version, Universal Studios originally cast Lon Chaney for the title role, but he died before filming and Lugosi was substituted.

"Dracula," Lugosi mused during a shipboard interview near the end of his life, "I don't know if it's a blessing or a curse. But Dracula never ends." Indeed, the role was the best and worst thing that ever happened to him. It made him a star (briefly), but the actor was immediately typecast as a boogie man. When he turned down the role of Frankenstein's monster (reportedly because he had no lines and makeup would obscure his face), the role went to Boris Karloff. Lugosi spent the rest of his life trying to play catch-up, before dying in 1956.

Celebrate the birth of the man who never dies with the original **Dracula** (1931). Yes, Tod Browning's direction is hopelessly stage-bound and downright inept after an intriguing first fifteen minutes, but Lugosi's performance is truly one of the stylistic originals of the movies—spooky, campy, sexy, and corny. His perfect inflection in the words "I never drink . . . wine" seems to sum up the man in one demented line. And savor the work of one of filmdom's great unsung heroes, the amazing Dwight Frye as Renfield, Dracula's fly-popping disciple.

october 21

There Goes the Sun

On this day in 2137 B.C., the first total eclipse of the sun to be recorded was observed in China. Imagine how frightening it must have been to witnesses.

Now imagine that you could go back in time and know exactly when just such an eclipse would occur. You could convince the clueless citizenry that you had godlike powers. That's exactly what happens to easygoing Bing Crosby as "Sir Guy" in **A Connecticut Yankee in King Arthur's Court** (1949), the delightful musical adaptation of Mark Twain's book. Modern-day New Englander Bing finds himself suddenly transported back to Arthurian England, where he finds himself in deep trouble with the king's magician. William Bendix is funny as his lunky sidekick, and Sir Cedric Hardwicke makes for a delightfully crotchety King Arthur. The trio's musical number together, "Busy Doin' Nothin'," is a lighthearted kick, full of that casual Crosbiness that only Bing could deliver. And Rhonda Fleming makes for one gorgeous maiden in distress.

october 22

Happy Eva After

On this day in 1946, a struggling and ambitious young actress and radio personality named Eva Duarte married Col. Juan Perón in a small and simple civil ceremony in Argentina. From then on, Eva Duarte was officially a thing of the past; all her movie performances were destroyed by fire, and the phenomenon of Eva Perón—forever after known as Evita—was born.

It's small wonder that after the success of their rock opera *Jesus Christ Superstar,* Andrew Lloyd Webber and Tim Rice chose Eva Perón as the subject of a musical—her life was the stuff of grand opera. She was born an illegitimate, poverty-stricken child in a small town in Argentina. Determined to make something of herself, she left home as a teen and journeyed to Buenos Aires, where she eventually became a celebrity, minor movie star, and popular radio personality. But that wasn't enough for her insatiable ambition, which was her biggest talent. She cornered Col. Juan Perón at a party one fateful night, and the rest is history. She helped guide his career to the presidency, in the process becoming "Evita," a goddess to the masses—the *descamisados,* or "shirtless ones." She was a brilliant propagandist and PR genius, distributing gifts among the poor while stockpiling great sums of her own money in the process. To some, she was a savior; to others, little more than an ambitious whore. When she died of ovarian cancer in 1952 at age thirty-three, the entire country mourned. Her body was mummified and preserved, but disappeared for several years, buried under a bogus name in Milan, Italy. It was finally shipped back home to Buenos Aires in 1971.

Madonna was, in many ways, the perfect choice to play the title role in **Evita** (1996); what she, too, lacked in talent, she made up for in sheer ambition, willpower, and charisma. And Alan Parker did an excellent job filming what many thought was unfilmable—Andrew Lloyd Webber's hit musical *Evita. Evita* is a mutated musical; filmed in real-life locations, with virtually no dialogue other than the libretto, and no choreographed dancing to speak of. In other words, a Hollywood musical that looks nothing like a Hollywood musical. Antonio Banderas tries hard as Che Guevera, but pales next to the memory of Mandy Patinkin in the role on Broadway. Still, *Evita* is a fascinating movie based on a fascinating woman, and it's Madonna's best movie by far.

october 23

Author, Auteur!

Is Michael Crichton an author or a franchise? Consider the number of books he wrote which have been turned into successful movies: *Twister, The Great Train Robbery, The Terminal Man, Congo, Rising Sun,* and, of course, *Jurassic Park.* He's no slouch as a director, either, having helmed *Westworld, The Great Train Robbery, Coma,* and others. After Shakespeare, he may be the single most filmed author ever. He was born this day in 1942.

Celebrate the birthday of this tremendously enterprising and creative money-machine with his most successful movie—Steven Spielberg's adaptation of his novel **Jurassic Park** (1993). Spielberg made substantial changes in the story details—in the book the kindly John Hammond isn't so kindly and doesn't make it to the end—but who can resist the fantasy of walking with dinosaurs? The special effects set a new standard in film; the dinosaurs are entirely convincing, imposing, and magnificent. Sam Neill, Laura Dern, and Jeff Goldblum are invited to preview an island theme park with living dinosaurs that have been created by extracting DNA from prehistoric mosquitoes (who had sucked on the blood of dinosaurs). Theoretically, they cannot breed, but as Goldblum's mathematician points out, "Life. . . . finds a way."

october 24

Banned in Boston

Isadora Duncan was the premiere performance artist of her time, a wildly bohemian dancer who bewitched continents and beguiled kings, leaving countless personal and political scandals in her wake. While dancing onstage at a prestigious Boston theater this night in 1922, she suddenly stopped in midperformance, looked at the audience, and announced, "Life is not real here!" while removing a red sash that covered her body and thrusting it in front of the audience. She stood naked onstage, pointing to the garment, and announced, "This is red! So am I! It's the color of life and vigor!" then she floated offstage to a chorus of boos. The following day, Mayor James Curley forbade her to perform in the city ever again.

Vanessa Redgrave was a perfect choice to portray the uninhibited, politically volatile dancer in **Isadora** (1968)—despite the fact that she couldn't dance. The two bohemian sisters shared the same penchant for bizarre, iconoclastic lifestyles, public scandals and love affairs, and outspoken, unpopular politics. *Isadora* casts a spell of a kind, much of it due to Redgrave's performance. An imaginative film bio of a fascinating woman, played by one of the best actresses of her generation, in her prime.

october 25

Do Two Henry the Fifths Make One Henry the Tenth?

"Once more, into the breach . . ."

—Henry V (St. Crispin's Day speech)

On this day in 1415, some six thousand English soldiers, archers, and men-at-arms followed King Henry V into battle against the French on a field at Agincourt, near Calais. The odds were overwhelmingly against them, six to one. When the English caught their first glimpse of the huge French contingent, Sir Walter Hungerford said, "I would that we had ten thousand more good English archers, who would gladly be here with us today." According to Shakespeare (who wasn't there), King Henry replied with the most incendiary monologue in all the Shakespearean canon, the St. Crispin's Day speech. The English, suitably fired up, went on to win the battle, with over six thousand French dead to less than a hundred English.

Commemorate this great event in English history (and not-so-great event in French history) with *Henry V*—but which one? There are two great versions. Sir Laurence Olivier's radically inventive and feverishly patriotic

Henry V (1946) was made at a time when his country was under attack by the Axis powers, and was created especially to fire up the patriotism and confidence of the citizenry. In his first directorial effort, Olivier emphasized the play's theatrical ancestry—the first part of the movie literally takes place on a re-created stage of the Globe Theater. Olivier's interpretation of the title role is coolly efficient, excepting the inspiring St. Crispin's Day soliloquy.

More fiery and colorfully contemporary is Kenneth Branagh's bravura version of **Henry V** (1989). Branagh's directorial debut is impressively muscular, devoid of pretension, and immensely energetic. Branagh is a passionate Henry, perfectly realized. And the supporting cast, including Paul Scofield, Ian Holm, Derek Jacobi, and Emma Thompson, is stellar. Branagh's re-creation of the Battle of Agincourt is a highlight of the movie—tremendously cinematic and graphic . . . and obviously influenced by Orson Welles's depiction of the Battle of Tewkesbury in *Chimes at Midnight*.

october 26

A Western Legend That's More than OK

The most famous shoot-out of the Wild West took place on this day in 1881 at the OK Corral in Tombstone, Arizona. The Earp brothers—Wyatt, Morgan, and Virgil—and their gambling companion Doc Holliday took on the Clanton family—Newman "Old Man" Clanton, sons Ike and Billy, and friend Tom McLaury. Some historians claim it was more of a mass execution than a gunfight, with the odds heavily in the Earps' favor.

The real-life Wyatt Earp was a decidedly seedy opportunist, a gambler and con man who only occasionally worked for the law, and who more often than not used his badge to achieve his own ill-gotten gains. The Earps had attempted to make themselves respectable in Tombstone, and had invested in its future. The Clantons represented the old ways. A showdown was inevitable.

The story of Wyatt Earp and the gunfight at the OK Corral has been depicted countless times in movies: Kurt Russell played Earp in *Tombstone,* which portrays the actual battle itself fairly accurately; the same year, Kevin Costner tried his hand in the exhaustive and ponderous *Wyatt Earp* (1994). James Garner plays a taciturn Earp in *Hour of the Gun* (1967), and Kirk Douglas puts his distinctive touch on the lawman in *Gunfight at the OK Corral* (1957). In each film, a different Earp emerges, along with a different version of the gunfight; together, they're like a Western version of *Rashomon.*

The best version is in John Ford's **My Darling Clementine** (1946). From a historic standpoint, *My Darling Clementine* fails miserably—the real-life Doc Holliday didn't die there, nor did Ike Clanton. But as pure filmmaking, it's a beautiful thing to behold and ranks among Ford's best westerns—which makes it one of the great westerns, period. Henry Fonda is the definitive (if idealized) Wyatt Earp, and Walter Brennan is one of the most vile screen villains ever as Old Man Clanton. The photography (the film was shot in Ford's beloved Monument Valley) is glowing, warm, and rich, and the film is packed with small, quiet sequences that are pure filmmaking magic—Wyatt's ability to nonchalantly balance himself on a leaning chair, the poetic community dance where Wyatt dances with Clementine on the floor of the unfinished church, and the climactic battle itself.

The real history of the West tends to get lost in transition to the silver screen. In John Ford's *The Man Who Shot Liberty Valance* (1962), a character observes, "When the legend becomes fact, print the legend." *My Darling Clementine* isn't accurate history, but it's accurate legend.

october 27

Say Cleese and Smile

He has created a gallery of some of the funniest comic characters ever. Consider his blustering sergeants, pompous executives, and upper-class twits in the Monty Python TV series and movies, or his obnoxious hotel manager Basil Fawlty in the television classic *Fawlty Towers.*

John Cleese, born this day in 1939, has done more to skewer the image of staid Britannia than the sinking of the pound. His first appearance was with Peter Sellers in a brief scene in *The Magic Christian* (1969), playing a typically stuffy museum attendant. He has appeared in several non-Python movies, his best by far being **A Fish Called Wanda** (1988) which he cowrote. Cleese plays an officious barrister who becomes unwittingly caught up in a robbery scheme. A great supporting cast aids and abets Cleese in this delightful comedy, including old Python mate Michael Palin, sexy Jamie Lee Curtis, and an inspired Kevin Kline as a not-too-bright armpit-sniffing hit man ("Don't call me stupid!"). Cleese created a disarming romantic crime caper comedy that was a nostalgic throwback to the gentle Ealing comedies of the '50s, as well as one of the funniest movies of the '80s. Nobody can sputter like Cleese.

october 28

Storm of the Century

It was an unprecedented convergence of nature's fury. On this day in 1991, Hurricane Grace converged with a Canadian cold front and a mid-Atlantic low-pressure system off the coast of Massachusetts, creating a 1,500-mile-wide tempest of unprecedented proportions. It skirted the coast, generating hundred-foot-high waves and winds up to 140 miles per hour. Several ships were caught in the middle. One of them, the *Andrea Gail,* a fishing trawler with a crew of six, didn't make it back. The resulting book, *The Perfect Storm,* became a best-seller in 1997 and a blockbuster movie in 2000.

The Perfect Storm is far from a perfect movie. Director Wolfgang Petersen delivers impressive CGI special effects, but botches the human element of the story. Like James Cameron in *Titanic,* Petersen makes incredibly inept and schmaltzy choices, right down to a maudlin and drippy scene (no pun intended) of a doomed young man telepathically sending a message to his true love as he goes under for the third time. George Clooney gives a stoic performance as the arrogant, macho fishing boat captain who stubbornly defies the elements (and any scintilla of common sense) and takes his entire crew to their doom. The movie would have you believe Clooney and his crew were the heroes—the last of a dying breed; the real heroes were the Coast Guard teams who attempted to rescue them and other, luckier seafarers. Where is their story? Back on land somewhere, because it's barely in this movie. Much of *The Perfect Storm* is pure speculation; no one was there to record what really happened. And Petersen reduces the characters to one-dimensional stereotypes.

The real, documented story is infinitely more compelling and moving. **The Killer Storm** (1999), produced by the History Channel, is a documentary that presents film and video of the real rescues and reconstructs the storm. Incredible footage captures several harrowing rescues, including one briefly depicted in Petersen's film, the jaw-dropping, stomach-tightening, awe-inspiring effort by a five-member Coast Guard team that ventures into the heart of the storm in a helicopter to rescue a sailboat crew. The attempt fails and the helicopter runs out of fuel, forcing its occupants to dive into the churning black sea. Ultimately it falls to rescuers to save the rescuers. A visceral, humbling testament to those who live by the creed "This we do, so that others may live."

october 29

A Hairy Anniversary

The musical that defined a generation, *Hair,* opened on this day in New York in 1967. Controversial in its time, it is now revived as a quaint period piece, no more threatening than *The Music Man* or *My Fair Lady*. But in its day it was revolutionary.

Remember the '60s with Milos Forman's film version of **Hair** (1979). John Savage plays a naïve young farmer who comes to New York and gets caught up in the hippy lifestyle thanks to head tripper Treat Williams. It's all here—the draft card–burning, the sit-ins, the loony cosmic consciousness. Inventive choreography by Twyla Tharp; words and music by James Rado and Gerome Ragni.

october 30

The Invasion That Never Happened

At 8 P.M. on this night in 1938, young radio star Orson Welles decided to play a pre-Halloween prank. The twenty-two-year-old wunderkind boomed "Boo!" to the whole country with his radio broadcast of the H. G. Wells sci-fi classic, *The War of the Worlds.* But he didn't deliver it as a radio play—he disguised it as a real-life "newscast," complete with flying saucers landing in New Jersey. "Newsbreaks" kept interrupting the "regular programming" with increasingly disturbing—and disconcertingly realistic—live remotes. The ruse was so effective that thousands of listeners were convinced we really were being invaded by Martians. The event skyrocketed Welles to fame and resulted in his being signed by RKO to come to Hollywood. It also led to stringent laws about what could be broadcast over the airwaves.

Commemorate the event with a double bill: **The Night That Panicked America** (1975), a better-than-average TV movie that re-creates the events of that memorable night. Then—just for fun—watch the kitschy classic **The War of the Worlds** (1953). The special effects, including the destruction of Washington, D.C., were pretty nifty for the '50s, and the invaders' stingray-like spaceships still look cool.

october 31

A Hollow Movie

Halloween—All Hallow's Eve—the night when the spirits of the departed return to earth to make mischief (hence the custom of wearing masks and costumes to confuse them) and eat lots of sugary sweets is the traditional night for scary movies. Actually, the holiday was originally celebrated by the Druids as the Eve of Samhain, the New Year of the Druids—when the Lord of Death gathered together the souls of all the wicked who had died during the passing year.

The wickedly maverick director Tim Burton was an inspired choice to adapt Washington Irving's classic early American tale *The Legend of Sleepy Hollow* to the big screen. In **Sleepy Hollow** (1999), Johnny Depp plays Ichabod Crane, a New York City constable in 1799 whose unconventional forensic approach to detective work alienates him from his colleagues. Ichabod's superior (Christopher Lee, in a nice cameo homage to his old Hammer films) sends him to the quiet hamlet of Sleepy Hollow to investigate a series of recent beheadings. The locals believe the grisly murders to be the work of a spectral Headless Horseman who haunts the nearby woods. Crane scoffs at the superstitious nonsense, until he goes head to—uh, shoulder with the boogie man himself.

Depp contributes his usual quirky characterization to the role of Ichabod, half determined detective and half cowering coward. Tim Burton's evocative visuals are stunning and spellbinding; the film is drenched in autumnal oranges and dark browns. As is often the case with Burton's films, the script is flawed, but it doesn't detract from the dreamlike atmosphere of foreboding which pervades the movie. *Sleepy Hollow* casts a perfect spell for a Halloween evening.

Already seen it?

The alternate possibilities are many: John Carpenter's classic *Halloween* (1978), with Jamie Lee Curtis starring in this granddaddy of all slasher films; any of the classic old Universal Studio standbys—*Frankenstein* (1932), *Dracula* (1931), *The Wolf Man* (1942), and the best of the lot, the campy, brilliantly designed *Bride of Frankenstein* (1935); *The Exorcist* (1973), William Friedkin's seriously scary shocker about a young girl (Linda Blair) possessed by the devil; or George Romero's primitive but primally effective *Night of the Living Dead* (1968).

For a spooky change of pace, why not sample one of the first, and scariest, omnibus movies, **Dead of Night** (1945)—a sort of O. Henry anthology of the supernatural from England's legendary Ealing Studios. A dinner guest at a country house party (Mervyn Johns) keeps experiencing an upsetting, escalating sense of déjà vu. Gradually, the other dinner guests begin relating a series of ghost stories, and soon we're in nightmare territory. Of the five "ghost story" episodes, two are exceptional: "The Haunted Mirror" (directed by Robert Hamer) and the famous "Ventriloquist's Dummy," starring Michael Redgrave as a mentally disturbed ventriloquist. The latter was expanded upon in the film *Magic* (1978), with Anthony Hopkins in the Redgrave role.

november

november 1

Porn Again

Who would have ever predicted that a purveyor of sleazy porn would emerge as one of the twentieth century's most eloquent spokespersons for civil liberties? Democracy makes strange bedfellows of us all: *Hustler* founder and publisher—and tireless champion of the First Amendment—Larry Flynt was born this day in 1942.

His fascinating rise to prominence and resultant battles with the law are recounted with great gusto in **The People vs. Larry Flynt** (1996). Milos Forman (*One Flew over the Cuckoo's Nest*) follows the only-in-America trajectory of Flynt's roller-coaster life, from a teenage bootlegging two-bit hustler to millionaire publisher, from shooting victim through his convalescence to his appearance before the Supreme Court fighting for his First Amendment rights against Moral Majority head Jerry Falwell. Woody Harrelson, in a bravura, breakthrough performance as Flynt, established himself as a major screen talent to be reckoned with. He's almost matched by Courtney Love's raw and nervy portrayal of Flynt's drug-addicted wife, Althea. A fascinating mixture of political fable, social satire, film bio, and a surprising tale of romantic loss.

november 2

When Radio Was King

On this day in 1920, radio station KDKA in Pittsburgh announced results of the Harding/Cox presidential election, effectively scooping the newspapers on a big story for the first time in history. Within ten years, radio would become the preeminent fixture in most American homes, connecting the entire country with an intimacy and immediacy never before possible. It wielded unprecedented influence on American life, rivaled only by television and the Internet today. In those days it was a truly magical medium, packed with sitcoms, variety shows, quiz shows, G-men shoot-'em ups, cowboy shoot-'em-ups, private eye shoot-'em-ups. The golden age of radio was rivaled only by the golden age of Hollywood.

Toast a wistful remembrance of glorious days past with **Radio Days** (1987), Woody Allen's enchanting nostalgic comedy about growing up listening to radio in the golden age of the 1940s. Allen painstakingly concocts some fictitious radio shows that capture the style and ambience of the day, including such pseudo-classics as *The Masked Avenger; Biff Baxter, G-Man of the Air; Gay White Way;* and *The Court of Human Emotions.* The "story" is really just a series of strung-together vignettes centering on a typical family in 1940s Brooklyn, and the legends of radio whose lives—both fictional and real—they followed. The great ensemble cast includes Mia Farrow as Sally, a cigarette girl who rises to radio stardom, Dianne Wiest as ever-hopeful Aunt Bea, Julie Kavner (the voice of Marge Simpson, and Rhoda's younger sister, Brenda Morgenstern), Josh Mostel, Jeff Daniels, Tony Roberts, Danny Aiello, and, very briefly, Diane Keaton.

A lovingly re-created period flavor permeates *Radio Days* like an intoxicating perfume, and the film is bathed in the golden glow of memory. And that, in the end, is what remains and lingers in this nostalgic slice of life that plays like *The Waltons* in Brooklyn. One of Woody Allen's most accessible, charming, and heartfelt movies. Allen narrates, but does not appear.

november 3

Hold On Tight—It's Going to Be a Bumby Presidential Erection—er, Election

On this day in 1992, William Jefferson Clinton, governor of Arkansas, was elected to the office of president of the United States. It would be one of the most productive—and controversial—presidential terms in history, fraught with scandal. His affair with White House intern Monica Lewinsky threatened to topple the presidency, and Clinton came within inches (no pun intended) of impeachment. Was Clinton a well-intentioned masterful leader with a fatal flaw, or a hypocritical, hollow man?

Commemorate the complex enigma that was Clinton's legacy with the insightful and hilarious **Primary Colors** (1998), based on the bestselling book by "Anonymous" (who was eventually revealed to be political correspondent Joe Klein). John Travolta delivers a layered performance as popular presidential candidate Jack Stanton, a "fictional" governor from Arkansas, a likeable optimist who believes in justice, equality, compassion, and, apparently, adultery—he can't keep his hands to himself. Elaine May's razor-sharp satirical screenplay offers plenty of ammo for both Democrats and Republicans, and director Mike Nichols deftly balances comedy, scathing satire, and compelling drama. Great supporting turns from Kathy Bates as a take-no-prisoners political consultant who will stop at nothing to dig up incriminating dirt, Billy Bob Thornton as live-wire consultant Richard Jemmons (modeled after real-life James Carville), and Emma Thompson as Travolta's much-tested wife.

For a look at the real machinations behind the scenes, drop by **The War Room** (1993), D. A. Pennebaker's absorbing documentary on the 1992 election campaigns. The focus is on the people running the campaign in the back room—the larger-than-life "Ragin' Cajun" James Carville and boyish, twinkle eyed, fresh-scrubbed, and soft-spoken George Stephanopoulos, Clinton's right-hand man. Revealing behind-the-scenes footage captures fascinating minutia—including Carvelle's forthright take on billionaire Ross Perot's doomed third-party campaign for president: "The most expensive single act of masturbation in history."

november 4

Watch One for the Gipper

It was the first time a man who had been divorced was elected president of the United States. He was also the oldest man ever elected to the office. Not only that, he was an actor. Well, allegedly.

On this day in 1980, Ronald Reagan was elected fortieth president of the United States. No, he didn't flub his lines at the swearing-in ceremony.

Good career move. His acting days were pretty much behind him before he was elected governor of California in 1966. As a star, he had never really broken through to the "A" list. He was pretty much a workhorse in "B" pictures for Warner Brothers. But as a politician, he prospered and became that rarity, an American life with a second act.

Before that midlife career change, given the chance and a suitable role, he could prove a credible actor. His performances in *King's Row* (1940; "Where's the rest of me?") and *Knute Rockne, All American* (1940; "Tell 'em to go out there and win just one for the Gipper") are solid, if not entirely Oscar material. But, like it or not (and we suspect he didn't), his cinematic legacy will forever be associated with his starring opposite a cantankerous chimpanzee in the innocuous **Bedtime for Bonzo** (1951). The surprise, for those looking for camp value (and there is a little of that, inevitably), is how breezy and enjoyable a comedy it actually is. The film was inspired by experiments which were going on at the time involving people raising chimps as if they were human children. PETA members are gonna hate this film. But it did manage to establish a bedrock of Reaganism: "Even a monkey, brought up in the right surroundings, can learn the meaning of honesty and decency." If you can get past the political incorrectness, watch this one for the Gipper.

november 5

Bombs Away

Up until this day in 1911, the airplane was more or less a sporting device for recreation. But on November 5, 1911, Italy became the first nation to experiment with air warfare by dropping bombs on an oasis in Libya—and suddenly flying wasn't so sporting. When World War I commenced just a few years later, aerial bombing evolved as an increasingly deadly and effective form of warfare.

Commemorate the birth of air bombing with the old-fashioned **Memphis Belle** (1990). In 1943, the crew of an American B-17 bomber prepare themselves for their twenty-fifth daylight bombing mission. If they succeed and make it back alive, they all get to go home on a PR tour. Exciting, involving, and crowd-pleasing entertainment; they don't make 'em like this anymore. The sturdy cast includes Matthew Modine, John Lithgow, Eric Stoltz, and David Strathairn. Make it a double bill with the star-studded World War II epic, **Thirty Seconds over Tokyo** (1944). Spencer Tracy heads a dream cast in this exciting World War II drama that chronicles the first aerial attack on mainland Japan by American forces. A great supporting cast includes Robert Mitchum, Van Johnson, and the always intriguing Robert Walker. Snappy, efficient direction and great action sequences by Mervyn LeRoy.

november 6

Hoop and Glory

The man credited with inventing basketball, James Naismith, was born this day in 1861. Actually, he didn't invent the game—our ancestors were probably playing some variation of the sport thousands of years before, but it was Naismith who gave us the rules and foundation we use today.

Celebrate the true glory of his invention with one of the great basketball movies—1986's **Hoosiers** starring Gene Hackman as the new coach of an Indiana basketball team who's determined to take his team to the state championships. *Hoosiers* transcends its sports-genre status by being an involving and uplifting drama, as well as one of the most exciting, crowd-pleasing, best-filmed basketball movies ever. In other words, non-basketball fans will enjoy this, too. Dennis Hopper deservedly won a Best Supporting Oscar nomination for his sympathetic portrayal of an on-the-skids coach who can't stop drinking.

For a look at the game of basketball in the "real world," make it a double bill with **Hoop Dreams** (1994), the extraordinary documentary that follows the lives of two very real but different inner-city basketball players as they pursue their dreams to become NBA players. Their lives change in ways which neither they, as participants, nor we, as spectators, have any say over, for better or for worse. Basketball is anything but a game to these hoop dreamers—it's a matter of life and death—and director Steve James keeps the camera going through all the twists and turns of their story. An unforgettable experience.

november 7

Catch a Hurricane

After serving twenty years in prison on a murder charge based on tainted evidence, former boxer Rubin "Hurricane" Carter is a free man this day in 1985, as U.S. District Court Judge H. Lee Sarokin hands down a decision to release him.

Imprisoned in 1965, Carter became a cause célèbre with the publication of his book, *The Sixth Round.* He received a major publicity boost in 1976 when Bob Dylan wrote and recorded "Hurricane," and star-studded benefit performances were held on his behalf in the mid '70s—but a second trial resulted in an upheld conviction. It took the resourcefulness of three Canadian students and a young American law student to get him out, long after the media and celebrities had turned away.

The Hurricane (1999) is a flawed but powerful account of the story of Rubin Carter's tempest-tossed life. Denzel Washington delivers a galvanizing performance in the title role, earning him a much-deserved Oscar nomination for Best Actor that year.

The movie occasionally falls into formulaic Hollywood dumbing-down—Dan Hedaya's cardboard-cutout corrupt cop and the four blended-in-a-vanilla-shake young activists who band together to get him out are standard-issue Hollywood hokum—but Washington's performance delivers a knockout punch that makes this movie a contender. He conveys the anger, the ego, the pride, and eventual salvation of a man on the ropes of life. "It was hate that got me into this place," he comes to realize. "It's love that's gonna bust me out."

november 8

A Star Is Not Born

It was a matter of simply being in the right place at the right time on this day in 1956 for a young Southern California clothier named Robert Evans. Actress Norma Shearer spotted the handsome young man poolside at a party in Hollywood Hills and became convinced he would be perfect to play the part of her late husband, movie mogul and legend Irving Thalberg, in the movie Universal was filming, *Man of a Thousand Faces.* Since Shearer had control over who got cast, Evans got the role; he was then cast as a bullfighter in *The Sun Also Rises* (1957) with Tyrone Power. But the young would-be star projected the charisma of a sedated mannequin in both movies, and he didn't get a third strike before he was out.

Instead, he became a producer, eventually making such films as *The Godfather, Love Story,* and others, and becoming one of Hollywood's most eccentric and best-preserved moguls. (For a wicked parody on Evans, see Dustin Hoffman in *Wag the Dog*.)

Salute a truly nonexistent performance by watching Evans in **Man of a Thousand Faces** (1957). James Cagney makes the movie worth watching (honest!) in his performance as real-life silent film star and master of makeup Lon Chaney, Sr.—and the movie is compelling entertainment. But just for laughs watch the parts where Evans appears as Thalberg. His golly-gosh all-American blandness washes out any set he appears in, and he's so stiff he makes Jack Webb look like Rudolf Nureyev by comparison. On behalf of film lovers everywhere, Robert, thank you . . . for becoming a producer. Mean it, baby.

november 9

It's Better in the Dark

On this date in 1965, if you were alive and in New York City—or anywhere in New York state for that matter—you probably remember where you were when the lights went out. At 5:16 P.M., right at the height of rush hour, the power went out throughout the entire state of New York, portions of seven neighboring states, and parts of eastern Canada. Thirty million people in the dark—and no electricity. People were stuck in darkened buildings, stalled elevators, immobile subway cars. The possibilities were endless, and more than a few people took advantage of them.

Where Were You When the Lights Went Out? (1968) evokes memories not only of the event, but of the times—more as a product of those times than as a depiction of them. Surprisingly, the movie was not based on the incident, but on a French play written twelve years earlier! Lots of familiar TV and B-movie faces, including Doris Day, Bobby Morse, Ben Blue, Jim Backus, and Terry-Thomas.

november 10

Walls and Bridges

After two thousand years, the Great Wall of China opened to commercial tourism on this day in 1970. Souvenir stands featuring T-shirts emblazoned with "My Mom and Dad Went to the Great Wall and All I Got Was This Stupid T-Shirt" started appearing within the hour. Built by China's first emperor in the third century B.C. as fortification against the Huns in the north, the Great Wall stretched an unbelievable, unbroken fifteen hundred miles.

A Great Wall (1986) is one of those small, magical movies that takes you out of your own life and familiar environment and transports you to someone else's experience and culture. A Chinese American family, long removed from their far away traditional Chinese culture, travels to China to visit relatives. The culture shock they experience is both comic and profound. The film examines both their old country's effect on them and, more subversively, America's effects on the old China. A remarkably insightful, quietly enchanting comedy of cultures from director Peter Wang.

november 11

Veterans Day

A day to pause in grateful remembrance and appreciation for those who served their country. On November 11, 1921—the anniversary of the end of World War I at eleven A.M. on November 11, 1918—an unknown American World War I soldier was buried in Arlington National Cemetery, while at the same time, other unknown soldiers were being buried across the Atlantic in England's Westminster Abbey and France's Arc de Triomphe. The occasion and day became known as Armistice Day, and it officially became a national holiday in 1938.

Finally, on June 1, 1954, the name was changed to Veterans Day in honor of all U.S. veterans. It is now recognized as a day to honor all those who served their country in the Armed Forces.

William Wyler's **The Best Years of Our Lives** (1946) follows the lives of three soldiers returning from World War II who face the challenges and difficulties of returning to civilian life. Fredric March plays a middle-class bank executive returning home to the bosom of his family; Dana Andrews is a blue-collar bomber pilot whose marriage to wife Virginia Mayo is not as solid as he thinks; and Harold Russell is a man who has lost both his hands in combat and is reluctant to reunite with his sweetheart (Cathy O'Donnell). All three are splendid and have great showcase scenes (both March and Russell won Oscars), and the film will leave you moved. *The Best Years of Our Lives* is remarkably adult and frank about its subject matter—unsentimental and unflinching in depicting the difficulties of returning to "civilian" life. There are no easy answers or trite resolutions, but there is enormous compassion here. A magnificent film; one of the best of our lives.

november 12

Shower the People

Andrew Ellicott Douglas, an early American astronomer, witnessed what is regarded as the first recorded meteor shower, on this day in 1799. Aboard ship, he wrote in his journal that "the whole heaven appeared as if illuminated with sky rockets, flying in an infinity of directions, and I was in constant expectation of some of them falling on the vessel."

Commemorate another close call with **Armageddon** (1998). You know that any film produced by Jerry Bruckheimer is going to be big, dumb, noisy, and packed with eye-popping effects—and *Armageddon* doesn't disappoint. A meteor is heading straight for earth, and NASA's executive director (Billy Bob Thornton in disheveled, harried executive mode) realizes that in eighteen hours the entire planet will be vaporized, so he gathers together a band of last-chance ragtag oil drillers to fly up, land on the asteroid, drill an eight-hundred-foot hole into its core, and drop off a nuclear bomb to divert it from earth. Piece of cake. Bruce Willis is—well, Bruce Willis—as the head astro-driller, assisted by Ben Affleck as the cocky young recruit who's engaged to Willis's earthbound daughter (Liv Tyler). Lavish, moronic, exciting, funny (sometimes unintentionally), and hugely successful; it grossed more box office dollars than any other movie in 1998. The always watchable Steve Buscemi livens things up as a looney lothario who goes space crazy once he's on the asteroid. See if you can tell the difference.

november 13

Ever Wonder Where "Wonderland" Came From?

"It's no use going back to yesterday, because I was a different person then."

—*Alice,* Alice in Wonderland

Thirty-year-old Rev. Charles Dodgson—soon to be known the world over as Lewis Carroll—sits down this night in 1862 in his tiny one-room living quarters at Christ Church, Oxford, and begins to write down *Alice's Adventures in Wonderland.* The whimsical, labyrinthine tale comes from a series of stories he has made up extemporaneously for twelve-year-old Alice Liddell, during leisurely summer boat excursions up the River Thames with her and her two older sisters. Whether or not Carroll was in love with young Alice has been debated for over 130 years. Liddell's mother destroyed all of Carroll's correspondences to Alice. But there is no doubt that Liddell was a special spark in the author's life. "I have had scores of child-friends since your time," he wrote to her after her marriage years later, "but they have been quite a different thing."

Alice has been filmed several times, most notably and successfully in an all-star 1933 version with Cary Grant as the Mock Turtle, Gary Cooper as the sweetly befuddled White Knight, and an unrecognizable W. C. Fields as

Humpty Dumpty. Disney produced an animated version in 1951 which retained little of the book's charm. Part of the trouble in transposing *Alice* to the screen stems from the fact that it is a fanciful story from another world and time altogether (Victorian England), and modern-day children have little patience for its languorous pace or knowledge of its intricate wordplay and outdated satire of long-forgotten political figures and poems.

Instead of watching *Alice,* ponder Carroll's mysterious motives and the enigmatic puzzle of his life with the intriguing and slightly surreal **Dreamchild** (1985). Now an old widow, eighty-year-old Alice Liddell (Coral Browne in an enchanting performance) visits New York City to celebrate the centennial of Carroll's birth. When she's confronted by a horde of reporters, Alice is forced to piece together the fragments of her life. *Dreamchild* is an appropriately dreamlike meditation on how the springtime of our childhood haunts our autumnal adult selves. The flashback sequences to Alice's youthful days on the English countryside (with Ian Holm perfectly cast as Dodgson) are evocative, and the re-creations of the *Alice* characters (featuring truly macabre puppets from Jim Henson) are marvelously surreal and, like Carroll's book, disconcerting. Not a film for kids, but for the kids that live on in all adults; elegiac, darkly nostalgic, and, ultimately, redeeming. Written by Dennis Potter (*The Singing Detective; Pennies from Heaven*).

november 14

A Really Big Dick

On this day in 1851, one of the great American novels hit the streets. *Moby-Dick,* by Herman Melville, was published. The symbol-laden tale of one man's obsession and quest to kill the great white whale that took off his leg is one of the great adventures ever written—as long as you skip every other chapter, wherein Melville goes into lengthy and boring detail about the history and anatomy of whales.

The seafaring adventure lent itself to Hollywood as far back as 1926 when matinee idol John Barrymore played Captain Ahab in the silent film, *The Sea Beast;* he was so successful that he again played Ahab—but this time with a tacked-on happy ending and sound—in the early talkie, *Moby Dick* (1930). These early versions were far from Melville's layered prose; in fact, in the 1930 version, Ahab lives, gets married, and lives happily ever after.

John Huston directed the best screen version of the tale, **Moby Dick** (1956). The screenplay (by sci-fi icon Ray Bradbury) is remarkably true to Melville's book; several passages are repeated verbatim—lending the film an authentically literary air. Gregory Peck is surprisingly effective as the vengeance-obsessed Captain Ahab. The underappreciated Richard Basehart keeps the story grounded as Ishmael, the narrator, who signs aboard the *Pequod*—a whaling ship out of New England. *Moby Dick* is one of those rare films which actually improve on the small screen; on a large screen, many of the effects (the giant whale, the sinking of the *Pequod*) look like obvious miniatures—but on television, disbelief can be easily suspended. Orson Welles—who was at that time starring in his own stage version of the novel called *Moby Dick, Rehearsed*—plays Father Marple; his lengthy monologue was done in one unbroken take. (By the way, Gregory Peck would go on to play Marple in the 1998 TV adaptation starring Patrick Stewart as Ahab and Henry Thomas as Ishmael.)

november 15

Watch a Real Long Shot

On this day in 1962, golfer Larry Bruce managed the near-impossible: a 480-yard hole in one at Hope Country Club in Arkansas. It still stands as the record for longest hole in one.

Celebrate this one-in-a-million shot with an all-golf-night marathon. Kick it off with W. C. Fields's uproarious twenty-minute short, **The Golf Specialist** (1933)—filmed on a single shabby indoor set. Then settle in for **Tin Cup** (1996), with Kevin Costner taking a break from making baseball movies to make a golf movie. Costner plays Ron "Tin Cup" McAvoy, a West

Texas golf hustler who has the magic touch, but is unsteady. When he decides to try for the U.S. Open, he consults psychologist Dr. Molly Griswold—who is also the girlfriend of McAvoy's longtime rival and successful PGA player, Don Simms (Don Johnson, surprisingly good). Needless to say, complications ensue. A sparkling, witty comedy-romance-sports film from writer-director Ron Shelton, who also worked with Costner on the hugely successful *Bull Durham.* Next, watch **The Caddy** (1953), one of Dean Martin and Jerry Lewis's better flicks. Dean's a professional golfer, and Jerry is his adoring, accident-prone caddy. Plenty of cameos from real golf pros like Ben Hogan, Sam Snead, and more.

Then, if you've still got the energy, top off the marathon with **Caddyshack** (1980), featuring inspired performances from SNL alumni Chevy Chase and Bill Murray wreaking havoc at the Bushwood Country Club.

november 16

Watch an OK Movie

The combined Indian and Oklahoma Territories were admitted to the Union on this day in 1907 as the state of Oklahoma, the forty-sixth state. The name was derived from Choctaw Indian words *okla,* meaning people, and *humma,* meaning red.

Celebrate the occasion with—what else?—**Oklahoma!** (1955), where the corn is as high as an elephant's eye. The musical revolutionized Broadway with its incandescent score by Rodgers and Hammerstein, and breathtaking choreography by the great Agnes DeMille (sister of C.B.). Gordon MacRae and Shirley Jones (fresh from their previous successful teaming in *Carousel*) star as the young lovers whose happiness is threatened by surly ranch hand Judd (Rod Steiger, miscast but game). The always glorious Gloria Grahame shines as Ado Annie, singing the show-stopping "I Cain't Say No." By the way, in case you're wondering, no, the movie wasn't filmed in Oklahoma; it was filmed in Arizona. Directed by Fred Zinneman.

november 17

An Asthmatic Film Geek Who Made Good

Martin Scorsese is arguably the most influential director of the last thirty years. Spielberg and Lucas have brought in more box office dollars, but Scorsese's artistic shadow falls over virtually all other directors, from Oliver Stone to Quentin Tarantino. A self-declared movie fanatic, he is a walking encyclopedia of film technique and history, and he is not afraid to embark on uncharted roads. As a director, his subjects may vary wildly—from *Mean Streets* to *Alice Doesn't Live Here Anymore* to *Taxi Driver* to *Raging Bull* to *New York, New York* to *The King of Comedy* to *The Last Temptation of Christ*—but his themes are consistent. He was born this day in Queens, New York, in 1942.

He was a hypersensitive, asthmatic child who found escape and inspiration in film—particularly the film noir of his youth and the work of director Vincente Minnelli. His first breakthrough success was *Mean Streets* (1973), a finely wrought study of the Little Italy in which he grew up, which also marked his first collaboration with the actor most associated with his work, Robert DeNiro. Their working collaboration has been one of the most fruitful partnerships in American cinema.

Assuming you've already seen *Taxi Driver* and *Raging Bull,* celebrate the birth of America's premier director with one of his more obscure gems, the seldom-seem, darkly comic **After Hours** (1986)—a small-scale, low-budget change of pace for the director. Scorsese fell in love with first-time screenwriter Joseph Minion's darkly surreal comedy script about one endless, nightmarish night in the life of a yuppie New York computer programmer (Griffin Dunne) who makes a date with a SoHo girl and gets much more than he bargained for. Minion's screenplay is a Kafkaesque labyrinth of construction—intricate as a Chinese box puzzle—and Scorsese's direction is at once economical, expansive, evocative, and surreal. The fabulous supporting cast includes Catherine O'Hara, Terri Garr, John Hurt, Rosanna Arquette, and Cheech and Chong. A dizzyingly inventive exercise in bravura filmmaking.

november 18

The World's Most Successful Four-Fingered Rodent

According to the official but dubious Disney dictum, Mickey Mouse was officially born this day in 1928. Actually, it was the day Steamboat Willie, Mickey's first cartoon, premiered at the Colony Theater in New York. The animated rodent was originally named "Mortimer"—until Walt's wife suggested "Mickey." And the voice was done by none other than Walt himself.

Celebrate Mickey's birthday with his creator's most visionary achievement, **Fantasia** (1940). Still a visual knockout and conceptually miles ahead of most CGI-generated animation, *Fantasia* was a gloriously bold, daring, and doomed experiment. Disney forsook linear narrative in a series of animated vignettes built around famous pieces of classical music. Purists objected to the bowdlerization of the original music (edited and rearranged for the film), and mainstream audiences of the '40s scratched their heads at the film's impressionistic tone after having come to expect the likes of *Snow White and the Seven Dwarfs*. It was a box office flop until it was reissued in 1969—when its success was widely attributed to the then-current drug scene.

Oh, yes . . . Mickey . . . he stars in the title role of *Fantasia*'s marvelous centerpiece sequence, Dukas's "The Sorcerer's Apprentice." As a mischievous assistant to a magician, he brings an army of broomsticks to life, with predictably disastrous results. It's Mickey's greatest performance, and he even gets to shake hands with conductor Leopold Stokowski. Not bad for an animated rodent born with only four fingers on each hand. (By the way, this sequence also appears in *Fantasia 2000* [2000], the long-delayed sequel to the original.)

november 19

An Address Everyone Should Know

On this day in 1863, Abraham Lincoln delivered the shortest speech of his career—and certainly the most eloquent. Speaking from a makeshift podium in the waning Pennsylvania autumn sun, he delivered what became known as the "Gettysburg Address."

He had been invited to attend the dedication at Gettysburg, the site, scarcely three months earlier, of one of the bloodiest and most decisive battles of the Civil War. The Battle of Gettysburg had lasted from July first to third, 1863. Casualties on both sides were horrific: the South lost 2,592 soldiers, with an additional 13,000 wounded, and the North lost 3,155 with approximately 15,000 wounded. It all came to a bloody head with Pickett's Charge, Robert E. Lee's disastrous offensive. Two of Pickett's three brigadier generals fell, and all fifteen regimental commanders were killed or wounded. Some 12,500 young men charged Cemetery Ridge; 5,000 returned. Pickett never forgave Lee, years later saying, "That old man had my division massacred."

Nobody expected Lincoln to attend the memorial and dedication of the hallowed ground on this day in 1863, but he accepted. The legend is that he hastily scribbled some notes onto an envelope on the train trip over. Actually, he had worked on the short speech for days.

The speech was over and done before anyone really knew it had begun. At a mere 268 words, it was over in less than two minutes. A cameraman didn't even have sufficient time to snap a photo before the president sat back down.

Not everyone was impressed. A writer for the *Chicago Times* opined that "the cheek of every American should be filled with shame as he reads the silly, flat and dishwatery utterences of the man who has to be pointed out to intelligent foreigners as the President of the United States." No one remembers who wrote that dismissive critique. But Lincoln's words are unforgettable. Contrary to his opinion that "the world will little note nor long remember," they endure.

Commemorate the anniversary with **Gettysburg** (1993), producer Ted Turner's exhaustive and painstakingly re-created account of the battle. At four hours, it manages to capture the flavor of the time in which it's set, and the various battles-within-the-battle are realistically staged by director Ronald F. Maxwell. Jeff Daniels and Richard Jordan make the best impressions from a large cast including Tom Berenger, Martin Sheen, Sam Elliott, and C. Thomas Howell. Ted Turner appears (barely) as an extra—wearing a Confederate uniform, naturally.

november 20

Come Blow 'Em Away, Horn

Outlaw Tom Horn was the last of a dying breed, a loner who made his living as what was euphemistically called a "regulator" in the waning days of the Wild West, when virtually all the frontier towns were tamed. He started out as an exemplary upholder of the law, and was responsible for tracking down Geronimo and negotiating his surrender (something an entire third of the U.S. Army couldn't accomplish). After capturing the World Championship title for steer roping in 1888, he was hired by the Pinkerton Agency, and single-handedly brought in notorious Hole-in-the-Wall Gang member "Peg Leg" McCoy.

But in the early 1890s, something snapped, and Tom Horn executed a 180-degree career shift, becoming a gun for hire. He abruptly quit the agency ("I had no stomach for it anymore") and became a hired killer. A western hit man, he worked for cattle barons throughout the west who wanted to eliminate their range war enemies.

His preferred method was bushwhacking, and he killed scores of men. In 1902, he went too far, killing a fourteen-year-old boy named Willie Nichell while lying in wait for Nichell's father, a sheep rancher he had contracted to kill. Horn confessed to the murder, tied his own hangman's noose, and met his Maker this day in 1903.

Horn lived life on his own terms and faced his death with stoic dignity. So, too, did Steve McQueen, in what would prove to be his penultimate role, in **Tom Horn** (1980). McQueen was fighting a valiant battle with cancer during filming, which adds a depth and resonance to his portrayal of the title character, a man whom time and circumstance have left behind. A great, richly nuanced script by Thomas McGuane and a stellar cast of veterans from westerns past (including Elisha Cook, Jr., Richard Farnsworth, and Slim Pickens) add to the authenticity.

november 21

. . . And a Dead Man's Chest

While diving in twenty-five feet of water off Beaufort, North Carolina on this day in 1996, diver Ray Giroux discovered the remains of *Queen Anne's Revenge*—the forty-gun flagship of Edward Teach. Teach was better known—and feared—as "Blackbeard," the most bloodthirsty, notorious pirate of the high seas. In his last days, he sailed the coast off the Carolinas, where many people think treasures are still stashed in long-forgotten hiding places.

Blackbeard was the quintessential pirate of yore, a genuine fire-breathing, seagoing pillager, cutthroat, and ladies' man (he is said to have had fourteen wives—a girl in every port, indeed). He was garnished from head to toe in weaponry—sabers, knives, and a brace of pistols—and his flowing black beard was festooned with colorful ribbons and, according to one source, burning hashish. Well, that's the embellished lore, anyway—mostly started by Daniel Defoe's book, *General History.* The truth is that, although he was irrefutably a pirate, there exists no evidence whatsoever that Blackbeard was the fearsome monster Defoe made him out to be.

He was born Edward Teach in Bristol, England, around 1680. A giant bear of a man, he launched his career as a legitimate pirate under the British Crown sailing out of Jamaica, raiding French and Spanish ships during Queen Anne's War. But when the war was over and the Bahamas outlawed piracy in 1718, he kept plundering, commandeering *Queen Anne's Revenge,* building up a substantial crew, and looting up to one hundred ships. A few months later, he was killed in battle. His head was put on display at the end of a spike at the entrance to Hampton Roads Bay in Virginia.

Drink a toast of rum to the old pirate by watching **Blackbeard the Pirate** (1952), a nearly forgotten high-seas potboiler that's got it all: sword fights, floggings, battles on sea and on land, buried treasure, torture . . . and William Bendix! Robert Newton plays Blackbeard in this action, adventure, and humor directed by Raoul Walsh. Look for a pre-*Beverly Hillbillies* Irene "Granny" Ryan as a blithering maid. Or you can enjoy Peter Ustinov's unlikely portrayal of the pirate in *Blackbeard's Ghost* (1967), a Disney movie that has both the charms and the drawbacks of the Disney live-action films of that period; it's really a revamped version of *The Canterville Ghost.* Still, Ustinov is a delight in just about anything.

november 22

Death of a President

Anyone who was alive at the time and old enough to remember will never forget where they were on this day in 1963. John F. Kennedy was in Dallas, Texas.

First of all, make no mistake about it: Oliver Stone's **JFK** (1991) is not history—it's a movie, an entertainment. Can entertainment be dangerous? Only when viewers are so pulled in to the experience that it becomes fact for them. Stone may be convinced that everyone from the CIA, FBI, A&P, PG&E, Castro, and the Mafia were active participants in plotting and carrying out the assassination and subsequent cover-up (as if all those disparate agencies could have possibly held such a volatile secret for so long), but he builds his lopsided case by blatantly rewriting history.

One of *JFK's* intrinsic "dangers" is its convincing cinematic sleight of hand—taking speculative events and positioning them as fact (hey, if we see it happening on screen, it must've happened, right?), and deliberately altering (or omitting) crucial events and testimony. One is easily swept up in Stone's majestic mosaic of a movie.

On the subject of how far Stone's movie deviates from the facts, I can only recommend the reader check out Gerald Posner's definitive and instructive 1998 book on the JFK assassination, *Case Closed.* It fairly convincingly makes mincemeat of Stone's conspiratorial neurosis.

But on the subject of Oliver Stone's *JFK* as a movie, in and of itself, I can attest that it is a powerful, stimulating, and tremendously absorbing experience. Kevin Costner stars as New Orleans District Attorney Jim Garrison, who became convinced there was a cover-up in the case against Lee Harvey Oswald and took his beliefs all the way to the Supreme Court. Gary Oldman is uncanny as Lee Harvey Oswald—it's downright scary how he manages to duplicate precisely the mumbling cadence of Oswald's voice. There are also flashy supporting turns from Tommy Lee Jones, Joe Pesci, Jack Lemmon, Kevin Bacon, and John Candy. (The real-life Jim Garrison appears briefly in a cameo as, ironically, Chief Justice Earl Warren.) And Stone's use of multiple film techniques, evocative of Orson Welles's out-and-out joy in slicing and dicing the medium, is dazzling.

So enjoy. It's a great movie. But it's *only* a movie; it ain't history.

november 23

He Must've Been One Ugly Baby

In Dulwich, England, on this date in 1887, William Henry Pratt was welcomed into the world. He grew up to be Boris Karloff. "I wasn't born a monster," he said. "Hollywood made me one."

Karloff was Hollywood's reigning bogeyman throughout the '30s and '40s. He was working as a character actor and extra in 1931 when then–horror king Bela Lugosi turned down the part of the monster in *Frankenstein.* According to legend, director James Whale spotted Karloff in the studio commissary and knew he had his monster.

And so he did. Karloff so perfectly embodied the part that he was initially billed in the credits as "?" His man-made monster is still one of horror movies' greatest achievements—frightening, powerful, brutal, but the child within comes out. Later, when Karloff took on speaking roles, his mellifluous, vaguely ominous voice suited his persona like a custom-made, skin-tight shroud. Witness his truly macabre evil priest in *The Black Cat* (1932), or his conspiratorial grave robber in Val Lewton's eerie *The Body Snatcher* (1945).

But his greatest part was his first reprise of the monster he created, in **The Bride of Frankenstein** (1935). The monster is back, and so is his creator, Henry Frankenstein (Colin Clive). Through the kindness of a blind hermit, the monster learns to speak, and he demands a mate for himself. Although Karloff himself didn't approve of the film (he believed that the monster should never have spoken), Karloff's performance is even better than in the original . . . particularly his scenes with the hermit who befriends him (which was so indelibly parodied by Mel Brooks in *Young Frankenstein* that one can't watch the original scene without smiling). A scene-stealing performance by the great Ernest Thesiger as the delightfully decadent Dr. Pretorious adds to the fun. James Whale's outrageously outré direction is spellbinding, the sets are spectacularly ersatz-gothic, and Elsa Lanchester's hairdo has yet to be topped. One of the greatest horror-fantasy films of all time, and the crowning achievement in the Universal Studios canon.

november 24

Into Thin Air

"No funny stuff!" the man yelled as he flashed something that looked like a bomb to the flight attendant, backing her toward the cockpit.

"D. B. Cooper" then informed the crew he wanted $20,000 and a parachute. The plane was diverted to Seattle Airport, where authorities met Cooper's demands and evacuated most of the passengers. Cooper then ordered the crew to fly the plane to Mexico, passing over Reno, Nevada, at a low altitude. After herding the rest of the crew into the cockpit, Cooper donned a parachute, opened the cabin door, and plunged into a raging thunderstorm with 150 mph winds and temperatures below zero. He was wearing only a thin suit and raincoat, along with a pair of wraparound sunglasses, and toting a suitcase full of money. It was on this night in 1971 that he tumbled out of the plane into the ever-fuzzy perimeters of history.

Did he make it or didn't he? People all across the country speculated on his chances; pretty much everyone secretly hoped he would get away with it, but few believed he could have survived the elements that night. He has yet to reappear, living or dead.

The Pursuit of D. B. Cooper (1981) speculates on what may have happened—all in an amiably breezy "what if?" scenario. Treat Williams is an appealing, charismatic, and roguish D. B. Cooper; perhaps too appealing. The real thing was no Cary Grant—imagine Harry Dean Stanton in the part! Robert Duvall plays yet another convincing variation on his "cop in pursuit" part. An underrated little gem of a movie. What do you think, D.B.?

november 25

The Band's Last Waltz

It was a Thanksgiving celebration to end all celebrations. On this night in 1976, the Band gave their farewell performance at Winterland in San Francisco.

In the beginning, they called themselves the Hawks—mostly because they had started as backup players for rowdy blues singer Ronnie Hawkins. While they were living in Woodstock and jamming with Bob Dylan—who was recuperating from his 1966 motorcycle accident—Dylan simply referred to them as "the band." The name stuck. It was a luminescent convergence of talent, vision, and musical styles that created an organic whole. The Band produced some of the most transcendent music of the decade—songs that seemed to have been written a hundred years ago and become part of the American heritage: "The Night They Drove Old Dixie Down," "Ophelia," "The Weight," "Arcadian Driftwood" and scores of others.

The musical alchemy didn't last forever. It never does. But it went out in style on this night in 1976 in San Francisco when the Band gave their last-ever concert with the original members with a grand farewell party and recorded it as **The Last Waltz** (1978). The royalty of rock were there to participate—doing their own material backed by the Band, who gave an extraordinary performance along with such guests as Bob Dylan, Joni Mitchell, Eric Clapton, Neil Young, and Van Morrison. The event was recorded on film by none other than Martin Scorsese (who had previously served as a second unit cameraman on *Woodstock,* and knew a lot about how to film a performance). Scorsese mixes footage of the concert itself, revealing interviews with the group, and a few in-studio set pieces that complement the rest of the film.

Magnificently shot and jam-packed with great music, *The Last Waltz* is one of the two best rock 'n' roll concert movies ever made. (The other is *Stop Making Sense,* directed by Jonathan Demme and featuring the Talking Heads.) A near-perfect film. If only they'd cut Neil Diamond's lackluster and dirgelike performance, it *would* be perfect.

november 26

An Educational Activity

On this day, the first official college fraternity was founded in America in 1825. The school was Union College, New York—and the fraternity was Kappa Alpha.

I say, "Food fight!"

It's the one day of the year you can watch **National Lampoon's Animal House** (1978) and say you're doing it to honor the prestigious history of fraternity houses all across America—particularly Delta House Fraternity, at Faber College, circa 1962. John Landis's classic comedy has only improved with age. John Belushi achieved instant cinematic icon status overnight as Bluto, the animalistic oversized oaf of Delta House with the feloniously hyperactive eyebrows and the bottomless appetite. Keep an eye on Donald Sutherland's increasingly red eyes during his pot-smoking scene; that was no film wizardry. Fun performances from Peter Reigert, Tim Matheson, Tom Hulce, and a young Kevin Bacon as a member of a rival fraternity. Mindless, brain-numbingly sophomoric humor—much like real fraternity life.

november 27

He Had the Cutest Little Baby Face

He wanted to be called "Big George"—but everybody called him "Baby Face." But not to his face. On this day in 1934, he went out in a blaze of sordid glory.

Lester Gillis—better known as "Baby Face" Nelson because of his deceptively innocent looks—was arguably the most vicious gangster in the age of the Public Enemy. Whereas John Dillinger and Pretty Boy Floyd killed only to protect themselves, Baby Face Nelson was an out-and-out, looney-tunes psychopath who craved killing and went out of his way to do it.

He was a punk, an unstable bantam-weight crook, when he hooked up with John Dillinger to rob banks. Unlike Dillinger, who carefully planned and orchestrated his heists like choreography, Nelson's idea was more like a demented rave —walk in and shoot everything and everybody in sight, grab the money, and run. After Dillinger was killed at the Biograph Theater in Chicago, Nelson became Public Enemy #1. It was a spot he had always perversely coveted—but he felt insulted when he saw that the feds were offering less reward money for him than they did for Dillinger.

On this day in 1934 he was driving with his wife and a friend near Fox River Grove, Illinois. Two FBI agents, Sam Cowley and Herman Hollis, spotted the car and started in pursuit. Soon, guns were blazing, and both cars pulled over. Nelson's wife ran to hide in the field, and a brief standoff between Baby Face and the two G-men began. After a few minutes, a frustrated Nelson grabbed his machine gun and started to stride purposefully—almost leisurely—directly toward the agents, who kept firing at the brazen fugitive, hitting the outlaw several times. Agent Cowley hit him with his machine gun, but Nelson walked right up to him, lifted his machine gun, and fired several rounds. Agent Hollis emptied his gun into Nelson's leg and turned to run but the resolute gangster still kept coming. Baby Face shot him down and then, his work done, turned and staggered toward the car, telling his disbelieving friend to drive. He lingered for a few hours; his bullet-riddled body was found the next day, dumped on a road, nude.

Mickey Rooney was an inspired choice to play the title role in **Baby Face Nelson** (1957)—both were pugnacious, egotistical, and volatile. Don Siegal directed this punk of a B movie with his usual zeal and economy. Skip the lame 1996 version of the same name starring C. Thomas Howell. Richard Dreyfuss, in his first meaty role, also gave a memorable, over-the-top performance as Baby Face Nelson in John Milius's *Dillinger* (1973), starring Warren Oates as America's Robin Hood.

november 28

When She Was Good, She Was Very Good . . . When She Was Bad, She Was Better

Gloria Grahame was the ultimate Hollywood Bad Girl with a Good Heart. Nobody could play a fallen woman or an errant wife like Grahame could. She had a unique ability to be trampy, sexy, wholesome, winsome, and conniving all at once, with a single flutter of her lashes or a downward turn of her pouty lips. She was born this day in Los Angeles in 1925.

Grahame first made an impression on audiences as Violet, the small-town bad girl of Bedford Falls in the classic *It's a Wonderful Life* (1946) who almost tempts Jimmy Stewart away from good girl Donna Reed. She won an Academy Award as Best Supporting Actress for her affecting portrayal of an upwardly mobile tramp seducing Kirk Douglas in *The Bad and the Beautiful* (1952). She gave a great, energetic performance in *Oklahoma!* (1955). After the late '50s, she pretty much retired from the screen, although she did return for one last curtain call in the delightful *Melvin and Howard* (1981). She was one of a kind, and that's putting it mildly.

Celebrate the bad girl's birthday with her most complex, layered performance—in Nicholas Ray's **In a Lonely Place** (1950). The lonely place is Hollywood, where scriptwriter Dixon Steele (Humphrey Bogart in unpredictably paranoiac mode) is suspected of murder, until his attractive next-door neighbor Laurel Gray (Grahame) provides him with a false alibi. Under pressure from the cops, their tentative relationship begins to unravel, and Dixon becomes increasingly distraught and violent. Is he the killer? An astonishing performance by Grahame abandons the femme fatale persona she excelled in, revealing a character of enormous complexity. A textbook example of film noir, still riveting and fresh and dark as its title, directed by Nicholas Ray (who was married to Grahame at the time of filming).

november 29

Did She Fall or Was She Pushed?

On this night in 1981, off a yacht floating near Catalina Island, actress Natalie Wood drowned under mysterious circumstances. She was forty-three years old.

She had been on a cruise with husband Robert Wagner and actor Christopher Walken, with whom she was then costarring in *Brainstorm.* Rumors had already started on shore that an inebriated Natalie was showing a great deal of affection and attention in Walken's direction, and Wagner was getting pretty steamed. Wood disappeared overboard sometime during the night; she couldn't swim and had a fear of deep water.

Wood had spent virtually her entire life as a Hollywood actress, from her memorable childhood role in *Miracle on 34th Street* (1947) through her teen years in *Rebel Without a Cause* (1955) and into steamy adulthood with *Inside Daisy Clover* (1966) and *Bob and Carol and Ted and Alice* (1968).

But her best performance may be her most unexpected (and unfairly criticized)—as the love-struck Maria in **West Side Story** (1963). Though she didn't do her own singing (the ubiquitous Marni Nixon handled vocal chores), Wood delivered a killer performance as the young Puerto Rican girl caught up in the blushes of first love and the mindless violence of gang warfare. The optimism, humor, despair, and aching romance are from the heart. Unfortunately, costar Richard Beymer as Tony proves sadly inadequate in the testosterone department—but Natalie Wood shines.

november 30

Apply for Clemens, See?

"Never put off until tomorrow what you can do the day after tomorrow."

—Mark Twain

Samuel L. Clemens was born on this day in Florida, Missouri, in 1835. As a young man he dreamed of traveling the Mississippi, and he became a riverboat pilot in 1857. It was there where he first heard the phrase *mark twain*—meaning two fathoms deep—and he found the nom de plume which he would use until his death in 1910.

Mark Twain became America's most celebrated popular author and wit, and several of his most popular works have been adapted for the screen. There was even a sudsy film bio, *The Adventures of Mark Twain* (1944), starring a heavily made up Fredric March. But the movies based on his work have been a mixed bunch, seldom capturing the sharp satirical timbre of Twain at his best. MGM's squeaky-clean version of *Huck Finn* is a typical example, starring Mickey Rooney as a somewhat overage Huck who was so spruced up that his fictitious namesake would not recognize himself. Probably the best Mark Twain adaptation on screen is 1938's **The Adventures of Tom Sawyer,** an early Technicolor movie starring young Tommy Kelly in the title role. Capturing much of the flavor of the novel, it also boasts one of the screen's all-time scariest villains: Victor Jory's "Injun Joe" is pure murderous menace, and the sight of him climbing the caves with a knife clenched between his teeth trying to kill Tom and Becky Thatcher is the stuff little boys' nightmares are made of.

december

december 1

Don't Boycott This Movie

On this day in Montgomery, Alabama, in 1955, Rosa Parks decided she'd had enough. After a surly white bus driver told the African American seamstress to move to the back of the bus, she refused. "I paid my dime," she said firmly. "I ain't got no reason to move."

She was arrested for violating segregated seating laws. A friend of Parks gathered together a group of nineteen of the area's most influential black ministers at a town meeting that night, and the group called for a boycott of the city buses. Among the group that night was a new Baptist minister on his first assignment, the young Martin Luther King, Jr., who was unanimously elected to be the leader of the newly formed Montgomery Improvement Association. Black Americans throughout Alabama responded in an unprecedented show of solidarity, boycotting the city's buses.

Celebrate the achievement and spirit with an inspiring and underrated film, **The Long Walk Home** (1990). Whoopi Goldberg gives an understated and moving performance as Odessa Cotter, a long-time maid in the Montgomery household of the affluent Thompson family. Sissy Spacek is Miriam Thompson, the Southern housewife who employs Odessa, and who is forced to confront her family's history and her own prejudices when she offers to give Odessa a ride to work during the boycott. The film chronicles the effect of the boycott on the lives and families of both women. Admirably, *The Long Walk Home* does not stereotype its characters—these are complex, well-rounded people with flaws, weaknesses, and failings, as well as compassion and untapped reserves of strength. Filmed on location in Montgomery, *The Long Walk Home* is an emotionally satisfying, historically accurate look at a crossroads moment in American history.

december 2

The Sadistics Can Be Alarming

"In order to know virtue, we must first acquaint ourselves with vice."

—Marquis de Sade

On this night in 1814, after a long life of decadence and debauchery, Donatein Alphonse Francois, Comte de Sade—better known as the Marquis de Sade—died peacefully in his sleep, at the ripe old age of seventy-four. That hard living will kill you every time.

He had been born to privilege; his parents were advisors in the court of Louis XV. As a young student he attended the prestigious Jesuit school Lycée Louis le Grand. While there, he was subjected to intense physical discipline, which included flagellation and whipping. It seems to have whetted his appetite.

He fought in the Seven Years' War with the prestigious King's Light Calvary and later married the daughter of a wealthy government official, fathering three children. But marriage proved boring for Sade, and his sexual pursuits knew no bounds. His behavior soon captured the attention of the French authorities, particularly after he tortured and mutilated his chambermaid. Eventually, after several more indiscretions, the French court sentenced him to prison. While serving time in the notorious Bastille, he wrote his best-known work, *120 Days of Sodom,* which graphically described deviant, violent sexual acts, including murder. In 1787, he produced *Justine,* which features such sophisticated inventions as "the whipping machine" and "the raping machine." After his release from prison, Sade left his wife and made a sparse living by publishing pornography. He was eventually sent to an insane asylum outside of Paris.

The provocative **Quills** (2000) is a deft combination of history, humor, and fantasy. Geoffrey Rush is suitably over-the-top in the role of the flamboyant, possessed writer de Sade. Kate Winslet plays Madeline, a laundress at the asylum where de Sade is incarcerated under the care of Abbe Coulmier (Joaquin Phoenix). When "alienist" Dr. Royer-Collard (Michael Caine) comes to oversee the asylum under the orders of Napoleon, the wheels of tragedy are set in motion. Great performances all 'round, an ingenious screenplay, and top-notch direction by Philip Kaufman make this one of the most outrageous, challenging, and controversial movies ever about artistic expression—and its repercussions. Definitely not for the kids, but Grandma may enjoy it. . . .

december 3

Catch a Ride on This Streetcar

A revolutionary night in American theater which would have major repercussions in Hollywood occurred on this night in 1947, when Tennessee Williams's *A Streetcar Named Desire* premiered in New York City. The frank, sexually steamy story elicited gasps from critics and audiences—as did the leading man. A young lion named Marlon Brando played New Orleans working stiff Stanley Kowalski—mumbling and scratching his way through the part like a caged animal with fleas. There was a method to his Method, and Hollywood jumped on him like white on rice.

Commemorate the debut with Elia Kazan's 1952 film version of the play, **A Streetcar Named Desire** (1951). Brando returned to reprise his stage role on film, costarring with Vivien Leigh (replacing Jessica Tandy from the stage show) as the deluded and damaged Blanche du Bois. For the most part, Kazan keeps his camera within the claustrophobic, dilapidated New Orleans slum stage set. A curious but effective mix of sweaty realism and high-humidity poetry. Brando is spellbinding, and never looked better, projecting a brutish, animal sexuality, explosive anger, and inarticulate vulnerability.

december 4

One Swingin' Club

When Duke Ellington and his band opened at the renowned New York City Cotton Club this night in 1927, they received a warm welcome—so warm that they stayed there for the next four years. Being the house band at the hottest swing club in the country certainly enhanced the Duke's chops and credentials, and by the time they left in 1931, the band was as tight as the cap on a bottle of Heinz 57 Ketchup. The Cotton Club became *the* jazz hot spot in Harlem, and the tales it could tell could fill a movie.

Celebrate the glory days of jazz, Prohibition, and gangsters with **The Cotton Club** (1984), Francis Ford Coppola's one-of-a-kind "musical gangster film." The story is fairly pedestrian (Richard Gere gives a particularly lackluster performance), but the musical numbers sizzle and pop, and Coppola's re-creation of the club in its glorious prime is ravishing. Bob Hoskins and Fred Gwynne take top acting honors as two tough gangsters, and the supporting cast features such luminaries as Nicolas Cage, Gwen Verdon, and, most impressive of all, Gregory Hines, tapping and dancing up a storm. Appropriately enough, Ellington's music is showcased throughout the film.

december 5

The Disney Version

Walt Disney's ultimate legacy may be that no filmmaker (or cultural icon, for that matter) has ever been so commercially and artistically successful and so reviled. His successes were all popular with mainstream audiences, but often denounced by the intelligentsia and the politically correct.

He was born this day in 1901. With the master animator I. B. Wurks, he created a series of popular cartoons in the 1920s, the most influential being *Steamboat Willie* (1928), which introduced his most lucrative and iconic creation, Mickey Mouse (it also introduced his voice; Walt provided Mickey's vocals for the first few years). His pioneer and entrepreneurial spirit spurred him to create *Snow White and the Seven Dwarfs* (1937), the first feature-length cartoon. By the time he filmed *Bambi* (1942), the artistry in his stable of animators was beginning to come to sweet, unparalleled fruition. But he came under attack for bastardizing the classics and fairy tales for mass consumption (a process that continues under the studio that boasts his name today) and homogenizing his product in more ways than one (minority performers were notably absent from the cast of his 1950s TV series, *The Mickey Mouse Club*). But, whatever his dubious cultural credentials, Disney became the single greatest artistic pioneer in the field of animation before going on to become a veritable franchise.

Although *Fantasia* (1940) takes top honors in innovative and daring use of the medium, **Bambi** (1942) is the quintessential Disney cartoon creation: lovingly rendered animation (the utilization of multiplane effects during the forest sequences is still breathtaking), combined with a simple, original story populated with lovable, anthropomorphic critters. The story of the life of young deer Bambi, as he's raised into adulthood, is packed with memorable moments—his clumsy first efforts to walk (derided by his best friend, the hyperactive rabbit Thumper), his first stirrings of love, and the most traumatic moment in all the Disney movies, the loss of his mother to a group of hunters. Here's a day to remember Disney the artist, not Disney the logo.

december 6

A Picnic Gone Bad

If *Woodstock* was the peak of the "peace and love" generation, Altamont was the apocalypse when it all came crashing down. On this date in 1969, the Rolling Stones decided to give a free concert in the San Francisco Bay Area, and settled on Altamont Speedway a few miles inland in Tracy, California. "It'll be a great picnic," crowed lead singer Mick Jagger. It was no picnic.

Things began to get ugly early on and only got worse. Three hundred thousand fans had jammed the grounds for the free show, and good vibrations among the crowd were few and far between. The Stones had hired the Hell's Angels as security guards—not the brightest move—and added fuel to the flame by paying them off in beer. During an opening set with the Jefferson Airplane, one of the Angels' "security crew" attacked singer Marty Balin onstage, punching him out. The atmosphere got increasingly volatile as the Stones dallied in their air-conditioned trailer. By the time they finally took the stage, any chance of music saving the day was gone with the sunset. Concert-goers rushed to the stage—forcing Jagger to impotently plead with them to be cool, losing his posing swagger in the process. Then one of the attendees, eighteen-year-old Meredith Hunter, made the mistake of getting too close to a Hell's Angel's chopper and was murdered for it. And his wasn't the only death at the so-called festival; one person drowned and two people were run over by cars as they slept in their sleeping bags.

It's all there to see in the Maysles Brothers' fascinating documentary, **Gimme Shelter** (1970): the music, the mayhem, and the murder (shown three times over the course of the movie). A nightmare come to life and captured on film, *Gimme Shelter* is a sobering reminder of what happens when you play with fire and offer sympathy for the devil. Altamont was indeed the dark side made manifest in a way Jim Morrison could only have dreamed of. Jagger expresses—or feigns—shock and innocence. Great footage of the Stones in performance at earlier shows and a truly unsettling example of mob mentality combine to make a visceral film that plays like a slow-moving rock 'n' roll traffic accident from which you can't avert your eyes—or your ears.

december 7

A Date That Will Live in Infamy

Today marks the anniversary of the Japanese bombing of Pearl Harbor in 1941, the cataclysmic event that jump-started the United States' entry into World War II. Recent evidence suggests that U.S. government officials—up to and including the president—had known of the impending attack.

Commemorate the anniversary of Pearl Harbor with **From Here to Eternity** (1953), which re-creates the event in spectacular fashion, helping to earn the picture an Academy Award for Best Picture of 1953. Square-jawed Burt Lancaster stars as First Sergeant Milton Warden, a career man in 1941 who's having an affair with Deborah Kerr, a fellow officer's wife on the island. Montgomery Clift delivers a sensitive performance as Corporal Robert E. Lee "Prew" Prewitt, a pacifist soldier stationed in Hawaii, who's in love with prostitute Donna Reed.

But the big surprise is Frank Sinatra's legendary performance as Maggio, the scrappy private who can't stay out of trouble and pays the ultimate price for mouthing off to bully Ernest Borgnine. The role literally resurrected Sinatra's career and won him an Oscar for Best Supporting Actor that year. Based on the best-selling novel by James Jones.

The attack on Pearl Harbor is also vividly captured in *Tora! Tora! Tora!* (1970), but with the added perspective of the story as told from the Japanese side (directed by Toshio Masuda and Kinji Fukasaku). The cast doesn't boast any major names—the most distinguished being Jason Robards, Martin Balsam, and Joseph Cotton—but it is expansive and expensive in its reconstruction of the events leading up to, and including, the climactic attack.

Oh, yes . . . and then there's Michael Bay's wanna-be blockbuster, *Pearl*

Harbor (2001), starring Ben Affleck as a patriotic hunk who wins the war. Two words: Bombs away.

december 8

The Dream Is Over

"Life begins at forty."

—John Lennon, who had just celebrated his fortieth birthday, in his last interview

Returning home from a recording session to his apartment in Manhattan late this night in 1980, John Lennon was shot dead by a fan whose name is not worthy of being printed here. Lennon was born during an air raid in Liverpool, England, on October 9, 1940. He was a troubled and sensitive child; his father, a seaman, left him when he was a toddler, and his beloved mother, Julia, was killed in an automobile accident when he was fourteen. Living with his Aunt Mimi in Liverpool, he found solace in American rock 'n' roll and began playing guitar. He formed a group first named the Quarrymen, then Johnny and the Hurricanes, then the Silver Beatles, and, finally, the Beatles.

In addition to being a pop culture hero and one of the most influential musicians in rock history, John Lennon had a charismatic screen presence and a genuine gift for comedy. His performance in the Beatles' first film, *A Hard Day's Night* (1964), is inventive and fresh, upstaged only by bandmate Ringo's doleful hangdog appeal. Lennon made only one film as a solo actor, in a supporting role as Private Gripweed in Richard Lester's antiwar satire, **How I Won the War** (1968). Lester had directed Lennon before in *A Hard Day's Night* (1964) and *Help!* (1965) and knew how to utilize his sarcastic, dry wit. Though Lennon's part is relatively small, it makes one wish he'd done more acting; he had a vibrant comedic presence and showed a real flair for understated delivery.

Michael Crawford (who years later would become famous as the first "Phantom" in Andrew Lloyd Webber's *Phantom of the Opera*) stars as the leader of a platoon of English musketeers in World War II. Much of the humor is pre–Monty Pythonesque, and the film is a daring and subversive piece of work, mixing theatrical humor with documentary-like, graphic realism. There is a spooky moment in *How I Won the War* which foreshadowed Lennon's real life: Trying to escape during the battle of Arnhem, Gripweed is fatally shot in the stomach. Lennon turns to the camera and says, "I knew this would happen. You knew this would happen, too, didn't you?" *How I Won the War* was a brave, decidedly dark experiment—and makes the antiwar sentiments in *M*A*S*H* seem provincial and pedestrian by comparison. Worth seeking out.

Imagine (1988) is a documentary on Lennon's life assembled by Andrew Solt under the—*ahem*—guidance of executive producer Yoko Ono. Packed with rare newsreel footage and home movies, *Imagine* is a disappointing whitewash. Some of Lennon's most endearing qualities—his skepticism, sarcasm and often scathing wit—have been excised from this lopsided documentary, which seems to be setting the foundations for proposed sainthood. It's like watching Dr. Jekyll without getting to see Mr. Hyde. Imagine a better movie.

december 9

The World's Most Famous Dimple

The jutting jaw with dimpled chin. The distinctive voice that sounds like a strangulated shout. The mercurial temper, the hyperdrive ambition and the prideful chip on the shoulder. There was only one Kirk Douglas.

He was born Issur Danielovitch this day in 1916, the son of illiterate Russian-Jewish immigrants, in Amsterdam, New York. He wrestled professionally to put himself through the American Academy of Dramatic Arts. He moved to Hollywood and played supporting roles until he literally made a big hit in *Champion* (1949) as an unscrupulous boxer fighting his way to the top. The role formed what would become Douglas's screen persona: ambitious, cocky, self-centered, confident, and forceful. **The Bad and the Beautiful**

(1953) perfectly captures the charismatic dichotomy of his appeal. Douglas plays an ambitious, egotistical producer who claws his way to the top of the Hollywood ladder, stepping on those who love him, only to fall past them on his way down. He starts out a sympathetic loner and ends up an abusive, maniacal heel with nothing left to lose except his soul. *The Bad and the Beautiful* is also one of the wittiest, most scathing exposés of Hollywood ever, and an engaging glimpse of a studio system that is now as extinct as silent movies.

december 10

Scandalous!

Quick. Name a Democrat. From Arkansas. Who got caught having an affair, creating a national sex scandal.

Wrong. Try again.

Rep. Wilbur D. Mills, Democrat from Arkansas, resigned as chairman of the Ways and Means Committee on this date in 1974, in the first public sex scandal in American politics. (What is it with those Democrats from Arkansas, anyway?)

Mills, who was married at the time, was pulled over by Washington police for driving at night with his lights off. He was drunk, his face was scratched, and he wasn't alone: Seated beside him was thirty-eight-year-old Annabelle Battistella, better known in certain social circles as "Fanne Foxe." The whole sordid affair set a precedent, ensnaring everyone from Gary Hart to Bill Clinton, which has ripple effects to this day.

A similar scenario figures into the little-seen **Striptease** (1995). Demi Moore stars as Erin Grant, a mother who loses custody of her child to her sleazy husband, and takes on a high-paying job at a Florida strip club to earn enough money to reopen the case.

Erin becomes the fixation of a right-wing congressman, David Dilbeck (Burt Reynolds), and soon the whole sordid affair leads to murder and the Mob. Reynolds's portrait of the smarmy politician with the Vaseline fetish and fixation on Erin Grant (Moore) reignited his career. Not long after, he was cast in the hugely successful *Boogie Nights* (1997). *Striptease* was directed by Andrew Bergman (*The Freshman*).

december 11

Scandalous!—Take Two

There was a whole lotta shakin' goin' on this day in 1957 when bad-boy rock 'n' roll hedonist Jerry Lee Lewis married his thirteen-year-old cousin, Myra. Newspapers all across the U.S.A. carried the lurid story on their front pages, and the young rocker became the object of one of the great rock 'n' roll scandals.

In a decade of milk and cookies, Jerry Lee Lewis was genuine, certifiable, combustible Southern moonshine. He once came to Graceland with a loaded shotgun to roust out Elvis Presley; this was one serious demented rocker. He appeared in musical cameos in a few '50s B-movie rock musicals like *Jamboree* (1957). But after his marriage he found himself persona non grata in mainstream media.

Dennis Quaid stars as Lewis in **Great Balls of Fire!** (1989). The musical sequences have fire and kick, even if Dennis Quaid never quite does justice to the man's demented genius. Alec Baldwin is actually quite good as his disapproving, Bible-quoting cousin. And Winona Ryder is both affecting and vulnerable as his young bride. But if Hollywood ever captured the real wild and crazy Jerry Lee Lewis on film, the screen would probably ignite in flame—or shoot itself.

december 12

Birth of the Blue Eyes

The poor skinny baby nearly didn't survive his own birth. He was rudely extracted by a doctor's forceps, leaving ugly scars behind his ears and the back of his neck which were there for the rest of his life. But the scrawny, sickly kid was a scruffy survivor—underweight, but a bantam fighter in the ring of life. Frank Sinatra was born this day in 1915 in Hoboken, New Jersey.

Of his musical contributions to our culture, there can be no overstatement. His career as an actor was, however, like the man himself, problematic but pugnacious. His early film roles were unchallenging, but he learned the ropes from some of the best. Gene Kelly taught him to dance and paired with him in *Anchors Aweigh* (1945) and *On the Town* (1949). Sinatra's lack of movie star good looks worked against him, his popularity waned, and by the early '50s he was starring in such turkeys as *Double Dynamite* (1951).

It all changed with his surprising, superb performance as the scrappy but doomed Private Maggio in *From Here to Eternity* (1953), for which he won an Oscar for Best Supporting Actor. From then on, he literally called his own shots, acquiring a stubborn reputation for refusing to do more than one take. (He walked off the set on the first day of shooting *Carousel* when he learned he'd have to film each shot twice for separate versions.)

Sinatra's period as a serious actor was brief but fruitful, turning in fine performances as a junkie in Otto Preminger's *The Man with the Golden Arm* (1955), an assassin in *Suddenly* (1954), and as entertainer Joe E. Lewis in *The Joker Is Wild* (1957). He even tried directing—once—for 1965's World War II drama, *None but the Brave.* But Sinatra's greatest film legacy is **The Manchurian Candidate** (1962), John Frankenheimer's sensational cold war thriller. Sinatra, who also produced, gives a superb performance as Korean War vet Major Bennett Marco, who is suffering from a series of horrific nightmares about his former commanding officer, Raymond Shaw (Lawrence Harvey). What neither man knows is that they were both brainwashed by the North Koreans during their combat duty, and that Shaw is a walking time bomb. A stunning movie, stylishly directed (the "ladies' luncheon" interrogation scene is brilliantly inventive), with a one-of-a-kind script by George Axelrod which veers from thriller to comedy and back. Angela Lansbury delivers a head-turning performance as Harvey's ambitious—and deeply disturbing—mother. (She had good reason to be deeply disturbed; Lansbury was only three years older than the man playing her son!) Sinatra had the film withdrawn from distribution after JFK's assassination, and it was unavailable for many years.

december 13

"Oh, *Rob . . .*"

He was one of the most physically astonishing comedians who ever took a pratfall. No less an authority than Stan Laurel was a huge fan and friend, and that's high praise and honor, indeed. TV funnyman Dick Van Dyke was born this day in 1925 in West Plains, Missouri. His phenomenally popular TV series, *The Dick Van Dyke Show,* ran from 1961 until 1965, and changed the high-water mark of sitcoms forever. Van Dyke's astonishing physical ability would have made him an ideal silent film star.

As it was, he never became a film star—though he contributed some fine performances (*The Clown* [1968]; *The Runner Stumbles* [1977]). His two best roles are probably as Bert the Chimney Sweep in Walt Disney's classic *Mary Poppins* (1964) and in a reprise of the role that made him a star on Broadway—Albert, a Tin Pan Alley songwriter in **Bye Bye Birdie** (1963). Albert is assigned to write a special musical number, "One Last Kiss," for popular teen sensation Conrad Birdie to sing on *The Ed Sullivan Show* before he goes away to the army. *Birdie* is that rare surprise: a '60s musical that holds up. Ann-Margret is the lucky teen selected to appear on TV to give Conrad his "one last kiss"—what more reason do you need for watching? Van Dyke sings the show's hit, "Put on a Happy Face," Paul Lynde is a hoot as Ann-Margret's flustered suburban father, and "Gotta Lotta Livin' to Do" actually rocks. (By the way, Van Dyke's TV costar, Mary Tyler Moore, has a birthday this month, too; see Dec. 26.)

december 14

A Human Enigma

"You should have first killed me, before I understand what it is to live."

—Kaspar Hauser

There are few stories as mysteriously and impenetrably sad as that of the enigmatic "Child of Europe," Kaspar Hauser.

On March 6, 1828, a sixteen-year-old boy in peasant clothes was found wandering the streets in Nuremberg. He did not know how to speak, use his fingers, or walk normally—he walked like a toddler, placing both the heel and the toe on the ground at the same time. On his person he carried a letter that read, "*I send you a boy who wishes faithfully to serve his king. This boy was left in my house the 7th day of October, 1812, and I am myself a poor day-labourer . . . since 1812 I have never suffered him to take a single step outside my house.*" The boy was capable of speech, but mostly incoherent; he managed to tell the mayor that he had lived his entire life in a small cell in Nuremberg, not knowing if it was day or night, living on bread and water.

The boy became a cause célèbre and a local curiosity. In 1829, Kaspar was taken in by a local family and began to make progress with reading and writing. When he announced he was going to write his memoirs, an assassination attempt was made on his life. He managed to recover, and commented, "I all men love; do no one anything. Why the man kill? I have done nothing. . . . You should have first killed me, before I understand what it is to live."

But on this night in 1832, he was lured to a park by a stranger and viciously stabbed in the chest by an unknown assailant; he lingered for three days before dying.

The Mystery of Kaspar Hauser (1974) is one of director Werner Herzog's most compelling, accessible, and moving films. Kaspar upsets the priests and professors who examine him, by disrupting their compacted view of the world. Herzog presents Kaspar as neither a feral child nor a Christ figure; in fact, the boy develops a cynical view of the world that alternately pities him, exploits him, and tries to convert him. Bruno S. gives a riveting, unsentimental performance as Kaspar; it is rumored that the actor was once confined in a mental institution himself. Breathtaking cinematography and an appropriately melancholy music score enhance this enigmatic film, which plays like a dream puzzle.

december 15

The Second Hottest Night in Georgia

It was the hottest night in Atlanta since Sherman marched through town with torches nearly seventy years earlier.

On this night in 1939, at precisely 8:15 P.M. at the Loew's Grand Theater on Peachtree Street in Atlanta, Georgia, MGM premiered **Gone With the Wind.** It was such a special event that the mayor of Atlanta declared a three-day holiday, and children were dismissed from their classes.

It was a magnificently gaudy night. Much of the cast were in attendance: Clark Gable (accompanied by wife Carole Lombard), Vivien Leigh (with husband Laurence Olivier), Olivia de Havilland, Evelyn Keyes, and the author herself, Margaret Mitchell. Leslie Howard was in England helping with the war effort. As for the black performers—including Hattie McDaniel, who would soon win the Best Supporting Actress Oscar for her role—they were notably absent from the festivities due to prevailing local pressure. It was a blemish on an otherwise festive evening.

A small screen really can't do justice to some movies. *Lawrence of Arabia, Around the World in 80 Days, How the West Was Won*—no matter what you may think of them as films, we'd all pretty much be in agreement that they're best shown on a large canvas, right? **Gone With the Wind** is one of those movies. Now more than ever (thanks to a loving restoration and remastering), it becomes another experience altogether on a big screen. It literally smolders and burns. The "burning of Atlanta" sequence is still one of the great pullback shots of all time.

With that as a qualifier, go ahead and watch it tonight at home anyway. It's not the same as on a big screen, but you can always sit six inches from your TV. It's too grand a film not to celebrate. (By the way, 1939 was a banner year for director Victor Fleming; he had also directed *The Wizard of Oz* that year.)

december 16

Battle of the Bulge

The single bloodiest battle of World War II, the Battle of the Bulge, began on this day in 1944, when Hitler ordered an offensive attack—largely using his Panzer division of tanks—on the Belgian Front. It had the potential to change the direction of the entire war—but was successfully repelled within days by Allied troops, who paid a dear price.

Commemorate the event with **The Battle of the Bulge** (1965). Henry Fonda and Robert Shaw head up an all-star cast as two military men on opposite sides of a battle of wits and survival. Shaw is especially good as the pragmatic German commander of a Panzer division. Originally produced for Cinerama (a special three-camera process that made the projected image three times as wide when projected onto three adjacent screens), *The Battle of the Bulge* is a refreshingly straight-ahead re-creation of events, neither patriotically gung-ho nor overly pacifistic in its execution. The excellent supporting cast includes Charles Bronson, Robert Ryan, and Telly Savalas.

december 17

Get It Wright the First Time

The flight itself was brief—twelve seconds. And short—120 feet. But it changed the world forever. It was 10:35 on a chilly but sunny morning on this date in 1903 when Orville Wright flew the first heavier-than-air mechanically propelled airplane, near Kitty Hawk, North Carolina.

Commemorate this high-flying day with **Those Magnificent Men in Their Flying Machines** (1965). A sort of international smorgasbord of comic actors who were popular at the time, the comedy is hit-or-miss—but you do get to see the finest display of existing early biplanes ever assembled for a picture that was made after 1912. The real joy of watching this movie lies in getting a good gander at those wondrous vintage aircraft in their true glory for one last go-round.

december 18

The Most Successful Filmmaker Ever

The single most successful movie director of our time, Steven Spielberg, was born on this date in 1947 in Cincinnati, Ohio, the son of a distant father who was a computer specialist and a doting mother who was a concert pianist. After moving to Phoenix, Arizona, he began directing movies as a boy, using an 8mm movie camera to film stories with his childhood friends, and at thirteen he won a competition for his war film *Escape to Nowhere.* While attending Cal State, he filmed a twenty-four-minute short, *Amblin',* which was shown at the 1969 Atlanta Film Festival and landed the twenty-year-old filmmaker a contract with Universal Studios. While at Universal, he directed the cult classic TV movie, *Duel* (1971), with Dennis Weaver as a lone driver being pursued by a gigantic truck on a desolate highway. The success of his impressive first feature film, *The Sugarland Express* (1974), led to what would become the turning point in his career—and one of the most successful movies ever—*Jaws* (1975); it cost $8 million to make and garnered $130 million in North American rentals. And Spielberg's unprecedented career was off and running.

The hits (and a few misses) came fast and furious: his epochal *Close Encounters of The Third Kind* (1977), his first folly, *1941* (1979), his brilliant homage to Saturday matinee serials, *Raiders of the Lost Ark* (1981), and the enchanting *E.T. The Extra-Terrestrial* (1982). Spielberg then ventured into his "serious" phase with the box office success *The Color Purple* (1985), the underrated *Empire of the Sun* (1987), his first Best Picture Oscar-winning film, *Schindler's List* (1993—the same year he directed the box office blockbuster *Jurassic Park*) and the disappointing but imposing *Amistad* (1997). For any film enthusiast, all are mandatory viewing.

If I had to select the quintessential Spielberg film, it would be **E.T. The Extra-Terrestrial.** No doubt you've seen it—probably more than once—but its magic is intact and timeless. In addition to his many other considerable talents and gifts, Spielberg is probably the single greatest director of children (note the naturalistic child performers in *Close Encounters,* and Christian Bale's excellent performance in *Empire of the Sun*), and his gift was never on better display than with the three main stars of *E.T.*—Henry Thomas, Robert MacNaughton, and, most especially, the (very) young Drew Barrymore. Look for the in-joke homage to his pal George Lucas during the "Halloween trick-or-treat" sequence. Possibly Spielberg's most popular, enchanting movie, *E.T.* is the ultimate example of his greatest strength: his ability to access the sense of childlike wonder in himself—and in us.

december 19

Spend the Night with Your Local Librarian

Seventy-six trombones led the big parade, filling the stage in New York as Meredith Wilson's Broadway smash, *The Music Man,* premiered this night in 1957. It went going on to become one of the most popular musicals of the twentieth century. It also gave a major career boost to film actor Robert Preston, who up until this night was pretty much relegated to supporting roles in B westerns.

Four years later, Hollywood filmed **The Music Man** (1962). Preston reprised his show-stopping performance as con man and quintessential American huckster Professor Harold Hill, who comes to the small town of River City, Iowa, to bilk the citizens out of their money under the ruse of forming a town band. What he doesn't count on is falling for mousey Marion, the town librarian (Shirley Jones, never more wholesome, winsome, or appealing). Preston's boundlessly energetic performance is invigorating to behold, and a cast of some of Hollywood's finest comic supporting players (including Paul Ford, Hermione Gingold, and Buddy Hackett—and a very young Ron Howard) add the icing on the cake. A crowd-pleasing, feel-good musical that even people who don't like musicals will enjoy. Featuring such classics as "Seventy-six Trombones," "Till There Was You," *and* "Goodnight, My Someone."

december 20

Around the World in 175 Minutes

One of the great fictional flights in history came to an end this day in 1892, in London, England, according to author Jules Verne. Phineas Fogg won his wager by managing to complete his round-the-world trip in eighty days. And he even made it home before Christmas.

Commemorate Fogg's impressive achievement with another impressive achievement, producer Mike Todd's **Around the World in 80 Days** (1956). A spiritual heir to P. T. Barnum, the entrepreneurial Todd did things in a big way. He had never made a movie before (though he did have a definite connection to the industry; he was married to Elizabeth Taylor). But he set out to make the biggest, brightest, most colorful movie adventure ever made, and came close to succeeding. David Niven stars as globe-trotting proper English gentleman Phineas Fogg, who accepts a challenge that he cannot circumnavigate the globe within eighty days. Utilizing whatever means are at his disposal—trains, carriages, mules, balloons, ships—he sets off on a series of adventures in exotic locales. *Around the World in 80 Days* was one of the first all-star extravaganzas—featuring a gargantuan cast of celebrities including just about everyone who was anyone in Hollywood. Filmed on-site in various exotic locales from Paris to India to Africa, *Around the World* moves at a predictably breathless pace, and is never anything less than dazzling—at least in its scenery. Winner of five Oscars, including Best Picture.

december 21

Great Scott

"No poor bastard ever won a war by dying for his country. He won it by making the other poor dumb bastard die for his country."

—General George Patton

George Patton was one of the most influential—and controversial—military leaders of the twentieth century. By 1945 his career was finished, and his timing for an exit was nearly perfect, even if the exit itself was a little messy. He was getting ready to return home to America for the holidays when he decided to go pheasant hunting near Mannheim on the Rhine River. On the way his Cadillac limo was cut off at an intersection by a U.S. Signal Corps truck, throwing him forward from the back seat. He suffered several concussions and a broken neck, and was paralyzed from the neck down, but was still conscious when they brought him into the hospital. When the attendant doctors recognized him as Gen. George Patton, he sensed their nervousness. "Relax, gentlemen," he said reassuringly. "I'm in no condition to be a terror now." He lingered for eleven days, before finally giving up the ghost this day in 1945.

General George Patton was a larger-than-life figure, and when it came time to film his story, a larger-than-life talent was required. **Patton** (1970) is a vastly entertaining screen bio, with George C. Scott delivering an Oscar-winning performance in the title role, capturing all the strength, stubbornness, brilliance, and wild contradictions about the man. Francis Ford Coppola's script beautifully delineates Patton's lust for power and the quirky eccentricities (designing his own uniforms; his passionate belief that he was a reincarnated Roman warrior) that made him one of the twentieth century's most fascinating personalities.

december 22

Break Away from the Pack with This Joyous Movie

The very first periodical devoted to the sport of bicycling, *American Bicycling Journal,* was published this day in 1877.

Celebrate the wonder of the two-wheeler with the uplifting and hugely entertaining **Breaking Away** (1979), one of the great "sleeper" movies of the '70s. High school student Dave (Dennis Christopher) and his friends (Dennis Quaid, Daniel Stern, and Jackie Earle Haley) enter to win the annual "Little Indy" bike race in their hometown of Bloomington, Indiana. Director Peter Yates has fashioned an enchanting story of small-town dreams and grown-up disappointments. Paul Dooley is both funny and affecting as Christopher's perplexed, bemused used car salesman dad; he has an extremely touching scene walking his son through one of the buildings he helped to construct as a "cutter" years ago. The rousing climax will have you up on your feet, cheering at your television set. One of those rare, small perfect gems of a movie—uplifting, funny, and inspiring. It'll motivate you to go out to the garage, dust off the old ten-speed, and start pedaling.

december 23

Just the Facts

He was never a major movie star, but he was an icon, and certainly one of a kind. As Sgt. Joe Friday on the popular radio and TV series *Dragnet,* Jack Webb was one of the most distinctive pop culture figures of the '50s and '60s. On this day in 1982, he died of a heart attack at sixty-two in his beloved home—"this is the city"—Los Angeles.

Many people forget he had a substantial movie career before and after getting into television. Throughout the '50s he distinguished himself doing variations on the tough wise-guy theme in such movies as *The Men* (1950) and *Sunset Boulevard* (1950). He created the hugely successful *Dragnet* radio series, transferred it to TV, and made it a gold mine.

As a director, he had a unique staccato style that almost bordered on self-parody. His best movie was **Pete Kelly's Blues** (1955), a uniquely Webb-style noir film about a jazz musician in New Orleans who gets mixed up with the Mob. A truly marvelous, spellbinding opening sequence promises more than the film itself delivers, but the movie is still worth seeing if only to catch Lee Marvin as a jazz player, along with a standout performance from Peggy Lee as a doomed singer. Ella Fitzgerald contributes a couple of songs, too. The film is beautiful but as stiff as Webb's ramrod-straight back. Jack Webb may not have been everyone's idea of a handsome leading man, but anyone who was married to Julie London must have been doing something right.

december 24

'Twas the Night Before Christmas . . .

It's Christmas Eve—as if you didn't know. Spend it with your friends and loved ones.

Everyone knows the old Christmas favorites (if not, I dicuss most of them in the next entry). So I'd like to suggest a substitute perennial for this year's consideration: Tim Burton's **Edward Scissorhands** (1990). With its depiction of a beneficent stranger in a strange land who is not accepted or understood by the people around him, *Edward Scissorhands* carries a certain seasonal resonance. It's a fairy tale—half-adult/half-childlike—framed around Christmas Eve, and Christmas comes to figure in one of the most enchanting sequences of the movie, when Edward creates a White Christmas, blanketing a suburban house in snow by shaving ice with his miraculously adept fingers. A funny, delicate, offbeat, enchanting, and ultimately heartwarming fable of love and acceptance, and Tim Burton's best movie to date.

december 25

Depending on how many rooms you have, you could have a different Christmas film for every room in the house. If you had to pick just one great Christmas movie that everyone in the family can enjoy immensely, you can't go wrong with **A Christmas Story** (1983), playwright Jean Shepherd's delightful comic recollections of his boyhood holiday season in small-town Nebraska circa 1940. All ten-year-old Ralphie wants for Christmas is a Red Ryder B.B. air-rifle—although everyone from his mother to his teacher tells him "You'll put your eye out with that thing!" As he counts down the days till Christmas morning, he must contend with neighborhood bully Farkas, a dreaded "triple dog dare" from his pal Flick, getting his mouth washed out with soap for saying the *F* word in front of the Old Man, and a department store Santa with a proclivity for kicking young tykes. *A Christmas Story* is a perfect blend of satire and nostalgia. Peter Billingsley is captivating as young Ralphie, and Darren McGavin and Melinda Dillon give marvelous performances as his unconventional parents. An absolutely delightful film that deserves its cult classic status for both children and adults—and those of us who were dumb enough to stick our tongue onto a metal flagpole after a snowfall.

For classicists, there's always that perennial seasonal ritual, Frank Capra's

It's a Wonderful Life (1946)—or **A Christmas Carol**—the Charles Dickens story that has been filmed countless times in so many configurations and permutations that trying to list them all is like counting snowflakes. The best versions are the classic 1951 British version with everyone's favorite Scrooge, Alistair Sim, and the 1984 TV version starring George C. Scott, possibly the finest Scrooge ever. Scott's underplayed Ebeneezer Scrooge is the most achingly accessible, the most fully rounded of all.

Feeling goofy? **National Lampoon's Christmas Vacation** (1989) has Chevy Chase as the ever accident-prone Clark Griswold in one of the series' best entries; a latex-encased Jim Carrey still manages to be recognizably Jim Carrey as the Grinch in **Dr. Seuss' How the Grinch Stole Christmas** (2000), director Ron Howard's feature-length adaptation of Dr. Seuss's classic Christmas tale, filled with delicious eye-candy colors; **Jingle All the Way** (1996) has Arnold Schwarzenegger in a comical quest for the year's ultimate Christmas present, an action figure toy, in a slapstick-heavy free-for-all; **The Santa Clause** (1994) is an unexpectedly endearing and entertaining holiday treat, with Tim Allen as a father who gradually and inexplicably metamorphoses into the *real* Santa; and Bill Murray does his take on the world's biggest skinflint—here a heartless TV executive (is there any other kind?) in **Scrooged** (1988), getting nice support from Carol Kane as a ditzy Ghost of Christmas Present and Bobcat Goldthwait as a modern-day Bob Cratchet.

Something for the kids? **Miracle on 34th Street** (1947) still works its magic, even if it is a little musty with age. A very young Natalie Wood stars as a little girl who doesn't believe the Santa Claus (Edmund Gwenn) who works at Macy's department store is the real St. Nick—but he does, and sets about trying to prove it. The smash hit **Home Alone** (1990), where eight-year-old Kevin (Macauley Culkin) is inadvertently left behind by his family for the holidays, is a sure-fire kid-pleaser, if not strictly in the spirit of the season; **The Muppet Christmas Carol** (1992) casts the popular puppets in a reworking of—what else?—Dickens's reliable chestnut. And Tim Burton's **Nightmare Before Christmas** (1993) is a charmingly macabre experiment, best appreciated by those over ten years old.

In the mood for a holiday-themed musical? Can't get much better than

Holiday Inn (1942) or **White Christmas** (1954; both with Bing Crosby, and both with "White Christmas"). Between the two, *Holiday Inn* wins by a nose thanks to Fred Astaire's hoofing. Or better yet, savor Vincente Minnelli's lovingly rendered, perfectly captured look at small-town Americana, **Meet Me in St. Louis** (1944), complete with Judy Garland's heart-breaking "Have Yourself a Merry Little Christmas." And there's always the little-seen musical version of that Dickens Christmas favorite, **Scrooge** (1970), starring a convincingly aged Albert Finney in the title role and Alec Guinness as the ghost of Jacob Marley.

If you're feeling a little Grinchy yourself, pop in **Black Christmas** (1974) starring Kier Dullea (Dave from *2001*) and Margot Kidder (*Superman's* Lois Lane), in a slashfest about a sorority house where the girls start disappearing one by one; or indulge in the season-bashing **Silent Night, Deadly Night** (1984), where a poor kid flips out, dons a Santa suit, and goes on a killing spree. Or check out **Santa Claws** (1997), a self-explanatory title. 'Tis the season.

Looking for a good kick-ass action flick to celebrate this day of peace? Both **Die Hard** (1988) and **Die Harder** (1990) are constructed around the holiday—but if you want something truly whacked out, try the undeniably demented **Santa with Muscles** (1996), starring Hulk Hogan as a Scroogy millionaire who gets conked on the head and is convinced by an evil elf that he's Santa Claus—so he goes around kicking the butts of everyone who doesn't get into the spirit of giving.

And there's always more . . . but if you find yourself at the video store reduced to having to choose between **Ernest Saves Christmas** (1988), **Santa Claus: The Movie** (1985), and **Santa Claus Conquers the Martians** (1964), you shouldn't have read down this far. Try roasting some chestnuts on an open fire, and Merry Christmas.

december 26

She Made It After All

Happy birthday today to everyone's favorite girl next door, Mary Tyler Moore, born the day after Christmas in 1936 in Brooklyn, New York.

The pert 'n' perky young actress got her start doing TV commercials, gallivanting around in leotards and wielding a magic wand as "Happy, the Hot Point Girl" for Hot Point appliances in the 1950s; she then played a secretary in the *Richard Diamond* TV series, although only her legs were seen—but they were great legs.

Her big break came when producer and writer Carl Reiner cast her as Laura Petrie, wife of comedy writer Rob Petrie (Dick Van Dyke) in *The Dick Van Dyke Show* (1961–1966). After a faltering first year, the sitcom became a huge hit with viewers who appreciated its adult humor and perspective. At first Moore's talents weren't really showcased, in favor of Van Dyke's excellent physical comedy, but she gradually revealed herself to be a gifted comedienne. She also started a nationwide fad by wearing capris instead of the traditional housedress on the series; arguably, Moore, Jackie Kennedy, and Audrey Hepburn were the most influential fashion forces of the early '60s.

After *Dick Van Dyke* left the air, she reached the pinnacle of her success as Mary Richards, news producer at WJM-TV, in *The Mary Tyler Moore Show* (1970–1977), which actually surpassed the popularity of Van Dyke's series.

Moore's ventures onto the big screen have been few, and for the most part in less-than-spectacular efforts. She was largely wasted as Julie Andrews's best friend in the misguided movie musical, *Thoroughly Modern Millie* (1967). She costarred as an inner-city nun with Elvis Presley in his last nonmusical role, *Change of Habit* (1969); apparently, she was one of Elvis's few leading ladies who did not succumb to the King's charms.

Her finest film role by far is in the extraordinary **Ordinary People** (1980), which tells the story of a well-to-do family coming to grips with the accidental death of a young son and the guilt-ridden suicide attempt of another. (Ironically, Moore lost her own twenty-four-year-old son to suicide that same year.) As the icy, emotionally distant Beth Jarrett, Moore plays against her warm image, portraying a neurotic, domineering wife and mother who is desperately trying to cover up her anger and sorrow over the loss of her son—trying in vain to hold her family together while simultaneously keeping them at arm's length. Her revelatory performance earned her an Oscar nomination that year for Best Actress. Also starring Donald Sutherland as her stoically suffering husband, Cal; Tim Hutton as her surviving son, who craves her love and blames himself for his brother's death; and Judd Hirsch (*Taxi*) as a psychologist trying to help him. The first, and possibly best, film directed by Robert Redford.

december 27

Do You Believe?

Peter Pan, the stage play based on J. M. Barrie's enchanting and immortal story of the little boy who refused to grow up, premiered this day in 1904 at Duke of York's Theatre in London. In a revolutionary bit of casting, Peter was played by a female, Nina Boucicault—a practice that continues to this day.

Celebrate the debut of the boy who never grew up with Walt Disney's **Peter Pan** (1953). Barrie purists will balk at the Disney-isms: a politically incorrect song by Sammy Cahn called "What Makes the Red Man Red?" and a Tinkerbell who looks suspiciously like Marilyn Monroe. But the overall charm is still intact, and Disney's use of Technicolor is gorgeous, particularly during the "I Can Fly" sequence over nighttime London.

For an interesting variation of the Pan story, check out Steven Spielberg's revisionist **Hook** (1991), featuring Robin Williams as the grown-up Peter and Dustin Hoffman as his old nemesis, Captain Hook. The movie's premise is brilliant, and the performers appealing, but the tale is ultimately botched in heavy-handed execution. But Julia Roberts almost makes up for it as a most fetching Tinkerbell.

december 28

Celebrate the Other Washington's Birthday

Denzel Washington was born this day in Mount Vernon, New York, in 1954. Perhaps more than any other African American actor since Sidney Poitier, Washington has broken through to become a mainstream star, delivering some of the most intense performances of the '80s and '90s.

His film performances have been consistently excellent: his proud boxer Rubin Carter in *The Hurricane* (1999); South African activist Steven Biko in *Cry Freedom* (1987); the runaway slave Trip in *Glory* (1989); the stubborn but inspiring head football coach in a racially divided town in *Remember the Titans* (2000).

Washington's shining moment is as Malcolm X in Spike Lee's riveting film bio, which is recommended in this volume for February 21. But he also delivers a galvanizing, layered performance as the homophobic lawyer who reluctantly represents AIDS-infected Andrew Becket (Tom Hanks in an Oscar-winning performance) in **Philadelphia** (1993). As his initial homophobic prejudice and discomfort dissolve into grudging acceptance and even admiration, Washington acts as the (mainstream) audience's surrogate conscience. It's not a showy role; Washington is generally not a showy actor. He tends to project quiet strength and resolve rather than grandiose and passionately emotional monologues. His solid performance in *Philadelphia* grounds the film, making it all the more effective.

december 29

Another Bloody English Martyr

One of England's legendary heroes, Thomas Becket, was murdered this day in 1170—under tacit approval by his king and supposed friend, King Henry II of England. Their friendship had gone back a long way; Henry had appointed the skillful Becket as chancellor in 1155. Becket proved a masterful and effective diplomat, and Henry trusted him, going so far as to nominate him for archbishop of Canterbury in 1162. King Henry had hoped his friend would help in his efforts to curb the church's power, but after his consecration, Thomas Becket became a powerful advocate for the church, pronouncing the church's right to determine its own destiny, and incurring the King's wrath. He was forced to flee to France, but was later reconciled with Henry, and in 1170 he returned to Canterbury amidst much public rejoicing.

Not long afterward, tension again came between Thomas Becket and the king. Henry, in a pique of temper, issued a public plea throughout his court: "What a parcel of fools and dastards have I nourished in my house, and not one of them will avenge me this one upstart clerk"—which was then the equivalent of broadcasting a bounty over the World Wide Web. A group of Henry's knights took him at his word and brutally murdered Thomas Becket in Canterbury Cathedral on this night in 1170.

Commemorate the anniversary of the deed with one of the most underrated great historical movies ever, **Becket** (1964). Richard Burton and Peter O'Toole both deliver mesmerizing, tour-de-force turns, at once dazzling and refined. Burton plays Becket as indomitably proud and righteous, unyielding in his convictions and passionate in his beliefs. Peter O'Toole makes Henry II both incredibly endearing and irresponsible, compassionate yet dangerous. Both deliver bravura performances, and their scenes together absolutely sing. A gripping story, an engrossingly literate script, and two of the century's greatest actors in their prime bouncing lines off of one another gloriously. (O'Toole would return in 1968 to the role of Henry—this time a much older version, opposite Katharine Hepburn's Eleanor of Aquitaine in *The Lion in Winter*.)

december 30

Happy Birthday, Tracey . . . Now Go Home!

Happy birthday today to multifaceted, multifaced comedienne Tracey Ullman, born this day in 1959 near Windsor Castle. A phenomenally gifted comic sketch artist, she first became a hit with American audiences in the popular *Tracey Ullman Show,* one of the first shows to premiere on the fledgling Fox Television Network. She played a dizzying variety of characters in the show, a gallery of fully drawn, wildly different creations. She moved to HBO for another series, the more explicit *Tracey Takes On . . .*

As impressive as Tracey is on television, on the big screen her success has been limited. She played Meryl Streep's best friend in *Plenty* (1985) and contributed a memorable cameo to *Jumpin' Jack Flash* (1986). Her best role to date has been as Rosalie, the Italian Bronx housewife who hires a couple of hit men to kill off her philandering husband, Joey (Kevin Kline), in **I Love You to Death** (1990). Written and directed by Lawrence Kasdan (*The Big Chill; Body Heat*), the film has a nice, sharp edge, and Ullman is both convincing and touching in a role which she made the most of. William Hurt and Keanu Reeves are out-and-out hilarious as the inept, stoned-out hit men she hires, and Kline is typically hilarious as the philandering husband who is seemingly immune to poison and bullets. Remarkably, it's all based on a true story. Ullman plays another working-class East Coast housewife in Woody Allen's first box office success in fifteen years, *Small Time Crooks* (2000).

december 31

New Year's Eve

Is there a single more dramatic moment in the calendar year than the moment before midnight on this night?

When Harry Met Sally (1989) covers several years of friendship and animosity between two traveling companions played by Billy Crystal and Meg Ryan. Nora Ephron's best script is packed with wry observations about the differences between men and women, plenty of laughs, one faked orgasm in a restaurant, and two delightful performances by Crystal (in his best screen role) and Ryan. It all comes to a suitably romantic conclusion on New Year's Eve. (*Note:* If you don't have someone to watch this movie with, avoid it at all cost!)

Can't get a date in the city for the big night? Perhaps you can relate to **200 Cigarettes** (1999), set on New Year's Eve 1981, in New York City. Director Risa Bramon Garcia gathers together an eccentric young cast (including Ben and Casey Affleck, Janeane Garofalo, Christina Ricci, Kate Hudson, Courtney Love, and Elvis Costello) in New York's East Village, all of them attempting to reach a New Year's loft party hosted by a very edgy Martha Plimpton.

Something a little more old-fashioned? How about **Holiday Inn** (1942)? Ah, they don't make 'em like this anymore—a glorious black-and-white musical starring croonin' Bing Crosby and dancin' Fred Astaire as Jim Hardy and Ted Hanover, two rival song and dance men who decide to transform a Connecticut farm into an inn that's only open on holidays. Not just one, not two, but three, count 'em, three New Year's Eve celebrations. Plenty of floating bubbles, hats 'n' tails, beautiful gowns, and great music. In addition to New Year's Eve (featuring a great dance by a "drunken" Fred Astaire), *Holiday Inn* covers just about every holiday in the book . . . Christmas (featuring Bing's first rendition of "White Christmas"), Thanksgiving, Fourth of July . . . it's all here with appropriate musical numbers.

And have a wonderful New Year!

APPENDIX

floating holidays

LABOR DAY

(First Monday in September)

First celebrated by the Knights of Labor in New York City in 1882 and 1884 as a way to honor the working man and woman (and give 'em a much-needed day off), the date was specifically selected to be spaced as far as possible from other holidays.

Enjoy a cold beer and savor **Blue Collar** (1978), writer-director Paul Schrader's heist-gone-wrong story of three blue-collar working stiffs who decide to get what's theirs. Auto-assembly workers Harvey Keitel, Yaphet Kotto, and Richard Pryor are beginning to have reason to suspect that their union is screwing them over just as much as their employer is. The three pull an amateurish robbery at their union headquarters, hoping to make off with some quick cash; what they end up inadvertently stealing is incriminating records linking the union to the Mob. Suddenly these guys are in way over their heads. Richard Pryor is a revelation as the increasingly paranoid working stiff–turned–thief; it's a shame he didn't have more such challenging roles. A masterful blend of heist movie, comedy, and social drama.

And don't forget your sisters in the union with **Norma Rae** (1979). Sally Field won a Best Actress Oscar for her dynamic depiction of a Southern mother and textile worker who rebels against the abusive management at her workplace. Ron Liebman is a New York labor organizer who encourages her to become a union activist, much to the displeasure of her husband (Beau Bridges). Terrific performances, inspiring story. Directed by "workingman's director" Martin Ritt.

EASTER SUNDAY

(First Sunday after first full moon following the spring equinox)

After the parade, the Easter egg hunt, and the traditional Easter supper (anything but rabbit!), settle in for one of the most festive of holiday musicals, **Easter Parade** (1948). *Easter Parade* marked the one and only pairing of two musical superstars, Fred Astaire and Judy Garland. Originally, Gene Kelly was cast in the lead role as a dance headliner who desperately needs a new partner, but when he broke his ankle in rehearsals, he reluctantly bowed out. He suggested that Fred Astaire take his place, and Astaire agreed (somewhat reluctantly, because he knew how difficult it could be at times to work with the insecure and temperamental Garland).

Astaire has some great showpieces, literally kicking the movie off with "Drum Crazy," and his brilliant "Steppin' Out with My Baby" is a stunning example of his art and magic. Garland looks like she's in transition and unsure of her character, but her charisma always steps in to back her up, and she is at her most fetching here. The two talents unite for the show-stopper "A Couple of Swells," its power all the more remarkable due to the relative simplicity of the piece. A killer backup cast includes the dazzling Ann Miller and a hopelessly miscast Peter Lawford. (If you've ever doubted your own musical ability, you will take great heart—and hurt—in his dreadful rendition of "A Fella with an Umbrella," one of Irving Berlin's understandably lesser known works.)

DAYLIGHT SAVINGS TIME

(Begins first Sunday in April and ends last Sunday in October)

These are the only two days of the year when we actually get to juggle time a little bit—well, the concept of time, anyway. We invented time. But we won't get into that here. Be that as it may, these are the only two days of the year where—zap! you get to accomplish "instant time travel," either one hour forward, or one hour backward—by doing absolutely nothing other than readjusting your watch.

Time travel has long proven to be a popular theme in movies, but never more entertainingly than in **Back to the Future** (1985), Robert Zemeckis's intoxicatingly inventive mix of sci-fi, comedy, and romance. Michael J. Fox plays teenager Marty McFly, whose dad (Crispin Glover) is a total wimp, and whose mom (Leah Thompson) is an inebriated ditz. Marty's best friend is an absent-minded professor, Doc Brown (Christopher Lloyd), who has invented a Delorean time-travel machine (Remember Deloreans? Those goofy "futuristic" cars with the doors that lifted upwards? Now that's time travel!). Marty journeys back to 1955, the year his parents met in high school. But the time continuum is threatened by the unsettling fact that teenage Mom now takes a decided fancy to her teenage offspring, presenting Marty with the sticky challenge of getting his parents together so as to ensure his own existence, while fending off his mother's advances. *Back to the Future* plays like a hip, mildly risqué Frank Capra movie, and Fox (fresh from his success as Alex Keaton in the TV series *Family Ties*), proves his box office appeal, becoming one of the very few TV stars to graduate successfully to movie roles. It was followed by two sequels, each one genuinely entertaining and inventive. Enjoy the trip.

MOTHER'S DAY
(Second Sunday in May)

Mother's Day came about largely as the direct work of one Anna Jarvis—who came to regret ever having gone to the trouble. When her mother died in 1905, Anna wanted to honor her memory, and spent the next three years persuading local pastors to hold Mother's Day services in their churches. She then single-handedly created a letter-writing campaign to U.S. governors, congressmen, and important clergymen—and on May 9, 1914, President Woodrow Wilson officially established the holiday.

But Jarvis immediately became discouraged with the holiday's rampant commercialism, and ended up an embittered recluse, chasing off reporters. That's the problem . . . you go to all the trouble of personally giving birth to a holiday, it doesn't turn out quite the way you expected, and it never calls you.

Celebrate the occasion—and the sanctity of motherhood—with **Mother** (1996), Albert Brooks's hilarious take on the ongoing "issues" between parents and children. *Mother* boasts a marvelous comeback performance from Debbie Reynolds, after a near twenty-five-year absence from the screen, as a mother who's more than the impassive maternal matriarch that first meets the eye. Brooks gives his usual dry, hilariously deadpan performance as a middle-aged yuppie newly separated from his second wife. Brooks moves back in with his mom in an effort to get to the root of his problems with women. His reaction upon discovering that his mother actually has sex is priceless. An insightful, funny, and forgiving look at the seldom-examined issues between middle-aged children and their parents.

Then, if you're up for a heart-tugger, watch **One True Thing** (1998), starring Meryl Streep as a dedicated mother who is dying of cancer. Streep wisely and luminously downplays any sentimentality; it's an honest portrayal that draws you in with its seeming simplicity. A three-hanky movie.

FATHER'S DAY

(Third Sunday in June)

Father's Day was first celebrated in Spokane, Washington, in 1910—spearheaded by Sonora Smart Dodd, a housewife whose father had raised six children alone after his wife died during childbirth. But it wasn't official until sixty-two years later, when Father's Day was proclaimed a federal holiday by President Richard Nixon.

There are plenty of Father's Day flicks to choose from. For sons and fathers, a consummate Father's Day film is **A River Runs Through It** (1992)—Robert Redford's elegiac adaptation of Norman Maclean's popular novel. Tom Skerritt plays a stern Presbyterian minister raising two sons (Brad Pitt and Craig Sheffer) in Montana in the early 1900s. A contemplative rumination on life, love, discipline, and fly-fishing. And for baseball fans, there's always **Field of Dreams** (1989), which has been known to make grown men cry. Kevin Costner stars as a baseball-loving Iowa farmer who receives a strange, ethereal message from the great beyond: "If you build it, they will come." Soon he begins his quest to build a baseball diamond in the middle of a cornfield. Great supporting performances from Burt Lancaster (magnificent and touching in one of his last film roles), as a doctor who long ago gave up his dream of playing in the major leagues, and James Earl Jones as a reclusive writer who is reluctantly caught up in Costner's vision. A game of catch between a father and son never elicited so many tears.

For daughters, there's a lot to appreciate in **On Golden Pond** (1981)—not the least of which is the affecting performances of Henry and Jane Fonda as an elderly, emotionally distant dad and his estranged daughter, who wants to reconcile with her obstinate father. Henry Fonda, in his final performance, won an Oscar as Norman, patriarch of the Thayer family. Katharine Hepburn contributes a typically great performance as Norman's wife. Or enjoy Spencer Tracy as the dad every girl wishes she had in the delightful and hilarious **Father of the Bride** (1950).

With two leading men like Robin Williams and Billy Crystal teamed up together, you'd think **Father's Day** (1997) would be much funnier than it is. When Nastassja Kinski's teenage son runs away after another fight with his dad, she calls ex-boyfriends Crystal and Williams, tells each of them they have a son, and they both go looking, mugging desperately along the way. Writers Lowell Ganz and Babaloo Mandel did much better work with Ron Howard's **Parenthood** (1989), which addresses the issues of fathers and sons with infinitely more humor, truth, and compassion.

Dad (1989) stars Ted Danson as a successful businessman who reluctantly comes home to care for his elderly father, Jake (Jack Lemmon), when his mother is hospitalized. The experience leads Danson to reassess his relationship with his own son (a very young Ethan Hawke). It gets a little saccharine, but Lemmon delivers an unsentimental and affecting performance.

But perhaps the ultimate Father's Day movie is the delightful **Life with Father** (1947), a nostalgic turn-of-the-century comedy starring the great William Powell in one of his last great performances as a harried, blustering but ultimately loving father. Look for a vivacious young Elizabeth Taylor in a small role.

GRANDPARENTS' DAY

(First Sunday after Labor Day)

And the Hallmark gift card opportunity holidays keep on comin', folks. Grandparents' Day was actually the result of the tenacious efforts of one Mr. Michael Coldgar, himself a grandparent. He went to visit his aunt in an Atlanta, Georgia, nursing home and was moved by the number of neglected grandparents. He used up his life savings making seventeen trips to Washington, D.C., over a period of seven years to lobby for a national holiday. Finally, in 1978, President Jimmy Carter signed the holiday into law.

To observe the occasion, enjoy **Cocoon** (1985), director Ron Howard's cinematic salute to serenity and senility. A trio of Florida septuagenarians (delightfully played by Hume Cronyn, Don Ameche, and Wilford Brimley) are in the habit of skinny-dipping in a neighbor's pool. What they don't know is that a group of amiable aliens is using the pool, too—for rejuvenating purposes. When the oldsters take a dip, the pool acts as a fountain of youth—restoring their energy, drive, and sexual prowess. It gets a little sticky toward the end, but overall, *Cocoon* is remarkably free of sentimentality (rare in a Ron Howard film!), and the performances are uniformly winning.

THANKSGIVING

(Fourth Thursday in November)

Notice to All Aspiring Hollywood Screenwriters. Wanted: One Classic Thanksgiving Movie.

For such a quintessential American holiday, you'd think there would be more movies centered around Thanksgiving. There are a few, to be sure, but none of them quite measure up to classic status.

In the meantime, after the game is over and the turkey and pie digested, sit back and enjoy John Hughes's Thanksgiving-themed comedy, **Planes, Trains and Automobiles** (1987). Steve Martin stars as harried and hurrying ad exec Neal Page, who's desperately trying to get back home to Chicago in time to enjoy Thanksgiving with his wife and family. Boisterous but endearing small-time salesman Del Griffith (John Candy, in his greatest performance) keeps blocking the way, one way or another. The comedy begins as formulaic and a little unsettling—but as the crises come, we grow fond of both characters. Writer and director John Hughes had previously worked magic with the youth market (*Pretty in Pink; The Breakfast Club; Sixteen Candles*), and here he went for something a little different. But it still has the heart that's apparent in the best Hughes films. Candy is especially good—exasperating, hysterical, and sympathetic.

For those who like a little more existential gravy with their Thanksgiving turkey, Woody Allen's masterful **Hannah and Her Sisters** (1986) is centered around three different Thanksgivings in the lives of three sisters and their various loves.

And if you prefer your Thanksgiving bird basted in vintage herb from the psychedelic '60s, may I suggest a true Thanksgiving treat, **Alice's Restaurant** (1969). Director Arthur Penn's amiable adaptation of Arlo Guthrie's cult song from the '60s recounting "a Thanksgiving dinner that couldn't be beat"—and the ensuing garbage disposal problem—is a true Americana Head Museum piece, but a fascinating and strangely endearing one. The movie was not a box office success; in fact, it's pretty much a forgotten film. But it does carry the whiff of the times that no other movie quite duplicates. Arlo Guthrie (Woody's son, and a genuine American folk hero in his own right) has an ingratiating but unassuming screen presence ("I was terrible," he says in retrospect), but the movie is not without its charms—especially for those of a certain age. On the DVD version, Arlo Guthrie delivers a marvelously droll running commentary that is every bit as entertaining as the movie itself—maybe more so. It's like having an old friend sitting beside you on the couch who just happened to be the star of that movie.

COLUMBUS DAY

(Second Monday in October)

This used to be a safe holiday; it has recently fallen into political and public disfavor due to its celebration of a man who committed genocide of a native people. Forty years ago, public schools used to begin their first history lesson with, "In fourteen hundred and ninety-two, Columbus sailed the ocean blue . . ." and, if not exactly enraptured, hundreds of thousands of baby-boomer kids got the short half of the real story.

1492: Conquest of Paradise (1992) tells the story behind the myth—well, a little more of the story than Hollywood usually does, anyway. Director Ridley Scott (*Alien; Blade Runner; Gladiator*) has a visionary director's eye, and it suits his subject. *1492* covers roughly twenty-five years of Columbus's life, from his early efforts to raise investors, to his adventures and triumphs, losses, and disillusionment. Gérard Depardieu gives an unexpectedly strong and sensitive portrayal of Columbus, and Sigourney Weaver is regally fetching as Queen Isabel. Spectacular visuals—but, at 155 minutes, it seems to last as long as the voyage itself.

FRIDAY THE THIRTEENTH

(Various ones scattered throughout the year—be on the lookout!)

The unluckiest day of the month for Christians, who believe that Christ was crucified on this day. To make it a double whammy, they believe thirteen is an unlucky number since there were thirteen present at the Last Supper. (But did they count the waiters, I wonder?)

Commemorate the occasion—and stay out of harm's way—with **Friday the 13th** (1980), the cheesy cult classic that helped start the whole string of young-nubile-promiscuous-girls-getting-shish-kebobbed genre. Is it a good movie? No—it's not even a competent one. But do you really want to push your luck today?